Travels in a Lifetime

by John Stuttard

Front cover: 1934 Rolls-Royce 20/25 (Harrison) with the author in
Arg-e Bam, South-East Iran, 1997

*For the inspiration to travel given by our 19th Century
ancestors who lived and travelled in distant lands*

Reverend James Midgley, Missionary in East Africa and Brazil

Louisa Harcourt-Rankin, Memsahib in India

Major General Robert Baker, Soldier & Tea Planter in India

**The McCall Family, Tobacco and Canned Meat Merchants in
North America, Uruguay, Argentina, Brazil and Tasmania**

I am grateful to my wife, Lesley, and to my friend, David Colvin
CMG, for reading a proof of this book and for pointing out errors.

ISBN 978-0-9933749-0-6

Published by John Stuttard, Shaftesbury

Travels in a Lifetime
by John Stuttard

Introduction

I was inspired to write this book while Lesley and I were visiting Zanzibar in February 2011. We had arrived from Dar es Salaam after travelling overland by train from Cape Town. During the 5,500km journey we read again the story of David Livingstone's African travels and the ending of the slave trade in Zanzibar in June 1873.

Also in June 1873, my great-great-great uncle, the Reverend James Midgley MA, left Zanzibar for his first missionary posting – Magila, on the East African mainland, in what is now Tanzania. While studying moral sciences at Cambridge, he had heard David Livingstone speak at the Senate House in December 1857 about his missionary work and travels in Southern Africa. He was greatly inspired and took the cloth. Then, in 1872, he read Henry Morton Stanley's account of *How I found Livingstone*. Doubly inspired, he joined the Universities' Mission to Central Africa (UMCA) and began his missionary life outside the UK. Although his stay in East Africa was brief, due to the onset of malaria, he recovered and spent 17 years as Consular Chaplain in Recife, Brazil.

During his retirement back in his home town of Todmorden, Yorkshire, he related his experiences of overseas travel to his great niece, Emily Whitehead, who cared for him in his old age. In her later years, Emily retold these stories. Quite probably the only subscriber, in Todmorden, to the monthly National Geographical Magazine, she cut out articles of interest which she sent to me and my brother, while we were away at boarding school in the Wirral in the 1950's. These stories and the articles were educational and, in due course, inspired me to want to travel – and I've never stopped.

Over the last 50 years I have enjoyed visiting some 77 countries and embarking on adventurous journeys. I am not sure that I would have travelled as much, for example spending a year in Borneo and five years in China, and visiting fascinating places, without this inspiration. Apart from being a source of endless interest, travel has been a stimulus for continuing education about geographies, histories, peoples and their cultures. But, to begin with, at an early age, being away from home was forced upon me for sound educational purposes. I spent five years at a boarding preparatory school on the Wirral between the ages of 8 and 13. Then I was sent to Shrewsbury for a further five years. 10 years away from home begins the process of travel, not least because my contemporaries also had the same experience. In the 19th Century and before WWII, those educated at *public school* expected an overseas life, serving the Empire. Travel, away from home, to faraway places, was the norm.

My wife, Lesley, had ancestors who were even greater travellers. In the 18th Century, Samuel McCall, had one of the first ships on the Clyde importing tobacco from Virginia; his son, also a tobacco merchant, owned land in America; and his grandsons became meat canners in South America. On the other side of the family, her great-great grandmother went out to India with the *Fishing Fleet* and married a major in the Army; he later became a tea planter.

When I began travelling abroad in the mid-1960's, the environment was very different. Journeying by train from Khartoum to Wadi Halfa or visiting longhouses in the jungles of Borneo were true adventures, although actually much safer than today. Now, air travel is cheap and the likes of EasyJet and Ryanair have made international travel accessible to all. But, with the onset of extremism and the breakdown of law and order, together with war in some countries, the world has become a much more dangerous place in which to travel.

I know that Lesley and I have passed on our love of travel to our two sons, Tom and Jamie. I hope that this book will, in turn, inspire future generations to enjoy the adventures and the pleasures that travel brings and, with it, a deeper understanding of other human beings and their different cultures. We are all richer for the experience.

Writing these accounts has been a labour of love, reminding me of past adventures and awakening memories hidden below the surface. My diaries and other written accounts have helped recall 50 years of journeys to faraway places.

The travelogues are described in the following chapters:

Sir John Stuttard, August 2015

Shakespeare in South Africa – July & August 1964

Shakespeare's Quatercentenary

1964 was the 400th anniversary of the birth of William Shakespeare.

At Stratford-upon-Avon, there were extensive celebrations. Under Sir Peter Hall's direction, a special programme of the *History Plays* was performed. In the presence of HRH the Duke of Edinburgh, a new Shakespeare Centre was opened, where visitors could study every aspect of the Bard's work. Representatives from over 100 countries of the world came to unfurl their national flags at Stratford on St George's Day, 26th April, the anniversary of Shakespeare's birth. Wreaths were laid. Souvenirs were manufactured. The Post Office in the UK produced a special issue of stamps. Sir Lawrence Olivier appeared in *Othello* at the National Theatre.

Commemorative celebrations of a similar nature took place all over the world. The town of Memphis, Tennessee organised a Shakespeare Festival. Stratford, Ontario minted a special medal. Pablo Picasso created drawings on the theme of Shakespeare's face and Louis Aragon wrote an essay to accompany the drawings. Even in Romania, a country from behind the Iron Curtain, a special postage stamp of Shakespeare was issued.

In South Africa, the English Academy of Southern Africa, which had been founded in 1961 to defend the English language against advocates of the Afrikaans language, wanted to celebrate the Quatercentenary. We had been told that representatives of the Academy had unsuccessfully approached Sir Laurence Olivier and, separately, Sir John Gielgud to visit the country to recite passages from some of Shakespeare's plays and sonnets.

South Africa in 1964

South Africa was, at that time, in the process of becoming a pariah state. Apartheid, which is an Afrikaans word meaning *separateness*, was introduced as a system of racial segregation by the National Party Government after their success in the 1948 national elections. Discrimination against the non-white population was legalised. Resistance against Apartheid began in the 1950's and led to demonstrations and arrests. In 1959, 69 people were killed by police at Sharpeville. The main black opposition party, the African National Congress (ANC), which included many liberal white supporters, was banned. For many years, the rule of *habeas corpus* had operated in South Africa so that no-one could be detained without trial. However, in July 1963, the most senior ANC members, most of whom had been living underground, were detained at a farm in Rivonia. To ensure continued imprisonment of these senior ANC members, legislation (known as the *90 Day Detention* Act) was rushed through Parliament and applied retrospectively, so that the people arrested at Rivonia could be detained (for 90 days) and held in solitary confinement, pending trial. In October 1963, some of the Rivonia defendants were formally charged. Nelson Mandela, who was already serving a prison sentence, was brought back to court. Two members of the ANC who were white South Africans, of Jewish origin, escaped from prison; some of the accused were acquitted, but Mandela and the others (including Sisulu and Mbeki) were eventually sentenced to life imprisonment and flown to Robben Island in June 1964 to serve their sentences.

In the context of this political turmoil, the English Academy of Southern Africa was desperate to find a solution to ensure that the Quatercentenary of Shakespeare's birth was duly noted and celebrated in South Africa.

The Cambridge Solution
One of the Academy's Committee members contacted her son, 22-year old Stephen Gray, a South African who had a degree from the University of Cape Town, and who was then studying for a Master's degree in English at Queens College, Cambridge in the UK. Stephen had become involved in amateur dramatics at Cambridge and had directed *Love's Labour's Lost* for the December 1963 tour of France and Switzerland by the Experimental Theatre Group (ETG) of Cambridge University. Stephen proposed a solution.

He suggested bringing a group of students from Cambridge University to perform two Shakespeare plays in South Africa. He was joined in this endeavour by Alexandra or Sandy Dane (nee Thompson), a fellow South African who had graduated from the

University of Cape Town Drama School. She had begun her professional acting career in South Africa before moving to London. She was later to appear in some of the *Carry On* films and, memorably, as *Busti*, the leader of the harem, in *Carry On Up the Khyber*.

Stephen approached members of the cast of the ETG's recent production to enquire if they might be interested. Some were and grasped the opportunity. But others reacted fervently (see below) against the proposal. Stephen approached other friends and contacts, to make up the cast, and formed the *Cambridge Shakespeare Group*, to take a party to South Africa to perform two Shakespeare plays, *Love's Labour's Lost* and *The Comedy of Errors*.

Given the political climate and the growing antagonism towards Apartheid, the idea of a drama group from Cambridge University going to South Africa caused a rift among those involved in amateur theatre in Cambridge. In May 1964, in a shocking act of vandalism, the words "*Free Mandela*" had been daubed on the east wall of Kings College Chapel, facing King's Parade. The strength of feeling against Apartheid was strong and very vocal.

A lengthy letter opposing the tour was sent to *Varsity*, the Cambridge University student weekly newspaper, which published it on 8th May 1964. This letter was signed by many luminaries of the then Cambridge stage, namely: Simon Baddeley, Stuart Clucas, Richard Eyre (now Sir Richard Eyre CBE and at one time Director of the *National Theatre*), John Grillo, Carey Harrison, Rob Knights, Robert Leach, Mark Lushington, Tony Palmer, John Shrapnel, Bernard Simons, Richard Syms, Neil Taylor, Tony Vivis, Jonathan Lynn, Graeme Garden (then President of the *Footlights* and subsequently a member of the *Goodies* and now an OBE), John Cameron, Tim Fell and Susan Bendall. They criticised the use of the university's name in the title of the touring company, and the fact that the company would be performing in front of some segregated audiences. The authors believed that the actors would inevitably be compromised by accepting hospitality from white South African families and would not be able to criticise the Apartheid regime as freely as they should.

Varsity responded with an editorial entitled "*Important Little Men*". It referred to "*the backbiting and intrigue which characterises Cambridge's acting world*" and derided the authors of the letter claiming that they wished to wreck the tour. The Editorial included the following paragraph "*It may come as a surprise to some members of the acting fraternity to find that despite their puffing and blowing, they cannot impose their opinions on others*".

Stephen had taken the precaution of consulting the Vice-Chancellor about the use of the town's name "*Cambridge*" in the name of the tour group (*Cambridge Shakespeare Group*) well before this letter had been written. On publication of the letter, the V-C commented that Stephen "*is clearly and genuinely alive to the issues and the motive of the trip is no way political, so that I can see no reason for objection to the name*".

As a result of this interchange, the cast and the support team were well sensitised to the political and human rights issues long before the company left Cambridge for South Africa.

The Journey from the UK to South Africa

Our return air fares to South Africa were generously funded by Harry Oppenheimer, the prominent South African businessman, who was Chairman of both Anglo American Corporation and De Beers Consolidated Mines. Born in South Africa, he was educated in the UK at Charterhouse and Christ Church Oxford. He was opposed to Apartheid and financed the opposition Progressive Party. He was also a great philanthropist.

The *Trek Airways* flight from the UK to Johannesburg took almost 36 hours, with the plane touching down in Luxembourg, Malta and Angola. Flying over the Sahara at night, we experienced a violent thunderstorm and the propeller driven plane bucketed and swayed from side to side. But everything was calm for the landing in Angola where our first African sunrise was spectacular and never to be forgotten, with magnificent colours and the sounds of wildlife and distant drums. Arriving at Jan Smuts Airport, we were surprised to be greeted with a rare snowfall.

<u>**Our Hosts in South Africa**</u>
To keep costs down, and to make the tour interesting for everyone, the English Academy had arranged for their members and friends to accommodate members of the cast at their homes. The group rehearsed in Jo'burg and then toured the country, playing at cities and townships during the two months of July and August 1964.

Staying in the home of a reasonably well off family in Jo'burg in 1964 was, for most undergraduates at Cambridge, the height of luxury. Most houses had swimming pools and the household had a number of staff: cook, gardener, cleaner and perhaps a butler. Some of the staff lived in the compound of the house, while others commuted from the nearest township where they lived. Apartheid had enforced a strict regime regarding dwellings, to ensure that races were physically separated.

Each house had a large garden, surrounded by a high fence, with security alarms and watch dogs. On the street corners guards kept watch all night with a simple hut and brazier to ward off the cold of the high veld. In July, being winter, as one drove through the wealthy suburbs, there were clouds from the wood fires and an intoxicating air of wood smoke which permeated the area. Even now, some 50 years later, on a January evening in the English countryside, I can almost recall that sweet and reassuringly secure smell.

Our hosts lived in the wealthy northern suburb of Lower Houghton, part of Houghton, whose Member of Parliament for many years was the famous Progressive Party leader, Helen Suzman DBE. As the single MP in Parliament who was not from the Nationalist Party, she fought against Apartheid and was the only white person permitted to visit Mandela in prison on Robben Island.

Another well-known anti-Apartheid campaigner at that time was Sir Robert Birley, former headmaster of both Charterhouse and Eton and, in the mid 60's, a visiting professor at the University of Witwatersrand, known as *Wits* (pronounced "*Vits*"). He was one of the few resident foreigners helping to keep a liberal tradition alive in

South Africa, against a hardening Nationalist regime, and he also showed an interest in our two Shakespearean productions.

Rehearsals and Preparation
Stephen Gray and Sandy Dane had arranged that we should rehearse the two plays at Wits. The university was founded in 1896 and is one of the great centres of learning in Southern Africa, with a fine academic record. Like the Universities of Cape Town, Rhodes and Natal, Wits stood out against Apartheid and, in fighting for academic freedom, had a multiracial admissions policy. During the 1960's there were many protests at the university against Nationalist Party policies; there were many police raids; and student leaders were arrested under the detention legislation. The English Academy had close links with the university where there were meeting rooms and a large stage for our rehearsals.

I was given the part of *Holofernes* in *Love's Labour's Lost*, a role that I had played on the ETG tour of France & Switzerland in December 1963. In *The Comedy of Errors*, I played *Antipholus of Ephesus*, while fellow undergraduate Piers Pendred of Trinity Hall played the other twin, *Antipholus of Syracuse*. There were certain facial resemblances between the two of us and we were roughly the same size; but, to ensure that our audiences would easily mistake one for the other, the director Sandy Dane arranged for Piers and me to visit a hairdresser in Sandton to have our hair dyed blonde. The *Dromio* twins also looked very alike and their hair was dyed black. And all four of us were given *Beatles* haircuts.

The Will Shake
Beatlemania was beginning to be an international musical phenomenon by the time of our South African tour. The Beatles' first film, *A Hard Day's Night*, was released in the UK in July 1964 and we saw the film when it came to Jo'burg later that month. The global music scene had started to erupt in the late 1950's with the *Rock-n-Roll* era of *Billy Haley and the Comets, Jerry Lee Lewis, Little Richard* and *Elvis Presley*. In the UK, pop groups such as *The Rolling Stones, The Animals* and *The Hollies* were being formed in the early 60's.

A number of us who enjoyed singing and playing music decided it would be fun to found our own pop group. So we formed the imaginatively named *Will Shake*, comprising Dick Lee (lead guitar), Piers Pendred (rhythm guitar), David Lascelles (piano), David Collins (drums), John Lornie (vocal) and me (lead singer). One of our hosts in Jo'burg, Ray Ackerman, was managing director of *Checkers*, the South African supermarket chain. He was becoming a very successful businessman and had a lot of imagination. He generously hired two guitars and a set of drums so that the six of us could rehearse songs, including several Beatles numbers, at his home, while his wife, Wendy, kindly provided a piano, refreshments and encouragement. Our repertoire included such well known pieces as *Please Please Me*, *I Saw Her Standing There*, *I Want to Hold Your Hand*, *She Loves You*, *Twist and Shout*, *Roll Over Beethoven*, *Needles & Pins*, *Long Tall Sally* and *Greenback Dollar*.

But Ray Ackerman also had a cunning plan. He arranged for us to sing these songs outside the Checkers Store in Rosebank on a Saturday morning. Duly promoted in the newspapers in advance, it was a great marketing idea. Not content with our first public performance, we played on other occasions, including the Bloemfontein University Hall. Later, when our skills had been finely tuned, we played in a theatre, after a performance one evening of *The Comedy of Errors*, at Evander, the gold mining town developed by the Union Corporation. That night the songs were so well received that we were asked to repeat the repertoire in its entirety. Sadly, by the following morning, after all that singing, I had lost my voice and this put an end to the recording session which had been arranged at the Pretoria office of the South Africa Broadcasting Company. Despite persistent enquiries at several chemist shops in Pretoria, the elixir for restoring broken voices was never found and thus the *Will Shake*, to the eternal disappointment of its fans, never cut a record.

Music in South Africa

The musical tradition in Africa is strong. In the US, the blues developed out of slave songs and rhythms that had originated on the African Continent. In the late 1950's, the music of Miriam Makeba had begun to make African music popular in the west. Her *Click Song* and the popular Swahili song *Malaika* were among her well known hits. She also starred in the all African jazz opera, *King Kong*. Given her frequent anti-Apartheid pronouncements, her South African passport had been cancelled while on a tour of the UK in 1960. This made her, even more, a symbol of oppression. She had been deprived of her human rights.

A more traditional form of music and entertainment was represented by the mine dances displayed by different African tribes on Sundays in the neighbouring mining towns. Each tribe would perform its own unique dance dressed in its own unique costume. It was very colourful and enjoyed by audiences and performers alike.

In Jo'burg, there was a rather special jazz club, known as *Dorkay House*, where African singers performed. We were delighted to be able to visit this establishment which was another venue for multiracial enjoyment of the arts.

<u>Touring the Country</u>

The rehearsals went well. The scene was set for a seven week tour of South Africa where the *Cambridge Shakespeare Group* would perform two Shakespeare plays to mixed audiences in Pietermaritzburg, Grahamstown, Port Elizabeth, Cape Town and Jo'burg and to whites' only audiences in Bloemfontein and Pretoria. Surprisingly, we were permitted to perform to blacks' only audiences in some of the townships, including Soweto, and this was rather special. I understand that we were the first white group to play theatre to all black audiences in South Africa. This is something that the anti-tour protestors back in Cambridge would never have thought possible.

BP Southern Africa (Pty) Limited had generously agreed to provide a bus to take the cast, costumes, props and set around the country. With no accompanying van, this meant that the set had to be small and, therefore, quite minimalist. The costumes similarly had to be simple. This worked well. It meant that the focus of both productions was the text and the direction. It also meant that it was easier to move from venue to venue with little set-up time.

The concept of touring a theatrical production to various cities was well known to Stephen, Sandy and many members of the cast who had participated in the ETG's production of *Love's Labour's Lost*. The ETG had visited seven cities in France and Switzerland in December 1963, when the cast also stayed with families in each town.

Pietermaritzburg

Our first stop was Pietermaritzburg, 275 miles south east of Jo'burg and just 50 miles from Durban. Pietermaritzburg was founded by the Voortrekkers in 1837 after the Battle of Blood River and named after Boer leaders. The British took over the city in 1843 and it became the capital of Natal Province. It has a large Indian population and is well known as the city where Mahatma Gandhi was ejected from a train for sitting in a first class carriage despite possessing a first class ticket. In 1962 Mandela was arrested in the nearby town of Howick, beginning his 27 years of imprisonment. Pietermaritzburg is also the home city of the controversial English cricketer Kevin Pieterson.

Pietermaritzburg is a gracious colonial city, with fine parks and boulevards, and grand Victorian buildings such as City Hall, the Museum, the Old Colonial Building, the Railway Station and the University of Natal (now renamed KwaZulu-Natal), where we performed.

We opened with *Comedy of Errors* which was reported the following morning (11th July) in the *Natal Witness* with a complimentary review *"In a uniformly excellent cast, the fine diction and lightness of touch (an essential in any comedy) were a sheer delight"*.

Grahamstown

The long, 400 mile, journey from Pietermaritzburg to Grahamstown took us through the Xhosa heartland of the Transkei, an area which had been designated for members of a specific ethnicity. It was given nominal autonomy in 1963 and existed for a while (until 1994) as a semi-independent region. It is now part of the Province of Eastern Cape.

For most of the journey through the Transkei there were green rolling hills, dotted with round thatched huts with white painted mud walls. The countryside was unspoilt and had a wild feel to it. Its capital, Umtata (now renamed Mthatha) was, at one stage, a prosperous trading post with some fine buildings. It is also the area from which some of South Africa's famous black leaders came, including Nelson Mandela, Steve Biko and Walter Sisulu.

Because of the long journey, we had little time to stop, but managed a quick bite in Umtata at the 1930's Savoy Hotel – sadly no longer in existence. Towards the end of the journey, we bypassed the busy sea port of East London and arrived late into Grahamstown, perhaps the most English of South Africa's cities.

Grahamstown is a centre of learning, with Rhodes University, the Anglican College of the Transfiguration and many secondary schools, including St Andrew's College, where we performed. The city is also home to South Africa's oldest independent newspaper, *Grocott's Mail*, established in 1870.

Not far away to the north is another very famous academic institution, the University of Fort Hare at Alice. Founded in 1916 as a college for non-whites, it has offered academic education of the highest quality to students from many countries in sub-Saharan Africa. Many of the black leaders of independent African countries have studied at Fort Hare and its better known alumni include: Govan Mbeki, Oliver Tambo, Joshua Nkomo, Nelson Mandela, Sir Seretse Khama KBE, Julius Nyerere, Robert Subukwe, Robert Mugabe, Kenneth Kaunda, Mangosuthu Buthelezi and Desmond Tutu.

On our theatre tour, we did not visit Fort Hare. There was insufficient time built into the busy schedule. Yet, given the quality of its students, Fort Hare would have been an obvious place for us to perform our two Shakespeare plays. This may not have been permitted by the authorities as the university was strictly segregated in 1960 and, at the time of our tour, was part of the Ministry of Bantu Education. Fort Hare was also a hotbed of liberal thinking against Apartheid and thus was carefully watched by the Nationalist Government.

Some 43 years later, Lesley and I were delighted to be taken to Fort Hare by the then British High Commissioner to South Africa, Paul Boateng (now Baron Boateng of Akyem in the Republic of Ghana and of Wembley in the London Borough of Brent). Paul has particularly close contacts with members of today's South African black elite, many of whom were educated at Fort Hare. With his deep knowledge of the facts of their struggle, he was able to explain the role of the university in shaping post-colonial history.

Over the two days, in Grahamstown, we performed each play twice – matinees and evenings. *Grocott's Daily Mail* trailered the productions well and then reviewed (on 15th July) *Comedy of Errors* generously: *"Successful University production: a happy marriage between William Shakespeare and Charles Chaplin"*; and *"a brilliant mixture of custard pie slapstick and evocative verse"*. And there was still further praise at the end of this review *"Of the gracefully played and beautifully spoken parts, it is only fair to mention the special polish in Piers Pendred's excellent Antipholus of Syracuse; that of John Stuttard as his brother; Colin Harris and Robin Harrison as the twin Dromios; Jean Dempsey's delightful Adriana; Sybil Ewbank's Aemilia and Joan (sic – should be Jann) Parry as the entrancing Luce and dancer. If only we could see much more like this"*.

Port Elizabeth

The journey to Port Elizabeth, or PE as it is known, is just 80 miles through a region which now has many game reserves, consolidated from former large farms. PE is one of South Africa's main sea ports and is linked to both Bloemfontein and Jo'burg by one of the country's main train routes. The city is also at the east end of the country's attractive *Garden Route* and is a starting point for tourists visiting that region of South Africa.

We played three performances at the City Hall, beginning with *Love's Labour's Lost,* which the PE's newspaper *East Province Herald* judged to be *"astonishing strange and astonishing good"*. The review went on *"The clowns made the best scenes. Andrew Brunt and John Stuttard were bizarrely brilliant. Piers Pendred, Richard Lee and Linda Kirk were cleverly bumpkin. Richard Huggett was neatly ridiculous. David Collins impressed in voice and manner. It was an experience not to be forgotten"*.

In a second review, the *Herald* reporter wrote *"The young actors, notably Piers Pendred (Costard, the country clown) and John Stuttard (Holofernes, the schoolmaster) showed a crisp sense of comedy and their scenes bubbled beautifully"*.

<u>Cape Town</u>

By this stage of our theatre tour, we had got used to our BP bus transporting the entire company of 21 and our minimalist set and simple costumes from one city to another. On each side of the bus was a huge banner, with the BP logo at either end and then in very large letters "CAMBRIDGE UNIVERSITY SHAKESPEARE GROUP".

Inside the bus, over the many hours travelling around South Africa, the student banter was maintained at a high level and there were more serious conversations about the political situation in the country. We were all grateful to be learning more about the history, tensions and difficulties. We were seeing South Africa at first hand and not as reported in the international media. Dick Lee and Piers Pendred kept us entertained with their guitars and there was a certain amount of singing. The time passed quickly and very agreeably.

After leaving Port Elizabeth, the road follows *The Garden Route,* a most attractive part of South Africa with a very mild climate that makes it popular for holidays, second homes and for retirement. Houses in towns such as Mossel Bay, Knysna and Plettenberg Bay are particularly in demand, with nearby sandy beaches, golf courses and good restaurants.

During the 500 mile haul to Cape Town, there was little time for sightseeing, although the views from the coach windows made the journey most scenic.

Culturally, Cape Town is perhaps the most sophisticated of all South African cities. We knew that the audiences at the Little Theatre at Cape Town University would be the most discerning. With 10 performances over five days (matinees and evenings), the Press had plenty of opportunity for critical review. Thus:

- Owen Williams on *Comedy of Errors* in the *Cape Argus* on 22nd July: *"Some style but little matter in Cambridge Shakespeare. In fact it was all over-stylised, over-rarefied to the point where it had little connection at all with the original work".*

- But Ivor Jones also on *Comedy of Errors* in the *Cape Times* on 21st July was kinder: *"Shakespeare ticks over to a very Arty-crafty beat"; "as a 'popular' entertainment, Miss Dane's production seemed to please the audience";* and *"Asked to award laurels, I would give them, preferably, to the male members of the cast, particularly the Antipholuses (Piers Pendred and John Stuttard), the Dromios (Colin Harris and Robin Harrison) and Andrew Brunt as the conjurer, Pinch*

- Owen Williams was also kinder in his review of *Love's Labour's Lost*, with *"Elegiac version of the play"; "the stylised production by Stephen Gray is a far better thing than the Company gave in similar idiom of that robust and earthy comedy, The Comedy of Errors"; and "David Lascelles and Robin Harrison squared off the quartet (of courtiers) in a pleasantly decorative way";* and *" there were four fine comedy performances. Richard Huggett was military bombast itself as Don Adriano, in perfect counterpart to Scholasticism in person, the rasping Holofernes of John Stuttard, and his foil, the timid cleric Nathaniel, well done by Andrew Brunt.";* and to conclude: *"We are beholden to the Cambridge players for two interesting versions of two rarely performed plays."*

- Ivor Jones was quite factual about the play and wrote the following conclusion of our rendition of *Love's Labour's Lost*: *"Once again the audience demonstrated its pleasure by the 'old approach' of applause".*

I can't now recall the names of all the families we stayed with in South Africa. But the family of De Kock in Cape Town stands out for their exceptional hospitality and generosity. Most families had large houses with guest wings and servants to match. The De Kocks went one step further – they hired a car for us to use while we were staying with them for the week. This meant that it was easy for us to get to the Little Theatre at the University and it was easy for us to sightsee.

We took advantage of their generosity and visited Table Mountain, Groot Constantia, Cape Point and Stellenbosch.

Cape Town is a most delightful city, set in a most delightful location, with most delightful food and wine. I have been pleased to revisit the city many times since.

Bloemfontein

A long 600 mile journey lay ahead from Cape Town to Bloemfontein, the capital of the Orange Free State (now renamed simply *Free State*) which was, between 1854 and 1902, an independent Boer Republic. For much of the route, the road passes through the Karoo, a semi-desert region where little grows. The indigenous Bantu Africans did not farm this area because of its harsh and arid climate. It was left to Bushmen who were hunter gatherers, until the Boers arrived in the mid 1700's, forced from Cape Colony by overcrowding. The Karoo is a lonely and inhospitable place and one which you pass through fairly quickly.

But, first, leaving Cape Town, our bus climbed the Hawequas mountain range that separates the fertile plains around the city from this barren area, until we reached Worcester, now an important town on the rail line that links the Cape to Pretoria and Jo'burg. From there we passed over the Matroosbergs to reach De Doorns in the Hex River Valley, a grape growing area and the last piece of good agricultural land before the Little Karoo and Great Karoo to the North West.

After the dusty road through the Karoo National Park, there are a few isolated towns, such as Hanover, which are little more than coaching stops. But not all of the Karoo is barren and around Colesberg, a former missionary station, there are sheep farms and also some very fine stud farms.

It was a long journey and we reached Bloemfontein in the evening. Next day, there was a performance of each of our plays to whites only in the University Hall. The following day, we played *Comedy of Errors* to the first of our non-white audiences in Heatherdale (now renamed Heidedal) Township, a segregated area reserved for Black

Africans and Cape Coloureds. The white, mainly Afrikaans, audience was polite and reserved, while the all-black audience loved the slapstick and buffoonery, as well as appreciating the text, in Sandy Dane's production.

The Press reviews of our performances were mixed. "R.A.S." of *The Friend* reported on the two plays very differently, as:

- *"The performance (of Comedy of Errors)....was a delight from beginning to end"* and *"This was all comedy without error".*
- Regarding *Love's Labour's Lost: "Love aside, they laboured and they lost"; "Poor John Lornie, David Collins, David Lascelles and Robin Harrison. On them fell the brunt of the work of making this curious interpretation actually succeed"; and "No, I didn't enjoy it, but I'm glad I saw it, for – and this is certain – this production will be a talking point among theatre-lovers for a long, long time. And, anyway, The Comedy of Errors made up for a great deal"*

It was in Bloemfontein that I first learnt how not to deal with the Press. It was a lesson that has stood me in very good stead over the years. And I have not repeated the mistake that I made on that unfortunate occasion.

A reporter from *Die Volksblad* in Bloemfontein interviewed a number of us about the tour, seeking our impressions of South Africa. I was complimentary about the country and volunteered that the hospitality had been outstanding. When questioned as to the reasons for this, I was, with hindsight, too analytical, without thinking about how my words might be interpreted. I referred to the lack of television, the introduction of which in the UK had given rise to families staying at home on their own. I referred to the practice, in South Africa, of households having servants to look after them, providing greater leisure time. I had observed the pleasure that South Africans experienced in hosting overseas guests who might be interesting and entertaining. The reporter responded *"So you mean South African hospitality stems from boredom"?* Without realising what had happened, that was the headline in the following morning's paper and the quote was ascribed to me!

When the text was translated into English by my Bloemfontein host, Mrs Aggie Wallis, both she and I were shocked. Stephen Gray very quickly arranged for me to be interviewed by another local newspaper, *The People's Weekly,* and, in the edition of 6th August, the main front page article contained an apology from me. It was reported that I *"looked so genuinely distressed"*. I said that I had been misunderstood. Mrs Wallis was reported as saying about me *"he could not stop talking about how much he liked the South Africans and the country"; and "that she and her husband had found him so friendly"*. The reporter's verdict was *"guilty, but dismissed. Come back and visit us again – you will always be welcome"*.

With hindsight, it was clear. White South Africans were, at that time, the subject of growing criticism, even hostility, by the international media. They were very sensitive to comment. I had not intended to upset, but I had not handled this first media interview at all well.

<u>Johannesburg</u>

Back at Wits in Jo'burg, we performed each play on five separate occasions, at the University's Great Hall. There were no fewer than nine newspaper reviews – some favourable, others less so. Extracts include:

- *Rand Daily Mail* of 1st August: *"Comedy of so-so errors"; "we are grateful to them for bringing a good student production"*; but *"Antipholus S and Antipholus E (Piers Pendred and John Stuttard) are quite characterless"*
- *Johannesburg Star* of 1st August: *"Comedy of Errors played with cheeky exuberance; The playing is close to tip top with special mention to all the females (Dempsey, Townsend, Ewbank, Kirk and Parry) as well as the two "servant" twins, Colin Harris and Robin Harrison"*
- *Sunday Express* of 2nd August: *"Bard's Comedy is Poetic, Merry"; and "the standard of acting can hardly be called professional"*
- *Sunday Chronicle* of 2nd August: *"Youth brings a light-footed Shakespeare"; and "The Cambridge University Shakespeare Group are a delightful bunch of Shakespearians, bright-eyed,*

nimble-tongued, clean-limbed and engaging as a parcel of puppies"

- *Johannesburg Star* of 3rd August on *Love's Labour's Lost*: *"Comic Satire in High Spirits: Different play, different director (Stephen Gray) but this alternating production has the same players equipped with the same sort of high spirits and bright ideas seen in Comedy of Errors"*
- *Rand Daily Mail* of 3rd August: *"Love's Labour's Lost – as good as any"; and "This is as good a Love's Labour's Lost as we are likely to see for a very long time".*
- *Sunday Chronicle* of 8th August: *"What other can an undergraduate actor do, for example, with old pedant Holofernes, than caricature him to the border of extinction? John Stuttard managed this without making the one last false step that would carry him over the brink"; and "David Collins's Berowne had dash and charm"*
- *Sunday Times* of 9th August: *"A zany Comedy of Errors – a fresh interpretation"*
- *Sunday Times* of 9th August: *"The English Academy is to be congratulated on importing this courageous and attractive group of young players"*
- *Sunday Express* of 9th August on *Love's Labour's Lost*: *"Group scores yet again"; and "I thought that David Collins as Berowne outstanding in his soliloquies".*

Based in Jo'burg, we played *Comedy of Errors* at village halls in the nearby mining towns of Evander and Springs, neither of which, we imagined, had seen a performance of a Shakespeare play before – at least not by a group from the UK.

Of even greater fascination and interest to us was the opportunity of performing at the townships of Daveyton, Evaton, Kwa Thema and Soweto. Playing to some non-white audiences was the Academy's quid pro quo for our being obliged to play to whites only audiences in Bloemfontein and Pretoria. I was led to believe that we were the first white group to perform a Shakespeare play in a South African township. Certainly the welcome we received was extraordinary. Typically those involved in this effusive welcome would comprise the local mayor, the head of the church and the headmaster at the local school. The audience would include schoolchildren, who might have a Shakespeare play in their English exam syllabus.

In a subsequent article by Stephen Gray which appeared in *The Guardian* (in the UK) on 23rd September 1964, Stephen Gray wrote: *"Members of the group were able to show that, in a country where human contact is aggravated by a rigid political system, communication by means of entertainment, particularly comic entertainment on and off stage, is increasingly vital. There was a certain lethargic distance between actors and audience in the predominantly European audiences, but not often in the African ones".*

In Soweto, we played at the Orlando East Community Hall. It was similar to a village hall you might find anywhere in the world. But for Africans, it had a special significance. Mandela had apparently used the hall for boxing training as well for meetings of the ANC Youth League in the 1940's. Albert Luthuli, Oliver Tambo, Alfred Nzo and Robert Sobukwe had all spoken there in the 1950's. Perhaps for these reasons, in the 1976 Soweto riots the Hall was one of the few Government buildings not to be torched. The Hall was of a good size, but the audience was so large that some people sat in the wings on either side of the stage; we had to climb over them to make our entrance. And that wasn't all; the *Guardian* printed a photo of an African boy standing on the seat of his bicycle watching the play through the window of the village hall. The performances (matinee and evening) of each play were extraordinarily well received. I remember coming on stage for the first time in one of those township performances and seeing a sea of grinning black faces.

There was also an opportunity to discuss the political situation in South Africa, but both Soweto residents and members of the cast had to be somewhat clandestine, to avoid potential problems with the authorities. I was delighted to return to the Orlando East Community Hall in 2007 when, as Lord Mayor, I visited Soweto; I stood again on the stage where I had performed 43 years earlier.

<u>**Pretoria**</u>

The seven week theatre tour of South Africa was reaching the end. The last venue was the Aula Theatre at Pretoria University. With over 1,000 seats, it was quite a place for a finale.

By this stage, the cast was not just word and gesture perfect, but very seasoned from a long tour in front of very different audiences, and from reading some very varying Press reviews. We had received accolades and brickbats. We had been euphoric and downbeat. As a 19-year old undergraduate, I was growing up very fast.

It was a pleasure to read the final review from the *Pretoria News* of 19th August, which read: *"Love's Labour's Won";* and *"The comic parts are the chief joy, with Piers Pendred as Costard – a most versatile clown – and Richard Huggett as Don Adriano de Armado – a fulsome child of fancy – in the lead though the lean Andrew Brunt as fantastical Sir Nathaniel, the Curate, and John Stuttard as Holofernes, the Schoolmaster, also make the most of their clever nonsense";* and *"In their freshness and originality, the Cambridge Group gives us the best Shakespeare we have yet had this Quatercentenary Year".*

And, in a gesture to celebrate our triumph, an after show party was hosted by Lady Stephenson, wife of the British Ambassador, Sir Hugh Stephenson, who thanked the cast for coming to South Africa, against the odds, and for keeping the lines of communication open during this very difficult time.

<u>**Postcript**</u>

As we now know, the political and human rights situation became a lot worse before things got better. 1976 was a low point, with riots and further imprisonment. But then, in 1994, the black majority elected the ANC as the first truly democratic Government of South Africa – some 30 years after our theatre tour. And as for the pre-tour kerfuffle in Cambridge – well, some of those *Important Little Men* had gone down after three years at the university, and word soon got around that the tour had been a great success.

Southern Rhodesia before UDI – August and September 1964

<u>Introduction</u>

Rhodesia was named after Cecil Rhodes, empire builder, politician, mining magnate and businessman. Born in Bishop's Stortford, the son of a clergyman, he was sent to South Africa as a 17 year old boy in 1870. A year later he went to Kimberley to work in the diamond fields. After brief periods back in England, at Oxford, to complete his studies, he succeeded in establishing his own diamond mining business and then buying up all the smaller diamond businesses, creating De Beers Consolidated Mines in 1888. He became a member of the Cape Parliament and, in 1890, Prime Minister of Cape Colony.

In 1888, he signed a treaty with Lobengula, king of the Ndebele in Matabeleland, for a mining franchise in the west and south west of present day Zimbabwe. Based on this, he obtained a charter from the British Government to found the British South Africa Company (BSAC), with powers to rule, police and obtain concessions over an area from the Limpopo River (the border with present day South Africa) to the Great Lakes of Central Africa. The BSAC had its own police force, the British South Africa Police (BSAP), which controlled Matabeleland and Mashonaland. Uprisings by the Ndebele and Shona people led to the two Matebele Wars in 1893-94 and 1896-97. The name *Southern Rhodesia* was officially adopted in 1898 for the southern part of this Empire and is known today as Zimbabwe. After his death, in 1902, Rhodes was buried, with the approval of the Ndebele chiefs, in the Matopos (aka Matobo) Hills, south of Bulawayo.

Rhodes wanted to expand his empire as he believed that the Anglo-Saxon race was destined for greatness. His vision was to create a British Empire in Africa from Egypt to the Cape linked by a railway that ran the whole length of the continent.

In 1923, the British Government decided not to renew the BSAC's charter. The 36,000 white settlers in Southern Rhodesia rejected the option of joining the newly formed Union of South Africa. Instead Southern Rhodesia was granted "self-governing" colonial status and given a great deal of control over the African population of over one million. A Parliament was elected based on voting rights for whites and a very few blacks based on property ownership. The all white Rhodesia Party won a landslide victory in the first elections of 1924. In 1953, Southern Rhodesia became part of the Federation of Rhodesia and Nyasaland, together with Northern Rhodesia and Nyasaland. The Federation fell apart in 1963, prior to the independence of Malawi and Zambia in July 1964 and October 1964, respectively. Southern Rhodesia was then renamed *Rhodesia*.

In Southern Rhodesia, the Land Husbandry Act of 1951 built on the Land Apportionment Act of 1930, which regulated the ownership and use of land in the country. This later act resulted in great tension between the white and black communities. Riots created a climate of fear among the white population, resulting in a security crackdown and the outlawing of the expanding black liberation organisations.

In 1965, Prime Minister Ian Smith won a mandate to pursue white independence and made a Unilateral Declaration of Independence (UDI) in November of that year.

After the successful imposition of sanctions by the world community and following a bitter guerrilla war, the white rule of the previous 90 years was ended and the country became the Republic of Zimbabwe in April 1980.

<u>Family connections</u>
My missionary ancestor, the Reverend James Midgley, from the Universities Combined Mission to Africa (UCMA) lived for a year in East Africa in 1873-74. Although he never visited Southern Africa, he had been inspired by the explorer and missionary, David Livingstone, whose journeys took him through the territory which became known as Southern Rhodesia. Livingstone's brother-in-law, John Moffat, had negotiated the treaty, on Rhodes' behalf, with King Lobengula in 1888. Based on these very distant connections, I always had an interest in Livingstone and in the countries he visited as an explorer and missionary.

Then, my mother's sister, Laura Ralph, had spent the Second World War years in Southern Rhodesia with her husband, Cyril, who served with the RAF, training air pilots. Auntie Laura and Uncle Cyril spoke fondly of the country and their life in Southern Rhodesia. Away from the austerity of war time Britain, in the African sun, with African servants, they must have enjoyed a "good war".

The Rhodesian Four

At the end of the Cambridge Shakespeare Group's tour of South Africa, there were five weeks remaining of the university's long vacation. It might be several years before I returned to Africa, so I decided to spend more time there before flying home. Apart from an interest in Rhodesia through family connections and from what I had read, there was so much to see in the country, not least the Victoria Falls and the Kariba Dam. With the breakup of the Rhodesian Federation and independence of countries to the north, this was potentially a very interesting time to visit the two Rhodesias.

In discussion with three other members of the cast, David Collins, Jann Parry and Linda Kirk, we decided to travel to Southern Rhodesia to tour the country, facilitated by Jann's parents whose home was in the country's capital, Salisbury (now renamed Harare).

David and Jann decided to fly from Jo'burg to Salisbury, while Linda and I thought we would try and save money by hitch-hiking the 650 mile journey – there and back.

The night before we left Jo'burg, the family (The Tomkins) with whom Linda had been staying pleaded, in vain, that we should take a flight. Hitch-hiking was dangerous and who knows what might befall us. Mrs Tomkins even offered to pay for the airfares. We did, however, accept the offer of a lift, from their son, Paddy, to the north side of Pretoria, from which the open road led north. Mrs Tompkins also kindly arranged for a chicken to be cooked and this would be our lunch on the first day of our adventure.

Hitch-hiking 650 miles from Jo'burg to Salisbury

Paddy drove Linda and me from Jo'burg to the north side of Pretoria and dropped us at 07.30 in the morning on 28th August outside a BP petrol station in the suburb of Les Marais. From there, the old main road, Route 101, (adjacent to the new N1) went north to Southern

Rhodesia. We would pass through Warmbad (now renamed Bela Bela), Potgietersrus (now renamed Mokopane), Pietersburg (now renamed Polokwane), Louis Trichardt (not renamed, following stiff opposition), Messina (now renamed Musina) and then the River Limpopo, crossing into Southern Rhodesia at Beit Bridge.

By 15.00 in the afternoon, we had travelled 150 miles to Pietersburg, about half way to Beit Bridge. During the course of the day, two cars, three vans and one truck had each stopped to give us a lift, in some cases for just a few miles. In this part of the Transvaal, it is very dry and sometimes there is no rain for several years. Every lift brought with it a tale of hardship. A farmer who had spent a great deal of his wealth drilling, unsuccessfully, for water showed us his drought stricken orange farm and, with typical South African hospitality, offered us some food and a drink. Another lift was from a breakdown truck. Linda went in the cabin with the driver, while I rode in the open back with an African mechanic. He had no education but was learning to be a car repairer. He was saving hard to start a business of his own in his home township of Benoni, where he had a wife and three sons. As we chatted, he demolished most of Mrs Tomkins' chicken and he told me how unfair the present South African Government was to his race. I sought to reassure him that the present situation could not last. It took a further 30 years before Apartheid was ended and Africans got the vote.

At Pietersburg, we stopped at the smartest hotel we could find for a wash and brush up and then found a lift from a farmer who took us about 20 miles and dropped us in the middle of nowhere, as the sun was setting. Trying, genuinely, to reassure us, he promised us a bed for the night if we found ourselves without a lift as darkness fell.

Some 40 minutes later, a Vauxhall with Rhodesian number plates came into view, with just a single person, the driver, in the car. We had learnt from the day's hitch-hiking experience that a car bearing a Rhodesian plate was normally full of luggage, children and grandmother. We were lucky. John Tomlinson, a chartered accountant from Jo'burg, was driving his firm's car to Salisbury, where he had relatives. He was excited about his visit to Salisbury as he was looking forward to seeing television which, at that stage, had not been introduced into South Africa. The Nationalist Government were fearful of the impact. While English language television programmes could easily be sourced from the US or the UK, there was no developed market for programmes in Afrikaans. There was a concern that the introduction of television would result in the English language becoming the dominant language in South Africa. John Tomlinson's firm's car had been registered in Salisbury six years previously and had to be taken out of South Africa to prevent car tax being payable on the purchase price. John clearly took pity on us as we stood beside the deserted road in the fading light of the Spring evening. He passed us and then, after 20 yards, stopped.

At about 20.00, in John's car, we were just short of Messina, when we came across an accident. An African had been knocked off his bike and was lying lifeless in the ditch. We got out to enquire if we could help and received a somewhat curt response from the white driver of a van that had probably knocked him down, "You can't help him. He's past it". While factually correct, the words did not convey an overly caring or sympathetic air.

An hour later, we reached Messina and headed for the first hotel, The Limpopo Inn. A South African Cabinet Minister was staying the night at the hotel, so dinner was not available to us there and we ate elsewhere. However, the Limpopo Inn was clearly the best hotel in town and gave us a good night's rest after our 300 mile journey through the Transvaal.

This part of South Africa is hot and dry. Low shrubs and thorn trees dominate the landscape, with occasional baobab trees. Despite long periods of drought, there are citrus, mango, tomato and date plantations. Messina is also known for its copper, discovered by the Musina tribe, from whom the town's name is derived.

In the morning, we crossed the Limpopo River. It was not, as described by Rudyard Kipling *great grey-green greasy*, but rather dried up and insignificant. Indeed it was possible, just five days after our crossing, for the Johannesburg railway station bomber, Dennis Hicks, to be driven across the dry river bed to escape arrest in South Africa.

Our first sight of Southern Rhodesian officialdom was the colonial customs house. Gone were the signs of *Whites Only* and *Non-Europeans Only* that we had seen on benches and public conveniences in South Africa. Our delight was soon shattered when we were almost refused entry into Southern Rhodesia as we had left our return flight tickets to London in Jo'burg for safekeeping. Initially £150 per person *assurance* was required but waved when I explained that I came from Lancashire. To this day, I am not sure why this hit the jackpot. My passport was duly stamped "*Beitbridge, Southern Rhodesia, 29 August, 1964*".

Soon after crossing the border at Beit Bridge, we took a right fork signposted Salisbury, a distance of 350 miles. After about 10 miles, we encountered the unique *strip road* configuration which I have only seen in Southern Rhodesia and which was to be a feature of our journey to Salisbury and around the rest of the country. These strip roads consist of a hard packed dirt road on top of which two strips of tarmac have been laid, in parallel lines, so that the four wheels of a car can be driven along the strips. The fun comes when another vehicle approaches from the opposite direction. As the two vehicles converge, the practice is for each to move to the left so that only the offside wheels of the two cars are on the left strip as they pass, while the nearside wheels are on the dirt road to one side. The temptation to play *chicken* is irresistible. While seemingly quite dangerous, it is possible to maintain quite high speeds while passing a vehicle in the opposite direction, providing you observe the convention.

Road traffic signs showing elephants were frequent sights, as were cattle wandering on the road. There were few cars but we were lucky and reached Fort Victoria (now renamed Masvingo) for an early lunch. Fort Vic is the oldest colonial settlement in Southern Rhodesia and seems inappropriately twinned with Middlesbrough in the UK. More important for African history, self-esteem and modern day African nationalism, it is close to the Great Zimbabwe Ruins which date from the 11th to the 14th Centuries. Inhabited by the Shona tribe, the area was home to over 10,000 people. It was abandoned in the 15th Century as a result of deforestation and the lack of available food from the poor quality of the land. Regrettably we did not have

sufficient time to see the ruins, as John Tomlinson had to reach
Salisbury by early evening. In retrospect, not seeing Zimbabwe, the
site of one of Africa's great civilisations, is something I regret.

It was around 17.00 when we drew up outside the 1960's Ambassador
Hotel in Salisbury and phoned the Parry's to announce our safe
arrival.

Salisbury in 1964

Southern Rhodesia in the 1960's was a prosperous country. The rich
farmland and the hard working and proficient white settler farmers
had created a successful agricultural industry, in beef, dairy, grain
crops, vegetables and tobacco. The rail network to Mozambique and
South Africa facilitated exports. The results of this success could be
seen in the architecture of downtown Salisbury where modern office
blocks (of 50's and 60's design) had crowded out the colonial
buildings that still graced other African cities. There were attractive
gardens and parks with statues of colonial heroes. The white suburbs
contained well-kept but fairly ordinary looking bungalows,
surrounded by white painted concrete walls or wire fences.
There seemed to be no shortage of cars and the shops were well
stocked with products and brand names that were familiar in Britain.
The Native or African population lived mainly in townships, but the
segregation was less rigid than in South Africa. There was less, albeit
growing, racial tension than in South Africa. The country seemed
more relaxed, with a more caring attitude among the white population
towards the majority of black Africans. But the dark clouds were
looming in the wake of changes in the rest of the Continent.

Jann's father, John Parry, was Director-General of the Southern
Rhodesia Broadcasting Corporation (SRBC) and a leading member of
the white community. The Parry's lived in the fashionable district of
Avondale.

We were informed by John, over a glass of brandy and coke (the
seemingly typical pre-dinner drink in 1960's Southern Africa) that
Linda and I would be staying with one of John's colleagues, DA
(Steve) Steven, his Assistant D-G, who lived alone, apart from
servants and domestic animals, in a large house nearby. Steve had

been in broadcasting in Malaya both before and after the War and spoke a Chinese dialect, probably Foochow. One of his animals was a Rhodesian Ridgeback bitch, called Heidi. Ridgebacks are loyal and intelligent dogs, excellent at guarding the house and family, but less aggressive than some other large dogs of the Alsatian variety. Steve's No 1 servant was away visiting his family in Malawi, so we were looked after by the cook, Gilus, who was helpful but clearly not as effective as No 1, whose name we never discovered. Linda and I stayed in the guest wing.

At that time, most well off, middle class, white families in Southern Africa had large houses in leafy suburbs, complete with swimming pool, a necessity in the hot summers. We spent lazy mornings by the pool, planning a programme for our three week stay in Southern Rhodesia.

In 1964, while South Africa had not yet introduced television into the country, the population in Southern Rhodesia had enjoyed black and white television since 1960. There was also a *Native Section* of SRBC, run entirely by Africans, broadcasting in Shona and isiNdebele, as well as in English. The SRBC attempted to be politically neutral and the Native Section was also determined to be even handed in its coverage of speeches by Joshua Nkomo and his rival the Rev Ndabaningi Sithole. John Parry showed us around the Native Section where we received comments about the length of our hair, which followed the fashion typical of British youth in the 1960's, and cries of *"Oh, look, there go the Beatles!"*.

John also took us to an auction at the Rhodesia Tobacco Sales. In those days, the country produced a huge amount of very fine tobacco. In the large auction shed, the auctioneer would walk along a gangway between lines of tobacco leaves, with the buyers following him and picking up leaves as they went. Based on the quality of each leaf, bids would be shouted out by the buyers and the posse moved on until all that day's stock had been sold. The speed of the auctioneers patter was such that we could not decipher what he was saying or the prices that had been realised. At one point, there was an outburst of laughter and we were duly informed that the auctioneer had put Jann up for sale and realised a quite exceptionally high price. We were not surprised. Jann was a pretty girl, with a fine gazelle like figure, and aspirations to be a ballet dancer. But she was small and not very heavy, so her total sales value would not have been that great.

After dinner one evening, we were taken to a drive-in cinema. We had never seen one of these before, although they had been quite common in the United States for some time, as we saw in some of the films starring James Dean. For countries with a dry climate, where land is cheap and movie goers possess a car, it is a popular way to watch a film.

White Politics in Southern Rhodesia in 1964

In the early 50's, under the United Rhodesia Party (later the United Federal Party), reforms were introduced, aimed at improving the education of the African majority. These reforms were pursued in particular by Sir Garfield Todd, who, as a young man, had emigrated as a missionary from New Zealand to Southern Rhodesia. As Prime Minister from 1953, he brought in programmes to divert Government revenues and private wealth to black schools, for example through a tax on Rhodesian property owners. He also pushed a Bill through the Colonial Office to introduce multi-racial trade unions. These measures proved to be most unpopular with the white voters, who controlled Parliament. Todd was forced to step down as Prime Minister in 1958 and was replaced by Sir Edgar Whitehead, who continued some, but not all, of Todd's policies. Whitehead negotiated the 1961 Constitution which increased black representation in Parliament. During his term of office, he also sought to reduce the extent of racial discrimination. However, these measures were of great concern to the white minority; yet they were insufficient to meet the demands of the black majority.

From the late 50's onwards, the white minority Rhodesians focused their efforts on trying to maintain their position and their rights in the country, which they regarded as their home. This resulted in the formation in 1962 of the right wing Rhodesian Front Party, opposed to change to majority black rule. Its founding principles included the preservation of each racial group's right to maintain its own identity; the preservation of proper standards through a policy of advancement through merit; the maintenance of the Land Apportionment and Land

Husbandry Acts which formalised the racial imbalance in the ownership and distribution of land; opposition to compulsory racial integration; job protection for white workers; and the maintenance of the Government's right to provide separate amenities for different races.

Todd's and Whitehead's policies were unpopular and, at the General Election later in 1962, the Rhodesian Front won 35 out of the 50 white seats, while the United Federal Party won 14 out of the 15 seats reserved for blacks.

The new Prime Minister was Winston Field, who was allegedly chosen as leader of the Rhodesian Front Party to lend an air of respectability. A successful tobacco farmer, he was solid and trustworthy and known not to be racist. His wife is later quoted as saying "*He didn't really want to take it on. He wasn't really a political animal*". During his term of office, Field negotiated unsuccessfully with the British Government to achieve independence before the Salisbury Parliament had a black majority. As a result of this failure, he was ousted as Party leader in April 1964 and replaced by Ian Smith whose Government, encouraged by winning all the white seats at the May 1965 General Election, unilaterally declared independence from the United Kingdom in November 1965.

John Parry knew Winston Field well and sympathised with his predicament. He suggested that the four of us might like to meet him. So we were driven out to the Fields' tobacco farm at Marandellas (now renamed Marondera), about 50 miles from Salisbury. They had a large estate, which was very productive. Around the house were attractive gardens and a lake nearby. We felt most honoured to be welcomed by a former Prime Minister, who suggested that we might like to spend a weekend at his cottage in the mountains near Inyanga. Sadly, our now well-developed plans for touring the country did not allow enough time for us to accept his kind offer. But we enjoyed an outdoor buffet supper and then returned to Salisbury.

Southern Rhodesian Television – The early days
Part of John Parry's empire was the new Rhodesian Television channel. John asked if we would like to visit the station during a live

broadcast and we arrived at the studio shortly before the start of a current affairs programme similar to the BBC's *Tonight* programme with Cliff Michelmore. The Rhodesian equivalent, Robin Brown, greeted us and I was able to stay and film some of the action using my 8mm triple turret Paillard Bolex cine camera.

A week later, on our return from a round trip tour of Rhodesia, we learnt that Rhodesian TV wanted to interview us, on their *Tonight* programme, about our theatre tour of South Africa. They also wanted us to perform a short piece from one of Shakespeare's plays; we chose the *Lovers' Quarrel* from *Midsummer Night's Dream*. Linda played *Helena,* Jann played *Hermia,* David played *Lysander* and I played *Demetrius*. After a glass of something with John Parry at the Salisbury Sports Club, we arrived at the studio and the *Lovers' Quarrel* was duly performed with the four of us reciting the words and the camera ingeniously focused on our feet to capture the action. An interview followed where the questions seemed quite naive – *"What did we think of Laurence Olivier?"* and *"Did we like Shakespeare?"* But then, Robin Brown asked about the new Chichester Festival Theatre and we were off, talking about Uncle Vanya and the cast which Olivier had assembled in 1962 and 1963.

The other items on the *Tonight* programme included an interview with a clock collector from Bulawayo. He had brought a few clocks with him, including a grandfather. Somewhat unfortunately, and amusingly, he was interviewed on the hour. The clocks struck and the interview came to an unexpected, but perhaps predictable, end. Then Desmond Lardner-Burke, who was the Minister for Law and Order and Justice, explained his actions in quelling disturbances and riots in one of the townships. In December 1963 he had ordered Robert Mugabe to be imprisoned, writing: "*whereas certain information has been placed before me and whereas due to confidential information which I cannot reveal, I am satisfied that you are likely to commit acts of violence throughout Rhodesia*". Lardner-Burke was one of the signatories to the 1965 UDI. Mugabe spent the next 11 years in prison.

The following morning we went to the Salisbury Show which was the most multiracial event we had witnessed thus far in Southern Africa.

Whites and blacks mixed freely. On a number of occasions we were greeted with the salutation *"Oh, the Shakespearians"* by those who had watched the TV programme on the previous evening.

A tour around Southern Rhodesia

There is much to see in Rhodesia and we were determined to visit the Kariba Dam, Livingstone (in Northern Rhodesia), the Victoria Falls and the Wankie Game Reserve. In total, this would a round trip of about 1,000 miles.

On Wednesday 2nd September 1964, the four of us set off from Salisbury in the Parry family car on a Rhodesian strip road similar to the type that Linda and I had experienced on our journey from South Africa. Taking the main road north to Lusaka, we reached Sinoia (now renamed Chinhoyi) after about 80 miles, which was a straightforward two hour drive. Here, Frederick Courtney Selous, the great British explorer, hunter and conservationist, had discovered the Sinoia Caves in 1888. The limestone cave system has some large pools of radiant cobalt blue water, including the main *Sleeping Pool* or *Pool of the Fallen.* The water is very deep and is used by expeditions for "ultra deep diving".

By lunchtime, we arrived at Maimi, in a tobacco growing area. Here we arranged for the car's engine to be examined at the local garage. The car had been pulling rather badly and we were fearful of not reaching Kariba that evening. By 16.00, the car had been fixed and we raced along the main road and then, less fast, for the last 60 miles to Kariba, along a dirt road that had originally been an elephant track. We learnt later that the huge generators now powering the hydro-electric facility at the Kariba Dam had been hauled along this road, taking two days to cover the 60 miles. About half way along this dirt road, we were waved to the verge by a Government official who requested us to drive through a corrugated iron shack where we were sprayed with insecticide as part of controlling the spread of tsetse fly.

Kariba

It had taken us all day to cover the 230 miles from Salisbury, including the enforced garage stop. It was a relief to check into the Lakeview Hotel, situated in an attractive spot adjacent to Lake

Kariba. The dinner of corned beef and sweet corn, all from a can, was less appetising than we had expected and didn't match the wonderful view of the lake.

The Zambezi River is the natural border between, what are now, Zimbabwe and Zambia. Running for most of its journey from west to east, it flows into the Indian Ocean through Mozambique. The first European to visit the upper reaches and discover the Victoria Falls was David Livingstone in his expeditions in the 1850's.

The concept of building a dam to produce electricity was conceived before WWII and in 1941 a survey was undertaken of its feasibility. The dam and the Kariba South Power cavern were built by Impresit of Italy between 1955 and 1959 at a cost of US$135million. The North Side Power Cavern was built by Mitchell Construction and completed in 1977. The World Bank assisted by providing finance. Today, the Kariba Dam supplies 1,266 MW of electricity to parts of both Zambia (the Copper Belt) and Zimbabwe. It is one of the largest dams in the world, standing 420 feet tall and 1,900 feet long.

By 1964, Lake Kariba had been formed behind the dam. 50,000 people, mainly from the Batonga tribe, and many thousands of animals had been displaced during the construction phase; the rescue of the animals was known as *Operation Noah*. The site on the south side near the dam was beginning to attract tourists and is, today, a popular spot for sunbathing, waterskiing and game watching. During our visit, seeing families bathing in the lake, we assumed that there were no crocodiles or bilharzia in the lake and took the plunge ourselves in wonderfully warm, clear water.

Our tour of the dam complex began with an inspection of the South Power cavern, with its enormous generators in vast underground galleries, the size of cathedrals. Massive sliding doors allowed huge lorries to enter these subterranean rooms. The film, Dr No, had been released in 1962 and Kariba's power cavern reminded us of the doctor's control centre on Crab Key. Crossing the Southern Rhodesian border post, we were able to drive to a parking place next to the dam wall, on top of which was a road leading across the river to Northern Rhodesia. The arch dam, designed by the French engineer

and inventor, Andre Coyne, is a thing of great beauty, holding back
Lake Kariba which is 174 miles long.

Driving over the top of the dam wall into Northern Rhodesia was
quite an experience. There was a huge drop (420 feet) to the river
below. And it was an interesting moment to cross the border.
Zambian Independence was just a few weeks' away. At Immigration,
two African officials were checking passports (mine was stamped
Kariba, Northern Rhodesia, 3 September 1964) while a white officer
looked on and checked the car's insurance documents. The officer
would soon be on his way, as most white Northern Rhodesians were,
we were informed, planning to leave the country.

Choma

After a very hot and dusty 150 mile drive west, to Choma, this view
was confirmed that evening as we sat at the bar of the Choma Hotel.
Sipping our brandies and coke, we listened to the concerns and
aspirations of the three white men who were drinking there. The local
policeman, the local bank clerk and the barman were each planning
their exits. All three were under 30 years of age, so a change of
location, with job opportunities elsewhere, was a viable alternative.
But it was quite sad that the prospect of an independent Zambia was
insufficiently appealing to these young men, whom the new nation
desperately needed.

Livingstone

Named after the great explorer, the town was, for many years, a
gateway for commerce and trade between the countries north and
south of the Zambezi River. In the 1960's, there were gracious
colonial official buildings and mansions, many of which were swept
away post-independence.

At that time, it was also a tourist destination for visitors to Victoria
Falls and the river excursions on the upper part of the river above the
Falls. The tourist business in Livingstone fell away after Zambian
Independence but has now recovered in the wake of the difficulties
which Zimbabwe has experienced in recent years.

We found accommodation, two simple huts at the Livingstone Rest Camp, on the Friday night. Being a weekend, we had to find an alternative home for the Saturday night and there were rooms at the Windsor Hotel, a fairly rough hotel on Victoria Falls Road. But this was a great location for an alfresco meal by the mighty river. Breakfast in the sun, watching hippos swim past, made up for the Windsor's faded curtains and grubby upholstery.

Less than a mile from the Falls, we could not avoid hearing the noise of the roar created by millions of gallons of water tumbling over the largest waterfall in the world. To get a proper view, we had to cross the border into Southern Rhodesia, over the road and rail bridge across the canyon, and then take a walk through the rain forest, aptly named because you get soaked from the spray.

My passport was stamped *"Victoria Falls, Southern Rhodesia, 6 September 1964"*. The Falls, known as the *Smoke that Thunders*, is an extraordinary sight; three miles long and 360 feet high, they are only matched by the Iguazu Falls in Brazil.

On the southern side, there is a statue of Livingstone, who was much liked by African people for his understanding of their culture and language and also for his role in abolishing slavery in parts of the Continent. Even today, almost half a Century since independence, his statue is still very much admired and photographed by visiting African schoolchildren. Some former freedom fighters in Zimbabwe would like to see it removed because it reminds them of the colonial era, while Zambians would like it to be re-erected on their soil because of their esteem for him – and, of course, he died in Zambia, where his heart was buried.

In the evening, back on the Northern Rhodesian side, we enjoyed a sundowner cruise with all the atmosphere that Africa can muster. Sipping our brandies and coke, there were animal noises, bird song, drums beating in nearby villages and, of course, the inevitable mosquitoes.

Sadly, we did not have time to visit or stay at the colonial Victoria Falls Hotel, built in 1904 on the south side of the Falls. Lesley and I did make up for this omission 46 years later when, in January 2011, we took the train from Cape Town to Dar es Salaam and stopped for a night at this grand hotel. There is a splendid view of the road and rail bridge over the gorge from its gardens where a traditional tea, with scones, jam and cream, is served. It is a great place to stay and a convenient base from which to see the Falls and to explore the area.

<u>Wankie and Bulawayo</u>

Our next stop was going to be the Wankie Game Reserve (now renamed the Hwange National Park). However, a stone thrown up from the road by a passing truck put an end to this plan. We could not be admitted to the Reserve with a broken windscreen.

So, after a rather unpleasant drive, with flies splattering our faces, we reached Bulawayo where a new screen could be fitted. Having been to the Kruger National Park in South Africa only the week before, we had at least seen animals in the wild. The priority now was to get the Parry's' car back to Salisbury in one piece.

Bulawayo is an industrial and business city, as well as being the home of the national railways. The city was founded by the Ndebele king, Lobengula, who settled there in the 1840's after the Ndebele people's great trek from Zululand. Much destroyed in the Matabele Wars, Bulawayo was rebuilt as an Edwardian colonial industrial town, with a few fine civic buildings. From Bulawayo, the 275 mile journey to Salisbury took the whole day.

<u>Return to Johannesburg</u>

After a few gentle and very agreeable days back in Salisbury, we said our thanks and goodbyes to Steve and the Parry's, who had been so generous in hosting our visit to Southern Rhodesia. Mirroring the offer made 10 days earlier by Mrs Tomkins, Mrs Parry wanted to fund the air fares for Linda and me to travel to Jo'burg by plane. But we set off again, at the crack of dawn, to hitch-hike the return journey.

Within 15 minutes, we had secured our first lift which took us 150 miles to Fort Victoria. After a second lift of just 40 miles, our luck ran out.

We waited for four hours with no prospect in sight. Standing by the side of the road, the only sign of civilisation was an African bar which pumped out loud music. Three different songs were repeated over and over again which limited our enjoyment of the entertainment. However, the occupants of the last car had volunteered a telephone number, in case we got stuck, of the person they were visiting at a farm in the bush. Paddy Heard, a graduate of Natal University and now a civil servant teaching modern farming methods, came to our rescue and, after a splendid dinner, we slept on camp beds on the floor of one of the store rooms. We were becoming accustomed to the extraordinary hospitality and generosity in Southern Africa.

Back on the road the following morning, we waited for another two hours, regaled again by the same three songs repeating from the African bar. Mid-morning a black constable from the BSAP cycled towards us and stopped. *"What are you doing here?"* he asked, in an official but caring manner. We answered: *"We are trying to persuade a car to take us to Beit Bridge and then on to Jo'burg"*. *"Don't worry"*, he replied, *"I'll fix it"*. He then waved down the next car travelling South, with the demand to the surprised driver *"Take these people as far as you are going, mun"*. The figure of speech *"mun"* was often used in Southern Africa to ensure that the statement was directed to the person, so that there was no confusion as to intention. It also seemed to be a slight term of endearment and was always taken as such.

So, with the help of the Southern Rhodesian constabulary, we got our next lift to the Rhino Hotel at the Lundi River. After that, another car took us on to Beit Bridge. There we experienced the same problem as a week earlier. Our return flight tickets to London were in Jo'burg for safekeeping. It took a couple of hours before the head of Immigration returned from lunch. He told us how very silly we had been and waved us on our way. My passport was duly stamped *"Beit Bridge, Republic of South Africa, 13 September 1964"*. After Messina, we had a long wait and wondered if we would reach Jo'burg that night.

Then along came a white knight, John Pocock, another graduate of Natal University who seemed to know everyone we had met in Southern Africa. He was fascinated to hear about our theatre tour of South Africa and the Southern Rhodesian Television appearance in Salisbury, so much so that he wanted to meet David Collins and Jann Parry as well. As a result, he drove us directly to Jann Smuts Airport, arriving at 23.00, to collect David and Jann off the plane from Salisbury. They were astonished to see us.

Then, we drove to the Tomkins house, where Mrs Tomkins was beside herself with relief. We had managed to hitch-hike both ways – a total distance of 1,300 miles – and we had returned to the safe haven of her home in Parktown.

Postcript
Our visit to Southern Africa came towards the end of the colonial period, although in some cases the finale was to take a further 30 years to play out.

Zambia became independent with little bloodshed, but resultant economic hardship, in October 1964. Botswana achieved peaceful independence in September 1966. Mozambique became independent in April 1974, following sporadic warfare. After UDI and a bitter war of independence, Zimbabwe was created in April 1980. Namibia fought for its independence which was granted in March 1990. In South Africa there was long struggle before black rule began, in April 1994, when Nelson Mandela was elected President.

The ending of the colonial period in Southern Africa was, in many cases, unpleasant, harsh and deadly, not least because the large minority white populations that lived in these countries wished to protect their livelihoods. They did not universally either respect or trust the black majority. Yet the majority merited independence. This has been a sad period in our global history. In many of the Southern African countries, while independence has brought freedom from dominant white rule and discrimination, it has also resulted in an increase in corruption and nepotism and a worsening of living standards.

The countries of Southern Africa need effective and benign leadership, as well as understanding and support from countries outside of Africa, to succeed. It will be a long haul. I wonder what my missionary ancestor in 1873 would have thought. I would have been quite frustrated at the lack of progress in the intervening 140 years.

Romeo & Juliet in Germany – June & July 1965

For those wishing to aspire to the dizzy heights of amateur theatre at Cambridge University, involvement in the *Marlowe Dramatic Society* should be your goal. This is particularly so if you wish to perform in a Shakespeare play or assist in its production.

When the Marlowe Society was founded in 1907 a play by William Shakespeare had not been performed in Cambridge for almost 20 years. The Society's aim was to correct this and also to perform other Elizabethan and Jacobean plays. Over the years, *The Marlowe*, as it is colloquially known, has become well known for the quality of its productions. To begin with, the Society performed mainly at the Cambridge University Amateur Dramatic Club (ADC) in Cambridge and then, from 1936, at the Cambridge Arts Theatre.

Many leading figures in the theatre world have acted and directed with the Marlowe Society. These include Sir Michael Redgrave CBE, Sir Peter Hall CBE, Toby Robertson, John Barton CBE, Sir Trevor Nunn CBE, Robin Midgley, Sir Ian McKellen CH CBE, Clive Swift, Sir Derek Jacobi CBE, Sir Richard Eyre CBE, John Shrapnel, Michael Pennington, Miriam Margolyes OBE, Eleanor Bron, Germaine Greer, Griff Rhys-Jones, Simon Russell Beale CBE, Emma Thompson, Stephen Fry, Hugh Laurie, Sam Mendes and Tom Hollander. In 2007, Sir Trevor Nunn returned to Cambridge to direct a production of *Cymbeline*.

From 1957 to 1964, in time to celebrate Shakespeare's Quatercentenary in 1964, with a commission from the British Council, the Society recorded the complete works of Shakespeare. This feat was arranged by the legendary George (known as Dadie) Rylands CH CBE. Dadie was an English don at King's College and a leading Shakespeare scholar, as well as being an accomplished theatre director. He was Senior Treasurer of the Marlowe Society and also (from 1946 to 1982) Chairman of the Cambridge Arts Theatre, where the Marlowe performed each Spring. During the 1940's and 1950's Dadie directed many of the Marlowe Society's productions at the Arts Theatre and some also in the West End.

A wealthy bachelor, Dadie acquired rooms in King's in 1928 where he lived, entertained and rehearsed for the next 70 years. Among his friends were Lord (John Maynard) Keynes CB, Lytton Strachey, Virginia Woolf, Sir Cecil Beaton CBE, Sir Frederick Ashton OM CH CBE, Constant Lambert, Lord (Noel) Annan OBE and Sir Patrick Leigh Fermor DSO OBE. For a budding actor or director, an invitation to Dadie's room for a party, meeting or rehearsal was akin to entering the inner sanctum of some holy order. There was much wit, a stretching of the boundaries of literary knowledge and a great sense of satisfaction in learning about the subject under discussion. It was reported that to be in one of Dadie's productions was a very happy and stimulating experience.

<u>Romeo and Juliet at the Arts Theatre in March 1965</u>
The Marlowe Society decided to mount a production of Romeo and Juliet at the Arts Theatre in March 1965, directed by Gareth Morgan. Gareth was a member of the Royal Shakespeare Company and had recently directed *The Miracles* at Southwark Cathedral.

Piers Pendred, a fellow Cambridge undergraduate, from Trinity Hall, had tipped me off about the auditions, which took place in November 1964. Piers had been made President of the Marlowe Society at the beginning of the academic year and he encouraged me to become Junior Treasurer. I met Gareth Morgan and was given the part of *Benvolio*. There was just enough time for a read-through before the Christmas break, during which I toured France and Switzerland with the Experimental Theatre Group's production of the *Merry Wives of Windsor,* directed by Trinity Hall undergraduate, Simon Baddeley.

Rehearsals began in January when there was also a Marlowe Committee meeting in Dadie's flat. Dadie recalled his own direction of the play, together with John Barton, in 1952, which he took from the Arts Theatre to Bournemouth and then to the Phoenix Theatre in London.

One of the very strange customs of the Marlowe Society is (or certainly was) the absence of the actors' names in the production programme. Only the *dramatis personae* and some of the production staff (director, set designer, costume designer, music composer and

choreographer) were named. Thus, 50 years later, when writing this
account, I can't remember the names of all those who took part.
However, some stand out either because of the quality of their acting
or because they were close friends (or both). Thus:

- Keith Rubidge played *Romeo*
- Jenny Peverall played *Juliet*
- John Grillo played *Mercutio*
- Piers Pendred played *Tybalt*
- Germaine Greer played *Lady Capulet*
- David Lascelles played *Paris*
- Liz Rietberg played the *Nurse to Juliet*

Shaun Curry, the director of the previous summer's production
(which toured Germany) of *A Midsummer Night's Dream*, was
invited back to direct and choreograph the stage fights. Playing the
part of Benvolio, I learnt to stage fight, using rapier and dagger, in the
grounds of Trinity Hall. Shaun showed me and *Tybalt* how to lunge,
thrust, parry and defend. It was a lot of fun. Our rehearsals took place
mainly in the Chetwynd Room at King's.

In my capacity as Junior Treasurer, I joined Piers, as President, for
meetings at the Arts Theatre with Commander Andrew Blackwood.
The "Commander", as he was known, was the General Manager from
1958 until his retirement in 1990. In an obituary of the Commander,
the then Box Office manager, Vivien Mayne, was quoted as saying:

*"He was a very modest man but very passionate about the theatre. He
was gentlemanly, very nice and had a droll sense of humour"*; and *"In
his 42 years, he pioneered audience development, established drama
groups for young people, generated funds for the theatre and
provided the city with a programme of entertainment that exceeded
anyone's expectations, while constantly battling with formidable
budgets and lack of funding"*.

I owe a lot to Commander Blackwood. I had met his PA, Judy Daish,
in the Cambridge undergraduate acting world and Judy (who later
became my sister-in-law) suggested that I should seek his advice on
my career post Cambridge. By the time of my second year at
university, I had observed that there were many other Cambridge

thespians who were better actors than me. I knew that the acting
profession was tough. But I loved being involved in the theatre. So
perhaps theatre management might offer an interesting career.
The Commander was incisive

*"It's a dog's life. You get all these prima donnas up from London
thinking they're God's gift to mankind. You're always struggling to
raise money. And you don't get paid much. Go and get a proper job.
Go and become an accountant or something like that. If you still want
to do it, you can go into theatre management later".*

The set for the production was quite stark, with vast grey blocks
which were rotated as required. Huge spikes extruded from the blocks
which gave an air of menace and danger, inherent in this play where
there is much fighting, death and sorrow. By contrast, the costumes
were extravagantly 1960's with capes made out of long strips of
coloured material.

We played *Romeo and Juliet* for five evenings and three matinees at
the Arts Theatre in March 1965. Regrettably I don't have any of the
Press cuttings of the reviews, but my recollection was that they were
reasonably favourable – and we enjoyed the production.

Planning for Germany

The Marlowe Society had toured Germany in the summer in each of
the previous two years, with *As You Like It* in 1963 and *A Midsummer
Night's Dream* in 1964, at the instigation, and with the support, of the
British Council. At a Committee meeting in Dadie's rooms, plans
were agreed to take *Romeo and Juliet* on a three week tour in June
and July. Inevitably, not all the present cast would be free to go, and
so Piers decided to find other student actors who would fill the gaps.
He then directed the "new" production himself, together with his
friend from Trinity Hall, Simon Hicks.

On this occasion, the cast list was published showing the names of all
the actors and support staff. This is reproduced in full, for the record.

Escalus	Charles Lemont
Paris	Robin Tomlin
Montague	Simon Hicks

Capulet	Peter Cochrane
Old Man	Chris Pinfield
Romeo	Keith Rubidge
Mercutio	Paul Bond
Benvolio	John Stuttard
Tybalt	Piers Pendred
Friar Lawrence	Richard Harris
Friar John	George McDowall (who also played *Abraham*)
Balthasar	Graham Smith
Sampson	Nigel Hall (who also played *Apothecary*)
Gregory	Julian Hartley
Peter	Peter Turley
Page	Mike Smith
Lady Montague	Jann Parry
Lady Capulet	Clare Ballantyne
Juliet	Jennifer Peverall
Nurse	Liz Rietberg
Citizens	Caroline Gray, Joanna Dodson, Julia Braybrook, Jenny Hanson

The cast had the following support:

Stage Manager	Rob Heap
Lighting	Mike Davies
Assistant Technicians	Judy Daish and Mike Vavrinek
Properties	Jenny Hanson
Wardrobe	Caroline Gray and Julia Braybrook
Costumes	Arts Theatre Wardrobe, designed by Judy Birdwood and Helen Fulcher
Music	Christopher Brown
Fights	Shaun Curry
Tour Manager	Nigel Hall

Rehearsals began in early June, just three weeks before departure.
Transport was arranged, comprising two mini buses, a van to carry
the set and the costumes, and Liz Rietberg's sports car which would

convey her and a friend. As in 1963 and 1964, the British Council again fixed the venues and made all the arrangements in Germany.

<u>The tour of Germany</u>

To keep costs down, many of the overnight stops were in youth hostels, the first of which was the Auberge de Jeunesse in Ghent. On the second day we reached Iserlohn, staying at the Jugendherberge for two nights, and for our first performance. The play was well received. Then onto Hamburg, to another youth hostel, the Jugendpark, and a performance in the enormous Auditorium Maximum, which holds over 1,500 people. The Beatles pop group was, by 1965, well on its way to meteoric stardom. For young undergraduates, a visit to the Star Club in the Reeperbahn was de rigueur and it did not disappoint. The excitement and the excesses of the night resulted in several members of the Marlowe cast slinking back to the Jugendherberge at seven in the morning, just as the German youths were about to begin their day's hiking.

Our visit to Heidelberg gave us a feel for another very ancient university town. The Alte Saal at the Heidelberger Schauspielhaus stands out in my memory as being a very fine classical building in which we performed. Performances took place in the Schauspielhaus or Staatstheater of many West German cities, including Munster, Kassel (at the newly built Kleines Haus), Solingen, Frankfurt, Mainz, Koln, and, memorably, Stuttgart.

In Stuttgart we played at the Kleines Haus, which had been bombed in the Second World War and was rebuilt afterwards, opening in 1962. The Grosses Haus, dating from 1912, was one of the few German Opera Houses to survive the war. Our visit in 1965 coincided with a special event. John Cranko had directed and choreographed the Stuttgart Ballet Company in a production of *Carmina Burana*, at the Grosses Haus, as a celebration of Carl Orff's 70th birthday. After seeing a performance of this work, we were thrilled to be invited to a late night party at John Cranko's house for the cast of both productions.

The atmosphere in the mini buses was typical of student group travel. There was plenty of singing and some courting. Alas, there was an accident on the autobahn in which Liz Rietberg's sports car suffered serious damage. While the tour seemed to go down well with the German audiences and was thoroughly enjoyed by the cast and the support team, sadly it made a financial loss. As Junior Treasurer, I was slightly ashamed of this. It made me even more determined to become an accountant, yet continue my dabbling in, and enjoyment of, amateur theatre.

Rumble in the Jungle – A Year in Borneo – 1966/67

A 1960's *Gap Year*

National Service was abolished at the end of 1960. Introduced originally in Britain in the First World War, this programme (*conscription*, as it was known) enabled the UK Government to require its citizens to perform a public duty, typically with the Armed Forces but also with the Merchant Navy, Fire Service or Police Force or in Industry or Agriculture, for as long as the Government specified. In peace time, those receiving "call up" papers would spend 18 to 24 months of their lives being trained and then performing a role in the Army, Navy or Air Force. Joining straight from school, they would interrupt their studies, if they had an ambition to go to university. But all would be trained and would gain experience and, in the process, they would be changed from boys to men.

Returning to academic life, conscripts were more mature, less prone to juvenile behaviour and had benefitted from the two year spell mixing with others from different backgrounds. It was all part of growing up and, in most cases, was beneficial as well as effective in producing a more experienced and stable being. *Hoodies* had not yet been invented.

By the time I came to leave school in 1963, National Service had been abolished. Boys and girls went straight to university. But, aged 21, when they graduated, they were quite raw and had not experienced any of the demands and challenges of those who had undertaken National Service.

The concept then developed of what we now refer to as a *gap year*. That is, either before or after university, the student might spend a year or two doing something else. This would provide a break either before university or, for graduates, before a serious career started and before one had to settle down.

Voluntary Service Overseas (VSO) was formed in 1958 when Alec and Mora Dickson recruited and sent 16 school leaver volunteers abroad, in response to a letter from the Bishop of Portsmouth asking for people to teach English overseas. It was designed to provide an educational experience overseas for school-leavers, initially only boys, before starting university. It was thought that energetic youngsters could add value, in the immediate post-colonial era, to developing countries which had insufficient educational resources. Sarawak, Nigeria and Ghana became early postings for volunteers. VSO soon expanded into an opportunity for graduates who would then take a break between university and a full time career. Volunteers offered untrained help in exchange for basic accommodation and pocket money. In 1962, a more recognized scheme of using qualified volunteers came about. By 1964, VSO had over 1,000 volunteers overseas, filling skills gaps in developing countries.

Many of my generation at Cambridge University did not want to go straight into a job which would then be their career for life. They hated the concept of working in an office immediately post university which, by the 60's, was a very liberal environment. Most of us wanted a certain amount of freedom, as we had experienced at university, and also time to mature a little and to reflect on career opportunities. VSO provided the perfect solution.

Of my contemporaries at Cambridge, Piers Pendred went to Trivandrum, Kerala in Southern India, David Lascelles to Kenya, Henry Marriott to Nigeria, Charlie Symes to Ghana and Tim Butchard to India. I was called for an interview by VSO and I suggested that I might prefer a country outside Africa, as I had spent three months in Southern Africa in 1964. As a result, I was sent to Brunei, on the North West coast of Borneo, for 12 months.

But, before doing so, I was asked to spend a week at Southlands College in Wimbledon, being educated in the objectives of VSO, the expectations of a teacher, some basic teaching methods and elements of South-East Asian culture. It was a broad syllabus and a week was not long or detailed enough to meet all the challenges that lay ahead.

Politics & the Economy in Brunei

Brunei is one of the three countries that together make up the minority (northern and western) portion of the island of Kalimantan. The others are Sarawak and Sabah (formerly North Borneo). The

56

majority (southern and eastern) portion of Kalimantan is part of Indonesia. The land mass of Brunei accounts for only 1% of the total area of Kalimantan, yet, with its reserves of oil and gas, it is the wealthiest part of this large island.

In 1968 the population of Brunei was estimated to be 179,000 (50% Malay, 28% Chinese, 16% local indigenous such as Murut, Dusun or Iban and 6% "other", mainly Indians & Europeans). Today, the population of Brunei is over 400,000. Two-thirds are Malay, 11% are Chinese, while most of the rest are mainly from local indigenous tribes. There are also expatriates, for example working with Brunei Shell Petroleum Company, and others of Indian, Sri Lankan, Chinese or Eurasian backgrounds. Malay was, and still is, the official language.

Today, crude oil and natural gas production accounts for over 90% of GDP. Brunei has the fifth highest per capita income in the world, of over £30,000.

Although Brunei had never been colonised, it was a British Protectorate from 1888 until full independence in 1984.

In 1959, a new Constitution Agreement was signed with the British Government, providing that:
- The Sultan was made the Supreme Head of State
- Brunei was responsible for its internal administration
- The British Government was responsible for foreign and defence affairs only
- The post of Resident was abolished and replaced by a British High Commissioner.

After the end of the Malayan Insurgency in 1959, the British sought to create a Federation of Malaya, Singapore, North Borneo, Sarawak and Brunei, a concept which was opposed by the Philippines and, particularly, by Indonesia.

The Sultan of Brunei was not convinced of the need to join the Federation as he could see no benefit, in the light of expanding revenues from oil production by the Brunei Shell Petroleum

Company at Seria. The Brunei Government was in favour of the idea of a Federation, while the Brunei People's Party (BRP), which had won 16 out of the 33 seats in the Legislative Council, advocated a new grouping, the North Borneo Federation, comprising the unified three territories of northern Borneo, under the Sultanate of Brunei. While this grouping would then have been strong enough to resist domination by Malaya or Singapore, the idea was rejected by the Sultan, who preferred to go it alone.

In December 1962, an armed insurrection by the BRP, under the name of the North Kalimantan National Army (TNKU), broke out in Brunei, led by a BRP politician, Dr Azahari bin Sheikh Mahmud. Within two days, British Forces parachuted in and suppressed the revolt, rescuing the Sultan. This rebellion helped to persuade the Sultan and the Brunei Government that their future would be best served by not joining the new Federation and, instead, by remaining a British Protectorate.

In 1963, in an undeclared war, Indonesia began a period of military confrontation against Malaysia. This armed struggle mainly took place on the island of Borneo involving British servicemen (particularly Gurkhas) and Commonwealth forces and lasted until 1966.

When I arrived in Brunei, at the very end of August 1966, the peace treaty to end Confrontation had been signed between Indonesia and Malaysia just 20 days earlier.

Journey to and arrival in Brunei Town (now renamed Bandar Seri Begawan)
In 1966, it took two full days to fly from London to Brunei Town. Stopping at Zurich, Rome, Delhi, Rangoon and Kuala Lumpur, the plane took 24 hours to reach Singapore, where it was necessary to stop for the night. From Singapore, an old DC3 provided the final leg, via Kuching, Sibu, Bintulu and Miri (all in Sarawak) to Brunei. At the Sarawakian air strips, British soldiers and military hardware were very much in evidence because of Confrontation. When I left Borneo a year later, this military presence had disappeared, although

regiments, particularly Gurkhas, were to remain in Brunei at the Sultan's request.

I was met at Brunei's small airport by Ian McKnight, a Yorkshireman married to a local girl from one of the Bornean indigenous races. Ian was Principal of the school where I would be teaching for the next year, Sultan Omar Ali Saifuddin (SOAS) College, the only school in Brunei which taught to the 6th form.

He showed me my flat at the school – two large rooms with kitchen and bathroom. The school had been built in the 50's and was of colonial tropical design – two stories high with verandas running along each side of the first floor to provide a shield from the sun and to catch any breeze. There was no air-conditioning at the school but large fans in the centre of each of the main rooms, including those in my flat. The windows had wire mesh on them to prevent mosquitoes flying into the room when the louvres were open at night.

Ian McKnight was a thoughtful and caring man. Apart from giving me dinner on the first evening that I arrived, he introduced me to some of the teaching staff at the school and then, the following morning, took me to an outfitters shop to purchase clothes appropriate for teaching at a school in the Tropics – white cotton shirts, white shorts and white long socks.

Brunei Town was fairly typical of South-East Asian cities and towns at that time – on a grid format; two storey buildings of a functional form; a raised walkway at ground level to prevent shops from being flooded in the rainy season, and covered so that pedestrians could walk from one end of the street to the other without getting wet; large monsoon drains running along the walkway; padangs or large open grass areas for markets, feeding cattle or playing sport; some civic buildings of which the most important might be the Post Office; and then the grand buildings such as, in Brunei's case, the mosque with its gold dome.

A particular feature of Brunei Town was Kampong Ayer (or water village) comprising wooden houses on wooden stilts above the Brunei River. The inhabitants of Brunei have lived in Kampong Ayer for over 1,300 years. It has been dubbed the Venice of the East, although it is quite simple by comparison. Today, 40,000 people live in this strange world, with water supply and provision of sewerage, walkways and its own hospital and schools.

In the centre of town were the shops, banks, restaurants, cinema and hotels that I was going to become familiar with over the next 12 months. In particular, I frequented the Union (a Chinese Restaurant), the Government Rest House (mainly for lunch), the OK Bar at the Brunei Hotel in Jalan Pemancha (at a time when the State permitted the sale of alcohol), the open stalls behind the Boon Pang Cinema (where one could buy a *curry udang* (prawn) or *curry ayam* (chicken) with a delicious *parata* or *puri* cooked on a very hot plate), and, finally, the Royal Brunei Yacht Club (which made the most delicious *Alaska Bombe*). The stalls (*Pasar Malam*, meaning Night Market) behind the Boon Pang Cinema had been declared out of bounds to British soldiers, who were based at the Army Camp at Bolkiah, on the grounds that they were a potential source of dysentery or even cholera. I was not so constrained. I was also a regular visitor to the town's Post Office to collect my incoming mail, where I had a lock box with the unforgettable number *PO Box 700*.

In the days that followed, I met a number of people associated with the school and the Brunei Government. Later, these contacts extended to the Brunei Shell Petroleum Company in Seria. The expatriate community in Brunei was small and extremely friendly. There was much party going. It was a carefree existence in the hot, steamy environment of the Tropics. Those with whom I would have a great deal of contact in the coming months were:

- Ian McKnight, Principal of SOAS College
- Douglas Boyd, a Eurasian, who was the Warden of the boarding part of the school. Douglas had served during the Second World War with Tom Harrisson (later the Curator of the Sarawak Museum from 1947 to 1966) in the campaigns of the Z Special Unit Semut Operations. These had harassed the Japanese Forces in Borneo and accounted for 1,700 Japanese soldiers killed. Douglas told me that, during the War, local head hunter tribesmen, who were offered one Malay dollar for every head brought to base camp, did not

always restrict themselves to bringing Japanese heads – Chinese heads could look quite similar

- Pat Ilomin, a Filipino, who was the wood work teacher at SOAS College and who owned a Mini. He was a regular companion for lunch and dinner, and at many late night drinking sessions, as well as being a supporter of drama at the school
- Hardy, a moody Eurasian teacher, in his 40's, who was responsible for the boarders and who had a complicated, and not always satisfied, love life
- Bob Tate, the State Geologist, a very agreeable companion, who had access to a boat for exploration and with whom we explored the Ulu (upriver) in the Limbang 5th Division of Sarawak and enjoyed dinners, parties and many late night drinks
- Jee, a Malaysian with a goatee beard, who worked for the Malay section of Radio Brunei. Jee lived at the Brunei Hotel, was a great socialiser and always ready for a challenge and an adventure. I never knew his full name and I believe that he might have also been a member of the Special Branch. He, too, was a late night drinker
- Pat Adamson, an officer in the Public Works Department (PWD) with whom we had many lunches and enjoyed many parties
- JR (Steve) Stevens, who became Acting Principal after McKnight left in April 1967
- Benedict Fair, a teacher from Sri Lanka and Principal of the Junior School
- Nigel Haslam, Chief Accountant at Brunei Shell Petroleum Company in Seria. Apart from being wicket keeper for the Panaga Cricket Team, of which I was a member, Nigel helped me to choose between three offers of employment back in the UK, from Cooper Brothers & Co, Price Waterhouse and Touche Ross. He recommended Coopers, not least because he enjoyed the company of John (Mac) McCormack who was Senior Partner of Coopers in Singapore responsible for auditing Shell's revenues on behalf of the Brunei Government

- Emilie Batteljee, a teacher at the Brunei Shell Petroleum Company's school in Seria, who was a close friend and my "partner" during my stay in Brunei
- Her colleagues, Bridget Barton and Anneke Glerum, who were fellow teachers at the Shell school in Seria
- Jean Noel, a geophysicist with Brunei Shell Petroleum Company, with whom we socialised a great deal until he went on leave in April 1967
- Peter Berry (now CMG) who worked with Harrisons & Crosfield, initially in Brunei in 1967, and later became Chief Executive and then Chairman of Crown Agents
- GV (Gerald) de Freitas, Director of Brunei's Broadcasting and Information Department, who gave me my first job in broadcasting
- John Lawrence, British Council representative in Kuching, with responsibility for VSOs in Borneo
- Dato Setia Bill Doughty, long term British resident of Brunei, who arrived in the country before the First World War and whom I interviewed for Radio Brunei

SOAS College

SOAS College was founded in 1955 to provide education for boys and girls to 6th Form level, with students taking General Certificate and Higher School Certificate qualifications in the Cambridge Exams. In 1966, there were 728 students in the Preparatory School and 721 in the Secondary School. Academic standards were not high, with only three passing HSC and three with GCE 'A' Levels in 1966. In the lower General Certificate Exams, only two students achieved Grade I passes and just 11 achieved Grade II passes. The low academic standards were not helped by the low entry qualification required to progress to the 6th Form – just three GCE passes.

Those who were considered bright enough, or who had an interest in further study, often went to school in the UK to obtain 'A' levels and so fit them for university. Yet, despite low standards, the School was growing fast and, by 1969, had a total roll of 3,173 students. It was a question of quantity rather than quality.

Since 1966, academic standards have improved greatly in the State and tertiary education is now available in Brunei, including Universiti Brunei Darussalam, The Brunei Institute of Technology and the The Paprsb Nursing College.

The Principal of SOAS College was, usually, of European origin – from Britain or one of the Dominions. The teaching staff comprised, for the most part, Indians and Sri Lankans from the Subcontinent or Malays and Chinese from Malaysia or Singapore. There were also a few Eurasians and Filipinos. Almost all the teachers in the Secondary School were graduates of a university from somewhere in the Commonwealth. I was not the first European on the teaching staff. A VSO volunteer, Peter Croucher, was my immediate predecessor.

Also, for almost two years (1958 and 1959) fellow Lancastrian, John Wilson (better known as Anthony Burgess) taught at the school as a member of the Colonial Service. During his time at SOAS he wrote *Devil of a State*, a parody on colonial life in an imaginary African country, Dunia, but actually based on Brunei. This was published in 1961. Burgess had to leave Brunei following diagnosis of a brain tumour. He later claimed that he had been driven out of the country for political reasons. Apparently his wife had said something "obscene" to the Duke of Edinburgh during an official visit and Burgess had supported the revolutionary opposition party, the BRP, and had become friends with Dr Azahari. His biographer, Geoffrey Grigson has written:

"He was, however, suffering from the effects of prolonged heavy drinking (and associated poor nutrition), of the often oppressive Southeast Asian climate, of chronic constipation, and of overwork and professional disappointment"; and further: "As he put it, the scions of the sultans and of the elite in Brunei "did not wish to be taught", because the free-flowing abundance of oil guaranteed their income and privileged status. He may also have wished for a pretext to abandon teaching and get going full-time as a writer, having made a late start".

Burgess is better known as the author of his Malayan trilogy of novels and also for *A Clockwork Orange*.

However, his comments on teaching in Brunei in 1958 and 1959
could easily be recognised when I came to SOAS College in 1966.
This was emphasised in the Principal's Report in the School's 1967
Annual Magazine in which the new Principal, JR Stevens, wrote:

*"Students are only too willing to take advantage of free tuition, free
exercise books, free text books, free transport, subsidised allowance
and Sixth Form allowance: there is never any lack of pupils asking
for money. When, however, it comes to giving something in return,
the response is somewhat different"*; and *"The best possible way in
which our students can serve the country is to study hard and play
hard, for education is Brunei's investment for the future"*.

For a year, I taught English, English Literature and Maths. I spent as
much time in preparation and as much time again marking exam
papers in each subject and marking IQ tests. Some classes seemed
interested and enthusiastic in the subject matter but not, in the main,
in studying at home or in revision. Many pupils regrettably did not
seem to have the incentive to put in extra time and effort. The State's
oil revenues guaranteed employment, as well as housing and interest
free car loans, for its Brunei Malay citizens. There were, of course,
notable exceptions and some pupils worked really hard.

Outside the academic world, my pupils' interest blossomed. Sport
was popular, as was music – both traditional Malay and 1960's pop. I
was encouraged to sing with one of the impromptu pop groups at an
event on the Brunei Town Padang. I managed to persuade the Public
Works Department (PWD) to lay a surface of tarmac, with a covering
of rattan carpet, for cricket nets. This was very popular. I had a great
editorial team for the school's annual magazine, of which I was the
Editor. And the one area where I felt most fulfilled as a teacher was in
the production of the play *The Importance of Being Earnest*, where
the cast and backstage support team applied themselves
enthusiastically to putting on a show of the highest quality.

The School Play
It was McKnight's idea that I should direct a play during my year at
SOAS College. *The Importance of Being Earnest* is a favourite at

schools because of the plot, the language and the humour. The production turned out to be quite a marathon, taking almost six months.

Auditions started on 10th October 1966 before the play was finally cast on 20th October. Lady Bracknell, Cecily Cardew and Lane, the Manservant, were Brunei Malays. John Worthing was Eurasian, while Algernon was the grandson of a member of a headhunting tribe. Gwendolen had Sri Lankan blood, Miss Prism was Chinese and the Rev Canon Chasuble was Indian. It was a magical cast and very representative of the different races at the school.

The first *run-through* took place, where the basic plot was discussed, followed by recitals and an explanation of the text. What, indeed, did *the unfashionable side of the street* actually mean? What/Where is *The Brighton Line*? For those living outside Britain, this strange world of Victorian England, Lady Bracknell and her charges, had to be explained.

None of the cast had acted before. It was necessary to teach the students how to move, how to make stage gestures, entrances, exits, pauses and, of course, how to project their voices. I would sit in the gallery at the top of the auditorium shouting *"can't hear, can't hear"* (imitating my drama teacher, Arnold Hagger, at my old school) until the fragile voices became louder and the words came out clear enough for a large audience to hear.

The school stage was in a chaotic state. The building had been used by the British Army paratroops who flew into Brunei at the time of the 1962 Rebellion. The stage curtains had been torn down and used as blankets. There was rubbish everywhere. After a general spring clean, new equipment was ordered – pulleys and ropes from a contractor in Brunei Town, curtains from Hong Kong, stage lights borrowed from the Army Camp at Bolkiah. Then the sets had to be painted and furniture acquired that might pass for being Victorian. Stage crew were recruited and shown how to shift scenery and how to change lighting and arrange sound effects. Costumes were made. The programme was printed.

After six months of hard work and three dress rehearsals, the first performance was in front of 600 schoolchildren from SOAS and the neighbouring girls' school, STPRI. The second performance was attended by over 300 adults and a few children. The third, on 9th April 1967, was the gala evening, with an audience of over 400, including VIPs such as the British High Commissioner, the Director of Education, the Attorney General and the British Council Representative from Kuching. It was a wild success, reported as such in the local newspapers and in the *Borneo Bulletin*. More important, it was a great learning experience, and a lot of fun, for the cast, as part of their wider education at SOAS.

It was therefore pleasing for me to hear, some years later, that my Lady Bracknell had been appointed the headmistress of the Girls' School in Brunei and that others had gone on to jobs in the Civil Service, in one case becoming a Government Minister. I was also pleased to welcome my Canon Chasuble to Mansion House while I was Lord Mayor and to learn that the cast had organised a 40th anniversary reunion in Brunei in 2007.

Radio Brunei

Radio Brunei had an English language channel. Gerald de Freitas, the Director General of Brunei's Broadcasting and Information Department, which was responsible for the radio station, preferred to have someone with a reasonable command of English, and preferably with an English accent, to read the News on the English Channel and also to act as "continuity" for introducing the programmes.

My predecessor as the VSO teacher at SOAS had performed this role and, immediately I arrived in Brunei, I was sent for, to be interviewed by de Freitas and given an audition. Fortunately, my acting experience at Shrewsbury School and at Cambridge University meant that I was able to speak fairly clearly and in a forthright manner. So I was hired, adding further income to my already generous pay as a volunteer; the Brunei Government insisted on paying me the local rate for a job as a teacher, the norm accepted by VSO, and in Brunei this was, indeed, very generous. As a volunteer, I was therefore considerably better off than my VSO contemporaries in Sarawak or Sabah and I put this to good use in funding holidays to other South

Asian countries in the two school holidays (December and April), as well as entertaining visiting VSOs from Sarawak and Sabah.

At that time, Radio Brunei was based in Radio House, which was a modest two-storey building about 100 feet by 30 feet. The ground floor consisted of two broadcasting studios, one for the Malay Section and the other shared by both the English and Chinese Sections. The two broadcasting studios were each equipped with two large tape recorders. Once in a while, especially during the night shift, the duty announcer would be able to see a rat or two going into these huge contraptions. Also equipped in each studio were two turntables capable of playing records in the three speeds: 78, 45 and 33rpm (revolutions per minute).

The role at Radio Brunei required me to arrive in good time to read either the 12.15 or the 21.15 News, several times a month. A jeep was sent to collect me and often arrived rather late, so that there was a scramble to get to the studio and read the text before live transmission. On a couple of occasions I had to beg a lift when the jeep failed to turn up.

The news always began by a statement about the activities of the Sultan in the previous 24 hours. On the first occasion in each bulletin that his name was mentioned, it had to be recited in full, thus: *Today, Al-Marhum Kebawah Duli Yang Maha Mulia Paduka Seri Baginda Sultan Haji Omar Ali Saifuddin Saadul Khairi Waddien visited abc.*

I progressed to *Continuity*, as well as the *News*, and then to being a member of the *20 Questions* team; this taught me the most effective technique of honing in on the likely answer, so that at least 10 of the last 20 questions would be guesswork. Peter Berry and I often worked out the right answer after only about 15 questions.

One of the more interesting features of my broadcasting career was recording an interview (on 28th July 1967) with Englishman Bill Doughty who had been in Brunei longer than any other expatriate. Born on 7th June 1886, William Henry Doughty, known later as *"Borneo Bill"*, arrived in Brunei aged 22, in May 1909, after a three month voyage in a four masted sailing vessel from Bristol. The interview was made at Bill's house at Mile 6½ on the Muara Road, with the sound of chickens and geese in the background, cars passing and Bill's clock chiming. While the questions (from me) were fairly amateurish, they did elicit some fascinating information:

- In 1909, there were five Europeans living in Brunei. One of these was the Resident, BO Stoney. Today he is remembered in the name of the road in Bandar Seri Begawan *Jalan Stoney*
- All the local population lived in the water village, Kampong Ayer
- Bill was employed as a junior engineer by the Island Trading Syndicate in its kutch making factory in Subok, Brunei Town. Kutch is bark from a tree which, when cooked, is used to strengthen fishing nets
- In 1912 he helped establish a similar operation in Sarawak
- After five years, in 1914, he returned home on leave, but was sent back to run the factory as others had been enlisted into the Army or were on sick leave
- He recalls the end of the First World War, in 1918, when a ship came steaming up the Brunei River with its flags unfurled
- On his next leave in 1919 he found England too cold and returned to Brunei
- In 1920 the first British warship, HMS Prince of Wales (built in 1902 and scrapped in 1920), came to Brunei
- In the 1920's he owned the first private car in Brunei with the registration number B2. The number B1 had been reserved by the British Resident
- He pioneered the beach road between Brunei Town and Kuala Belait
- During the Second World War, he was initially compelled by the Japanese to manage a sugar factory at Subok but was later interned in Kuching
- After the Second World War, he briefly went home to recover from internment, but then returned to Brunei
- Bill had a house on the nearby island of Labuan and married a local girl

- On the occasion of the Sultan's 50th Birthday on 23rd September 1966, Bill Doughty was honoured with the award of *Pehin Dato' Seri Laila Setiawan Jasa*. This was the highest honour to be afforded to a foreigner

Bill died in 1971, by far and away the oldest European resident of Brunei. His grandson, Daniel Doughty, is now living in Kota Kinabalu and runs an Internet networking company, known as BorneoColours.com.

Up the Ulu

In Malay the word *Ulu* means remote. In Borneo, there are many remote places which are inaccessible because of the dense jungle. Transport between villages is easiest (sometimes only possible) by river. And, in Sarawak, there are five geographical divisions (or regions), based on the five great rivers. Closest to Brunei is the 5th division, located around the River Limbang. This land was disputed by the Sultanate of Brunei when Rajah Charles Brooke annexed it in 1890. The 5th division now separates the two halves of Brunei.

The 5th division of Sarawak is, even today, not well served by roads as there is much jungle. In 1966 the only way to access the villages of the hinterland was by boat.

A party of five, including the Brunei State geologist Bob Tate, who was a regular visitor to the Ulu, Jee, Emilie Batteljee and Bridget Barton, set off by boat from the Brunei Wharf at 08.15 on 11th November 1966, after breakfast at the Government Rest House. Our intention was to travel up the River Limbang, and its tributary the Medamit, to visit and stay at some of the long houses in the 5th division. In preparation for the hospitality in store we loaded the boat with a case of Chinese brandy to be given as presents to our hosts.

We reached Limbang by about 09.00. After a stop at the DO's house and to see some VSO volunteer teachers, we took a taxi (on one of the few roads outside town) to Rumah Ghani, our first long house, where we met a Peace Corps couple, Bill and Eleanor Revelle. From there we hired a long boat up the River Medamit and then another long boat to take us further upriver to Rumah Layang, an old decrepit long house, where we spent the night.

Long houses are designed to provide accommodation off the ground at first storey height, away from nasty wild jungle animals, with the domestic animals (eg pigs and chickens) penned at ground level. On the first floor, there is a long veranda, named a *ruhai*, where the men (and visitors) sleep and where the meetings of residents of the long house take place. In parallel behind the *ruhai* are separate rooms known as *bilek*, where the family (mother and children) lives (and sleeps and cooks) and where the husband is invited from time to time.

The tradition in long house hospitality is that the hosts provide the rice and perhaps some fish or meat, while the visitors bring with them a present that the villagers might enjoy. In our case, the Chinese brandy was very much appreciated and led to plenty of singing and dancing, with rural musical instruments being played and the tribesmen dressing up in traditional costume. On the walls of the long house were several, rather frightening, heads – relics of a previous era when headhunting was a normal pastime.

After a further ride through rapids we were shown a Murut burial cave and then the furthest long house, Rumah Imang, before returning down the Sungai (meaning river) Medamit to Rumah Ghani, another long house where we spent the night, amid further singing and dancing.

In those days, long houses were not much visited by Europeans. Our arrival prompted speculation about some major happening, the announcement of which was, presumably, the reason for our visit. *"Had the Great Queen died?"*

For indigenous Kelabits living furthest in the Ulu along Sungai Limbang, it would take five days paddling by boat to reach the small town of Limbang. The journey back home, with the current against you, would take even longer. I imagine that, with the availability of outboard motors, life is very different today.

<u>The Social Scene in Brunei</u>
Brunei attracted a large number of expatriates, who were welcomed by the Government providing they added value and behaved. The

Religious Affairs Department was quite strict in ensuring a proper dress code for local women (but not as strict, at that time, as in some other Muslim countries) and ensuring that there were no (or, at most, very limited) relationships between Muslim girls and foreigners.

In 1966, alcohol was freely available in clubs, bars and restaurants, although this was later to change. Expatriates were highly thought of, with no discrimination or envy, perhaps because Brunei had never been a colony. The Sultan and his extended Malay family had always been in control and it was they, rather than a foreign Government, that made the decisions, as the Government of the country. Because of the oil revenues, there was no need for any direct or indirect taxation. Brunei was, therefore, an attractive environment for expatriates, who came from many Commonwealth countries.

Some expatriates worked for the Brunei Government while others were employed by international companies operating in South-East Asia, such as the Hong Kong Bank (now HSBC), Standard Chartered, the Borneo Company, Harrisons & Crosfield, Sime Darby and Jardine Waugh.

The last four of these organisations were engaged in all manner of trade and commercial activity – on the one hand: supplying tractors, cars, generators and travel arrangements; on the other hand purchasing timber, rubber and local produce. The goods would be transported by the many vessels that plied between Singapore, Malaya, Sarawak, Sabah and Brunei, many owned by the Straits Steamship Company.

Peter Berry, who took over as head of the Kuala Belait branch of Harrisons & Crosfield, had an ingenious idea for selling air-conditioning units and generators. Travelling to shops in remote villages, he would visit the local shops (*kedai*) owned by the Chinese merchants (*tawkis*). In those days, men of substance (or perhaps of aspiring substance) would own a fighting cock. As one sat on the veranda of the *kedai*, there was a rail protecting the owner from the street and the monsoon drain below. The cocks would typically perch on the rail and, from time to time, there would be a warm sensation as the cock did its business down the bare leg of the person immediately next to it. In furthering the financial goals of Harrisons & Crosfield, Peter would embrace innovative sales concepts. For example, he would bring to the attention of each *tawki* the alleged results of research studies, which had concluded that sex was more satisfying when the room temperature was 72 degrees Fahrenheit or less. As a result, Peter was able to increase the local sales of air-conditioning units. In addition, since not all the villages were linked up to a national electricity grid, he was able to increase the local sales of electricity generators.

In Seria, the Brunei Shell Petroleum Company employed many expatriates, particularly from the UK and the Netherlands. And Shell's suppliers and partners, for example Schlumberger, would also bring in experienced expatriate staff. Expatriates would spend typically two to four years in the country. There were just a very few expatriates, such as Bill Doughty, who had lived in the country for more than 10 years. Some had arrived before the Second World War and had been interned by the Japanese. They were Orwellian characters, as in *Burmese Days*, with fascinating stories to tell.

There were few hotels in Brunei in 1966 – the downtown Brunei Hotel being an exception. Government and other visitors could stay at a Government Rest House, of which the main one was in Brunei Town. There were a few bars and restaurants, but expatriate life mainly centred on the clubs:

- Foremost among these, in Brunei Town, was the Royal Brunei Yacht Club (RBYC). It was a delightful relic of Somerset Maugham days, with expats (often inebriated) drinking and dining in a huge dining room and on the long veranda opening directly onto the Brunei River. There were non-whites who were members of the club but this rather depended on their occupation. So, for example, the Indian Deputy Head of the Special Branch was totally acceptable and, indeed, welcomed. The RBYC had a small clubhouse and jetty at Muara, 17 miles from Brunei Town, which was an excellent place from which to sail to some small islands for snorkelling in clear, blue waters. The RBYC served excellent European food and the chef excelled at *Baked Alaska*. Jonny Boucher and Connal Rankin of the Hong Kong Bank were regular dining and drinking pals. The British High Commissioner, de Freitas, as well as McKnight and Adamson were also frequent visitors, for bridge and a drink, as was I

- The Brunei Sports Club in town was a mixed race club, which offered soccer, tennis, bridge and a lively bar. I frequented the Club often for tennis with Indian colleagues and bridge and late night drinking with Peter Berry, Bob Tate and Jee

- The Panaga Club in Seria was, effectively, the Shell Club. I was able to join, through my links with Emilie Batteljee and Jean Noel. The club had a large swimming pool, tennis courts, a rather smart air-conditioned restaurant, and fielded both a hockey team and a cricket team. I played for the cricket team. Typically, to even things up in friendly cricket matches, for example against the Gurkhas, if a bowler took too many wickets or if a batsman scored too many runs he would be obliged to down a can of *Tiger Beer* and the cans would then be piled up against the wicket, until the bails, stumps and the cans fell with a clatter when the wicket was next hit. The official and actual Dutch and British Queens' Birthdays were opportunities for further celebrations – tulips would be flown in from Amsterdam by KLM or the RAF Band would come especially from Singapore. Other nationals were not left out and Bastille Day, the Swiss National Day and, of course, the Brunei National Day, were also celebrated

- The Hash House Harriers (H3) originated in 1938 in Kuala Lumpur, when a group of British colonial officers and expatriates began meeting in the evening once a week to run a paper chase, typically through jungle, and then finish in a clearing where several beers would be drunk and rugger songs would be sung. It was allegedly an attempt to rid oneself of the excesses of the previous weekend, but ultimately led to yet more intake of alcohol. H3 was named after the Selangor Club Annex, known as the Hash House, where several of the original hashers happened to live and dine. After the War, it restarted in KL and further branches were set up in Singapore, Brunei and along the north coast of Sarawak and North Borneo. The concept in Borneo was that the merchant ship bringing goods to each town would leave Singapore on a two week round trip, stopping at each port (Kuching, Miri, Sibiu,

Brunei Town, Jesselton and Sandakan) on the way out and again on the return trip. H3 clubs were established so that the traders on board could enjoy a Hash in each port, on a different evening, if they wished. Today, there are 2,000 H3 clubs around the world, the Brunei club being the 4th oldest, founded in February 1963. I was pleased to join the Brunei Hash and to be given my green tie with "H3" on it. There was, at that time, a suggestion that the Sultan should become the Honorary President so that the Brunei chapter could be elevated to "H5" – His Highness's Hash House Harriers" but this never materialised. Our regular routine was to run through the jungle as fast as possible to avoid wild animals and insects. Reassuringly, we were informed that snakes could hear us coming and would slither out of the way. The only exception to this are pythons who, we were further informed, are stone deaf and enjoy hugging people. My diary records the names of Harriers who have long since left Brunei such as: Rod Tickler, Bill Hudson, Aloysuis Mettler, Will Rodgers (aka Dill Bodger, the *Master of Hash Words*), Norman Frigout, Graham Moffat and Peter Veck. They were all great drinking companions, after each Hash. Where are they now?

There were also some wonderful sandy beaches at Jerudong and Padjagong. They stretched for miles and were completely empty. In those days the facilities at the beaches were very basic, perhaps a tumbledown hut if you were lucky. But they offered a totally private sunbathe on soft sand and an exclusive swim in the South China Sea.

There was also a very 30's boat club in Kuala Belait which had several sliding seat single skull rowing boats. To go sculling on the Sungai Belait, with crocodiles, allegedly, waiting for you to "catch a crab" and fall in, was a frightening experience. There were also sailing dinghies with a hazardous sliding seat for the crew to sit out on. Capsize or simply falling off was frequent and hazardous. I only learnt later that, actually, there are no crocs in the Belait River; it had all been a typical expatriate scare story.

In the evenings, there was a varying selection of films at the Boon Pang Cinema back in Brunei Town. On one occasion, Peter Berry told us that the projectionist showed the reels of Graham Green's film, *The Comedians*, in the wrong order. He claimed to be the only person in a full house to notice this.

Climbing Mt Kinabalu

At 13,435 feet (4,095 metres), Mount Kinabalu in Sabah is the highest mountain in South-East Asia. It is a huge mass of igneous rock towering over the west of the country, about 60 miles from the capital, Kota Kinabalu (formerly Jesselton). From the Rest Camp in the National Park, which is at about 6,000 feet (cool after the heat and humidity of coastal Borneo), it is a two day walk to the summit and back. Depending on whom you believe, the origin of the mountain's name is either the Kadazan word, *Aki Nabalu*, meaning "*the revered place of the dead*" or *Cina Balu*, meaning "*a Chinese widow*". Either way, the mountain is overbearing and looks formidable. It is not, actually, that inviting. But, being the highest mountain in the region, it calls out to be climbed. Like Kilimanjaro, which Lesley and I climbed in 1971, it is a walk. No climbing ropes are required.

With Jee and a New Zealand volunteer, Rick Vallance, whom we met on the plane from Brunei to Jesselton, we hired porters (to be precise, they were bare footed Kayan ladies, who carried 20 kilos on their backs) and set off at 07.45 the day after our arrival at the Rest Camp.

The morning's walk, climbing 3,000 feet, takes one to Carson's Camp, where we stopped for lunch. In the early afternoon, the walk became steeper and we were soaked through, as it rains on Mount Kinabalu almost every day after about 09.00 in the morning. By 18.00 we had reached our hut for the night, Panar Laban, at 11,000 feet and it was getting quite cold.

After a very early supper, we were in bed by 20.00. Poor old Jee, used only to the heat of South-East Asia, was positively shivering and beginning to wonder why he had joined the expedition.

To reach the top as early as possible, before the morning clouds start drifting across the summit, we had breakfast at 04.00 and started walking at 05.00, while it was still dark. We passed the very top hut at 12,000 feet and then started ascending the rock face, which can easily be climbed without ropes. At this point, as the sun rose, there were spectacular views of Ranau, in the valley below, and we crossed a saddle on the mountain, resembling a lunar landscape with enormous boulders which we jumped over. By 07.45 we had reached the summit, Low's Peak. There, the view was incredible. We could see all over North Borneo. I particularly remember watching the sun rise to touch the tops of the mountains to the South West (all around 10,000ft). The light then spread into the jungle below and, for a moment, took on a sort of green glow before the full daylight began – strong and tropical. In those days, there was a metal box fixed in concrete to one side of the summit and the tradition was to write your name in the book kept in this metal box. I wonder where that book is now?

Leaving the summit, after three hours, at 11.00, it was a straightforward 7,000 foot descent, to the Rest Camp, but there were thousands of steps which were murderous on the knees. We were back in Jesselton in time for dinner, preceded by a hot bath.

<u>Travelling to other countries from Brunei</u>
One of the great bonuses of being a teacher is the length of the school holidays. While much of the holiday period might be spent preparing for the next term's work, there is plenty of time for leisure, including an opportunity to travel.

In the Christmas break, I visited the Philippines, Hong Kong (for turkey, Christmas pudding and mince pies, which were not easy to come by in Brunei) and Japan. In the Easter holiday I had climbed Mount Kinabalu. In the summer, I travelled to Sarawak, Singapore, Malaysia, Thailand and Cambodia. In the mid 60's, there was still a sense of adventure when visiting countries which would later become popular tourist destinations. One felt very privileged and could stay at colonial hotels before they were renovated in the 1970's and 80's (Raffles in Singapore, The E&O in Penang, The Oriental in Bangkok, Le Royal in Phnom Penh). The magical Auberge Royale des Temples, built in 1909 in quiet gardens immediately facing the entrance to Angkor Wat, was very sadly destroyed by the Khmer Rouge.

<u>**Return to Britain**</u>
Before I left Brunei, I was delighted to learn that, after much prodding on my part, the Brunei Government and VSO had agreed that I should be succeeded by another VSO, Peter Maingay, an English graduate from Selwyn College Cambridge and a native of Norfolk.

For me, it was a terrible shock to return to Britain after a year of such adventure, fun, achievement and interest. The UK was cold. Harold Wilson was Prime Minister. Nationalisation was in full swing. The oil tanker Torrey Canyon had run aground near Land's End and was bombed by RAF planes to sink it. The UK decided to apply to join the EEC and De Gaulle blocked the application. The pound was devalued.

At Cooper Brothers & Co, the accountancy firm I had joined, my first year's salary was less than what I had earned in Brunei (as a volunteer, plus being a radio broadcaster). The firm's Staff Handbook included a requirement that all staff, including articled clerks (such as me), should wear white shirts with detachable collars, and bowler hats when out of doors. And my first assignment was the audit of Ford Motor Company at Dagenham.

What a very different world.

Haile Selassie's Empire – September & October 1971

I first met Piers Pendred at Cambridge University, where we both spent much of our undergraduate days on the amateur stage. Some theatrical productions in Cambridge were also taken abroad and we toured France & Switzerland, South Africa and Germany with three of Shakespeare's plays – *Love's Labour's Lost*, *Comedy of Errors* (in which we played the Antipholus twins) and *Romeo & Juliet*. We had a lot of fun.

Piers was a year ahead of me academically and graduated at the end of my second year, in 1965. Prior to joining the British Council in the Sudan, he spent nearly two years teaching as a volunteer with VSO in Kerala, Southern India. In 1969, we holidayed together, with Bernard Simons and Lesley, in Morocco, touring the whole country, visiting Tangier, Meknes and Fez and the desert areas south of Marrakesh. Following a lengthy bout of Hepatitis A, which both Piers and I contracted in Morocco, he was then transferred from Khartoum to Addis Ababa. At the end of his tour of duty in Ethiopia in 1971, he suggested that he might take some local leave and that we should spend three weeks together touring the country.

Ethiopia is the fabled home of the Queen of Sheba, who allegedly slept with King Solomon and bore a son, Menelik, from whom successive kings of Ethiopia claim descent. Its civilisation and its dynasties can be traced back over 2,000 years; the last of these gave rise to a spectacular Coronation, in 1930, of Emperor Haile Selassie, well documented by the author and journalist, Evelyn Waugh.

Its people are *Semitic* with almost 80 different ethnic groups. Their language is mainly *Amharic*, which is the second most spoken Semitic language in the world, although there are many other languages spoken in the country. *Coptic Christianity* (now known also as *Ethiopian Orthodox*) was introduced to the country via Egypt and became the official religion in the 4th Century. A large part of this landlocked country lies above 6,000 feet and Ethiopia's inaccessibility has undoubtedly prevented it from becoming a Muslim country, unlike its neighbours, Sudan and Somalia.

The country has, over the years, been sometimes known as *Abyssinia*, from an Arabic word meaning *mongrel, mixture* or *confusion*, on account of the mixed character of its people. Yemenites settled in the north of the country around the town of Axum in the first millennium BC. The central and southern part of the country has been known, for centuries, as Ethiopia, from two Greek words meaning *I burn* and *face*, together meaning *the land of the scorched faces*. As successive Emperors wished to emphasise their European rather than Middle Eastern heritage, the name Ethiopia has been increasingly used. However, it was not until the Second World War that *Ethiopia* became the official name of the country.

After many centuries of independence, in the 19th Century Ethiopia attracted Imperial interest. The brief detention of British nationals in 1867 led to an army of 12,000 men, under the command of Sir Robert Napier, being sent to rescue them. The following year, at the ensuing Battle of the Fortress of Magdala (then the capital of the country), the British won a decisive victory but had no desire to remain and colonise the country. In the second half of the 19th Century, Ethiopia was unsuccessfully invaded by Italian forces, culminating in their heavy defeat at the Battle of Adowa in 1896.

But Ethiopia submitted to an Italian invasion in 1935 when, for six years, the country became part of the Italian Empire. This short lived colonisation brought some benefits as a result of significant expenditure on infrastructure but, alas, also brought much torture and wanton killing. Emperor Haile Selassie sought to defend his country on the international stage, appearing before the League of Nations and, in 1935, he was voted *Man of the Year* by *Time* magazine.

Following Ethiopia's liberation from the Italians by the British Army in 1941, Haile Selassie introduced many measures to reform the country. In 1955, a new Constitution gave greater powers to Parliament. He helped found the Organisation of African Unity with its headquarters in Addis Ababa.

By the time of our visit, in 1971, Haile Selassie was beginning to show his age. Venerated almost beyond belief by many of his citizens, his ability to introduce the necessary reforms was beyond him. He had six children, four of whom had died. His elder son had been killed in a car crash. His surviving daughter, Princess Tangna Warq was highly regarded, but his younger son, Crown Prince Asfa Wassan, was deeply unpopular, having led a coup against his father in 1960. There were concerns as to who might succeed him. The struggle by Eritrean liberation groups for independence was unsettling, causing rifts and military losses. Famine (mostly in Wollo Province and parts of Tigray) led to an estimated 200,000 deaths. Inflation, corruption and high unemployment in Ethiopia had also caused serious unrest. Certain regiments in the Army mutinied. These factors conspired together to create the environment for a coup, in 1974, led by junior officers who formed a committee known as the Derg. Thus Haile Selassie's long reign of 44 years came to an abrupt end. The former Emperor died, in mysterious circumstances in 1975, with the leader of the Derg, Mengistu Haile Mariam, allegedly implicated. Haile Selassie's remains were given an Imperial style funeral in 2000. And his name lives on as the God incarnate of the Rastafari movement. Ras Tafari, Prince Tafari, was his name before he took the name Haile Selassie at his coronation. As *Conquering Lion of the Tribe of Judah* he was viewed as the Messiah who would lead the African people and the African diaspora to freedom.

As a result of its fascinating history and ancient religion, Ethiopia has some magnificent heritage sites. The 12th Century rock churches of Lalibela have been described as the 8th Wonder of the World. The castle at Gondar and, in particular, the interior of the church of Debre Behan Selassie are stunning. The ancient city of Harar is now included in UNESCO's World Heritage List. Lake Tana in the north of the country is the source of the Blue Nile which exits the lake near the spectacular Tissisat Falls. Ethiopia has some stunning scenery, but it is not a country frequented much by tourists. Tourism is not well developed and the country is not well served by international communications. Ethiopia is, however, visited and appreciated by serious travellers with a spirit of adventure.

It did not take long for Lesley and me to respond positively to Piers' invitation to visit the country and we prepared for a five week holiday in East Africa, including three weeks in Ethiopia.

<u>**Saturday 18th September**</u>

In January 1971, we had completed the renovation of our home, Number 11 Fitzroy Road, Primrose Hill. We were not therefore exactly flush with spare cash. Flying to East Africa and enjoying five weeks' holiday had to be arranged as economically as possible.

The concept of cheap charter flight tickets had been developed by the international tourist industry in an attempt to encourage travellers with modest budgets to fill otherwise empty seats on scheduled airlines. To qualify, under IATA rules, you had to be a member of a *club* for six months. This requirement did not seem to concern many of the holiday bucket shops which had grown up in the late 60's and clubs with fanciful names provided the requisite low cost tickets at the drop of a hat. One of the bucket shops in London had arranged our return flights, via Air France, to Nairobi at a cost of £120 each, as a result of our membership of the *Tropical Socio Society*.

<u>**Sunday 19th September**</u>

Travelling via Paris, Cairo and Entebbe, we arrived in Nairobi some 30 hours later, expecting to be met by our host for the night, Hugh Sweet, a manager from Cooper Brothers & Co in London, on secondment to Coopers in Kenya. Hugh was nowhere to be seen and could not be contacted by phone. So we set off in a taxi and spent the next two hours being driven around the leafy suburbs of Nairobi until we were deposited outside an empty house covered in bougainvillea. Copies of accountancy magazines on the window sill gave us hope that this was, indeed, Hugh's home and, fortunately, this turned out to be the case.

At the time of our brief visit to Nairobi, Kenya had been independent for just six years. Colonial architecture still dominated the city centre and its suburbs. Newer buildings included the Hilton Hotel with a swimming pool some 50 feet above street level – quite a novelty in those days – and the Kanu Building, with a roof in the shape of an African hut. Princess Elizabeth Avenue had been renamed Uhuru Avenue and a flourishing black market had developed for those wishing to exchange pounds sterling for Kenyan shillings.

<u>Monday 20th September</u>

After dinner with Hugh at the Intercontinental Hotel, we were back at the airport early on Monday morning for a 08.30 Ethiopian Airlines flight to Addis Ababa.

Compared with Nairobi, Addis was decidedly *Third World*. A few modern buildings appeared in the tourist and official photographs of the city but the reality was a chaotic jumble of tumble-down buildings linked by mud pavements and open drains. Cows vied with cars on the main streets. We learnt that in the entire country there were just six traffic lights, five of which were in Addis. There seemed to be little order. Frankly, it was a mess.

Piers drove us to the house of a friend, UN statistician Andy Flatt, who had initially come to Ethiopia as a VSO. Andy had become a legend in Addis for his hospitality to volunteers from other countries. The house, with its name *TransLoveEnergies*, colourfully displayed on an arch above the corrugated iron battered gates in a sort of flower-power 60's manner, was a hive of youthful activity, with alternative music constantly playing loudly – known by the inhabitants as *Andy Flatt music*. Scarcely a meal went by when there were fewer than eight sitting down to table.

Piers was staying with Andy, having relinquished his own accommodation some weeks before leaving the country. Ethiopia's exit visa requirements were strict. An unpaid debt would prevent the requisite exit permission being granted. Indeed there was a tale of a servant arriving, with police escort, at the airport on the day the foreigner was about to leave the country and the foreigner being prevented from doing so by a claim for an unpaid wage. So departing foreigners, like Piers, were cautious and vacated their property well in advance of the planned date of departure.

That evening, before dinner, in order to get some exercise after three days of flying, I challenged Piers to a game of squash. There was one squash court in the city (perhaps even in the country) at that time – at the Addis Ababa Golf Club. The club was in a much smarter district, reserved for diplomats and foreign executives, with houses built originally for an American mapping mission. The squash courts were rather primitive and scruffy. And, at an altitude of 7,400 feet, the air was thin, which didn't help breathing or running. But the exercise was much needed and stimulated an appetite for the dinner that was to follow back at Andy's house, with the usual minimum of eight at the table.

<u>Tuesday 21st September</u>

After a brief hunt for Calor Gas canisters, tinned food and a torch, we set off in Piers' car, a Cortina Estate, for the Lakeland area of Ethiopia, some 150 miles to the south. The road (now named Route 6) was one of the best in the country, being the main route to northern Kenya. It was surfaced, at that time, with tarmac, for a considerable distance. Throughout the day, we descended into the Rift Valley, stopping for lunch at the town of Mojo where another road turns eastwards towards the Red Sea. A meal of Minestrone soup and Spaghetti was complemented by Goudar Makinissa, a local red wine, and gave us a first impression of the Italian legacy to the country.

In the afternoon we journeyed further south, passing Lake Ziway and then turning off the main road, via a dirt track, to see Lake Abiata and its flocks of flamingos. They resembled a huge cloud of pink candy floss floating on top of the water and drifting off into the distance. There must have been tens of thousands of birds. It was quite a sight. Continuing on the main road for a short distance, we turned off on to another dirt road and, in a while, reached our destination for the night, the shore of Lake Langano.

After pitching our tent and finding a local helper to light, and look after, the fire, we drove a further 10 miles south to see the sulphurous Lake Shala. Hot water bubbles from springs on the northern shore and cools as it passes over solidified lava to reach the lake. 20 miles long and 10 miles wide, Lake Shala is barren and its only use, so far as we could see, was a natural place to enjoy a picnic, albeit a smelly one because of the sulphur. The locals would bring sweet corn to be cooked naturally in the boiling water by the side of the lake – sustainability at its very best. Before we left, we collected small pieces of pumice stone which we still have in our bathroom today.

Returning to Lake Langano, we watched the sunset, sipped a gin and tonic, or two, and enjoyed an evening meal cooked on the camp fire. Our idyllic setting was soon disturbed when a car load of noisy Italians arrived and attempted to pitch their camp just 20 feet away from ours. We observed, with some amusement, as they spent over an hour trying to erect their tent before finally giving up and retiring to a local hotel just a mile away.

<u>Wednesday 22nd September</u>

20 miles to the south of Lake Langano lies Shashemene, the most important town in the south of the country and the centre of a Rastafarian community. This Rasta community grew up following a grant of land in 1948 by Haile Selassie who encouraged members of the Rastafari movement to move there from Jamaica.

At the time of our visit, in 1971, the road had no tarmac beyond Shashemene. It is now a more prosperous town and an overnight stop on the Trans-African Cairo to Cape Town Highway 4.

Turning east off the main road on to a dirt road, some two hours later we reached the town of Soddo, where the local market sold everything from vegetables to shoes to goats. Here Lesley bought some most attractive fabric for a dress for 20 Ethiopian dollars (about £3). And we stopped at a local bar for a beer and ate a simple picnic drawn from the cans acquired in Addis.

After Soddo the road deteriorated further, not helped by local streams which had overflowed during the recent rainy season. Our descent into the Rift Valley continued and the rough Ethiopian high plateau gave way to arid, brown, grassland, interspersed with acacia trees. Two fully grown water buck ambled across the road in front of us. And, after a few more hours of awful road, we passed the northern shore of Lake Abaya and on to Arba Minch, our destination for the night.

Arba Minch, the southernmost provincial town in Ethiopia, is the back of beyond and swarms with mosquitoes. Our hotel, perched on a hill overlooking Lake Abaya, was managed by a middle-aged woman who appeared to be half Ethiopian and half Italian. The accommodation comprised a number of separate chalets similar to those you find in ski resorts and game parks. With French windows leading onto wooden terraces they provide a private facility for lounging outdoors and for alfresco meals. That evening, amid talk of lions prowling in the scrub in front of our chalet, we drank beer, played cards and tried to avoid being bitten by mosquitoes.

Thursday 23rd September

By morning, it was clear that we had failed in this last endeavour. The little blighters had got into our room and had reached parts that we did not believe possible. Lesley had been bitten savagely on the backside and this was to prove unfortunate, if not nearly disastrous, as our story will reveal.

We breakfasted on the wooden terrace using the remains of the previous day's picnic, complemented by fresh bread rolls, while the gas canister hissed away, boiling water for our black coffee. But our peaceful and leisurely breakfast was disturbed by the arrival of a friendly ostrich. Actually, he might have seemed friendly to his owner, the hotel proprietor, but to us and to our breakfast he was as aggressive as any animal can be. Not fully appreciating the culinary difference between Piers' arm and the bread rolls, standing some seven feet tall, he pecked away at everything in his sight. The animal kingdom had won again and we fled, after paying our bill, and set off to explore Arba Minch and the surrounding countryside.

The region must have spawned an important political figure. For, despite the town being very run down, a dual carriageway tarmac road had been built on the outskirts. The Imperial Highway Authority (IHA) had constructed a store nearby of building materials, including semi-circular drainage cylinders which the local children had converted, with great ingenuity, into a giant see-saw. This was development in the Third World at its very best! Aid used for the betterment and benefit of the people was being appropriately exploited.

Returning on the road to Addis, we stopped for the night at Soddo, where we hoped to find Tim Heffernan, a British aid funded engineer responsible for supervising the construction of a radio transmitter on a hill above the town. The transmitter would enable educational programmes to be broadcast across Wallamo Province and assist in the education of its people. The hill was a former fortification of Emperor Menelik used in his campaigns in the south of the country. The lines of the former fossa were clearly discernible, spreading geometrically from the top of the hill. At the summit, all that remained was a pair of stone gate posts heralding the entrance to the inner part of this encampment.

Tim had been testing the transmitters and loud Scottish music most inappropriately drifted across the valley below. But his weather forecasting proved to be extraordinarily accurate as he predicted heavy rain. Sure enough, as we left Soddo, there was a torrential downpour and the road became a river.

Our destination that night was a house, some 25 miles to the east of Shashemene, where a young Swedish volunteer, Elizabeth, was managing a cattle farm, with hundreds of Ethiopians and thousands of cattle. Her project, sponsored by the Swedish Government, was to cross the sturdy humpback Ethiopian breed, which is capable of surviving on the high plateau, with Kenyan Friesians, who are prolific milk producers.

Because of the rain, our journey had been slow and it was 17.00 before we reached Shashemene. It would be a further 20 miles drive to the next village where we would turn off on to a dirt road to the farm. Our concern was that, having reached the village, we might be prevented from leaving. Because of the threats from *shifta* (local bandits), villages were cordoned off at night with barriers across the access roads. Fortunately the barriers were in an upright position as we passed and we arrived at Goba Farm at around 19.00, just in time for dinner.

Being a Swedish aid project, the farmhouse comprised pre-fabricated Scandinavian wood chalets, decorated in Nordic style. Albeit hugely functional, it looked decidedly out of place on the Ethiopian plateau. And, regrettably, this had not resulted in much work for the local craftsmen who might otherwise have been gainfully employed.

That evening, Elizabeth was entertaining a family of Ethiopians. The daughter had been working for her as a servant and wanted to return to school. Elizabeth supported her view. The father wasn't convinced. He wanted his daughter to be financially independent of the family. He was concerned that if she became too educated, then no-one would want to marry her. It was clear that female emancipation still had some way to go in rural Ethiopia.

Our dinner was traditional – *injara, wat* and raw meat. I've never been a fan of steak tartare and the Ethiopian equivalent was no better. *Injara* has been correctly described in many tourist guide books as *cold wet foam rubber*. It is a fermented bread made into thin round sheets, about two feet in diameter, which are laid out on a large plate. The diner tears off a piece of *injara* and dunks it into a bowl of *wat*, which is a spicy stew. This traditional menu is certainly an acquired taste and one that I never seemed to be capable of acquiring.

After dinner, we learnt the conclusion of the evening's deliberations. The father had carefully considered Elizabeth's well-meaning and well-chosen words. He had enjoyed his dinner. He appreciated the importance of the issues at stake but he would defer his decision until after another dinner at Elizabeth's house the following week. After thanks and much kissing, the guests departed, having enjoyed themselves enormously.

We never did hear the final outcome but I imagine that Elizabeth might have had to host a few more dinners to get the result she wished for.

Friday 24th September
Elizabeth had arranged for us to visit the vast acreage of her farm on horseback. Piers, Lesley and Elizabeth were all accomplished riders. But I had never ridden anything more serious than a seaside donkey. Fortunately they gave me a reasonably quiet mount. But Lesley's horse turned out to be quite frisky.

The Ethiopian grooms had prepared the horses and all we had to do was to mount – as it turned out on the opposite side to European practice. And the saddles looked similar to those you would find in a cowboy film. Off we went, galloping across the open countryside and through a hamlet where villagers, peering out of their *tukuls*, gazed open mouthed at the amateur nature of our riding skills – Ethiopians are fine horsemen.

Then, after riding for about an hour, we came to a sharp wooded incline. Piers went through the wood at breakneck speed. Elizabeth and I set off for open ground to the right. But, Lesley's horse, by now the controlling agent in the partnership, took off, hurling Lesley to the ground. In a flash, she was surrounded by some of Elizabeth's cowmen attempting to thrust small lumps of earth into her mouth, presumably because of the moisture content or was it some herbal remedy. Fortunately she recovered soon enough not to eat too much. Elizabeth swapped horses and Lesley was brought back to the farm house to recover.

It was there that she and I discovered that the day's ride has caused her mosquito bites to turn rather nasty. Bandaged and padded, she was able to walk but found sitting down for lunch to be most uncomfortable.

The discomfort was partially relieved by observing the antics of Elizabeth's Dalmation dog, Otto, who was chasing vultures away from the bones he had been given for his lunch. This had developed into quite a game. He would allow the vultures to strut closer to the bones and then, at the last moment, he would rush towards them, causing them to fly away. This was repeated again and again until Otto got tired or bored. At this point, the vultures had the bones to themselves.

That afternoon we left Goba Farm to drive to Dinsho, in the Bale Mountains. Here we would stay with Bob Waltermire, a Peace Corps volunteer who had been seconded to the Ethiopian Wildlife Conservation Organisation (an Ethiopian Governmental organisation). His remit was to help form, and then manage, as Park Ranger, the Bale National Park.

Bob lived in a large, solid house 10,000 feet up in the mountains, above Dinsho, from which there was a magnificent view of the surrounding countryside. The house had been built in the 1960's by a Belgian, BN Weerts, who had the idea that the mountain land would be suitable for sheep farming. He suffered heavily, and went bankrupt, when thousands of his sheep died from disease. The house, built of local grey stone, had been tastefully designed and planned, with a large fireplace in the spacious reception area and smaller fireplaces in each of the bedrooms, as the outside temperature drops significantly at night. Now the headquarters of the Peace Corps in Bale Province, it was an excellent base for Bob and his colleagues to develop the Park with a particular focus on Mountain Nyalas and Ethiopian Wolves. Today, I understand that the dream has been realised. The Bale Mountains National Park is a reality and the house is a lodge used by visitors to the Park.

Arriving at the Bale Peace Corps HQ at around 19.00, it was clear that Lesley was suffering after the long journey. We went to bed early with a fire blazing in our bedroom hearth. But before doing so, we visited the house's only loo, which was outside – a 50 yard walk down a muddy slope. The following morning we were informed that the howling sounds we heard during the night were those of a nearby hyena looking for its dinner.

<u>Saturday 25th September</u>

The plan for the day was to visit the Sof Omar Caves, approximately 100 miles to the east of Dinsho. The longest system of caves in Ethiopia, they were first seen, and documented, by a European at the end of the 19th Century. Allegedly named after a Muslim holy man who lived there, the complex of caves is rarely visited because of its inaccessibility.

Lesley reluctantly decided to stay behind at the house, nursing her wounds, and would be cared for by the house boy. I set off with Piers, Bob Waltermire, another Peace Corps volunteer (a lawyer, Basil Karmazyn), and a volunteer from the UK (Richard) in Bob's Toyota Jeep. For a dirt road, the first 70 miles to Goro were not too bad. Goro has a grass landing strip, robust enough for an Ethiopian Airlines DC3 plane, and this may have accounted for the quality of the surface of the access road. However, further east towards Sof Omar, the road was no more than a track of dried mud. There was little human habitation and we had the impression of being in a game reserve as there was plenty of wildlife – baboons, a fox, dik-dik, a hyena and many wild birds. A camel train confirmed Bob's information that we were crossing the main camel route between Addis and Somalia.

About a mile from Sof Omar, the road became impassable. So we left the jeep and scrambled down the steep hillside to a gulley formed out of the limestone through years of wear by the Web River. The entrance to the cave was about 50 feet above the present level of the river and led us, walking downhill, to a tributary of the river which we could cross by climbing over huge boulders. This led in turn to a huge wall of limestone with a six foot high hole, through which we could pass into a passage, which eventually led to an enormous cave the size of a cathedral. The main river roared below, swollen by the heavy rain in recent weeks. The sight was amazing and the sound was deafening.

Moving on, we found an exit to the cave and the daylight brought us to the rather nondescript village of Sof Omar. By then it was raining hard and, with the river level rising, there was no alternative but to cut our visit short and return to the Jeep for the journey home.

About a mile from Sof Omar, we realised that we were in trouble. The dirt road had been transformed into a sea of glutinous mud. We stopped for a while, hoping the mud might dry out in the sun, as the rain had stopped. We set off again but the acacia trees on the side of the road prevented our driving on drier land, so we had to follow the track. After a further half mile, the Jeep was up to its axles in mud and we came to sticky halt. By then it was 16.00 and would soon be getting dark. Vain attempts were made to free the Jeep using tree branches under the wheels, but the vehicle seemed to sink further at each effort. The harder we tried, the worse the situation became. Darkness fell. We were stuck for the night on, or rather in, a mud road, far from civilisation.

Meanwhile, back at the Peace Corps house in Dinsho, an English girl on holiday with her Ethiopian boyfriend had come to stay with Bob. Finding the house empty, except for Lesley and the houseboy, she realised that Lesley was about to develop septicaemia and needed an antibiotic fast. She had wisely brought a medical kit with her and administered tetracycline, which duly prevented further deterioration to Lesley's health. When the "cave party" had not returned by sunset, the English girl made reassuring noises about the state of the roads, but became more anxious as the hours past. Lesley wondered if she was about to be prematurely widowed on the eve of our first wedding anniversary (26th September 1971).

With the Jeep stuck in the mud, Piers and Richard decided that they would go looking for help and food. They set off with torches and strict instructions from the rest of us not to stray from the road. About an hour later, they returned with five dry slabs of unleavened bread and some rather dirty looking water, which they had been told was tej, a local beer, having encountered one of the camel trains. At least we had something to eat and drink, but the night passed slowly. A Toyota Jeep is not large enough to permit five grown men to sleep.

Sunday 26th September
Lesley was woken by the English girl who was now quite concerned that the cave party had not returned. She had decided to go in search and she would be taking the house boy with her. Lesley was thus left in the house on her own, not knowing what fate lay in store.

Meanwhile on the road to Sof Omar, it had fortunately stopped raining during the night. As the morning temperature rose, the mud began to dry out. Still more fortunate, we were relieved to find a Volkswagen Beetle coming towards us from the west on the now dried up road. About 400 yards away it stopped. The occupants got out and came to greet us. They announced that they were representatives of *Voice of the Gospel* from Addis, spreading God's word, and offered to help. We had, indeed, been saved.

They had long tow rope and, after a short while, we were freed and on our way back to Dinsho. So overjoyed by our good fortune and our release, we stopped at every village on our return and called at each local bar. Some hours later, the occupants of the car had thoroughly celebrated their new found freedom and by the time they reached Dinsho there was an overblown air of euphoria.

Lesley was relieved, and somewhat bemused, to see the Peace Corps Jeep weaving its way up the hill to the house. After much hugging and recounting of adventures, we celebrated our first wedding anniversary with a very welcome dinner and then a surprise firework display on the hillside – the Peace Corps cater for every eventuality.

Monday 27th September

After a group photograph on the front steps of the house, we said our farewells and set off for the return journey to Addis Ababa, which took most of the day.

On arrival we drove Lesley directly to the main hospital who confirmed her lucky escape, thanks to timely dose of antibiotics.

Tuesday 28th September

The day was spent recovering from our eventful first week in Ethiopia and recounting the tales of our adventures.

Piers suggested we might go and inspect the train to Dire Dawa, as his car was playing up and needed attention. A train journey followed by a taxi ride to Harrar would provide time for repairs to the car and a welcome change from driving on poor roads.

The concept of a railway from Addis Ababa to Dire Dawa, and then on to Djibouti, dates from the end of the 19th Century. Concessions were granted by His Majesty Emperor Menelik II and the French Somalia authorities and, in 1896, the concessionary company founded the *Compagnie Imperiale des Chemins de Fer Ethiopiens* (the *Imperial Railway Company of Ethiopia*). Work continued but technical problems were experienced and many landowners and villagers were hostile. Faced with mounting debts, the company filed for bankruptcy in 1907. In 1908, a new company, the *Compagnie du Chemin de Fer Franco-Ethiopien* (the *C.F.E.* or *Franco-Ethiopian Railway Company*) was formed to continue the work. By 1917 the 500 mile railway line between Djibouti and Addis Ababa was complete. The Addis Ababa station (La Gare), designed by French architect Paul Barrias, came later and was inaugurated in 1929.

At the time of our visit in 1971, the railway had been nationalised but
was still running both to Dire Dawa and Djibouti. At the time of
writing, the service had stopped some years ago as result of heavy
financial losses. Crumbling embankments, decaying bridges and poor
general maintenance of the track caused frequent derailment of trucks
and carriages. The Ogaden War between Somalia and Ethiopia in
1977 and 1978 had caused considerable damage to the eastern part of
the railway. In 1985 a train derailed at Awash (between Addis and
Dire Dawa) plunging four of its five carriages into a ravine; the crash
was estimated to have killed in excess of 400 people and injured 500
more of the 1,000 on board. It was the worst rail accident in Africa. It
is believed that the cause of the crash was the excessive speed of the
train round a curve on a bridge across the ravine. Clashes in 1991
around Dire Dawa between the Ethiopian Government and the Oromo
Liberation Front and the Issa and Gurgura Liberation Front furthered
the problems of the railway and, by 2008, it had ceased to operate.
However, a year later, funded by the European Union, work had
started on restoring the 100 year old Imperial railway. After Eritrean
independence in 1993, once again the railway became Ethiopia's only
means of access to the sea, via Djibouti.

Our main purpose in inspecting the train the day before our intended
date of travel was to decide which class of ticket to buy. In First
Class, there were comfortable arm chairs. In Second Class, the chairs
were wooden and, in Third Class, the seating comprised benches. We
chose Second Class.

After inspecting the train, we were quickly hustled out of the station
as the railway officials wanted to offload the boxes of cigarettes
which had been smuggled from Somalia and were hidden under the
carriages.

Wednesday 29th September
Piers stayed in Addis to attend to his car, while Lesley and I set off
for Harar. The train pulled slowly out of Addis railway station, La
Gare. And throughout the length of its journey to Dire Dawa (over
300 miles) the pace remained slow. In many parts of the journey,
hawkers ran alongside the track, clambered aboard, sold their wares
and got off again.

The track and embankments were in a poor state of repair and the train's speed was limited. But, we were in no hurry. We had assigned the whole day to reach our destination and there was plenty to see en route as we stopped at small station halts and observed the colour and simplicity of rural Ethiopia.

The French and Italian influences on the railway were strong. For example, the staff spoke better French than English. Then, at about midday, the train slowed and stopped for 30 minutes at a halt in the middle of nowhere. Passengers alighted and many of us took lunch at the station restaurant. The menu was spaghetti.

By the end of the afternoon we had reached Dire Dawa and stayed the night at the relatively upmarket Ras Hotel, with a swimming pool and excellent food.

Thursday 30th September

Apart from experiencing the train journey, the main purpose of our visit to Dire Dawa was to see the ancient walled town of Harar, some 35 miles to the east and close to the border with Somalia.

Legend has it that around 1,000 years ago religious leaders from the Arabian Peninsula settled in Harar which became a great centre of culture and craftsmanship, as well as a trading and commercial hub. In the 16th Century a high protective wall was built around the city and this still exists today. According to UNESCO, it is considered the fourth most holy city of Islam, with 82 mosques, three of which date from the 10th Century, and 102 shrines.

After a longer than expected taxi journey from Dire Dawa, we spent the best part of a day admiring the ancient shops and mosques, no doubt similar to those observed by Sir Richard Burton on his visit to Harrar in 1854. The great explorer was probably the first European to enter the city, disguised in Arab dress – there was a prophecy that the city would decline if a Christian were to be admitted inside. And, during our visit, we did notice a lack of warmth and many wary looks as we wandered about the narrow streets, Even today, Harar does not see, or extend a welcome to, that many Europeans.

To ensure we had sufficient time to see the rest of Ethiopia's main attractions, rather than returning to Addis by train, which would take another whole day, we took an Ethiopian Airlines flight from Dire Dawa airport.

Friday 1st October

The day was spent in Addis, preparing for the final leg of our adventure – to the north. The car had been repaired and there was time to catch up with the basics, not least our laundry.

Saturday 2nd October

By Ethiopian standards, based on the poor quality of the roads, the 350 mile journey to Bahir Dar was a long drive. The landscape changed, being agricultural farming at the outset and then, for most of the journey, high veld plateau with quite rugged scenery.

During the journey, Piers told us about a legendary figure, Brigadier Dan Sandford, who owned a farm north of Addis. In 1940, he encouraged Haile Selassie, whom he knew well, to return from exile in England to lead a force of Ethiopian irregular forces to harass the occupying Italian Army. Sandford visited resistance fighters, pledging British help to push out Mussolini. After the war he was appointed as the Emperor's principal military adviser. In 1946 his wife, Chris, founded the Sandford School which, at the time of our visit, was one of the best schools in Ethiopia.

It was also during this journey that we stopped to give a lift to an old man who was walking very slowly along the road. Piers had a sufficient command of Amharic to convey our offer and then to hear the old man's reaction - thanking Haile Selassie, God and then us – in that order.

About 140 miles north of Addis is the Blue Nile Gorge. It is one of the most spectacular gorges in the world - bigger, wider and deeper than the Grand Canyon in the United States.

We were late reaching Bahir Dar and the first hotel we tried was fully booked. We were now on the tourist trail to nearby Lake Tana, the Tissisat Falls and Gondar. Our accommodation for the night was a rather down market truck driver's stopover.

Sunday 3rd October

Lake Tana is the source of the Blue Nile which flows from the lake and then over the magnificent Tissisat Falls which are 150 feet high and 1,300 feet wide. The falls are 20 miles from Bahir Dar and are reached from the road down a rocky and muddy path. Slightly unnerving was the sight of two rather sinister characters, dressed in fatigues and carrying rather ancient rifles. We weren't sure of their purpose but they obviously saw themselves as the local guides and escorted us to see the magnificent falls – the finest in the northern half of Africa.

Lake Tana is also a religious centre, associated with the Emperors of Ethiopia. The lake has as many as 45 islands and no fewer than 19 monasteries, dating from the 14th to 17th centuries. In the monasteries, guarded by priests, are sepulchres and the mortal remains of many emperors, treasures of the Ethiopian church, as well as ancient manuscripts. Seven of these churches (and the most accessible) have been chosen for conservation by UNESCO. One of these islands, Seghie, has a church dating from the 14th Century, with the most sensational wall paintings.

After admiring the church, we were astonished to be shown by the priest in charge what appeared to be crown jewels together with huge Ethiopian crosses and some very ancient illuminated books. We were, indeed, very privileged to see these amazing objects stored, by modern museum standards, in extraordinarily primitive conditions.

That night there were rooms available at the Blue Nile Springs Hotel, yesterday's first choice. By the side of the lake it had most attractive gardens and served excellent food.

Monday 4th October

It was just over 70 miles from Bahir Dar to Gondar, for 200 years Ethiopia's capital. Emperor Fasilides built a castle there in the 17th

Century. Other famous buildings included the 17th Century church of Debre Birhan Selassie with its stunning ceiling of angel's faces and a splendid wall painting of Saint George slaying the dragon.

When the Mahdist Forces of the Sudan sacked the city of Gondar in 1888, they burned down every church in the city except Debre Birhan Selassie. According to local legend, when the soldiers approached the church, a swarm of bees descended on the compound and kept them back, and the Archangel Michael himself stood before the large wooden gates with a flaming sword. The Imperial capital was moved, in 1866 by Emperor Tewodros II, to Magdala, which was devastated two years later by Napier's Army.

One of the more attractive ways of getting around Gondar and seeing the sights is via a gharry – a small carriage or cart pulled by a horse. Gharries are the main source of affordable transportation of goods and people over short distances in many parts of Ethiopia. In Gondar they are an attractive part of the visitor experience.

Tuesday 5th October

After our stay in Gondar, leaving the car at the airport, we flew to Lalibela in an Ethiopian Airlines DC3. These planes are very reliable for hopping over mountains and landing on grass runways, of which there were many in Ethiopia. DC3s also have a reasonable safety record despite the poor quality of local maintenance and the conditions in which they have to operate. We were alarmingly advised that the maximum altitude for a DC3 was lower than the height of the mountains through which we had to fly.

The 12th Century ruler, Saint Gebre Mesqel Lalibela, was given his name due to a swarm of bees said to have surrounded him at his birth. As a youth he spent time in the Holy Land and visited Jerusalem. The layout of the rock churches in Lalibela is said to be a copy of the patterns he observed there, in an attempt to create a new Jerusalem after the capture of the old Jerusalem by Saladin in 1187. Many features have biblical names and even the town's river is known as the River Jordan. Lalibela was the capital of Ethiopia from the late 12th Century, although some of the churches have been dated to the 10th Century. Today, Lalibela is a place of pilgrimage as well as a major tourist site. In the mountainous area of Northern Ethiopia, with its proximity to surrounding Muslim countries, the 11 churches of Lalibela were hewn out of the rock such that the roofs are at the same level as the surrounding area. Below ground level, the rock was further chiseled out, forming doors, windows, columns and various floors. There is an extensive system of drainage ditches, trenches and ceremonial passages, some with openings to hermit caves and catacombs. Thus the churches could not be seen by unfriendly visitors unless they were almost on top of them. Perhaps this accounts for their longevity and the lack of damage or destruction during their 800 year history.

Each church is different, some cruciform and some rectangular, although the basic design and layout are the same. We walked down a flight of very steep steps cut into the side of the rock until we reached the floor of the church some 60 to 100 feet below. Once there, we entered huge doors which led to chambers, halls and places of worship. On the floors were woven carpets which we found later, to our discomfort, were riddled with fleas. The priests, dressed in white, acted as guides.

Lalibela is very special and justifies being considered *The Eighth Wonder of the World*. We were pleased that Piers had planned this as the last place for us to see during our visit to Ethiopia. It was a memorable finale.

Tuesday 6th October

After a night in a tourist hotel in Lalibela, we waited for most of the day on the grass landing strip at the primitive airport, before the DC3 arrived to take us to Gondar to collect the car. Because of the delayed flight, in order to have the evening at Andy's house before leaving for Nairobi early the following morning, Lesley and I flew back to Addis, while Piers drove his car back, leaving Gondar in the evening and driving through the night. This cannot have been easy, given the mountainous terrain and the state of the roads.

Wednesday 7th October

Piers had completed the 10 hour journey from Gondar to Addis in time to drive us to Addis airport. With grateful thanks to Andy for the accommodation, but most especially to Piers for organising a most interesting and thrilling three weeks, we left Ethiopia.

Returning to Kenya for the next stage of our East African holiday, we took with us some extraordinary memories as well as some very persistent Ethiopian fleas, a souvenir of Lalibela. It wasn't until after our clothes had been boiled by Hugh Sweet's dhobi in Nairobi that we finally rid ourselves of fleas, one of the least welcome legacies of our visit to Haile Selassie's Empire.

Postscript

On reflection, our tour of Ethiopia in Autumn 1971 caught the tail end of Emperor Haile Selassie's long reign, at a stable moment, before things got really bad. To come, in the ensuing three years, were geopolitical interference, famines, the 1973 oil crisis which caused inflationary pressures and world recession, and the desire for reform in the country. But, in 1971, the economy and society were just ticking along. The railways still ran. And there was hope of gradual progress – not least through the involvement of NGOs and the other aid agencies. Sadly the traumatic changes brought about in 1974 set the country back many decades to a low point from which, with a more benign Government and with international help, it is only now slowly beginning to recover.

Kilimanjaro, the Roof of Africa – October, 1971

Climbing mountains

"*Because it's there*". Perhaps one of the most famous quotes in the history of climbing, this was the answer given by George Mallory when asked "*why do you want to climb Mount Everest*".

He elaborated, "*It is of no use. There is not the slightest prospect of any gain whatsoever. Oh, we may learn a little about the behaviour of the human body at high altitudes, and possibly medical men may turn our observation to some account for the purposes of aviation. But otherwise nothing will come of it. We shall not bring back a single bit of gold or silver, not a gem, nor any coal or iron. If you cannot understand that there is something in man which responds to the challenge of this mountain and goes out to meet it, that the struggle is the struggle of life itself upward and forever upward, then you won't see why we go. What we get from this adventure is just sheer joy. And joy is, after all, the end of life. We do not live to eat and make money. We eat and make money to be able to live. That is what life means and what life is for*".

At Shrewsbury, where Mallory's climbing companion, Andrew Irvine had been educated, I joined the Rovers, which arranged weekends in Snowdonia. There, we conquered Tryfan and the Glydyrs and climbed the Idwal Slabs and the Parson's Nose on Snowden. These were tame compared to climbs in the Alps and the Himalayas, but they had given me a taste for adventure. In 1967, I reached the top of Mount Kinabalu, the highest mountain in South-East Asia. Now, in 1971, a holiday with Lesley in Ethiopia, Kenya and Tanzania gave us the prospect of having a go at Kilimanjaro.

Kilimanjaro – the facts

At 20,000 feet, Kilimanjaro is the highest mountain in Africa. When the borders were fixed, in the arbitrary partitioning of Africa, a line was drawn from Lake Victoria to the coast which is straight apart from a curve around Kilimanjaro. There is an apocryphal story that the Kaiser complained to Queen Victoria that she had two snow-capped mountains, Mt Kenya and Mt Kilimanjaro; and so the Queen gave her cousin the latter as a birthday present. Thus, today,

Kilimanjaro lies in Tanzania, although it can be climbed from both countries.

The first recorded climb was in 1889 by a German, Dr Hans Meyer. Since then, it is estimated that over 25,000 people have attempted to conquer the mountain; of these, approximately two-thirds have been successful. Those who don't make Uhuru Peak normally turn back because of altitude-related problems. The oldest person ever to climb the mountain was an 87 year old Frenchman, Valtee Daniel. The youngest was seven and the fastest took just nine hours to run up the mountain and back.

Our climb in October 1971

Lesley and I had spent three weeks in Ethiopia before flying to Nairobi, hiring a Volkswagen car and then driving through the Masai Mara and Serengeti Game Parks as well as the Ngorongoro Crater.

En route we had camped in the security of game lodges and seen a variety of animals, including some friendly monkeys who joined us for breakfast. They were bold and would, literally, take eggs from a pan of boiling water and then crack the egg against their teeth to get at the yoke which then dribbled down their chest. Licking gooey egg off one's chest is not easy but it makes for an amusing sight.

We were ill-prepared for the Kilimanjaro climb as we had no boots, protective clothing or medicine to combat the effects of altitude. If we had thought hard about it and consulted a doctor or pharmacist before leaving the UK, we might have brought with us Diamox, which relieves the adverse symptoms of altitude sickness.

In those days, there were two hotels in Moshi, from which most climbs began, the Marangu and the Kibo. The Kibo was the oldest, built in 1896, while the younger of the two, the Marangu was a 1930's gem, family run, with single storey cottages in attractive gardens, from which there was a wonderful view of Mt Kilimanjaro towering above. We chose the Marangu and enquired about guided and portered trips up the mountain.

We were out of luck. No guides or porters were available. We should come back next week. Well, that was out of the question as we had a plane to catch. After a pause, during which he reflected on the consequences of losing two customers, the helpful manager of the hotel announced that there was a party of five white men, from Ndola in Zambia, who were leaving for the climb the following morning and they might accept an English couple as part of the group. They did – and they were charming company.

The hotel arranged boots and clothing, as well as bedding and food for the five day journey, during which we would be staying in mountain huts. There are several routes to the top and we would be taking the popular and most used Marangu Route, which would involve walking almost 50 miles over five days.

Day 1 (Marangu at 6,102 feet to Mandara Hut at 8,907 feet – 5 miles)

At first light we rose and breakfasted quickly. The first day's walk was at relatively low altitudes and would be quite warm. We dressed accordingly. Prior to setting off, we gathered in the garden with our belongings and the porters arrived. We had one porter each and they would carry everything – food, bedding and other essentials. Each porter knew that he would receive a bonus if he managed to assist his chosen client to get to the top. The seven bed rolls and personal effects of each of the seven climbers were laid out on the grass and each of the seven porters then stood by a roll. We stepped forward to our respective load to meet the porter who would carry everything for us. As Lesley went to greet her porter, his face fell; there goes my bonus, he must have thought.

From the hotel we were taken by jeep to Marangu Gate, which is four miles from the hotel. The gate is the entrance to the rain forest and the trail, which is a red mud path, climbs through the lush forest to the Mandara Hut. The walk took about four hours, climbing almost 3,000 feet. It was hot and we took it slowly, ensuring we didn't overexert on the first day.

The huts on the slopes of Kilimanjaro are quite basic, with wooden beds, on which our porters placed rather thin bedding. Mandara Hut is situated on the edge of a spring, so there is both drinking water and water for washing. After a simple meal, we had an early night.

Day 2 (Mandara to Horombo Hut at 12,155 – 7 miles)
African dawns are magical, with freshness in the air and a cacophony of birds singing. After a large cooked breakfast, we left the Mandara Hut by about 09.00. The first half hour or so continued through the rain forest after which the trail emerged into alpine moorland. The day was clear and we had splendid views of Kilimanjaro's twin peaks, Kibo and Mawenzi, and also of the plains stretching away below the mountain. The vegetation was spectacular, with different types of heather, red hot pokers, protea, lobelia and giant groundsel, as well as other flowers. The day's walk took about seven or eight hours to Horombo Hut which was less sheltered than Mandara, but quite comfortable.

Day 3 (Horombo to Kibo Hut at 15,518 – 6 miles)
From Horombo we took what is described as the *upper route*, which is an older path, involving a steep climb of around 2,000 feet to the foot of Mawenzi. The path then descends to the saddle, where there is a high altitude desert between Mawenzi and Kibo. At the end of the saddle, the route becomes a gentle uphill climb and then, for the final hour, a steep climb to Kibo Hut, at an altitude of 15,518 feet. The day's walk had taken another seven or eight hours.

Day 4 (Kibo to Summit at 19,340 feet, then back to Horombo Hut – 13 miles)
The fourth day is one of the most exciting, as climbers are woken at about 23.00 on Day 3 to begin the assault on the summit before the sun melts the frozen scree which separates the Kibo Hut from the rim of the crater.

Lesley decided that this final leg was a step too far and that she had achieved a huge amount already. So she stayed behind at Kibo Hut, while I dressed, grabbed a drink and we set off shortly after midnight. By the light of the moon, we were able to walk uphill around large rocks. But the going got tough as we reached the scree, which was very steep and we had to climb in a zig-zag fashion.

By 06.00, we had climbed to the edge of the crater and reached Gillman's Point just as the sun was rising. It was an extraordinary sight, with Mawenzi towering above the East African countryside. I duly signed the book in the metal container at Gillman's and felt elated but nauseous from the altitude.

From Gilman's it is a further hour's walk around the crater to the Summit at Uhuru Peak and, sadly, for me that was not to be. I saw the snow and the ice cliffs on the top, but I couldn't put one foot in front of another without feeling the adverse effect of altitude sickness. We should have been better prepared and perhaps taken an extra day to climb the mountain to get better acclimatised. But, I had reached Gilman's Point at 18,650 feet and I had seen the most amazing sunrise.

After resting for about an hour, we descended back to Kibo Hut, taking about three hours and, then, after a further rest and a meal, continued our descent, with Lesley, to Horombo Hut, taking a further three hours.

<u>Day 5 (Horombo to Marangu Hotel – 17 miles)</u>
As one descends a mountain, there is more oxygen in the air and the body is given an extra boost. One feels fitter and able to achieve much more.

As a result, after waking early, we decided to get up and start walking, with the idea of having breakfast at the lower Mandara Hut. Unbelievably, we walked seven miles before breakfast, taking just two hours to reach the hut. We felt invincible. We could do anything.

After breakfast, there was a short walk, of another two hours, to Marangu Gate where the jeep would take us to the hotel. However, we arrived too early, after our pre-breakfast trot, and the transport hadn't yet shown up. So, still full of energy and chutzpah, we walked the final leg to the Marangu Hotel. I arrived at the hotel in the first group, downed a beer and then commandeered the jeep to take a crate of beer back to the stragglers. There on the path, surrounded by lush vegetation, we celebrated our achievement.

After the Raj – The Indian Subcontinent – October 1973

Introduction

As Neil Tweedie and Peter Day wrote in *The Telegraph*, *"1973 was the year of Watergate, the Arab oil embargo and the three-day working week. On 1st January 1973 Britain entered what many regarded as a bright new era in our history as a member of the Common Market - even if the Union flag was flying upside down outside the EEC offices in Brussels"*; and *"By December the country was coming to a near standstill, plunged into darkness by industrial strife, economic mismanagement and cuts in Arab oil supplies in the wake of the Yom Kippur War. Food prices spiralled and the European butter mountain was sold to Russia at less than a third of the price in the shops. Pensioners were given butter vouchers."*

While the Heath Government was unable to control wage rises and price inflation, for Lesley and me things weren't so bad. I had just been promoted to the grade of Senior Manager at Coopers & Lybrand in London, with a team to lead, and my salary kept increasing more than the cost of living. We had a very nice house in Primrose Hill and inflation was gradually reducing, in real terms, the amount of mortgage loan we had to pay off. We spent weekends at the Old Rectory in Gussage St Michael in Dorset and, not yet with a family, we were free to spend time on long holidays.

So, encouraged by a squash playing Indian friend, Sonjoy Chatterjee, we were encouraged to spend a month in India, based at his father's house in New Delhi.

We were away on the Indian subcontinent for four weeks – the whole duration of the Yom Kippur War, which lasted from 6th to 25th October. Apart from being another life changing moment for both Israelis and Arabs, this war heralded the oil embargo and the oil price hike, which led to huge global price rises, a painful recession in 1973/74 and the start of a rebalancing of wealth between the Middle East and oil-consuming Western countries. The Secondary Banking Crisis ensued in the UK and this contributed to the UK's worst post war economic situation, which did not recover until the 1980's.

During all of this, Lesley and I were in India and Nepal – happily away from all the mayhem.

<u>Our fascination for India</u>

At the time of our visit, *Freedom at Midnight, Staying On, Jewel in the Crown and A Passage to India* had been published but not yet filmed. Richard Attenborough's film *Gandhi* was yet to appear in UK cinemas. But as children, the story of the British Raj and of Empire was part of our schooling and our history. We had both come across Anglo-Indian teachers at school and, in Lesley's case, she had ancestors who had served in India in the 19th Century.

One of Lesley's great-great grandmothers was Louisa Edith Harcourt-Ranking, baptised at St Mary's Church, Cambridge. Louisa's great grandfather had founded Mortlock's Bank in Cambridge and her grandfather had also been Mayor and was knighted as a Commissioner of Excise. Louisa therefore came from *a good family*. But misfortune struck in 1864 when her mother died and her father, Dr William Ranking, suffered a stroke and became an invalid. Louisa was considered by her immediate relatives to be too well bred, and too pretty, to become a governess and, so, at the age of 19, she and her sister Marion were sent to India to stay with an uncle (Lancaster Ranking) and, hopefully, to find husbands. Within a year, on 14 July 1866 she was married to Major Robert Baker at St Stephen's Church, Ootacamund. In April 1867 they moved to Hoshungabad in the Central Provinces where Robert was posted and where their eldest child, Violet Baker, Lesley's great grandmother, was born on 29th September 1867. In her later years, Louisa wrote an account of her passage to India in 1865 and of her time both in India and England. It makes fascinating reading as it records the challenges of daily life in India for an English lady in the third quarter of the 19th Century and describes the sea journeys backwards and forwards. Separated from some of her children for very many years, as they were sent back to England for schooling, and with transport around India in bullock driven coaches, before the advent of the railway, it must have been hard. And with hindsight, it should be recalled that India was still not actually totally safe from rebellion or dissent. Her arrival in India, in 1865, was just eight years after the end of the Indian Sepoy Mutiny of 1857/8. On the other hand, stability had been restored following the

British Government taking over the government of India from the British East India Company and the strengthening of the British Indian Army, of which Major Robert Baker was a part.

So our image of India was very much influenced by our reading of the history of the British Raj and of Louisa's account of her life as a British India Army General's wife. There were tales of travelling in a sedan chair and by bullock cart as well as, later, by train, dealings with servants, snakes in the bathroom, bringing up a baby when life expectancy was low, crocodiles as well as corpses in the river, riding, shooting, trying vainly to make a success of a tea plantation that Robert acquired after retiring from the Army, parties at Government House and of a general pioneering atmosphere in a very British yet very Indian environment. Our image of India turned out to be hugely outdated, as the country had just completed its first 26 years of independence – a whole generation since the British left.

Das Kushak Road

Kushak Road is less than one mile from the centre of New Delhi and the main Government buildings. Here, a broad, tree-lined avenue fronts onto spacious plots which contain the most desirable of single storey colonial mansions, used by ministers, senior civil servants and military officers. Sonjoy's father, Lieutenant-General SN Chatterjee MC, Director General of the Indian Armed Forces Medical Services, lived at number 10 (or *das* in Hindi).

SN had been trained in the Indian Army when the country was under British rule. He had been befriended by a British family and admired the British way of life. His MC had been won in the Second World War, prior to Indian independence in 1947. We understand that, at one stage, he had an English girlfriend but, in the end, he married a Mukherjee, from the wealthy Bengali steel-making family, and they had two sons, Sana and Sonjoy. Sadly SN's wife died in 1953, shortly after Sonjoy was born, and SN later took a mistress, the wife of an Army Major. Strangely to us, both mistress and her military husband also lived at Das Kushak Road, together with their daughter, a product of their lawful marriage. The mistress was euphemistically referred to by Sonjoy as *Auntie*. Both boys had been sent to public school in India and Sonjoy told us that in his time, boys could bring their own elephants, and presumably also elephant wallahs, to school. Sana had studied at Cambridge University. Sonjoy had been sent to London to be trained as an accountant, something which he sadly did not achieve, as we discovered when he used us and our London postal address as the recipients of his exam results. However, in 1973, he was an ace squash player and someone who was full of the joys of life. Fresh faced, full of enthusiasm and very companionable, he had acquired the nickname *Sunshine*. Sonjoy had been introduced to us in London by another squash playing Indian friend, Ashok Bhatia, a chartered accountant whom I had known at Coopers in the late 60's and who has remained a great friend ever since.

After an overnight Air India flight from London, listening to sitar music and drinking large gin and tonics with a group of Canadian tourists, we had a long, early morning wait to be processed through immigration at New Delhi airport. On arrival at Das Kushak Road, the guest bedroom was peaceful and restful as we slept for a few hours before lunch. The dark interior, made more so because of the rattan blinds outside as a protection from the sun, was cool with high ceilings and ceiling fans. Sonjoy told us of the practical joke at his public school in the Himalayas where boys would place an ink pot (with no lid) on the blade of a fan in the classroom and then ask the teacher to switch on the fan. It worked every time.

Outside the house, the General's official car, a 1950's Ambassador, was waiting, with driver to take him, members of the family and guests to their next appointment or pleasure. There were some smaller Ambassador cars in attendance. But, representing the next generation, Sana Chatterjee owned a BMW and, as a sign of the times, since spares for BMWs were hard to come by in India, we had been asked by Sonjoy to collect some key parts from a depot near Heathrow and bring them out to India for Sana. I am not sure that this was the only, or even main, reason for our delay in being processed through Customs at New Delhi airport. Sana was delighted to receive the spare parts.

Das Kushak Road was gracious and quiet. In at least two acres of grounds, there was a small *"farm"* comprising one cow and a few chickens, providing fresh milk and eggs. One or two farm wallahs were in attendance. In fact it seemed that there were many wallahs in attendance, for different duties and purposes. Labour in India was cheap and the military ensured a good supply of personnel to cater for every one of the General's needs, including *Auntie*. But SN was modest and restrained. A medical man, he was more interested in curing ailments and in saving lives than living an extravagant lifestyle. The internet contains essays written by him on medical subjects relevant to conditions in India. He was a gentleman military officer of the old school.

After a few days of relaxation and getting to know the family, we learnt that SN was about to retire and that Das Kushak Road was to be vacated by the end of October. It was kind of him to allow us to stay in the house during his final weeks there. Indeed it was a perfect base to plan our travel itinerary for the next four weeks on the subcontinent.

Lesley was invited into the kitchen, after the rats had been ushered away, to be shown how to cook Indian dishes. She watched *roti puri* being made, with great attention and enthusiasm. She saw how *curries* were made from scratch, with natural ingredients. And, of lasting legacy to the Stuttard household, she learnt how to make ginger potatoes, a most appetising variation of *aloo chaat*.

A few days in Delhi

Delhi comprises two cities, at least – the old part, much of which dates from the 16th and 17th centuries – and New Delhi, the creation of the Raj after the capital was moved from Calcutta, following the Imperial Durbar of 1911.

Sonjoy was keen to show us around and, interspersed with visits to travel agents and the Air India office to book hotels, trains and flights, we saw the magnificent sights of the city.

In old Delhi, we visited the Red Fort, built by Shah Jahan dating from 1639 when he moved his capital from Agra. The principal mosque of Delhi, the Jama Masjid, was completed in 1656 and is a magnificent example of Moghul architecture, with its domes and pepper pots, which were copied as an architectural style by the British Raj.

Chandni Chowk is Delhi's main marketplace, also created by Shah Jahan. Much older is the Qutub Minar, a tall red sandstone tower, built in the 13th Century as a sign of early Muslim domination of India and used as a minaret to call the faithful to prayer. And we visited a Hindu place of worship, the Laxminarayan Temple, built in the 1930's in honour of the goddess of wealth, Lakshmi, and inaugurated by Mahatma Gandhi. And we paid homage to the great man by visiting his memorial, a black marble monument with marigold flowers placed on the top, in Raj Ghat on the banks of the Yamana River. There was much to wonder at and to take in. Cycle rickshaws vied with cows on the road, bullocks pulled large grass cutting machines on the Medan and hawkers sold everything from *kebabs* to *samosas* to *lassi*, a popular yoghurt based drink. There was a general buzz about old Delhi, with thousands of people rushing about on bicycles, autorickshaws and by bus, the most common form of transport. In those days, tourists were besieged by souvenir sellers offering everything imaginable.

By comparison, New Delhi was more stately and refined. There were more cars but less hassle. With its wide open spaces and grand avenues, New Delhi has the appearance of a great and important city. Conceived before the First World War as the place of Government, after Calcutta became too large, industrial and crowded, New Delhi is a testament to the British Raj and to town planning and architecture on a grand scale. Planned by the British architect, Edwin Lutyens, the city is well laid out and contains some stunning buildings designed by Lutyens and fellow architect, Herbert Baker. At its heart runs Rajpath (meaning King's Way) which is the main wide avenue through the centre of the new city, flanked by lawns, canals and rows of trees. For decades it has been the venue for large scale parades of regiments with brightly coloured uniforms. In the middle stands India Gate, a memorial to Indian soldiers who died in the Afghan Wars and in the First World War. At one end, on a hill, sits the former Viceroy's Palace, now the Presidential Palace. On the slopes of this hill, flanking Rajpath, there are the Secretariat Buildings and the Parliament House with their familiar pepper pots, so typical of British Raj design influenced by Moghul architecture.

Some 34 years later, as Lord Mayor of London, I paid a visit to the Finance Minister, P Chidambaram, whose office was in one corner of the North Secretariat building fronting Rajpath. Perhaps not surprisingly, it had a feel of HM Treasury in Whitehall before its recent renovation, with open courtyards in a style similar to that found in Florence. There were large rooms with splendid views for Ministers and senior officials, small rooms for junior officials and some even smaller rooms for brewing tea, with cubby holes for the janitors. There seemed to be very many supernumeraries hanging about and a bevy of cleaners with metal buckets and mops transferring dirty water from one corridor to the next.

<u>Third class to Agra</u>
The construction of India's railways began in earnest in the 1850's. By 1929, there were 41,000 miles of track and 7,500 stations, making it one of the largest rail networks in the world. Today, the national Indian Railways employs over 1.4 million people. At the time of our visit, the train was an obvious means of visiting cities and tourist sites in Northern India.

Our first experience was the train to Agra, taking just three hours and leaving at 07.00. Arriving at Delhi's Nizamuddin Railway Station was a revelation. Thousands of people were milling around, a sea of humanity looking for the right platform, looking for food and drinking tea in small clay pots which were subsequently discarded on the track. We had not undertaken our research thoroughly enough and assumed, incorrectly, that there was little justification for travelling first class for such a short journey. So we had booked third class. We were informed that, leaving at 07.00, we would be served breakfast en route, if we wished. The third class accommodation was crowded, with families camped as if for long journeys, and it had hard wooden seats. There was a very basic lavatory at the end of each carriage and, just outside, on a platform between the carriages sat our chef, cooking greasy omelettes with ghee in a frying pan over a small coal fired stove. We had been warned about eating in India – no salads, no iced drinks, no fruit that another human being might have touched. But, with no other prospect of breakfast, we concluded that the omelettes had been freshly prepared even though the circumstances of their preparation were insalubrious and even if we couldn't guarantee the quality of the raw material. We survived.

A cycle rickshaw took us to the Taj Mahal. At that stage in our lives (I was 28 and Lesley was 27), our hips and bottoms were of modest proportions and so it was possible for the two of us to sit together in one rickshaw. This had two benefits – first, the obvious, it cut the price of a journey by half; the second, perhaps as important in India, it meant that you could stick together and we often heard the plaintiff cries of, typically, American ladies with a wider girth whose rickshaw was trailing behind that of her husband *"Elmer, please wait, I'm getting scared and who knows what will happen to me if we are separated"*. With her age and looks, she need not have worried.

To say that we were bowled over by the Taj Mahal is an understatement. It was breath taking. Built of white marble on the orders of Shah Jahan, to commemorate the death of his third wife, Mumtaz Mahal, it was completed around 1653. Of Persian design, it has a central dome, four smaller domes at the corners and then four tall minarets on the outside square. Set in attractive gardens, it lies between Agra town and the Yamuna River. Shah Jahan described the building in the following words:

> *"Should guilty seek asylum here,*
> *Like one pardoned, he becomes free from sin.*
> *Should a sinner make his way to this mansion,*
> *All his past sins are to be washed away.*
> *The sight of this mansion creates sorrowing sighs;*
> *And the sun and the moon shed tears from their eyes.*
> *In this world this edifice has been made;*
> *To display thereby the creator's glory"*.

Shah Jahan was deposed by his son and put under house arrest at the nearby Agra Fort from which he was able to gaze over the river and admire his creation in the sadness of his old age. When he died, he was buried in the mausoleum next to Mumtaz.

After a morning's sightseeing, a local restaurant gave us the opportunity of sampling a superbly cooked roghan josh, a Kashmiri lamb dish of Persian origins known for its aromatic flavour and liberal use of chillies. In 1973 wine was not easy to come by in India. There was a locally produced gin which, when combined with tonic and its quinine content, was allegedly a deterrent to bugs of all sorts. This was probably a tale from the Raj when housebound memsahibs looked for any excuse to drink away the lonely hours when no-one apart from the house servants were at home. But the main drink for Indians and foreigners alike was beer, of which the most popular in the 1970's was Lion Beer, which had been first brewed in India 130 years earlier.

The afternoon was spent travelling by rickshaw to the Agra Fort to visit the scene of Shah Jahan's incarceration. En route, we came across a couple of large brown bears in chains, ready for either dancing or fighting. We were not sure that the RSPCA would have approved. Like the Taj Mahal, Agra Fort is now a UNESCO World Heritage site. With its origins in the 11th Century, it was redesigned during Shah Jahan's time but the monumental Delhi Gate dates from the 16th Century. Apart from Shah Jahan's imprisonment the Fort is famous for the fact that in a battle in 1526 the Moghuls captured much treasure including a diamond later known as the Koh-i-Noor. Then, much later, in 1857 during the Indian Mutiny, the fort was the scene of a battle which caused the end of the British East India Company's rule in India, leading to direct rule by Great Britain. As with the Red Fort in Delhi, there are some wonderful buildings of limestone and marble and walls of rooms inlaid with precious stones.

We imagined that it would be romantic to visit the Taj Mahal at night, when the moon would light up the stunning white marble. Since it was a clear night, we set off from our hotel, after dinner, and paid our entrance fee. We hadn't bargained for the fact that thousands of other people, mainly Indians, had the same idea. The gardens of perhaps the world's most beautiful building turned out, that evening, to be reminiscent of the scrum outside a football stadium in the UK, with shouting, jostling and, to Lesley's displeasure and discomfort, bottom pinching. We beat a hasty retreat.

A visit to Fatehpur Sikri made up for the previous evening's disappointment. Founded in 1569 by Akbar, Shah Jahan's grandfather, the city was the capital of the Moghul Empire in the late 16th Century. Made largely out of red sandstone, the buildings are based on the arrangements of a Persian court, with halls of audience – public: *Diwan-i-Am* and private: *Diwan-i-Kas* – and a splendid mosque, the *Jama Masjid*, containing the tomb of the 16th Century Sufi saint Salim Chishti. The Imperial complex was abandoned in 1585 due to a shortage of water but the splendour of its buildings, demonstrating the imagination of Akbar and his architects, remains.

Lucknow and Cawnpore

The names of both Lucknow and, especially, Cawnpore rank high in the list of places that were the subject of key events in the history of the British Empire. Cawnpore stands for nefarious barbarism at the hands of local rebels who killed almost all of the British soldiers and then murdered around 120 women and children at the infamous Bibighar, throwing corpses and some still alive down a well. Like Cawnpore, Lucknow had also been besieged by rebels but was relieved and then evacuated and thus Lucknow stands for salvation and victory against evil forces. Both cities were casualties of the Indian Mutiny of Sepoys in 1857, which ended the rule of the British East India Company and of the last Moghul Emperor. Perhaps worse and something which has only recently been highlighted is the fact that millions of Indians, Sepoy rebels, alleged supporters and innocent bystanders were ruthlessly slaughtered by a British Army whose Mother country was incensed at the way its subjects, particularly women and children, had been treated. It was a question of revenge. But for the people of India, it meant continuing domination and subjugation that took a further Century to remedy.

The Mutiny and the final slaughter at Cawnpore had taken place almost exactly a Century since the Battle of Plassey on 23rd June 1757 which led to the expansion of British rule in India. One of the driving forces of the Sepoy rebellion was a prophecy which predicted the downfall of East India Company rule in India exactly one hundred years after this Battle.

But the real reasons lay in the various grievances of some Indian rulers and the Sepoy troops who were also incensed, on the introduction of the new Enfield rifle, when they believed that the

116

cartridges for this weapon were greased with a mixture of beef and pork fat, which was felt would defile both Hindu and Muslim Indian soldiers.

Cawnpore (or Kanpur as it is known in Hindi) is roughly 300 miles south east of Delhi. It was also the home of Sonjoy's brother, Sana, and his wife Meera. Sana was the managing director of a division of the British India Corporation and lived comfortably in this large industrial town. Our train journey from Delhi took most of the day and we met them for dinner at our hotel, a government guest house in well-tended and watered gardens. The following morning we visited All Souls Cathedral (now renamed the Kanpur Memorial Church) erected in memory of those killed in the Indian Mutiny and in the massacre of Cawnpore.

Sana and Meera took us to lunch at the Cawnpore Club (still retaining its original name) which had been founded in 1890, acquiring a colonial style mansion dating from 1833. It is a fine place, in spacious grounds, and regarded as one of India's foremost clubs with traditional codes and rules to match. A 19th Century brass plaque in Reception confirmed its credentials as a colonial St James's club. Today's members are reminded that, inter alia:

- *A member should carry himself like a gentleman*
- *Use of abusive language is strictly prohibited*
- *Talking loudly/Shouting is not allowed*
- *Servants / Ayahs / Driver / Pets are strictly not allowed in club premises. Any servants / Ayah / Driver if seen with the member in club premises, general committee will have power to take disciplinary action against him*
- *Rs. 5000-/ will be fined for eating and spitting of Pan or Pan Masala in the club premises*
- *Entry will be denied to such person*
- *If a member or guest or dependant is seen eating or spitting pan or pan masala in the club premises, strict disciplinary action will be taken against such a person*
- *Sitting or lying on the Billiards table is not allowed*

It was a hot day and we lounged on the lawn and swam in the pool before enjoying traditional Uttar Pradesh *Awadhi* cuisine, which is based on cooking over a slow fire, using rich spices such as *cardamom* and *saffron*. After a starter of *samosas*, we tasted chicken *curry, pasanda lamb kebab*, complete with *daal, raita, shahi paneer* and *puri*. Indeed, during our time in India, we became great fans of *roti puri* which, if properly prepared and cooked, are deliciously light. We saw them being made by the ladies at SN's new house in Delhi (of which more anon) and the secret seems to be spending hours preparing the puri mixture before it is cooked.

Meera was heavily pregnant with their first child and she relaxed on a lounger on the Club's lawn, looking most attractive in her green sari. Over lunch she complained about her servants. Her mother had always been quite tough and strict; this resulted in her being given enormous respect. Meera, on the other hand, was overly generous, for example giving them air-conditioning in their bedrooms, and they took advantage of this relaxed approach and were not nearly so attentive or obedient. It dawned on us that some of the liberal attitudes popular in the west in the 1970's had reached India and had had similarly unfortunate consequences.

While there is little remaining in Cawnpore of the aftermath of the Indian Mutiny, in Lucknow there are many ruined buildings in the former Residency compound. The siege in Lucknow, in two phases, lasted a total of 148 days and saw great bravery. In fact, on 16th November 1857 no fewer than 24 Victoria Crosses were earned, the largest number ever awarded in a single day. There was fierce hand to hand fighting and, in the first siege, women loaded muskets for the men. After the relief of the second siege, in November, the British Army left the city and it was held by the rebel forces until the following March, when it was retaken.

Lesley and I wanted to see the Residency compound and to try and envisage the events of 1857. A taxi brought us from Kanpur to Lucknow and then we hailed another, local, taxi whose driver didn't speak English. "*Residency*", we said, only to find out that he was taking us to the Bara Imambara, an impressive 18th Century religious monument from which you have a magnificent view of the city. We were glad to see it but our main aim was the see the Residency. So *"Residency"* we shouted, hoping that volume would make up for our lack of Hindi. No luck as our next stop turned out to be the Lucknow Zoo, which was not altogether uninteresting, as we discovered behind the zoo near some sheds an enormous statue of Queen Victoria which had obviously been removed from a more prominent position somewhere in Lucknow. What, indeed, would the once mighty Empress of India have thought of her present location – at the back of a zoo, where only the porters, dhobis and cleaning wallahs could see her? Finally, our taxi driver brought us to the Residency.

There is something very eerie about the site of a battlefield or massacre. These are holy places, where the ghosts of the departed haunt the living. The Lucknow Residency is a collection of buildings which are ruined shells, with walls pockmarked by cannon shells and with no roofs. During the siege it was a refuge for over 3,000 British inhabitants and the ruined church contains the graves of 2,000 British soldiers who died in the revolt.

For the Indians, the Mutiny is commonly known as the First War of Independence.

India's holy places
Over 80% of those practising a religion in India are Hindu and the most holy place in India for Hindus is Varanasi on the banks of the River Ganges, itself a holy river.

We caught an overnight train from Lucknow which arrived at a station close to Varanasi at about four in the morning. From there we grabbed a taxi and were in a rowing boat on the river by sunrise, when the worshippers and bathers begin their morning prayers and ablutions. And what an extraordinary sight it was. We had not seen religious fervour and devotion quite like this before. Holy men, with three white horizontal painted stripes across their foreheads and chests, chanted away while men, women and children said prayers as they took their morning dip and wash. The burial ghats, where the funeral pyres are lit, were also chilling to see and emphasised the holy nature of this river into which funeral ashes were cast after cremation.

From there, it was a half-day's drive to Bodh Gaya, where Buddha gained enlightenment. For Buddhists, this is the most holy place on earth. The main attraction is the Mahabodhi Temple and the Bodhi tree, a sapling of a tree in Sri Lanka which itself was a sapling of the original Bodhi tree under which he reached enlightenment.

A short visit to Nepal

To have visited the two most holy sites in India in one day was perhaps rushing it a bit, but we had to press on in order to travel to Nepal and then to Bengal in the east and Kashmir in the north west. After a night in nearby Patna, we flew Nepal Airlines to Kathmandu.

In the 1970's, encouraged by those on the hippy trail, the Kingdom of Nepal had gained a reputation for being very *alternative*. Drugs were easy to come by. The authorities turned a blind eye to the excesses and eccentricities of long-haired, bearded foreigners who spent time there either bombing out, bombed out, chilling out or, in the case of Americans, avoiding the military *Draft* which would have sent them to less hospitable Vietnam. With few international newspapers arriving in the country, and before the invention of the internet, cafes were meeting places for exchanging information, enjoying shared experiences, meeting potential mates and, of course, acquiring a joint.

Lesley and I were very correct. We neither smoked nor inhaled. Our pioneering days were not yet over but we liked to be looked after. We were developing a taste for the good life. We had therefore booked into the very grand five star Hotel Yak & Yeti, a former palace with marble clad rooms and set in spacious grounds with antique fountains. It was a central location from which to visit the city and nearby Patan. Interestingly, some 24 years later in 1997, when I was driving my 1934 Rolls-Royce on *The Peking to Paris Motor Challenge*, we stayed for two nights at the Yak & Yeti which was a haven of rest after the discomfort of camping and after one ghastly hotel we experienced when journeying through Tibet.

It was harvest time in Nepal and everyone seemed to be drying rice, wherever they could. Roofs, the courtyards of temples, even side streets were covered with the results of agricultural labour. And, in the holy places, there were offerings of rice and marigold flowers to the Hindu gods. Many of the buildings in Kathmandu were made of wood and some of these were very old with intricate carvings and tracery. In the ancient part of the city, there were some most attractive buildings – temples, palaces, shrines – in three Durbar (meaning place of palaces) Squares. At that time, Nepal was still a monarchy, before the awful massacre by the Crown Prince Dipendra of King Birendra and family members in 2001 and the elections of 2008, which resulted in its abolition. At the time of our visit, King Birendra had been on the throne just 20 months, following the death of his father, Mahendra, who died of a heart attack while shooting at Tiger Tops. One afternoon, we learnt that the king was to pass through the city and we witnessed his cavalcade, with rows of admiring schoolchildren, seated or squatting by the side of the road, waving flags and flowers. Also, of interest on our 1997 rally was meeting the sick and ill-meaning Crown Prince Dipendra at a Kathmandu reception where he told us rather sheepishly that his own, elderly, Mercedes was too young to compete in our challenge. Who would have thought that four years after meeting him on the rally he would murder his family in cold blood?

Patan is a suburb of Kathmandu that was once a separate village and has some very old wooden buildings and narrow streets. Lesley and I, in a Jules & Jim moment, hired two bicycles and cycled the short distance to Patan to see this attractive town. And then we indulged in a very typical tourist moment – we signed up for a plane journey around Mount Everest. The weather was fine and it turned out to be memorable, flying over the Himalayas covered in snow.

Another tourist moment followed – a taxi ride to the Chinese border. In the 1970's, both Russia and China were alien places, potentially dangerous and potentially threating to safe Western existence. In the north of the Kathmandu valley, the river from Tibet brought power generation to Nepal and was also the crossing point to China, which by then had absorbed Tibet. So we took a long journey, through pretty Nepalese villages, just to see the Chinese border at Friendship Bridge.

On our motor rally in 1997, after a very arduous few miles descending from the Tibetan plateau, we were delighted to reach Friendship Bridge and the relative safety of the Kathmandu Valley.

24 years later the road had been tarmacked and the standard of living of the villagers had risen quite significantly. On that occasion, since our team had been raising funds to support the Red Cross in Nepal, we were welcomed at every village by members of the Red Cross offering cups of tea and schoolchildren waving flags.

<u>Calcutta, the former capital of India</u>
After the granting of a licence to the East India Company in 1690, Calcutta became the most important city and the main trading port for the British in India. Before the Second World War, the three great cities of Asia were Shanghai, Rangoon and Calcutta. But, its perceived geographical disadvantages and growing Bengali nationalism resulted in the capital shifting to New Delhi in 1911.

The splendour and economic might of Calcutta gradually faded, particularly after independence in 1947, as a Marxist branch of the Indian Communist Party took over the Government of Bengal and militant trade-unionism deterred investment. Many factories closed and unemployment soared. In 1973, we witnessed this decline and the fading of this once glorious city. Everything seemed grubby, with rubbish in the streets, buildings showing lack of maintenance, gutters overflowing and moulded plaster falling off the walls. It was quite sad to see.

We stayed at the Oberoi Grand, a fine colonial building dating from 1911. With a neo-classical façade and grand pillared entrance it is a fusion of Victorian architecture and Indian style, reflecting the city's history and its heritage. From the peace and calm of the hotel's courtyard garden we were able to make sorties onto Chowringhee Road and, travelling by cycle rickshaw, see some of Calcutta's splendid monuments to the British Raj. The Victoria Memorial is the most impressive. Initiated by Lord Curzon in 1906, it was modelled on the Taj Mahal, with four pepper pots at the corners, but its dome has a hint of St Paul's. On top of the dome is a huge figure of the Angel of Victory – hardly an Indian symbol. Curzon had intended that this museum should be a history lesson to all who came to see it. There are many paintings of the British Royal family, miniatures of the Moghul school and early sketches by the Daniells. There is a huge bronze of Queen Victoria seated in an Imperial pose. Inside there are sculptures of famous leaders of the East India Company and Viceroys, including Hastings, Cornwallis, Clive, Wellesley and Dalhousie. This huge wedding cake of a building sits in splendid grounds and is worth a visit at night, when floodlit, as well as being a must on any tourist's list of things to see during the day in Calcutta.

We found the city charming in its decadence. Calcutta looked very British but was becoming very Indian. In 2001, the city changed its name to Kolkata and the State of West Bengal became the State of Bangla.

A day in Rajasthan

Rajasthan is full of ancient cities and rich sights. But time was against us, despite spending four weeks in the country. So, we decided to fly from Delhi to Jaipur for the day. Catching an early flight there and a late flight back should have given us time to see the key sites. Alas, the plane took off three hours late and we had just a short time – for a pleasant lunch at the very grand Raj Palace Hotel, a visit to the pink Palace of the Winds and an inspection of the 18th Century observatory, the Janta Mantar. We got a feel for the culture and architecture of the Rajputs, but did not do Rajasthan justice and vowed to return.

A new house for SN

Meanwhile, back in Delhi, SN had retired from the Army and had completed the construction of a new house in an up and coming district known as Vasant Vihar. This new house was *architect designed* and architects were designing, in the 1970's, some revolutionary and some downright hideous concepts. Made out of concrete, painted all white, the new house looked irregular in every way – windows were not symmetrical, the rooms on each floor seemed to be at different levels with many steps, there was much open plan. While it might have won an architectural award, the new house looked decidedly uncomfortable and was a far cry from the grace and style of the old colonial house in Kushak Road. But this was progress. This was an example of the new India demonstrating its confidence and seeking to distance itself from the Raj.

We visited the house on a couple of occasions, while thankfully not actually staying there other than on our final night in the country. On one visit, there was a religious ceremony to bless the new house involving a Hindu priest and SN dressing up in white robes – Sonjoy looked most embarrassed, even ill at ease, at this event.

Chandigarh – a Statement of Modern India

At the time of Independence, India was partitioned and the State of Pakistan was created. The Punjab was split in two and its capital, Lahore, became part of Pakistan. Indian Punjab needed a new capital and plans were made by the famous architect, Le Corbusier, in 1951. He envisaged a grid structure with buildings, parks and roads based on clearly defined functions for living, working, care of the body and spirit, and circulation. The city complex comprises three architectural masterpieces: the Secretariat, the High Court and the Legislative Assembly, separated by large piazzas. In the heart of this complex stands the giant metallic sculpture of *The Open Hand*, the official emblem of Chandigarh, signifying the city's credo of "*it is open to give and open to receive*".

Having been educated at Churchill College I was not unfamiliar with 1950's architecture, with rectangular shapes, sharp edges, flat roofs and concrete finishes. Later, I got to know the architecture of Alvar Aalto in Finland. Despite this familiarity, I have never been a great admirer of this period of architecture. However, Chandigarh works as a city. It boasts the highest per capita income of any Indian city and, according to studies, is India's cleanest. In 2007 we visit Brasilia, the brainchild of Oscar Niemeyer and we were reminded of our visit to Chandigarh.

The Bhakra Nangal Dam

During the 1950's, there was a spate of very large power generation and irrigation projects in the developing world. Upper Volta, Kariba, Indus River Basin are fine examples of these. At the time of partition, the canal irrigation system in the northern Indian subcontinent was interrupted by the new national border and most of the water from the hills went west to Lahore, the capital of pre-independence Punjab. A massive project was devised to extract water from the Sutlej River on the borders of the new Indian State of Punjab and of Himachal

Pradesh to provide hydro-electricity and irrigation. Two dams were built close to each other, the Bhakra Dam which is considered to be the highest straight gravity concrete dam in the world and the Nangal Dam, some 8 miles downstream. The project, like Chandigarh, was another product of modern India and SN was very keen that we should see these as well as the historical sites.

Bhakra Nangal is 70 miles from Chandigarh and we took a taxi to see this wonder of modern engineering. The area around the dam was a military zone and we needed our passports to get into the area. Stupidly we had left them back at the hotel in Chandigarh. But, I had my shotgun licence with me and, surprisingly, with its official Dorset Police stamp, the licence was official enough for Lesley and me to be allowed through to see the dam complex. The project had been funded by the World Bank and by many governments who had stipulated that their own country's manufactures had to be used. This meant, regrettably, that each of the power generators, and supplementary equipment, was unique and thus none of the spare parts was interchangeable. This did not make for efficient operations. But we were impressed by the scale of the Bhakra Nangal dam.

Jammu to Kashmir
Tracing our steps back to Chandigarh, we then caught the down train to Jammu, the only region of Jammu and Kashmir State with a Hindu majority. Like Amritsar, Jammu is close to the Pakistan border, and the start of the steep climb of almost 200 miles that leads to Srinagar, the State's summer capital. There are no trains between the two cities and this was a chance for us to take our first long distance Indian bus, with a journey time of nine hours. We had been warned; take every opportunity to go to the loo whenever the bus stops, regardless of the cleanliness of the local facilities. And, take food with you, but only something which no human hand can have touched – so nuts, bananas and Coca-Cola bottles with unopened tops sustained us during the long journey.

Kashmir has had an unfortunate recent history of political turmoil and violence. With its large Muslim majority population, at the time of Partition in 1947, Kashmir should have been ceded by the Maharaja to Pakistan, which launched a guerrilla campaign to put pressure on him. But, being a Sikh, he appealed to Mountbatten to send troops and Kashmir became part of India. Promises of a plebiscite never materialised and led to war between the two countries in 1965 and 1999. Tensions remain and Kashmir had never regained its stability sufficient to benefit fully from commercial success, including the latent tourist trade.

Despite this, with its gardens and lakes, surrounded by hills, Srinagar has long been considered, by Indians and British alike, a holiday destination where one can escape the oppressive heat of the plains in summer and enjoy the cool mountain air. There are two main lakes, Dal and Anchar, on which there are many houseboats that can be rented, complete with staff to cook meals and service the accommodation. The houseboats are reached from the shore by a shikara, a wooden boat, with awning to shield passengers from the sun, rowed by one shikara wallah and holding up to six people. Our houseboat had the grand title of the *Hilton Supper* (sic) *Deluxe* and was complete with master bedroom, bathroom, huge drawing room with wood burning stove, dining room, kitchen and other facilities. Our staff cooked the meals and we were visited, each day, by a succession of shikaras, each offering different products and services – flowers, tailoring, hairdressing and photography. It was this last that caught us out. Running short of 35mm slide film we purchased two reels of Kodak from the photography shikara. It was only after we returned to the UK and had the negatives developed that we discovered the scam. The film had been taken from a camera that had been stolen and carefully wound back so that when I took a photograph, there was a double exposure. In our case, there was an Indian lady in an attractive sari superimposed on most of the photos of our time in Kashmir and on Lake Dal.

<u>Retrospective and Farewell</u>
Back in Delhi, we gathered together the souvenirs of our month's holiday – two hand-engraved tall copper vases (to be made into lamps), decorative marble plates inlaid with flower motifs, table cloths with exotic designs and fur-collared embroidered coats from Kashmir. Our thanks to SN for his hospitality and advice and to Sonjoy for showing us around Delhi and Cawnpore were effusive and sincere. A final thanks resulted from our being ushered through the

VIP channel at the airport, the last vestige of SN's senior role in the Indian Army. And the journey home, with sitar music on the headphones in the Air India flight, gave us an opportunity to reflect on what we had seen.

India was in transition from colonial British Raj to modern developing country. Not yet a BRIC, it was still emerging from the legacy of British rule. The train network was impressive – you could travel almost anywhere. The cultural heritage was rich. The monuments – Moghul, Hindu, Victorian and Lutyens – were extraordinary. Attitudes were influenced by the Hindu caste system but also the English class system. There was much bureaucracy, a legacy of British rule or perhaps of earlier Moghul influence. There was a disparity of wealth and a degree of poverty that we had also witnessed in Africa. There was much begging, which we found dispiriting and annoying. The Hindu religion was all pervasive, with cows wandering in the streets and an acceptance, by the poor, of the lot one had inherited. With so many people, it was a busy place and in many areas a dirty place. But with such colour, music, magnificent sights and charm, India had been an educational and enjoyable place for us to see, as part of our understanding of the wider world in 1973.

In Kitchener's Footsteps through Sudan & Egypt - April 1974

In March 1974, I had been working for the international accounting firm, Coopers & Lybrand, in London for 6½ years and had been promoted to the grade of senior manager. Lesley and I were living happily in a refurbished four-storeyed terrace house in Primrose Hill. Things were going well. The firm had introduced, in the UK, a brand new (and quite sophisticated) approach to auditing its client companies. They wanted to roll this out to their offices across the world. I was asked to spend two weeks in South Africa, lecturing to the local partners and managers (at that time all white) about these new procedures.

Time spent lecturing and in discussion in Jo'burg, Durban and Cape Town was pleasurably interspersed with fine dinners and excellent South African wines. The visit re-introduced me to Southern Africa, where I had spent six weeks some 10 years earlier.

At the end of this assignment, I had the opportunity of taking a few days' holiday en route back to the UK, potentially breaking my journey in Mauritius, East Africa or Egypt. Our holiday in Ethiopia and East Africa in 1971 had introduced me to a region which, 100 years earlier, had been the centre of Victorian drama, as adventurers sought the source of the River Nile. And, my Uncle James had played a small role as a missionary in East Africa in the wake of Livingstone, his inspirer. In preparation for our 1971 holiday, we had read Alan Moorhead's compelling books, *The White Nile* (1960) and *The Blue Nile* (1962). I had also read, many years earlier, Winston Churchill's *My Early Days* including his account of his time in the Sudan and the Battle of Omdurman in 1898. The Nile beckoned.

And so, returning from Jo'burg to London, I took a British Airways flight to Nairobi, an Ethiopian Airways flight to Addis Ababa, and then a Sudan Airways flight to Khartoum. I had learnt that the train from Khartoum to Wadi Halfa, on the border of Sudan and Egypt and by the shore of Lake Nasser, left once a week at 06.00 on a Sunday morning, reaching Wadi Halfa 24 hours later. From there, a river cruiser took a further 24 hours to cross Lake Nasser to the Aswan High Dam, which had been completed in 1970. At the time of my journey, the lake was filling up, reaching its capacity some two years later. From Aswan it was possible to take a train all the way to Cairo, to catch a flight home.

I wanted to see for myself this inhospitable part of Africa which had been the scene of many tales of derring-do in the second half of the 19th Century.

Speke had found Lake Victoria Nyanza to be the source of the River Nile in 1858. His dispute with fellow explorer, Burton, the death of Livingstone in 1873 and the amazing tale of Livingstone's body being carried across Africa to be brought back to England conjured up a picture of discovery and thrilling adventure. The accounts of the journeys of Grant, Stanley and Sir Samuel Baker added to this image. The abolition of slavery in East Africa and the Upper Nile was a cause much admired back home.

Every schoolboy (and schoolgirl) has been told the story and seen images of General Gordon being speared to death on the steps of the Governor-General's Residence in Khartoum, at the hands of the fanatical Mahdi, Mohammed Ahmed. He was portrayed as the brave Christian representing the best of Empire. The fact that Gordon had been instructed by the British Government to evacuate Khartoum, rather than to try and hold it, had not altered his esteem in the eyes of the British Public. Following pressure on the British Government, over a year after the siege of Khartoum began, a relief force under General Sir Garnet Wolseley was sent from London but it arrived two days after Gordon was beheaded on 26th January 1885.

News of Gordon's death led to an "*unprecedented wave of public grief across Britain*". A memorial service was held at St Paul's Cathedral. The Lord Mayor of London initiated a fund raising campaign to establish the Gordon Boys' Home in Woking. In 1888 a statue was unveiled in Trafalgar Square. The statue was removed in 1943, to protect it from war damage, and re-erected on Victoria Embankment in front of the post-war Ministry of Defence building. There is also an effigy of Gordon in St Paul's Cathedral and a bust in Westminster Abbey. Other statues were erected elsewhere around the Empire, including Aberdeen and Melbourne.

After failing to relieve Gordon and his Khartoum garrison, General Wolseley's force went home. An expeditionary force, under Sir Gerald Graham, was sent to Suakin in March 1885. Although this was successful in the two actions it fought, it failed to change the military situation in the Sudan. These events ended British and Egyptian involvement in Sudan, which then became controlled by the Mahdists.

During the 1880's and 1890's, Egypt's economy was being gradually rebuilt and the Egyptian Army reformed by British administrators under the control of Sir Evelyn Baring, the British Agent and Controller-General, later to be ennobled as the First Earl of Cromer.

Egypt had not renounced its claim over the Sudan, and the British authorities considered that claim to be legitimate.

Mirroring a vision floated by Cecil Rhodes in 1892, Baring publicised the idea of a "Cape to Cairo" chain of British colonies to keep foreigners, not least the French and the Germans, out of Africa. Lord Salisbury, who had become Prime Minister in 1895, agreed that Baring could begin preparation of the reconquest of the Sudan providing only Egyptian forces were used. It would therefore be seen as having been authorised by the Egyptian Government. Baring arranged for Colonel Horatio Kitchener to be appointed Sirdar (Commander in Chief) and promoted to the rank of Major-General in the Egyptian Army. In 1898, the British decided to reassert Egypt's claim on Sudan. It therefore took 13 years before the British were to avenge the death of General Gordon and put an end to the Mahdist regime in North Africa.

By 1896 Kitchener's army of 18,000 men had reached the Third Cataract on the River Nile. But their supply lines were stretched and they needed support. He appealed to London for additional funds and then began the task of getting his men south to Khartoum.

The idea of a railway linking Cairo and Khartoum had been mooted by the Egyptian ruler, Ismail Pasha, but like many of his projects it did not materialise. The railway never reached the Third Cataract of the river on the great bend in the Nile and, when travelling south, it took a week by boat to navigate the huge bend in the River Nile south from Wadi Halfa.

Kitchener decided that it would be more effective to transport his army not by river but via a new railway 234 miles across the Nubian Desert, thus avoiding the cataracts. As they constructed the railway, each day the railhead pushed further into Mahdi territory, returning each night to the safety of the guarded camp for supplies (food, water, more wooden sleepers and rails). By late October 1897, his army had completed the building of this stretch through the desert from Halfa to Abu Hamed and the journey took just 24 hours. Lord Salisbury then sent over 8,000 British troops to strengthen the campaign.

After crossing the desert, the building work of the newly formed Sudan Military Railway continued along the River Nile, with the idea of completing the 149 mile journey to the Atbara River, south of Berber and south of the Nile's Fifth Cataract. Here, at Fort Atbara, gunboats, complete with military hardware, could be reassembled on the Nile, after their train journey from Halfa. They were used to ply up and down the river looking for the enemy and ensuring a safe passage for the army.

In April 1898 the new leader of the Mahdist Army, Abdullah al-Taaishi, sent 14,000 men to attack the British but they were badly defeated and suffered 3,000 dead. As Kitchener prepared for the final push, Abdullah raised an army of 52,000 men centred on Omdurman. On 1st September, British gunboats shelled Omdurman from the River Nile, while Kitchener's army gathered for the final assault. Kitchener's Army of around 26,000 was heavily outnumbered by the Mahdist forces which totalled 60,000 tribesmen, but the former were well equipped with modern rifles and Maxim machine guns, supported by artillery and the gunboats on the Nile. By comparison, the Khalifa's army was poorly equipped and Winston Churchill described it as nothing so much as *"a 12th Century Crusader army, armed with spears, swords, and with hundreds of banners embroidered with Koranic texts"*.

By lunchtime on the 2nd, Kitchener was the victor. In the battle, the Mahdist forces lost almost 10, 000 killed, 13,000 wounded and 5,000 captured. By comparison, the Sirdar's troops had suffered just 47 dead and 340 wounded.

Khartoum was recaptured two days later, after which Kitchener was despatched to Fashoda (now renamed Kodok) in the south of the Sudan, where a French force had arrived by boat from Brazzaville followed by a year-long trek across Africa and the Sudanese desert. Intent on expanding the French sphere of influence, the expedition was halted by Kitchener's presence. After skilful diplomacy, the Fashoda Incident was brought to a close some weeks later with the French Government ordering its force to withdraw. Then, in March 1899, the British and French Governments agreed that the source of the Nile and the Congo rivers should mark the frontier between their colonial territories.

From 1899 to 1955, the Sudan was under joint British-Egyptian rule, known as the condominium. Independent from 1956, the country then split into two in 2011, following years of civil war and genocide in the south.

With this fascinating history, I was determined to visit the Sudan and to travel overland from Khartoum to Cairo, taking the railway built by Kitchener's Army prior to the reconquest of the Sudan in 1898.

Friday 5th April
When I arrived in Khartoum on Friday evening, I found the temperature to be still over 35 degrees centigrade. Situated at the confluence of the Blue and White Niles, Khartoum is a bustling, commercial city where Africa meets the Middle East. Hot, dusty and dirty, in 1974 there was little to recommend it, apart from the excitement of coming to a place steeped in history, particularly that of the late Victorian British Empire.

I left the much under-used Khartoum Airport and headed for Nile Street, one of the prettier roads in Khartoum, with the Blue Nile on one side and attractive, albeit decaying, colonial buildings on the other. Many had become Ministry buildings. The National Museum and the Presidential Palace are also on Nile Street. But my destination was the Grand Hotel, now renamed the Grand Holiday Villa Hotel. At one time administered by Thomas Cook, this colonial hotel had seen better days. The state rooms longed for a lick of paint. The plumbing needed upgrading. But, with commanding views over the Blue Nile, the bar served cold beer and the restaurant produced an excellent curry. It was a good place to start my journey.

<u>Saturday 6th April</u>
The concierge was helpful and told me where to buy a train ticket to travel to Egypt. After a short taxi ride to Khartoum North station, I waited in a queue for 30 minutes to buy a First Class ticket for the train (from Khartoum to Wadi Halfa) and then I waited in another queue for a further 30 minutes to reserve a First Class cabin on the boat from Wadi Halfa to Aswan High Dam. The train would depart at 06.00 the following morning, a Sunday.

After successfully accomplishing my mission, there was sufficient time to see the prominent sights of Khartoum and I taxied to Omdurman, over the old metal bridge across the White Nile. The silver dome of the Mahdi's tomb dominates the sky line, but was not open to visitors, particularly infidels like me. Instead I visited Almourada, one of the city's old neighbourhoods with its flourishing fish market, confirming the Nile as a great provider.

I spent a good hour at Khalifa's House, the residence of Abdullah al-Taaishi, who took over as leader of the Mahdists after the death of Mohammed Ahmed. The house is now a museum and contains various historical documents, including newspaper reports of the British battles in the Sudan. Memorable exhibits were a painting of Gordon's fortifications in Khartoum; two horse drawn carriages; an enormous bath; the first motorised vehicle to be used in the Sudan; letters sent by General Gordon to his sisters during the year-long siege; and a copy of Queen Victoria's sympathetic letter to one of Gordon's sisters:

Dear Miss Gordon,

"How shall I write to you, or how shall I attempt to express what I feel! To think of your dear, noble, heroic brother, who

served his country and his Queen so truly, so heroically, with a self-sacrifice so edifying to the world, not having been rescued! That the promises of support were not fulfilled—which I so frequently and constantly pressed on those who asked him to go—is to me grief inexpressible."

General Gordon's diary was found and sent to his sister. Its last entry was, *"I have done my best for the honor (sic) of our country. Good-by (sic)"*. His Bible was presented by his sister to the Queen. It was placed on a cushion of white satin in an exquisite casket of carved crystal with silver mountings. *"This is one of my greatest treasures"* the Queen often said, as she sadly pointed it out to her friends.

Sunday 7th April

After several more cold beers and another curry on the previous evening, I left the Grand Hotel as day was breaking to catch Kitchener's train north to Atbara and on to Wadi Halfa.

Khartoum North station was as busy as you might expect for the departure of the one train each week linking two countries. Looking shabby, it had clearly suffered from a lack of maintenance over many years. The 06.00 *Down Train Express* to Wadi Halfa matched the station. It looked very *down* and could hardly have been described as *express*. Pulled by a diesel of late 1950's vintage, the train looked decidedly Soviet in character, perhaps a legacy of the Cold War era when North and Central African nations were being wooed by Communist bloc countries posing, we now know misleadingly, as anti-colonialists. The carriages had no lounge or dining car and each compartment had bench seats with an upper layer that could be folded away except when needed for night journeys. The train was not air-conditioned and there was one loo to each carriage.

I had been allocated one of the compartments, sharing it with a Sudanese family, of Arab rather than African origin, on their way to see relatives in Egypt. They were polite and companionable. *"Weren't the British wonderful? – honest, reliable, upright and with a sense of fair play. What was I doing in the Sudan? Why was I on this train? What was my ultimate destination?"*

The conversation was as interesting for me as it was for my travelling companions. Outside, through the train windows, we glimpsed views of the Nile, as the train continued its journey north. By mid-afternoon, we had reached Atbara and, before sunset, Abu Hamed. From there, our journey across the Nubian Desert began. By the time we pulled down the upper bunks to create beds, there was the sight of sand on either side of the track and, by the time we woke up the following morning, shortly after sunrise, there was still sand on both sides. From the time taken and the distance covered, I worked out that the *Down Train Express* to Wadi Halfa was probably travelling at around 30mph.

Monday 8th April

On Monday morning there were occasional stops at desert halts. Food sellers came down the train selling bread, cakes and melons. Then before we knew it, the train arrived at the new station of Wadi Halfa. Much of the old town had been flooded when the Aswan Dam created Lake Nasser. The new town was decidedly 'one horse' with hastily built shacks acting as Immigration and Customs check points. Everything was searched. Vaccination certificates were meticulously examined. I was glad that mine were up to date, as a rather used-looking hypodermic needle was strategically placed in front of the Health Officer, waiting for an excuse to be thrust into, and thereby pass some awful disease onto, a hapless victim.

Border crossings between emerging countries are always fascinating places to experience. There is a heavy dose of officialdom, a petty and sometimes vindictive adherence to rules and a resigned but frustrated air – in the case of Wadi Halfa heightened by sitting in the sun with the temperature soaring to the mid 30's and the tea break a long way off. I should add that, because of the heat, I had decided to wear white shorts, white long socks and a white shirt – all acquired during my VSO days as a teacher in Brunei. Looking decidedly official, if not colonial, this seemed to expedite my compliance with both Sudanese as well Egyptian formalities.

Border checks completed, we carried our bags across the sand to embark on the ship that was to take 24 hours to cross Lake Nasser to Aswan. There were three decks to the boat and the few First Class cabins were, as one would expect, on the top deck. With shower, wash basin and loo en suite, this was sheer luxury compared to the Wadi Halfa 'down train'.

After the ship had set sail across the lake, a passable dinner down below was followed by an early but not, as it turned out, an uneventful night. Probably about midnight, there was a fearful banging on my cabin door with someone shouting *"Doctor, doctor, come quickly, a girl is very ill"*. My all white outfit had led to my being taken for a medic and I was escorted down below to find a young girl in her cabin, writhing and screaming hysterically. Returning to my cabin to collect my medical kit, I took the view that a good dose of Aspirin would put her to sleep and defer consideration of the cause of her distress until the morning. Within a few minutes, she was asleep and I retired to bed, awaiting my fate which, as it turned out, was favourable.

Tuesday 9th April

The following morning I was greeted with handshakes and words of congratulation. The young girl had slept well – very well. The Aspirin had done the trick. She had woken fresh and much recovered from her *turn* of the previous evening. What was the cause of her ailment – the sun or the excitement of the journey? Either way, she was better, and in good spirits. I was the hero of the hour. Regrettably during the night, under cover of darkness, the ship had slid past the temple of Abu Simbel which had been raised to its new position after the flooding of the Nile. It was to be a further 30 years before Lesley and I returned on holiday to Egypt to see this ancient wonder.

The High Dam at Aswan, the electricity generation equipment and the surrounding dock and rail facilities had been completed only recently, largely with Russian help, and looked state of the art compared with infrastructure in the Sudan. But the short journey to the Old Cataract Hotel, built in 1899, revealed a bygone era, still much appreciated by travellers seeking to avoid the European winter. The hotel, made famous in the film of Agatha Christie's novel *Death on the Nile*, had not by 1974 been modernised. The spacious bedrooms sported original brass bedsteads. Waiters in uniforms with shabby white aprons served large gins, with fresh lemon, as the customers enjoyed a stunning sunset, looking down from the cocktail terrace to the River Nile far below where the feluccas navigated the sleepy waters. In the distance the Mausoleum of the late Aga Khan could be seen. It is a delightful and relaxing spot. I often think that if I was suffering from a terrible illness, yet able to travel, the Old Cataract Hotel would be a restful place to recover or to contemplate the next life.

Aswan is a typical, busy Egyptian town, with a bustling market and with traffic that knows no rules. What is not so typical is the unique quality of granite (Syenite) that is quarried here and which was highly treasured by the ancient Egyptians when commissioning statues and obelisks some 3,500 years ago. These included the three Cleopatra's needles now located, respectively, in London, Paris and New York.

Wednesday 10th April

The train from Aswan to Luxor took about four hours, arriving in the late afternoon. I grabbed a taxi to the Winter Palace Hotel (now the Hotel Sofitel Winter Palace Luxor), built in 1886 on the east bank of the Nile. Confidently expecting to find a room without having booked, as in Khartoum and Aswan, I was shocked and, later, extremely disappointed to find that it was full and that most of Luxor's other respectable hotels were fully booked that night. The only available hotel was *for locals* on the left bank, which was convenient for the Valley of the Kings but not as clean or as safe as I would have wished. With no lock to the bedroom door, a stout wooden chair came in handy to jam the door shut as I tried to sleep in the heat and noise of an Egyptian night.

Thursday 11th April

That did not deter me nor stifle my enjoyment of the amazing sights that Luxor has to offer – the Temple of Karnak, the Temple of Hatshepsut, the Colossi of Memnon and the tomb of Tutankhamun. A day was not long enough, but whetted my appetite for a later visit to Egypt and a cruise on the Nile many years later. By good fortune, the Winter Palace had found a room for my second night in Luxor and I relived the splendour of late Victorian travel with another large gin and fresh lemon before an excellent meal and a good night's sleep.

<u>**Friday 12th April**</u>

Rather than catching the train again, a short flight in the early morning from Luxor to Cairo gave me the opportunity of a few hours in the capital city. I also had to be back in the UK for Easter.

There was just enough time in Cairo for a brief visit to the El Ghorya Bazaar, but insufficient time to see the Museum, the Pyramids or the Sphinx. They would have to wait for a later visit. That afternoon, I flew back to London with a water melon and several lemons in my hand luggage, together with a blue kaftan for Lesley.

<u>**Saturday 13th April**</u>

The Easter weekend was spent at the Old Rectory, the house we shared with my brother at Gussage St Michael in Dorset. Together with Lesley's parents, Geoffrey and Elizabeth Daish, we were joined by Jacques and Laurette Gamard, the parents of Lesley's French pen friend, Jacquie.

Recounting to them my recent adventure and my journey along the Nile, in Kitchener's footsteps, I felt a great sense of achievement.

Our elder son, Tom, was born exactly nine months later!

Down the Irrawaddy – December 1982

<u>Introduction</u>

The recent history of Burma has been dominated by the stifling consequences of autocratic military rule and by the struggle of Aung San Suu Kyi in her fight for democratic freedom.

Burma gained independence from Great Britain in 1948. A military coup in 1962 brought General Ne Win to power and the introduction of the *Burmese Way to Socialism*. A "One Party" system of government was introduced into the constitution. Businesses were nationalised. Burma began its long road to economic decline. Isolationist, cut off from foreign investment, and with a Soviet style economy, the country remained in a time warp. By contrast, some neighbouring countries, including China, India, Thailand and Vietnam, modernised and surged forward, with high rates of economic growth.

In 1989 the name of the country was changed by the military junta to the *Union of Myanmar* and the city of Rangoon was renamed *Yangon*. These changes have not been accepted by many Burmese or by the international community and both country and city are often still referred to by their former names. In 1990 free elections were held and Aung San Suu Kyi's National League for Democracy won 80% of the vote. Yet, still, the military junta refused to cede power and she was detained under house arrest in Rangoon. But the attitude of the regime began to change as a result of continuing UN sanctions. A realisation that other countries were faring better, savage riots in 2007 after food price rises, and a natural disaster caused by a cyclone in 2008, all helped to create a change in attitude. Despite winning the general election in 2010, which the international community judged to be fraudulent, the military regime began to introduce reforms towards liberal democracy and a mixed economy. In the process, Aung San Suu Kyi was released from house arrest. These reforms are far-reaching; productive contact with foreign governments has been renewed and the country has opened up to foreign trade and tourism.

A rich history and a benign environment

According to some, not least the Burmese, the word *Burma* means *"The first inhabitants of the world"*. However, historians now generally believe that the country was first populated from the north and the north east about 2,600 years ago.

The first group to arrive were the Mons, whose descendants inhabit parts of Thailand and Cambodia today. Legend has it that, in about the 6th Century BC, they laid the foundation stone of the Shwedagon Pagoda that is one of Rangoon's great sights.

Next to arrive were the Pyu people who migrated from Yunnan Province in China in the 2nd Century BC. After this, city states were developed and Buddhism was introduced to the country following extensive trade with India. In the 9th Century the Pyu civilisation was overthrown by an invasion of Tibeto-Burman people from the kingdom of Nanzhao, also from Yunnan.

From a small settlement in Pagan (aka Bagan), an Empire of Burman-speaking people developed in the 10th to 12th centuries and this Empire ruled over an area covered by modern day Myanmar, until the Mongol invasions at the end of the 13th Century.

The River Irrawaddy was the route by which invaders entered the country and by which the civilisations spread. During its course through Burma the river runs for 1,350 miles, bringing water for irrigation and for the villages beside it. The British called it *"the Road to Mandalay"* and for centuries it has been the country's main transportation route.

During the period of the Pagan Empire, the Burmese culture and language developed; literature and art flourished; and Theravada Buddhism became the primary faith. One of the stunning legacies is the remarkable complex of hundreds of stupas and temples at Pagan. Marco Polo described them, in 1298, as *"one of the finest sights in the world"* and today, for serious travellers, Pagan is invariably on the list of Top 10 global attractions.

Over the centuries, different ethnic groups have held power in the region – Mons, Pyus, Shans, Mongols, Arakans and Burmans, with periodic incursions by Chinese, Kampucheans, Laos, Thais, Portuguese and Dutch. During the British colonial period which began in the mid-19th Century, Indians and Anglo-Burmese helped to manage the country, but with periodic protests and riots from the Burmese and the ethnic minorities in the border regions.

Influenced by events in neighbouring countries, such as India and French Indochina, Aung San Suu Kyi's father, Bogjoke Aung San sought independence for the country from Great Britain. He co-founded the Communist Party of Burma in 1939. When Burma was invaded in 1941, Aung San and his colleagues sided with the Japanese as a means of achieving independence, but after three years they became disillusioned. They transferred their support, including an army of 10,000 soldiers to the Allies, and this helped the British recapture Rangoon in 1945. Thereafter Aung San continued the fight for independence. His assassination in 1947 on 19th July (now *Martyrs' Day*) is said to have hastened the achievement of this objective, in January 1948.

Because of its rich history, Burma is a fascinating country to visit. There is a wealth of ancient sites, with attractive temples containing hundreds of wooden Buddha statues, some shaped like Modigliani figures. Burma also has natural advantages. There are high mountains and there are large rivers. The land is fertile, irrigated by the great Irrawaddy River, and with a hot and wet climate the environment is perfect for agriculture. The country has coal and other minerals, as well as precious stones such as sapphires, jade, rubies and emeralds. Its teak forests are second to none in the world. Its people are, generally, placid and content, based on their non-confrontational Buddhist religion, which also makes them very devout. George Orwell's *Burmese Days* is a must read for any traveller to the country wishing to understand the character of Burmese (and also certain characters in the British Raj). The availability of food means the population is well nourished. But, it is a land of many different peoples and religions and, from time to time, violence erupts. The country has a stormy history and, for years, many held the view that the only way to keep the country together was through strong military rule. Indeed, today, there are still many of that opinion.

Burma in 1982

When I first visited Burma, in 1982, the country had been *on hold* for 20 years. Economic development had, in a nutshell, not taken place. With businesses nationalised and investment limited, there was little change for the better. People went about their daily life in much the same way as they might have done prior to the Japanese invasion in 1941, albeit freed from the colonial yoke, but with less economic freedom. The Press was stifled. There was no challenge to the ruling military regime.

The buildings looked the same as they had done at the time of independence. The 1960's had come and gone, without making any of the blots on the landscape that we experienced in the UK. There were genteel 1930's villas in the suburbs of Rangoon that mirrored those in Carshalton or, at the smarter end, in Reigate. The government buildings were fine copies of *"Birmingham municipal"*, complete with cupolas and neo classical frontages. These temples to British Imperialism included the Supreme Court, the Accountant General's Office, the Custom House, the Port Authority and the magnificent Central Post Office. The Anglican and Presbyterian churches possessed bells that might have been forged in the Whitechapel Bell Foundry.

All these buildings had been sadly neglected and their edifices, as well as the interiors, were crumbling through lack of maintenance over a 40 year period. Shops in the centre of Rangoon still had vestiges of the colonial era, such as one with a sign over the door *"Tailors to Officers of His Majesty the King and the Glasgow Captains of the Irrawaddy Flotilla Company"*. Vehicular transport was constrained by a 300% duty on cars, so that 1950's Chevys, Buicks and Fords were still the best available cars, used also by taxi drivers. With a lower import duty, trucks were being increasingly used for the transport of both passengers and goods.

The country had been known, pre-war, as the rice basket of Asia. Huge quantities of teak had also been harvested and exported to foreign lands, including Britain. Burma had been known for its precious stones. The war and the post-independence environment had put a stop to much of that. The country had been devastated by the conflict. On the Irrawaddy River, transport had suffered following the scuttling of hundreds of ships in the wake of the Japanese invasion of 1942. 600 of these vessels were from the Irrawaddy Flotilla Company alone. They had not been replaced. There was no money in the post war period to do this. There was no Marshall Aid. And the human resources had not been replaced after the exodus of competent, but not terribly well loved, British expatriates during the Second World War. So, by the time of our visit, Burma was a net importer of rice. The standard of living was lower than it had been for almost 40 years. Yet, it was a very safe country for a foreigner to visit and travel, even to the remotest parts. Many of the Burmese living in the area of the big river are, by nature, peace loving and caring people, as we were to discover. However, there has always been tension between the many ethnic groups in Burma and, occasionally, this erupts into violence of an extreme kind. This comes as a surprise, given the Buddhist faith and the non-confrontational attitude of many of its people.

Travel to Burma and initial impressions
In 1982, a foreigner was permitted to visit Burma for a maximum of just seven days. Few tourists actually travelled to the country partly because of its ostracization by the world's governments and press and also because of the lack of facilities (hotels, restaurants and transport) to attract even the most interested of travellers.

My old school friend, Tim Butchard, was working with the British Council and had been based in Bangkok for three years. While he was posted to South-East Asia, he was keen to explore as much of Burma as our seven day visa would allow. Tim and I were joined in this endeavour by Tim's Thai male partner, Thaweep Piyatharathibes (known as Mee).

We arrived at Bangkok Airport at 08.00 on Saturday 11th December to catch the Burma Airways daily Fokker F28 Jet service to Rangoon. The plane took off an hour late. We speculated as the reasons for the delay. At that time, there were many Kampucheans (Cambodians) fleeing to the Philippines, taking up valuable aircraft time and space.

Bangkok airport was chaotic. Of the 60 passengers on our flight to Rangoon, only about 30 appeared to be tourists, demonstrating the low level of tourism to Burma at that time.

The members of the cabin staff were *Soviet* in their attitude to service. A chicken sandwich was thrust at each passenger with the command "*Eat*". This was not an organisation that promoted customer service, even less one which would listen to the views of its passengers. In Burma, the hierarchy had decided on its objectives and looking after airline customers was not one of these. The junta had other priorities.

It was a short flight to Rangoon's deserted airport, where there were two forlorn Fokker Friendships parked near the terminal. Here we encountered the bureaucracy and restrictions of a closed economy. There were three customs forms to be completed: one for currency, a second for travellers' cheques and a third for high value items, such as cameras and binoculars, which might be sold in the country. It was a requirement that every currency transaction we made would need to be recorded on one of the first two forms.

To obtain local currency (*kyats*) at a better rate than the official government rate, we had been advised to bring with us a carton of cigarettes and a bottle of Johnny Walker Red Label. But our taxi driver, in his 1950's Buick, had an even better plan. He took us to the Russian built Inya Lake Hotel. There we exchanged US$240 of our legally declared currency, at the official rate of 7.45 kyats to the US dollar, to purchase Winston cigarettes, which he immediately purchased from us for 2,880 kyats, giving us an effective rate of 12 kyats. It was good to learn that free enterprise was thriving in this stifled economy.

Situated close to the British Embassy and the Burma Airlines office, and close to the river, the Strand Hotel in downtown Rangoon was our base in the capital city. The Strand was built in 1896 and operated by two of the Sarkies Brothers whose family also ran the E&O in Penang and Raffles in Singapore. These great hotels catered for the famous and the wealthy of the 1920's and 1930's – Charlie Chaplin, Sir Noel Coward, Douglas Fairbanks, Rudyard Kipling, Somerset Maugham, Lord Mountbatten, George Orwell and Sun Yat Sen.

It was while staying at the Strand Hotel that Noel Coward was, allegedly, inspired to write *Mad Dogs and Englishmen*. And, thus:

> *"In Rangoon the heat of noon*
> *Is just what the natives shun*
> *They put their Scotch or rye down*
> *And lie down".*

The hotels owned or managed by the Sarkies Brothers suffered during WWII, and during the immediate post war years. Now each has been renovated and affords, once again, the height of luxury for travellers to the Far East.

However, in 1982, the Strand did not look as though it had received much more than the odd lick of paint since the 1930's. There were bedside cupboards for potties; in the bathroom there was a high ceiling with a fan; the bath and wash basin were of a sea green colour that was a popular feature of Art Deco; the lift had open sides and a concertina door; the telephone exchange was an old *Strowger*, with plug and wires – ideal for receptionists commissioned to eavesdrop conversations; the scruffy bar displayed liquor prices by the *half peg*; at the main reception, there was a *lost property* cabinet with a glass front containing articles carelessly abandoned over the last 35 years – ladies' fans, a wrist watch, a bracelet, a rusty razor, unrecognisable currency, several cufflinks and a host of buttons.

An early task was to ensure that our arrangements for travelling around Burma were in order. Being an employee of the British Council in Bangkok, Tim had sought the help of a member of staff in the British Embassy in Rangoon. Sadly Tim's contact had messed things up. He had made a reservation for us at a hotel in Pagan the day after our return flight to Rangoon. Everything had to be unscrambled. But it was a Saturday and the Embassy was closed for the weekend. The duty officer could not be contacted.

Fortunately, Tim did have a note of the home telephone number of the Cultural Attaché at the Embassy, Richard Hale, who came to our rescue. The offices of Tourist Burma, which was responsible for hotel accommodation, and Burma Airlines were open and, after much bureaucratic haggling, the travel arrangements were sorted out and we also had an invitation to the Hales' house for buffet supper that evening.

But before that, there was time for some initial sightseeing.

The streets of Rangoon were empty of cars and the local boys played football in the middle of the road. On the other hand, the pavements were crowded with hawkers selling all manner of consumer goods – cigarettes, betel nut, leather belts, old fashioned round pin electric plugs and food. Asians are fond of grazing and there was plenty to choose from – noodle dishes, fried rice dishes, soups of all kinds, biryani chicken or mutton, chapatti with boiled peas and, for pudding, various semolina dishes. Because they are freshly cooked, the risk of tummy problems from street food is low, but if your tummy is delicate the stalls are perhaps best avoided. There seemed to be a complete mixture of races – Burmese, Indians, Chinese and the many ethnic tribes.

Burmese people, particularly the girls, are most attractive. With a soft brown complexion and long black hair, they move graciously in their ankle length longyis, made from fabrics of a beautiful design and with stunning colours. Following ancient customs, they paint their faces with a fragrant smelling cream made from the wood of the Thanaka tree. The yellowy white paste is applied to the cheeks in the form of a circular patch, or in stripes, or of a leaf pattern, and acts as protection from the sun as well as a cosmetic to enhance a girl's beauty.

Even the older women and older men display a graceful elegance and, as George Orwell put it in *Burmese Days*:

> *"The Burmese do not sag and bulge like white men, but grow fat symmetrically, like fruits swelling".*

Kandawgyi Lake, formerly the Royal Lake, was created by the British to provide a clean water supply to Rangoon and is now a place for recreation, with a huge concrete replica of a Burmese royal barge, which also houses a buffet restaurant. From there the view of the sunset at five o'clock, framed by palm trees and the Shwedagon Temple, was quite breath-taking. The nearby Kandawgyi Palace Hotel, formerly the Rangoon Rowing Club, built in 1934, was a great place for a sundowner.

The Hales house, built in the 1930's of red brick, looked like something from Gerrards Cross. The long drive, circling before the house, enabled cars to deposit guests at steps leading to a grand portico. The garden was full of bougainvillea and jacaranda, lovingly planted, one imagines, by a memsahib whose husband worked in colonial administration or was one of those much esteemed captains of the Irrawaddy Flotilla Company.

The guests were an interesting mixture of foreign and local. The English comprised an adviser from BT helping to modernise the country's antiquated telecoms system, the chief accountant of a cigarette manufacturing company and an advisor on grain from the UK Institute of Tropical Products. The Burmese included a senior officer in the Burma Navy whose friendship with General Ne Win had enabled him to send his two sons to be educated in England, a lecturer in English at Rangoon's only university and the university's librarian.

With such a diversity of backgrounds and possible persuasions, our diplomat host ensured that the discussion danced around politics but could be firmly focused on the economy and everyday life. There was tacit, if not general, agreement that income levels were declining and that there was little incentive for personal effort. Wealth was concentrated in a few hands. There was too much bureaucracy in the country. With a shortage of foreign currency, there was a thriving black market. Scott's Market in the centre of Rangoon was a place where you could buy anything and everything, smuggled in from Thailand, but at inflated prices. No change was expected in the near future. It was a realistic, if not somewhat depressing, introduction to the economy of the country.

<u>Dawn in Rangoon</u>
In the seven days we spent in Burma, we saw four dawns. Each was special as there was a recurring, magical start to the day – a

witnessing of the beginning of life. Being such a religious country, this was somehow even more special.

After a 5.00am wake up call, we took a samlor (a three-wheeled bicycle with a rear passenger seat) through the deserted streets to the southern stairway of the entrance to the Shwedagon. This Buddhist temple is one of the wonders of Asia. 2,500 years old, it is 98 metres high and covered in gold leaf. Hair relics of the Buddha are believed to be contained in a casket in the middle of the stupa. Three huge bells, one weighing over 40 tons, are housed in pavilions around the stupa. Another of these bells, the Maha Gandhi, was cast in 1779 and was dropped in the Rangoon River while being transported away by the British in 1825. It was subsequently raised from the river bed and reinstated in the Shwedagon.

At the top of the steps, around the upper platform of the Shwedagon stupa, near the foot of the monument, we encountered hundreds of people, in deep prayer. There were lines of, mainly, men who were trance-like in their morning's obeisance. Occasionally a worshipper would strike one of the triangular gongs. It was a very mystical moment. I was deeply impressed by the religious fervour of those early morning worshippers.

On the descent, we encountered the usual barrage of street sellers, one of whom had cooked the most wonderful Burmese fish soup (*mohinga*) on sale at a noodle stall. After an early breakfast, we visited other stalls selling antiques and statues carved from sandalwood. I bought one of these as a special reminder of our first, very religious, dawn in Rangoon.

Back at the Strand, we enjoyed our second breakfast of the morning in the high ceilinged dining room, interrupted by a boisterous Chinese party, but with a more English fare of boiled eggs and a local reading of the *Rangoon Guardian*. This was the junta's newspaper and focused on the accounts of the visits of local Party chiefs to schools, townships and conferences.

Just around the corner from the Strand is the National Museum, whose showcase is the *Lion's Throne*, once the seat of King Thibaw

at Mandalay Palace. Taken from Mandalay by the British, the throne
and the spectacular royal regalia were outside the country when the
Mandalay Palace was burnt to the ground in 1945 and so survived.
They were returned to Burma by the V&A in 1964. The Museum
contained a number of fine paintings and photographs but the walls
and the corridors were in the most awful state and one feared for the
preservation of the museum's treasures.

A 1959 Chevrolet taxi took us to the airport for our flight to
Mandalay. Two hours later we were still waiting for repairs to be
completed to the plane, but we were saved by some delicious curry
puffs in the airport lounge. Eventually our Fokker F28 jet (yes, it was
a jet) brought us to Mandalay in the late afternoon.

Mandalay

As at Rangoon, the airport in Mandalay was deserted. One propeller
driven plane was on the tarmac loading passengers, baggage and
chickens. Then we found a jeep to take us into town and deposit us at
the Mandalay Hotel. A quick look at the standard rooms did not
impress and so, at a cost of US$20 each, we reserved two suites.
Standards of accommodation and service in Burma in 1982 were not
high. But the food at the Mandalay Hotel was excellent and the staff
were desperate to please.

Ensuring the certainty of future travel arrangements was uppermost in
our minds. A visit to Tourist Burma secured the entire *State Cabin* on
the upper deck of the local passenger boat for the day's journey (on
14th December) from Mandalay to Pagan for the grand cost of US$15.

We had heard about the *night market* which sold goods illegally
imported from Thailand and China, representing everything that the
average Burmese might desire to purchase. There was also
entertainment in the night market in the form of Chinese opera with
puppets and a rifle range. While there were plenty of food stalls in the
market, we decided to be safe and found a Chinese restaurant which
served the most delicious fried noodles and sweet and sour prawns,
cooked in an enormous *wok* which might have been capable of
driving out any germs that the kitchen harboured.

Our return transport to the hotel was a *tonga*, whose horse was barely able to trot and pull the vehicle. The fare cost less than £1; this seemed poor reward for what appeared to be its final dying efforts.

Up before dawn, we had a full day to explore Mandalay which, in 1982, was a vast sprawling city of over 500,000 people. Today, the population has grown to over one million.

Like Timbuktu, Mandalay has an exotic image.

It was Rudyard Kipling who immortalised the city, for many of us, in his famous poem. Writing in 1890, he was on his way back to England after seven years in India. The passenger ship had set off from Calcutta and called in at Rangoon. There Kipling was struck by the beauty of Burmese girls and wrote:

> *"I love the Burman with the blind favouritism born of first impression. When I die I will be a Burman ... and I will always walk about with a pretty almond-coloured girl who shall laugh and jest too, as a young maiden ought".*

Kipling's poem was published in 1892 as part of a collection in *Barrack-Room Ballads, and Other Verses*. It was made into a popular song in 1907 and has become a favourite ever since. The poem describes the nostalgia and longing of a British soldier for Asia. It is these sentiments, as much as anything else, that still today draw British travellers to the city.

I have reproduced the first verse, which begins to convey the alluring image of Mandalay in the British mind:

> *"By the old Moulmein Pagoda, lookin' lazy at the sea,*
> *There's a Burma girl a-settin', and I know she thinks o' me;*
> *For the wind is in the palm-trees, and the temple-bells they say:*
> *Come you back, you British soldier; come you back to Mandalay!*
> *Come you back to Mandalay,*
> *Where the old Flotilla lay:*

We hired a WW2 Willis Jeep to take us around town. Sadly Mandalay lost its key visitor attraction, the Royal Palace complex, which burnt to the ground in the final months of the Second World War. The Japanese and some Burmese soldiers were holed up in the old Mandalay Fort which housed over 100 exquisitely carved teak buildings. In the process of dislodging the enemy, British bombs and shells set fire to everything.

With a huge moat around it, the walled fortification and its gates have been restored and are worth a visit, as is the one surviving teak palace building, Shwenandaw Kyang. Built in the 19th Century on the orders of King Mindon, who died there, this palace was moved in 1880 from the Royal Palace complex to its present location and is now used as a monastery. The floor is eight feet above ground, on stilts, as a protection against the rain, while the walls and the roof have elaborately carved images of Buddhist legends. The original 100 or so buildings would, today, have been made a world heritage site if they had survived.

Dominating the city is Mandalay Hill, which rises 774 feet above the surrounding countryside. Under a covered walkway, there are 1,729 steps to the summit and we counted them all. The walk was not particularly arduous but, at eleven in the morning, the day was getting warmer. On the way up there were stalls selling puppets, brass bells, scissors, knives and cold drinks. One seller offered us lemon and barley, which sounded most refreshing until we discovered a layer of mould in the neck of the bottle. However, I did buy a temple bell which hangs at our present home, guarding against evil spirits. Towards the summit, behind a wire mesh, is a stone tablet inscribed to the memory of men of the 2nd Battalion The Royal Berkshire Regiment who fell during three days of hard fighting to recapture the hill in March 1945.

Another stunning visitor attraction in Mandalay is the Kyauktawgyi Pagoda, a fairly plain building, which houses a giant white Buddha, carved from a single slab of marble. Legend has it that it took 10,000 men 13 days to haul it from the River Irrawaddy to its present location.

The day finished with a visit to a shop selling lacquer ware, antiques and precious stones, where I acquired some lacquer ducks and a blue sapphire. Dinner back at the Mandalay Hotel was agreeable and gave us the opportunity to order three lunch boxes for our journey downriver the following day.

<u>The River Irrawaddy</u>
The Irrawaddy is Burma's main transport artery, linking the north with the south of the country. We were to travel on a local passenger ferry for the 200 miles from Mandalay to Pagan, a fraction of the river's total length of 1,350 miles.

Our morning call was at 04.00, followed by a Jeep ride across town to the wharf where our boat had berthed overnight.

On arrival, we found that the cabin we had booked was full of sleeping Burmese, who were ushered out on the arrival of the ticket collector. Actually, to call it a cabin was an understatement. It was a state room, some 20 feet long, with four bunks, a table, chairs, and windows on three sides. The wood panelling and louvres around the windows gave it a colonial feel. Positioned on the top deck at the bow of the boat, the cabin provided the most marvellous view of the river and the countryside around it.

The ferry was about 120 feet long and rose 20 feet above the river. Its passengers seemed to be mainly country folk, with baskets of belongings, travelling between villages on either side of the river. Its cargo varied from maize and fruit to chickens and, at one stage, three horses. There were two decks – the upper deck exclusively for passengers and the lower deck for both passengers and livestock. At the stern, there was a small café selling small items of food, bread, cakes and soft drinks.

Wrapped up in our cabin, against the cold of the morning, we saw a spectacular sunrise (which I captured on camera) before the boat cast off at 06.30, pulled by its Glasgow manufactured Kelvin diesel engine, one of the most reliable motors of the 1930's.

To journey to Pagan, the boat travelled northwards initially from Mandalay, before turning to the west and then finally joined the main river flowing south. There was plenty of room in our cabin, while the rest of the boat was packed. The pressure in the boat was eased a little when the ferry made its first stop at Sagaing, a small town which was briefly capital of Burma in the 14th Century. The town and surrounding area were covered in temples and pagodas. There is a rail and road bridge linking Sagaing with the town of Ava on the opposite bank. Originally built in 1934 of box girder construction, the bridge was blown up in 1942 in the face of the Japanese advance. It was not rebuilt until 1954 and, at the time of our visit, was the only bridge across the River Irrawaddy. Others have been built since.

Being a local passenger service, the ferry stopped at innumerable villages en route. Sometimes there was a jetty, but mainly not. The passengers and livestock waded in the shallow waters at the edge of the river to clamber aboard on a wooden plank. At each stop, dozens of young girls would descend on the boat selling fruit, corn on the cob and curry puffs. Amid lots of shouting, goods were exchanged and then, with much bell ringing, the boat would set off again.

The day passed safely and leisurely as we drifted downstream. There was much to see on the river, with flocks of birds as well as countless large and small boats. Each stop proved to be interesting, not least when there was a struggle to get the three horses to the shore on a narrow gangplank. One fell into the river, amid much laughter. While the sun was hot, the roof of our cabin gave protection and there was a breeze with the windows wide open.

The Mandalay Hotel's lunch box lived up to expectations, supplemented by numerous curry puffs purchased both on the boat and from hawkers at the various stops. But the journey was slow, as the river level was low. There was a risk of becoming stuck on a sandbank. We had been warned. Fortunately, the captain was experienced and we avoided that problem. However, the slow speed meant that we would not reach Pagan that day. Instead, we finally docked for the night at 20.30, at the small town of Pakokku, some 20 miles north of Pagan and too late to hire a taxi for the rest of the journey.

Pakokku is a small town not often visited by tourists and not, in 1982, listed in any of the guide books. It was with some trepidation that we sought somewhere to stay for the night. Of course we could have slept in our cabin on the boat but, with no mosquito netting, we would not have had a very pleasant night.

As we disembarked we saw, among the many hawkers and greeters, one man who carried a large piece of cardboard on which was written *"We have nice hotel. Good food. Wife speaks English"*. On approaching him, the man produced a school exercise book containing names and addresses of Europeans and Asians, who had stayed the night at the hotel, complimenting it with favourable written testimonials. Some spoke of the friendliness of the hosts, others of the food, while some had even attached photographs. There was a backpacker feel to the referees. With no other option, we followed our man (Tint San) to his hotel, Mya Ta Nar Inn, No 2288 Lanmataw Street, where we met his charming and gracious wife, Daw Mya Mya.

The Mya Ta Nar Inn was simple. There were some small rooms but we were housed in a dormitory with six foot high partition walls separating the wooden beds which were covered with mosquito nets. The dormitory had a monastic feel to it and there was a long walk through the garden to the bathroom facilities. But what impressed us most was Daw Mya Mya. Our hostess seemed to be in her late 40's or early 50's. Her great grandparents had emigrated from China and she was half Chinese and half Burmese. She was exceptionally beautiful and had a very calm, composed manner. She had learnt English at a Roman Catholic school in northern Burma and subsequently taught the language in the kindergarten of another missionary school. She showed an interest in a wide range of subjects including enquiring about life in the UK and the reasons for our travel. She said she preferred the cooler climate of the northern hills. Meanwhile, her daughter cooked the most delicious fried rice (with meat and egg) that I think I have ever tasted.

After a restful night, we were woken at about 04.00, before carrying our bags to the nearby wharf. The ferry departed at 05.00, shortly before dawn, using a powerful spotlight positioned above our cabin at the bow of the boat.

Below Pakokku, the river was shallower and we had to moor up and wait until it became light. Then, with the crew testing the depth of the water with long poles, we inched forward, reaching the small town of Nyang-Oo at around 07.30 for our first breakfast of the day – samosas and nuts. It was then just a short journey further downstream to Pagan.

<u>Pagan</u>
Pagan had no jetty and so the only way to disembark was via the means we had observed in many places on the river – a gangplank. As we left the boat, our state cabin was again commandeered by other passengers. Waiting on the bank were three or four tongas, with canopy roofs. One of these took us the three miles to the Thiripyitsaya Hotel, our base for the night, where we took our second breakfast of the day and a much needed shower.

Pagan is one of the wonders of the ancient world. Of the 15,000 or more temples and pagodas that were built during a 230 year period from about 1060, many were destroyed by the Mongols hordes that descended on Pagan in 1287 and more were subsequently destroyed by earthquakes. But a staggering 2,000 to 3,000 are still standing. Made from local stone or brick, they vary greatly in size. Some are a mere 20 to 30 feet in height. The largest temple, the Thatbyinnyu, rises to 200 feet. Some have been restored and painted white, while others have been left as they are, with the bare brick or stone showing. Unlike Angkor Wat in Cambodia, Pagan has been the site of a living religion over the last 1,000 years and this may have assisted in the preservation of so many of its structures.

Sightseeing by tonga is a most convenient method of ensuring that the experience is not rushed. Shielded from the sun, the traveller can take photos and stop to inspect temples. The only downside is the slightly bumpy ride. First on the list was the Gawdawpalin Temple, significantly renovated with much concrete after the disastrous earthquake in 1975 which threatened the whole of Pagan. Architecturally it seemed to be a blend between a Hindu temple and a Buddhist stupa. Gawdawpalin was constructed at the end of the 12th Century, about the time that plans were being drawn up for our great English cathedrals.

Next on the list was the stunning Ananda Temple, built in 1105, and the most representative of the early Pagan period of architecture. The layout is cruciform, with several terraces, above which is a small pagoda or stupa, covered by a hti, which is like an umbrella. Inside are four standing Buddhas. Outside, in the north-west corner, there is a courtyard with a pool containing fish and a huge Banyan tree providing shade. Ananda is one of the most visited temples in Bagan and has been described as The Westminster Abbey of Burma.

We spent a full day being driven around and stopping from time to time to see other temples and visiting the town, with its shops, cafes and restaurants. The Government school of lacquerware was a fascinating place to visit. Although most Burmese smoke, our tonga driver begged us not to, so as not to disturb the horses. Apparently Burmese cigars have a habit of bursting into flames and scaring the animals.

By late afternoon the light was fading and we had been advised to watch the sunset from the top of the Thatbyinnyu Temple. It was a good tip. A long climb about three-quarters of the way up the 200 foot monument provided a great vantage point to see a remarkable sunset, flanked by hundreds of temples. The dust of the plains, kicked up by the tongas, made the light diffuse and my photo of Pagan at dusk matched, for quality and atmosphere, the photo I had taken 36 hours earlier of the Irrawaddy River at dawn.

That night, it appeared that Pagan was out of beer. Neither the Thiripyitsaya Hotel nor the hotel next door seemed to have any of the amber liquid. But our tonga driver proved more innovative and three quart sized bottles were produced at a steep black market price. After a delicious dinner, we spent much of the evening trying to calculate how much of our currency had been converted legally at the government rate and how much on the black market. Our conclusion was that the immensely bureaucratic forms that we were obliged to complete were extremely ineffective at curbing black market transactions. Our actual rate worked out to be 10 kyats to the US dollar, compared to the official rate of 7.45 and the unofficial rate of 12.5.

After a restful night, we woke a little later – this time after dawn. Both Tim and I were suffering from sore throats following the changing temperatures on the boat and also because of the dry and dusty air of Pagan. Unlike Thailand, Burma does not suffer from humidity in December, although the moisture can escalate at other times of the year.

We had just enough time to see two more sights, the Dhammayaungyi Temple, which was never completed as its builder king was killed, and the Bupaya Pagoda near the Irrawaddy River. After a hurried lunch at the Nation Restaurant in Pagan, a rickety old bus took us to the airport for an elderly Fokker F26 propeller driven plane to fly us to Rangoon.

<u>The last 24 hours in Rangoon</u>
At the Strand, we enjoyed a delicious (and inexpensive) lobster in the freshly painted green and white dining room. Mee ordered a dessert, described as *Coupe a la Strand*, consisting of pink jelly with strawberry and vanilla ice cream, topped with small cubes of more pink and some green jelly. With the fans whirring away, the scene was positively colonial pre-war, confirmed when a rat ran quickly across the floor towards the end of our dinner.

It was not the result of the rodent incident that made us to seek another hotel for our final night in Burma, but more because we wanted to experience a night's stay at the old Rangoon Rowing Club, now the Kandawgyi Palace Hotel.

Our final day in the country was spent visiting some of Rangoon's interesting, and unspoilt, colonial buildings. These included the

Bogyoke Market (formerly Scott's Market and renamed after Aung San Suu Kyi's father) which sold everything from fish to longyis; the iconic Central Post Office; the High Court and its clock tower, dating from 1905; and the 1920's City Hall. And we returned to the Shwedagon for a final glimpse and feel of this holy place. At one of the stalls I bought three small bells, with leaf shaped clangers, which make a tinkling sound when the wind blows, reminding me of Burma.

We returned to the Kandawgyi for our final evening. It was there, with a sundowner in my hand, that I began to read George Orwell's *Burmese Days*. I was ready for it. After six days in Burma, it was easier to relate to his descriptions of expatriate and Burmese life. The lobster, for a second time in two nights, matched up to the standard of the Strand. But the rooms didn't. With paper thin walls and a very basic bathroom the Kandawgyi scored higher on nostalgia than luxury. But it was cheap – just US$25 for a deluxe room. Indeed all our hotels had been cheap. We had not spent that much money in Burma.

At Rangoon airport, currency and other formalities were less onerous than we had imagined. Before boarding our plane to return to Bangkok we had chance to have a quick conversation with the British Ambassador, Nick Fenn, to whom my FCO friend David Colvin had written on our behalf. Nick had been showing a senior colleague from the FCO, Sydney (later Sir Sydney) Giffard, around Rangoon and Pagan. Giffard offered the view that Burma would open up very slowly, with little prospect of commercial development for many years. His comments were echoed by Justin Staples, then British Ambassador to Thailand, whom we met at a party in Bangkok a few days later. He was not at all sanguine.

It did, indeed, take a further 28 years for Burma to begin to change.

The 78km Finlandia – February 1987

Introduction

Who in their right mind would wish to ski, cross country, in freezing temperatures, for a marathon distance of 78kms, taking almost 11 hours, for fun? Who indeed?

I had been working in Finland, on and off, since December 1983, when we embarked on the listing on the London Stock Exchange of shares in Amer Group Ltd, a Finnish company listed on the Helsinki Stock Exchange. The directors of Amer considered that they had expertise in managing brands and in marketing. Amer made Marlborough cigarettes and Koho ice hockey equipment, published books under the name Weilin + Goos and ran a garden centre business called Kukkameri. After this Stock Exchange success, in April 1984, we went on to list the shares of a manufacturing conglomerate, Rauma-Repola, in June 1985, of Nokia in June 1987 and of Outokumpu, mining and metals company, in October 1987. This all took place because Finland changed its legislation permitting shares in Finnish companies to be owned by foreigners with effect from 1 January 1984 and I was called in to assist these Finnish companies take advantage of this change. Those businesses which had started manufacturing and selling products in many countries, also wished to internationalise their shareholder base. I was contacted by Lars Blomquist, a Finnish auditor and accountant, whom I met at a conference I arranged in Amsterdam 10 years earlier in 1974, when I was engaged in the audit of Ford Motor Company in Europe, and Lars was in charge of Coopers & Lybrand's Helsinki office. He asked if I knew anything about listing companies on the London Stock Exchange, which I did, and so I travelled to Helsinki for a briefing meeting in December 1983, the week before Christmas.

My first encounter with Lars' fellow audit partners was bizarre. The plane from London was delayed, because of poor weather and snow in Helsinki. Lars met me at the airport, explaining that the others had already gone to the sauna. When we arrived at the Hotel Intercontinental, Lars took me to the sauna complex, bade me undress and, with a towel around me, enter the sauna. There I was introduced to Antti Helenius, Aunus Salmi and Tauno Haataja. You could say that I had been immediately presented with the naked truth.

Finnish business was, in the 1980's, and to some extent still is, a very male dominated affair. This is surprising given the fact that more than 50% of Finnish MPs are female and that ladies in Finland were among the first in the world to be given the vote. But the business environment in Finland seems different. It is still, at least at senior levels of management, very much an all-male preserve. Large companies have country cottages to entertain customers, to relax, fish, ski and to shoot wild animals (the Finns call it hunting). The animals seem to get larger as the season progresses. Starting with duck, pheasants are next to be shot and the winter finishes with elk – nothing escapes. These seem very much male interests and pastimes. At the time I started my love affair with Finland, a day's work usually finished with a sauna (men only of course) followed by a dinner where alcohol was not spared. Ladies did not seem to feature.

The Finns have a great appreciation for the countryside and for nature. Most families have a summer cottage where they spend the, usually warm, month of July, when the country closes down. Every cottage has a sauna and this is invariably situated close to a lake or by the sea. So the sauna is often combined with a skinny dip. For Finns, the concept of sauna goes back to time immemorial. In northern Russia, from which their ancestors allegedly came, there were no baths or showers at home, but a communal bathing facility where stones were heated and water poured over them to produce a hot steam, thus providing an effective way of washing. The concept of Turkish bathing is not dissimilar. After each sauna, when one was relaxing, the affairs of the village would be discussed and resolved. When the sauna was slightly cooler, it was a place where women could give birth to their babies, as the heat made their bodies suppler. So, the sauna has a special place in Finnish culture and legend.

After the first few weeks in Finland in early 1984, my enjoyment of the sauna increased. It was a place to freshen up and, when relaxing afterwards, a place to discuss matters of great importance and put the world to right, over a cool beer or two. Having a swim in the lake or sea afterwards seemed very healthy and was all part of the ritual. This got rather out of hand on one occasion when the Vice-President Finance of Amer Group, Seppo Salminen, arranged for us to take a sauna at the Krapihovi Hotel on Tuusula Lake in February and then take a dip in the freezing water through a hole in the ice. It is of passing interest that the temperature of the water under the ice was invariably warmer than the temperature of the air at that time of the year. And his boss, the heavy drinking Heikki Olavi Salonen insisted on going to the sauna when I asked him what the strategy of the Amer Group was. There, on the top floor of the office block of the Amer Tupakka factory, we enjoyed a sauna in the executive suite, followed by a roll in the snow on the roof of the factory where Heikki's employees were making cigarettes on the factory floor below. Only then, over a beer, would Heikki outline the company's strategy.

It was during the exercise to prepare Amer Group for listing that I first met Eira Palin, a lawyer working for Procope & Hornborg, who was later to move to Union Bank of Finland and be posted to London with her husband, Lasse Lehtinen, when he was appointed Press Counsellor at the Finnish Embassy in London. Eira and Lasse, like Lars and Ritva Blomquist, and, later, Kalle and Ammi Isokallio, became great friends with whom we have partied and spent weekends together over the years.

At one of the many business dinners I enjoyed in Helsinki, in January 1985, my host was the Vice-President Finance of Rauma-Repola, Dr Stig-Erik Bergstrom. "*Stigu*", as he was known, had been an academic and was now leading this major company to a share issue in London. He was an agreeable dinner companion and could, on occasions, particularly when sufficient wine had been consumed, make flamboyant gestures. As the evening wore on, the conversation turned to Finnish likes and pursuits – hunting, saunas, Koskenkorva vodka, marinated Baltic herring, ice hockey and cross-country skiing. Stigu spoke about the skiing marathon, the Finlandia, which started on the frozen lake in Hämeenlinna and finished, some 78 kms later, in the Ski Stadium at Lahti. In 1985, for the first time, there was to be a prior event on the Saturday, before the main Finlandia Marathon Race on the Sunday, for those who were slower and less competitive. These lesser skiers would have to carry their own lunch in a backpack and there would be no *service stations* on the way. This prior event, known as the *Reppu Finlandia* (or Backpack Finlandia), would cover exactly the same route. Stigu dared everyone present to enter the Reppu. Those of us at the dinner – Lars, Tauno and I immediately accepted the challenge, although I had never cross-country skied in my life.

We had five weeks to prepare. I was taken, immediately, by Eira Valtanen, the Coopers & Lybrand Helsinki office manager, to a ski sports shop next to Stockmann, the department store, to buy skis, sticks, ski clothes and a bobble cap. Lars suggested lessons and training at a hotel and seaside resort, Haikko Manor at Porvoo, about 30 minutes' drive from Helsinki. Here, Lesley and I enjoyed a weekend with Lars and his wife Ritva and, because it was flat and frozen, the sea was the ideal place to learn to cross-country ski. My style was the old fashioned up and down Nordic style not the skating style used by those more adept. But, I could propel myself at a reasonable speed. Over the next few weeks, we practised every evening on the snow covered, floodlit, footpaths of Helsinki's parks, with sauna and soup after skiing. It was demanding, exercising every muscle in one's body and preparing us for the challenge ahead. By this time, Stigu had dropped out with a damaged shoulder, a reason or perhaps even an excuse that we all thought pretty pathetic. And then the day came. Gathering on the frozen Hämeenlinna Lake at 06.30 for a 07.00 start, it was still dark, with the red glow of daylight beginning to appear. The sky was clear and it was cold, in fact very cold, with the mercury recording minus 24 degrees. In Finland, at minus 27 degrees, sporting events at schools are called off, as the freezing air temperature can damage human lungs. However the Reppu Finlandia was started since it was only minus 24. Despite the fact that it was a military area and there were no maps, every few kilometres, Lesley and Ritva managed to find us. They brought juices and warm blueberry soup, to keep up the blood sugar levels and to replenish the water we had lost through the vigorous exercise.

But the weather became colder as the morning progressed and, half way, at Lammi, the recorded temperature was minus 29. An official stopped Lars and told him that if he continued, he might lose his nose, through frostbite. On hearing this, Lars responded that he was very attached to his nose. So we stopped, having been beaten by the weather. 1985 turned out to be the coldest winter in Finland for a Century. But this was not to be the end of our attempt to finish the Finlandia.

Logistics were against us in 1986 but in 1987 we began work on the listing of shares of Nokia Corporation, then a conglomerate before it focused on mobile and portable phones based on wireless technology. The Vice-President Finance, Kari Haavisto, was a keen skier and so the training started again, in earnest, in January and February. We were joined by Lars, Tauno and also Clive Suckling, a senior manager working for Coopers in London. And, this time, the temperature at the start on Hämeenlinna Lake was a very mild minus 5 degrees – just perfect for cross-country skiing. As each ski slides over the snow, friction creates heat. At anything warmer than minus 5, the snow becomes too slushy and wet. On the other hand, if it's too cold, the surface doesn't become slippery enough. So, in perfect conditions, with Lesley and Ritva providing sustenance en route, we completed the 78 kms Marathon.

Out of our group, Kari came in first, followed by Tauno and Lars. My time was 10 hours and 57 minutes. We had been skiing all day, with hardly more than eight breaks of five minutes each. Lesley had been teased that on arrival in the Ski Stadium at Lahti we would finish by skiing down the long ski jump. After skiing all day, thankfully this was not required. In fact we could hardly stand up. And, I was so dehydrated that, after a much needed sauna, I drank 23 cups of tea, one after another. We were euphoric. It was an enormous sense of achievement to have completed the course. We had demonstrated, as the Finns say, true *sisu*, which is interpreted as strength of will, determination and perseverance. But there was no great rush, on our part, to repeat the challenge. Once was enough.

Hungary, Romania and Yugoslavia
Before the Iron Curtain Fell – August 1987

Introduction

Soon after his election in March 1985 as General Secretary of the Soviet Politburo, Mikhail Gorbachev announced that his primary goal was to revive the economy by introducing domestic reforms. *Glasnost* (openness), *perestroika* (restructuring), *demokratizatsiya* (democratisation) and *uskoreniye* (acceleration of economic development) were the guiding principles by which change was to be introduced. The initial purpose of his reforms was to resuscitate the planned economy, not to introduce market socialism. However, as time went on, it was clear that far greater reforms were in prospect with potentially far reaching consequences. In 1988 he announced that the Eastern bloc countries should be allowed to determine their own internal arrangements. In August 1991, after a failed coup attempt by hardliners, Gorbachev resigned as Party Secretary and then as President of the USSR. The Soviet Union itself ceased to exist in December 1991.

In August 1987, this extraordinary period of change was clearly underway but with the outcome unclear. In most of the Iron Curtain countries, the old guard remained in power – Kádár in Hungary (but only until May 1988), Honecker in East Germany (until November 1989), Husák in Czechoslovakia (also until November 1989) and Ceausescu in Romania (deposed in December 1989). In Yugoslavia, the seeds of disintegration had been sown with Tito's death in 1980 when religious and ethnic tensions began to surface again. A storm was brewing across Eastern Europe and the whiff of change was in the air. It was also becoming easier for foreigners to travel to Eastern Bloc countries whose people were increasingly looking to the successful and wealthy West for inspiration and guidance.

Our friends David and Caroline Colvin were living in Budapest. David was in the Foreign Office and number two at the British Embassy to Len Appleyard (later Sir Len and British Ambassador in Beijing where I was to get to know him while running the Coopers & Lybrand business in China). I had met David when we were both on secondment to the Cabinet Office in 1983. Lesley and I and our two boys, Tom and Jamie, drove out from London to Budapest in our Range Rover and stayed initially with the Colvins at their FCO provided house in Bimbo Ut, in a leafy suburb on the Buda side of the Danube. The plan was to travel together, in two cars, to Romania which David had not yet visited and then for Lesley, me and the boys to drive on to Yugoslavia. In Belgrade we would meet up with another friend, Bernard Simons, and travel to Montenegro, then still part of Yugoslavia, and spend a few days in Sveti Stefan, an island village on the Dalmatian coast converted into a rather smart hotel.

A few days in Budapest

We arrived in Budapest on Wednesday 19th August, having driven almost 1,100 miles across Europe, through France, Germany (stopping for the night in Straubing) and Austria in our second hand Range Rover. There were long queues at the Austro-Hungarian border but, thankfully, with UK number plates we were waved through. Tom was aged 12 and Jamie was to enjoy his 11th birthday two days later at a delightful Hungarian restaurant with Gypsy music by the name of Margitkert near the Margaret Bridge on the Buda side of the Danube.

By coincidence, the Colvins' house had been occupied by another FCO English family, Mike and Jessamy Reynolds, whom I had known at Cambridge. It was believed, at that time, that the Hungarian secret police or AVO had regular clandestine access to the house, as there were frequent strange occurrences, such as the fridge door being left open over night when no-one resident in the house had been into the kitchen. True or not, confidential matters were discussed in the garden or in a special sound-proof "safe room" in the British Embassy where, allegedly, personal relationships were known to develop. Hungary in Communist times was always bristling with intrigue.

Of great interest within the FCO was of course the likely impact of Gorbachev's new policies on the Eastern European satellites. Self-determination was on the agenda and the issue for the Western governments was the extent to which they should encourage this and, perhaps in the process, risk prompting a backlash among Kremlin hardliners. The "wait and see" policy while encouraging change and developing wider relations with each country was to pay off, as we witnessed some two years later when the USSR started to fall apart.

Hungary was also of interest to my firm, Coopers & Lybrand, who had worked successfully with Tito's Yugoslav Government in the 1970's and 80's, training national and local government accountants in international auditing procedures. At the time of our visit, one of my partners, Neil Payne, was actively exploring opportunities and potential relationships. This proved to be very productive as the successor firm, PwC, has developed a major presence in Hungary.

Budapest is a most attractive city, bisected by the Danube into Pest on the eastern side and Buda, with its rolling hills, on the west. In the three days before we left for Romania, there was a great deal to see, despite the city's near destruction in the Second World War. Highlights included the neo-Gothic Parliament building which apes Westminster in Pest; Castle Hill and the Castle District of Buda now a UNESCO World Heritage Site; the 700 year old Saint Matthias' Church; Heroes Square in Pest; the fine newly restored Hungarian State Opera House; and, of course, the famous bridges, all of which were destroyed in the war but some, such as the Chain Bridge, rebuilt to their original design.

Sadly, we did not visit the Király Baths, a thermal spa built in the second half of the 16th Century during Ottoman rule. But David and I made up for this by spending hours working up a good sweat on the squash court at the Duna Intercontinental Hotel on the east bank of the River Danube. History does not relate the score but photographs show David "*down*" and even "*very down*" at the Duna.

Thursday 20th August was Hungary's National Day, with military parades and a fly past of jets over the River Danube. By coincidence, or more likely by design, this was also the festival of St Stephen, a popular saint in Hungary and the King who reigned from 1000 to 1038. It was also marked with a traditional harvest parade through Buda with beautifully decorated horse drawn carts. This was followed, in the evening, by a most impressive firework display over the Danube, which we watched from the terrace of the Duna Hotel

Jamie's birthday on the Friday was an opportunity to celebrate. The Margitkert (St Margaret's Garden) proved to be just the right place – a restaurant serving Hungarian food, with outdoor tables, where we were serenaded by a gipsy quartet playing music from Transylvania. Jamie's interest in music was developing at that time, with proficiency in piano and the tuba. He was later to secure a position in the National Youth Orchestra and was awarded a Music Exhibition at Emanuel College, Cambridge at the end of his first year. The songs also helped us get into the right frame of mind for our forthcoming week in Romania.

But first, there was the question of victualling for our journey. David had been advised by FCO colleagues in Bucharest that food in Romanian hotels and restaurants was awful, except in certain places in the capital. So we spent a good hour at the Diplomatic Shop in the Embassy stocking up with cans of every food imaginable, packets of biscuits and dried fruit, bars of chocolate, cans of fizzy drinks and bottles of beer and wine.

Sunday 23rd August – Budapest to Cluj Napoca via Szolnok and Oradea – 255 miles

With the food safely deposited in David's Ford Sierra station wagon, bearing Hungarian CD plates, we were confident of protection from taxes or, worse still, confiscation by the Romanian Customs. Thus we sought to ensure a week's supply of something edible in the event that the stories of awful meals in Romania proved to be true. And, sadly, they did. Over the next few days, we had the most appalling dinners fortunately balanced by the most delightful picnic lunches from our own provisions.

The journey from Budapest to the Romanian border of 190 miles was not of great interest as it covered the wide eastern plain of the country before ascending the Carpathian range of mountains. David, Caroline and their four year old son, Thomas, had diplomatic visas and travelled in the Ford, with its diplomatic number plates, while the four of us with tourist visas were in the Range Rover. Just before the border Caroline and Lesley swapped places so that at least one member in each car had a diplomatic visa. This worked well and gratifyingly confused the border officials. We were not searched, in contrast to others who had their cars literally taken to pieces. The border crossing took little more than half an hour.

We arrived in Romania on the national holiday. Red, yellow and blue Romanian flags were everywhere. Some were so faded that they looked like the French tricolour. All public buildings were draped in Soviet style bunting with a portrait of the great 'conducator' or conductor. National holiday apart it was clear that the manufacture of political signs and slogans was one of the more successful and enduring sectors of Romanian industry. Every town, every village, every factory and certainly every important building carried slogans praising the Romanian Communist Party and its leader, Comrade Nicolae Ceausescu. The most frequent of these being:

> *Ceausescu si poporul*
> *Patria si tricolorul*

Other slogans identified Romania with the cause of peace and disarmament, occasionally denouncing the forces of imperialism. For David, the contrast with Hungary could not have been more extreme.

The drive from Oradea to Cluj was spectacularly beautiful as we climbed into the Carpathians – Cluj is 1,200 feet above sea level. The beauty of the Transylvanian landscape here and around Bistrita, Sighisoara and Sibiu helps to explain Hungarian bitterness at the loss of part of their empire that was ceded to Romania in 1919. It also helps to explain Romanian zeal to justify and digest what they regained after 900 years of Magyar rule. Despite the majority of the population speaking Hungarian, in western Romania, all road signs were in Romanian.

Cluj-Napoca, to give it its full name, is quite a grand provincial city and, after Bucharest, the second largest in Romania. Under the Roman Empire, Cluj was the capital of what was known as Dacia and has been for many years the unofficial capital of Transylvania. In the Middle Ages it became part of the Kingdom of Hungary and Saxons were encouraged to migrate to Transylvania to help develop its agriculture. A scion of Cluj, Matthias Corvinus, became King of Hungary in 1458 and allied intermittently with the notorious Vlad the

Impaler in his efforts to ward off Turkish invasions. A statue of Matthias Corvinus astride a horse can be found in front of the 14th Century St Michael's Church. Vlad is better remembered not just for impaling tens of thousands of his enemies on stakes but also as the inspiration for Bram Stoker's Dracula. The origin of this name is the Romanian word "drac" meaning "dragon" and thus Vlad the dragon, the slayer of Turks. With both Hungarian and Romanian populations, Cluj has always suffered from ethnic tension and, during the late 19th Century, there was dissent from the then Hungarian rule. Attempts were made to stifle Transylvanian and Romanian influence and to integrate the city more into the Austro-Hungarian Empire. The architecture of some of the municipal buildings reflects this, a prime example being the National Theatre, completed in 1906. This splendid structure with neo-baroque facade was one of the many theatres and opera houses designed by architects Fellner and Helmer who were responsible for literally dozens of these buildings constructed in the Austro-Hungarian Empire between 1874 and1913. Every important town had to have one. In Cluj, the theatre housed the Hungarian National Theatre from 1906 to 1919. Then it was taken over by the Romanian National Theatre and Romanian Opera until 1940 when it became the Hungarian National Theatre again. But this was short lived and it has now been romanised again. So as if to emphasise this, in 1987, a huge red flag had been placed across the top half of the front of the theatre, with a photo of Nicolae Ceausescu in the middle, below which there was a Roman wreath and the words *"Partidul – Ceausescu – Romania"*. We learnt later that this was the title of a song played before the main news every evening at 7.00pm showing Ceausescu, his family and his visits around the country on official duties. Based on a 19th Century patriotic song, *"Tricolorul"*, between 1977 and 1990 it became an anthem glorifying Ceausescu and his reign. By placing the flag on the face of this gracious building, we gained the impression that apart from demonstrating the President's paranoiac need for self-aggrandisement, it was yet another example of the suppression of the Hungarian people in Romania. These impressions were enhanced by what we were to observe in the days ahead.

That night we endured our first unlovely hotel, the Hotel Belvedere, which turned out to be not as bad as others we encountered later in the week. But following our first unlovely dinner, the emergency rations received their first onslaught. We were also warned to remove anything from the cars that could be removed, for example windscreen wipers, when parking up for the night in the street. Actually, we needn't have worried since members of the Securitate, the secret police, had been assigned to watch our every move and that included watching (and therefore guarding) our cars. We and our vehicles were quite safe in Romania.

Monday 24th August – Cluj to Cimpulung Moldovenesc via Dej, Beclean, Bistrita and Vatra Dornei – 165 miles

Before leaving Cluj, David had a duty to perform, at the request of the British Hungarian journalist, Lady Listowel. Born Judith de Marffy-Mantuano in Hungary, she won a scholarship in 1926 to study economic history at the London School of Economics, where she met Billy Hare, the future 5th Earl of Listowel. The couple were ill-suited; initially they travelled together around Europe and then separately for the rest of the decade. After war was declared, Lady Listowel urged both Count Ciano, Mussolini's son-in-law and Foreign Minister, and her kinsman, the Hungarian Prime Minister, Paul Telecki, not to side with Hitler. Now in her 85th year, she asked David to deliver medicines, coffee and a bottle of sherry to someone, in difficult straits, who was descended from aristocratic families with large estates in pre-War Hungarian Transylvania.

Madam Bojthe Peterne, the former Baroness Christina Banffy, lived in a shabby house (No 28 strada Cetatil, 3400 Cluj) with what looked like a small mixed farm in the backyard. Her wealthy landed ancestors, from the illustrious Banffy and Wesselenyi dynasties, owned castles which had been seized or destroyed by the Red Army at the end of the War. The Cathedral in Cluj has a large marble tablet to the Banffy family and Christina Banffy had a few remnants of her aristocratic past: an oil painting of her grandfather riding to hounds; an 18th Century oil painting of the wife of Count Istvan Bethlen; and an enormous canvas depicting the conversion of King Istvan to Christianity – she told us that this had been one of a set of six paintings and that hers had been buried for some years in WWII. Clearly these few relics helped her sustain a defiant sense of cultural identity in the face of relentless Romanisation. We received a warm welcome from Christina and her friends and much useful advice about where in Transylvania to visit. The state in which she lived testified to the difficult economic conditions in Cluj but all seemed remarkably good humoured and cheerful. The mask only slipped once when one of her friends referred, in German, to the fact that "*die Schweinhunde*" were destroying the perfect medieval town of Sighisoara, of which more below.

We also had time to look at some of the shops in Cluj, hoping perhaps to supplement our stache of emergency supplies. The grocery cum supermarket seemed to have just one product on its shelves – row after row of jars of bottled cooked tomatoes, presumably the result of this year's harvest. In collectivised Romania, the townsfolk enjoyed, if that's the right word, the results of the single agricultural production line, which would no doubt process a different vegetable next month. It was diversity of a sort which we had not experienced before, not even in Socialist Britain of the 1960's. But, it was a concept that Tony Benn would have warmed to as he sought to idealise the proletariat, centrally plan and nationalise all means of production. At another shop, which sold books, the few on display seemed to be either about President Ceausescu or were written by President Ceausescu. Christina Banffy seemed to bear all this state controlled horror and megalomania with great forbearance.

The route along this part of the Bistrita Valley was one of the most attractive during our week in Romania. There were high mountains with soft fields below, covered in wheat being cut manually by dozens of farmers, wives and friends, who waved as we drove past. It was hot and the women had stripped to their bras displaying arm muscles to match those of the men. The roads were deserted with very few foreign vehicles. In fact during our entire time in Romania we encountered only six foreign registered cars and one Finnish coach (Finnmatkat), taking Finnish tourists around Transylvania. Then from nowhere, there was a procession of combine harvesters, perhaps ten of them, as if going to a meet. But it was the absence of mechanisation in the fields that most struck us. There were horses and hay carts and hayricks, with the whole village pulling together, to see the harvest in and then to celebrate. We imagined that this was as England used to be before WW1.

The picnic that day was by the side of a river, not far from the village of Beclean which amused the children (and the adults) as we drove through it, after capturing a "Selfie" next to the town sign. The river had geese feeding on its banks and our picnic comprised peaches for dessert. After trying to intimidate the geese with peach stones, the boys called it the *"Peach Stones and Geese Picnic"* – each day's picnic was given an appropriate name.

That night we encountered our least lovely hotel, the Zimbrul at Cimpulung Moldovenesc. The bed linen looked dirty, the dinner comprised polenta and little else, the service was surly and the lights were turned out at 10.00pm, either through lack of power or because the hotel had failed to pay the electricity bill. We were due to spend two nights there but decided after dinner to cut this short. At breakfast the following morning the staff seemed to know that we would not be returning for a second night. Had they overhead our conversation or was our room bugged? No matter. We set off for the Bukovina monasteries.

En route we pondered as to the reasons for the appalling quality of hotels in Romania. Later in Russia we were to experience similar horrors. It seemed as though service did not come naturally. In general, the closer to the Soviet border, the worse the service and the food. To qualify as a Grade 1 hotel a television set has to be provided in each bedroom; it is so provided, but it never works. Hot water goes off at night and returns in the morning and one has to remember to turn the taps off at night to avoid being awakened by the sound of running water. There was always something wrong or something missing: leaky plumbing, no bath plug, no soap and a small smelly towel with holes in it. In the restaurant, there was no menu card or a la carte, but a fixed meal, with no choice, thrust on the table with the command *"eat"*. The wine was surprisingly pleasant, but then the country did have a Roman tradition and alcoholism was rife in all Eastern Bloc countries. Telephones failed to work (in a pre-mobile age) and everything shut down at 9.00pm. The management of the restaurant in each hotel was different from the management of the hotel, making it impossible to put the cost of dinner on the hotel bill. When questioned about this, the somewhat illogical response was that to combine the two would involve recruiting more staff. This was Communism at its very best. Thankfully it would all be over soon.

Tuesday 25th August – Cimpulung Moldovenesc to Suceava via Moldovita, Sucevita, Putna and Humorului – 135 miles

Our journey continued north east through the Carpathian Alps to Bukovina in the Moldavian Region for one reason only – to visit the remarkable painted monasteries. We did not regret the decision to make this lengthy detour. Apart from the monasteries, this area was frozen in a time warp. A true peasant culture was still alive and well, with decorated carved wooden houses and fences, a countryside of scythes, rakes, ricks and stooks, where driving hazards are the ubiquitous horse and cart, geese crossing the road and wandering cows.

We visited four monasteries: *Moldovita* (small, charming, almost English in character, a working nunnery); *Sucevita* (the largest and grandest, fully walled, excellently restored, more like a castle than a monastery); *Putna* (modern, restored in 1968, plain with no wall paintings, disappointingly bare but come back in two centuries when it will have aged; and *Humor* (in rather poor shape but the paintings inside the church are particularly fine). In total there are eight churches, seven of which enjoy UNESCO World Heritage Site protection. They are well known for the quality of their painted exterior walls decorated with elaborate 15th and 16th frescoes featuring portraits of saints and prophets, scenes from the life of Jesus and images of angels and demons, heaven and hell. As with stained glass in western European cathedrals and churches, the purpose of the frescoes was to make the story of the Bible and the lives of the most important orthodox saints known to the villagers, through the graphic use of images. In some cases, the wall paintings have been disfigured by the deeply etched names of 18th and 19th Century visitors. Vandalism is by no means a 20th Century phenomenon.

We were thankful for another picnic in the fields near Bukovina before a further visit to the monasteries and then to another unlovely hotel in Suceava. Once the seat of the Moldavian princes and then a major city in the eastern extremity of the Austro-Hungarian Empire, Suceava was heavily industrialised and there was no desire to linger.

Instead, the next leg of our journey took us through more attractive countryside and some fascinating towns, many of Saxon origin.

<u>Wednesday 26th August – Suceava to Sibiu via Falticeni, Tirgu-Neamt, Piatra-Neamt, Bicaz, Gheorgheni, Odorheniu, Sighisoara, Medias – 240 miles</u>

The first part of the day was less interesting than the second half. While ancient and with some historical places of interest, the towns of Falticeni, Tirgu-Neamt and Piatra Neamt lay to the west of a wide plain and had been crudely industrialised, particularly Piatra-Neamt which was enveloped in heavy pollution and a thick yellow smog.

As we turned south west and climbed back into the mountain range, everything changed. The landscape became more varied and interesting, with streams, attractive villages and old houses with carved wooden tracery. Back again alongside the Bistrita River, we found a small tributary and a spot for our day's picnic. Just outside the small town of Bicaz, on a very quiet road, we chose a patch of grass next to a stream and close to a bridge which accessed the nearby farm. After another wholesome lunch, making up for the soggy polenta of the night before, the farmer came over to say hello. He was a Hungarian speaker and delighted to find that after a fashion he could converse with David. He was determined to show us around his modest farm, including his prize possession, a fairly large horse, onto which he placed Jamie for a photo opportunity. The Bistrita River was already dammed, providing hydroelectricity for Bucharest, and there was talk locally about building another dam closer to the farm. It seemed as though our farmer's simple bucolic existence might be under threat.

A few hours further on, after passing through the small town of Gheorgheni, we followed the Târnava Mare River until we reached Sighisoara, one of the highlights of our visit to Romania. During the 12th Century, German craftsmen and merchants, known as the Transylvanian Saxons, were invited to Transylvania by the King of Hungary to settle and defend the frontier of his realm. Others were asked to farm the uncultivated countryside. At that time, the town was known as Schaäsburg in German and Segesvár in Hungarian. The city played a key strategic and commercial role at the edges of Central

Europe for several centuries. Sighişoara became one of the most important cities of Transylvania. Its craft guilds and its trade flourished. Being on the crossroads of east and west, it benefited from trade but also suffered from invasion. In consequence large and impressive fortifications were built around the city.

In 1987 however, Schaäsburg or Segesvár or Sighisoara was rather a sad place. The ancient brick and wooden buildings were in an advanced state of dilapidation. This perfect medieval Saxon town was gradually being abandoned by its former inhabitants – Saxons who now numbered just 2,000. They were fleeing to East Germany to escape the oppression of the Ceausescu regime. Although as a result of history, the city's graveyards were full of Wagners and Müllers, the coming generation of Sighisoarans appeared to be gypsies who had begun to take over houses left by the departing German speakers. Perhaps this influx only served to quicken the exodus.

Yet, at the same time, we encountered East German tourists fascinated by the architecture and lifestyle of their Saxon ancestors and yet horrified at the low standard of living of their 20th Century cousins. Even life under Honecker was better.

While walking around Sighisoara, we were approached by a well-spoken (local) Saxon who wanted chocolate *"fur die Kinder"* in exchange for Romanian lei. When we gave him the chocolate but refused to accept money, he insisted that we wait while he went into his house; he then emerged with a churn of honey from which he doled out a generous payment. It was delicious.

The old city is on the top of the hill, surrounded by fortifications. Today, as in 1987, the major attractions are its 12th Century citadel with spectacular views from the remaining nine towers, the covered stone staircase leading to the Church of St Nicholas on the hill (with its Saxon graves), the ancient houses in the medieval streets, and a bust of Vlad the Impaler on a wall just around the corner from his birthplace.

The more modern part of the city, dating from the 19th Century, is further down the slope and nearer the river. During our visit, demolition was taking place in this lower part, doubtless to pave the way for the appalling workers' flats, of grey cement, which disfigured every Romanian town we saw – a legacy of Comrade Ceausescu.

We were subsequently delighted to learn that Sighisoara had become a UNESCO World Heritage Site, with all the protection that this status affords. We were also amused to learn that, in 2003, strong opposition from local civic society groups and the media prevented the construction of a Dracula theme park in a nearby nature reserve.

Our scenic drive continued along the river through Medias to Sibiu. En route we stopped to photograph some most attractive farms with elaborately carved gate posts, all influenced and once owned by Saxon farmers. In Slimnic, near Sibiu, we stopped to admire one stunning example of this architectural genre, where David began a conversation in German with a local farmer. The farmer explained, with pride, that a number of his relatives now lived in West Germany. He had also heard that conditions in Hungary were much better than Romania. He gave an eloquent shrug at the state to which his own village had been reduced, revealing that the packet of Kent cigarettes which David presented to him represented one day's work. Another two East German tourists that we met visiting the ruins of the castle overlooking Slimnic were moved to say that it was incredible that such poverty existed in Europe in the latter half of the 20th Century.

That night, the Hotel Continental in Sibiu proved marginally better than its predecessors but once again failed to offer dinner. So we attempted to locate the *highly recommended* Golden Barrel Restaurant. As the witching hour of 21.00 hours approached when restaurants stop serving, we stopped at a bar to ask for directions. The barman happened to be a friend of the proprietor of the Golden Barrel and offered to climb into our Range Rover and take us there. Unfortunately, we arrived shortly after 21.00 and the kitchen staff had already gone home. Without further ado, our friendly barman got back into the car and took us to a restaurant next to his bar and prevailed on them to serve us dinner. Three petrol coupons (a month's ration) had a remarkable effect and we enjoyed a wonderful meal.

Next morning, before leaving Sibiu, we visited the bar to thank our rescuer who served us a memorable frappe, the ingredients for which deserve to be recorded:

- *Ice cream*
- *Brandy*
- *Coffee essence*
- *Syrop of sugar*

The final touch was a real straw to drink it through.

I'm not sure if it was the result of three of these frappe which gave us a rose tinted view of Sibiu but we certainly found it a remarkable town. Much larger than Sighisoara, it has some grand buildings from the 18th Century as well as medieval streets. It has gracious squares – including a Grand Square and a Lesser Square. The city also has an unusual architectural feature in the older houses - dormer windows cut into the roofs and resembling eyes, with eyebrows above them. Since the roofs are at least as high as the walls of the buildings beneath, the houses look top heavy and the eyes dominate, watching over passers-by and potential intruders. With its complex of five museums, Sibiu was judged European Capital of Culture in 2007.

Thursday 27th August – Sibiu to Râmnicu Vâlcea, via Călimăneşti – 97 miles

After a morning in Sibiu, it was a short drive to Râmnicu Vâlcea, which had nothing to commend it other than the fact that it was on the way to the Iron Gates, a gorge on the River Danube, where we were to cross to enter Yugoslavia. Half way, we stopped at Călimăneşti, a spa town with a 14th Century monastery by the side of a lake.

Driving on in convoy, we were waved down by a police car. Two officers got out and on seeing our British number plates allowed us in the Range Rover to continue. But they were less generously inclined towards the Colvins whose Hungarian number plates suggested the prospect of a bribe, until they realised, with crest fallen faces, that these were diplomatic.

On arriving in Râmnicu Vâlcea, it was plain to see why this was not on the tourist circuit. In the 1980's, the city had been completely rebuilt in a style combining Socialist realism with local vernacular architecture. It was truly ghastly, as was the Hotel Alotus which, thankfully, no longer exists.

<u>Friday 28th August – Râmnicu Vâlcea to Belgrade, via Tirgu Jiu, Drobeta-Turnu Severin and Pozarevac – 250 miles</u>

South of the Carpathians the countryside is much less interesting and compelling than Transylvania. Our increasing depression as we passed through soulless modern towns was worsened as our cars became separated while passing through, or maybe was it around, Tirgu Jiu. We turned right at some traffic lights while the Colvins went straight on – and we were separated for a good 30 minutes. Knowing that the remaining day's picnic lunch was in the back of the Colvins car caused our sons some anxiety. Tears began to flow. What were we to do? Fortunately after each driver had gone around the block a few times, we met up. And the picnic that day proved even more special – by the side of the Danube River, before driving over the top of the Iron Gate Dam and leaving Romania.

As on our entry into the country, Caroline and Lesley swapped cars again and the formalities were completed fairly quickly. We crossed into Yugoslavia.

It was time to reflect on our six days and five nights in Romania.

We had seen some stunning countryside. We had visited attractive towns and villages. We had glimpsed a rural and urban lifestyle that died out in Great Britain with WW1.

It was impossible in such a short visit of this kind to reach any serious conclusion about the extent to which the Hungarian minority was being culturally or linguistically threatened and assimilated into the Romanian way of life. For the Saxons it was clearer, they were leaving and emigrating to East or West Germany, the latter if they were lucky. The tensions between the Hungarians and the Romanians stem from history, their separate and distinctive culture and language, and as much from the economic differences and philosophies. The Hungarians we met in Cluj were similar to the middle class in Hungary – cultured, charming, intelligent and, where permitted, enterprising. In Ceausescu's Romania, these virtues would have been considered vices.

In 1987, the country had a third world feel to it. In marked contrast to Hungary, there was little evidence of integration into, or even connection with, the world economy. Industrialisation was haphazard and ramshackle. The road network had clearly seen no development since the 1930's. There were few cars on the roads and little by way of a developing trucking system. Heavy goods went by rail and the rail network was 19th Century. In the countryside, harvesting was by traditional means, namely by hand, with horses to help pull carts and do the heavy lifting. Consumer goods were in short supply, with none imported from abroad that we could see, and consumers took second place to the collective production system. The country was also a police state, with the ever present and watchful Securitate, the secret police agency that kept an eye out for dissent. Near one village in Transylvania, we stopped to chat to some farm workers who were hay making, when a sinister individual, better dressed than the others, joined the group to overhear our conversation. Ceausescu and Communism had brought the Romanian people little in terms of economic and social welfare. Fortunately all this was set to change following the ousting of Ceausescu in December 1989.

We had made reservations in Belgrade at the five star Hotel Metropol, our first comfortable resting place for a few days. There we met Bernard Simons who had flown in from London to join us for our journey along the Dalmatian coast. Having been deprived of fine dinners, luxuries and choice in Romania, we ordered caviar and vodka from Room Service and felt back in some sort of civilisation.

<u>Travel to the Adriatic and then civilisation</u>
In 1987, Yugoslavia was still a Communist country, with all the disadvantages that went with that regime. There were few consumer products, but many restrictions and many regulations to adhere to. En route to the Adriatic Coast from Belgrade we made one overnight stop, in a town whose name we omitted to remember because of its awfulness. In our hotel for the night, apart from recording every detail about ourselves, we also had to sign a declaration about the contents

of our room. Previous occupants must have stolen the fridge or the television or perhaps even the bed.

After travelling through the mountains, we reached Podgorica, the capital of Montenegro, now a separate country but then part of Yugoslavia. It was a town, rather than a city, with some grand 19th Century buildings dating from the era when Montenegro gained its independence from the Ottoman Empire and was, for a while, a kingdom. In 1987, it still looked sad, as part of the Socialist Federal Republic of Yugoslavia.

By contrast, the island village of Sveti Stefan on the coast was, even then, international and quite sophisticated. This was certainly not Eastern Europe. In fact, although inspired by Tito, Sveti Stefan was an early example of a Western capitalist upmarket tourist resort in this otherwise dreary part of the communist Balkans. In the 15th Century Sveti Stefan was a fortified village on an island with a causeway to the coast, impenetrable at high tide. It was built to defend its people against the Turks and later became a haven for pirates of the Adriatic. Initially, the island with its fortress had just 12 families but it grew from a hamlet into a large village in the 1900's, when the population numbered about 400. Then in the post WWII period, all of the buildings were acquired by the Yugoslav government and turned into a hotel. Between the 1960's and 1980's, the place was visited by many celebrities, including Orson Welles, Elizabeth Taylor, Sophia Loren, Princess Margaret, Carlo Ponti, Ingemar Stenmark and Kirk Douglas. The resort was described as a 1970's Adriatic playground on a hilly peninsula that is barely connected to the mainland. It also hosted political conferences and was an occasional chess venue, attracting top-class players such as Boris Spassky and Bobby Fischer. For Lesley and the boys, this was a most attractive coastal paradise after the horrors of the hotels in the Communist countries through which we had travelled.

Journeying north along the Dalmatian coast, we visited the ancient town of Kotor, in a Gulf which was a natural and quite large shipping harbour, developed by the Venetians with architecture reminiscent of their lagoon city. But, some days later we were to revisit the horrors of the Eastern Bloc. After dropping Bernard Simons at Dubrovnik airport, we motored north westwards along a stunning coastal road before seeking a refuge for the night. It turned out to be the dreadful Hotel Alan in Starigrad Paklenica, a coastal resort in what is now Croatia. In 1987, it was a sort of Butlins for steel workers from East Germany. The food and service suited the clientele well.

It was therefore something of a relief to reach Trieste and enjoy an Italian lunch on the quayside before bettering this and spending a night at the Grand Hotel Villa Serbelloni on Lake Como. This was a hotel of the fin de siècle, with extensive grounds looking northwards over the lake, superb dining and, to demonstrate its real style, linen mats, which were daily laundered, on either the side of the bed, so that you didn't tread on the carpet when you got up in the morning.

We had seen some wonderful countryside, splendid cities and glimpses of life as it was before WWII. But, after tasting, for two weeks, what the Eastern European countries of the USSR had to offer, we were thankful that we had been born west of the Iron Curtain.

With the Finns in Russia and Estonia – July 1990

<u>Introduction</u>
In 1988 and 1989, the countries that made up the USSR were beginning to stretch their national muscles. This had been encouraged by political developments in Russia and, in particular, by Mikhail Gorbachev's policies and utterances about *perestroika* (restructuring or reform) and self-determination. With their history as part of Europe, looking west and south rather than east, the three Baltic countries of Lithuania, Estonia and Latvia were in the forefront of Soviet countries seeking to leave the USSR.

On 24th August 1989 half the adult population of the Baltics formed a human chain stretching the entire length of the three republics to protest against the 50th anniversary of Soviet rule. Unbelievably, the Soviet authorities had imagined that the anniversary would be viewed as a celebration, rather than an opportunity for a protest.

On 11th March 1990, the Lithuanian Supreme Soviet proclaimed the re-establishment of Lithuanian independence. This shocked the Kremlin which replied in the only way they knew how. Tanks were sent in on 22nd March and five days later Soviet troops occupied strategic buildings. Estonia and Latvia were not far behind Lithuania, declaring independence on 30th March and 4th May respectively. Economic sanctions were applied by the USSR but these had as little impact as the military actions before them.

Although legal independence and formal acceptance by the United Nations of independence of the three Baltic countries did not occur for a further year, by 1990 the die was cast.

I had been working in Finland on various business assignments since 1983 and had heard from colleagues and clients about their experiences of doing business in Russia and in Estonia – and about life behind the Iron Curtain.

After the Second World War, in which Finland was on the losing side, the country had to pay substantial reparations to Russia. These were often in kind – telecommunications equipment, electricity generators and ships. There is an apocryphal story about an ice-breaker being built by the Finns for use by the Russians in the Baltic Sea. True to tradition, the Finnish shipbuilder ensured that there was a sauna on board, with the finest wooden seats. On inspection, the Russian apparatchiks determined that modern steel, rather than traditional wood, was more appropriate for seating in the sauna. One can only imagine, with amusement, knowing the thermal conductivity of steel as opposed to wood, the scene of those first Russian seamen, in the newly delivered ship, taking a sauna with such over-cooked seats that they must have had rather hot behinds.

The reparations and the bilateral trading agreement with Russia from 1950 to 1990 paradoxically benefited Finland. This stimulated and protected Finnish manufacturing industry when many other European countries, particularly the UK, suffered a decline, in the face of growing competition from Asia. Finnish companies entertained Soviet officials at country cottages in Finland, to build relationships, and some Finnish companies (for example Nokia and Rauma-Repola) established operations in Russia. The Finns got to know the Russians quite well – this time in peace rather than war.

Finland's ties with Estonia were also close – the origins of the people, their culture and language were similar. They came from the same stock, a racial grouping in the northern part of Russia from which they migrated. While their subsequent histories had been different, they were also geographically close, with Helsinki being just 55 miles from Tallinn, across the Gulf of Finland. During Soviet times, Estonians could listen to, and understand, Finnish television that was easily accessible to them. Finnish companies had also established operations in Estonia, where the price of labour reduced the costs of production and services of Finnish companies.

<u>Planning our tour</u>

I suggested to Lars Blomquist, my erstwhile colleague at Coopers & Lybrand Helsinki, that we should take advantage of the gradual *Opening-Up* by driving through the Baltic States to Leningrad (as St Petersburg was then named). Lars discussed this idea with another Finn, Heikki Hakala, who was the Executive Vice-President and Chief Financial Officer of one of Lars' clients, Rauma-Repola, whose shares I had helped list on the London Stock Exchange in 1985 and which had a business venture in Russia.

Heikki advised against this as he believed that our car tyres and the windscreen wipers, and perhaps even the cars themselves, would be stolen and there was a risk that we might be robbed or worse. He suggested, instead, that we should hire a mini-bus, with a Finnish driver experienced at driving in Russia, and travel from Helsinki to Vyborg (in Karelia), then onto St Petersburg, Novgorod, Moscow, Pskov, Tallinn (in Estonia) and back to Helsinki. We would be accompanied by a Russian guide and Heikki would book the hotels through Rauma-Repola's offices in Russia.

The journey begins

Lesley and I arrived in Helsinki on 30th June 1990, with our 13 year old son, Jamie, who was one year into his time at Harrow School. His older brother, Tom, was in Virginia on an exchange with the son, Robbie, of another partner of mine from Coopers & Lybrand, Bob Walters, who sadly died soon after retiring.

The following morning, we met Lars and his wife, Ritva, and Heikki and his wife, Eiva, in Kasarmikatu, the street outside our hotel, Hotelli Rivoli Jardin, where we always stayed in Helsinki. Instead of a mini-bus was an enormous 40-seater coach – the bus company didn't have anything smaller. In addition to the seven of us, there was the driver (Veho – a traditional Finnish name), and an American, Jack (whom we referred to, in Finnish, as Jääskö, and who, we always imagined, might be a member of the CIA looking for an opportunity to visit Russia under cover of a very good excuse as our country guide) and a Russian interpreter, Natasha (who wore lurid coloured shell suits, then very popular amongst the young, although Natasha was no longer young). These ten very different travellers were to share the 40-seater bus for the next 11 days, joined when we came to a major city by a local guide.

Karelia

The distance from Helsinki to Leningrad is 240 miles and, with the coach well stocked with beer and soft drinks (kept cool in a fridge), the holiday mood started early. Finns enjoy a good drink and the next

11 days was to be no exception. The passage through immigration and customs at the border was smooth and fast, assisted by Russian officials wearing those ridiculously outsize caps with a large upstand at the front to hold large medals. The presence of Natasha, a Russian speaker, helped speed our transit.

From the present national border to the outskirts of St Petersburg is a region which was once the Finnish Province of Karelia, a name close to the Finnish heart and captured forever as the title of a suite of orchestral pieces by Jean Sibelius, who had a particular affection for Karelia's folk music. There is also a favourite Finnish pastry dish, the cholesterol laden Karelian pasty, which is another symbol of the region's culinary heritage. Not surprisingly, Karelians had the highest incidence of heart disease in the world. Sadly Karelia was overrun by the Russian Army and lost to Finland in WWII.

The Finns describe WWII as three separate wars: the Winter War of 1939-40, in which the Finnish Army fought bravely against the Russian invader; the Continuation War of 1941-44 in which the Finns sided with Nazi Germany but lost to the Russians; and finally the Lapland War of 1944-45 when the Finns fought the Germans to make them retreat from the north of the country.

At the end of the Continuation War, Finland was obliged to cede Karelia, resulting in the enforced westward migration of over 400,000 Finnish people, who were dispersed in large groups to help resettlement. As well as the personal trauma of so many evacuees, this seizure by the Russians resulted in Finland losing as much as 80% of its wood pulp producing capacity, one-third of its hydro-electricity supply and its maritime access to the Gulf of Finland via the Saimaa Canal. It was a national disaster of unbelievable proportions and on an unbelievable scale.

Today, over 80% of the people living in Karelia are Russians, many of whom were moved there by the USSR and then occupied the houses and farms of the departing Finnish Karelians. For Finns, Karelia evokes feelings of sadness, representing a lost part of the nation's soul. And, in 1990, the region looked very sad to us as the buildings had not been well maintained, the roads were in poor condition and the region had been badly affected by state ownership, lack of investment and a decay that characterised the Soviet regime.

The capital of today's Republic of Karelia is Vyborg, or to use its Finnish name, Vipuri. In Medieval times it was an important Hanseatic town. And, before the Second World War, it was Finland's second most important city, linked to Finland's western lakes via the Saimaa Canal, built in 1856. During Czarist times and in the early part of the 20th Century, there had been a thriving timber trade between Karelia and Great Britain. Vyborg has a few very old buildings, including the 13th Century castle, heavily restored in the 19th Century, and the Round Tower dating from the 16th Century. Of great interest to our visiting Finns was the Vipuri Library designed by the distinguished Finnish architect, Alvar Aalto, and built between 1927 and 1935 in a functionalist style. At the time of our visit, the Library was closed for renovation, which had been ongoing for many years.

The main markets of Vyborg (both closed and open) are in the centre of the city and sell a very limited range of products. Of interest, though, was the Soviet memorabilia on sale (some of those ridiculously large caps, as well as medals and some guns) and most attractive woven Karelian linen table cloths. Despite the Soviet blanket which had smothered Karelia for 45 years, the minority non-Russian Karelians still produce traditional products with ethnic designs and they were very attractive and inexpensive.

The first floor of the 16th Century Round Tower, accessed via a stone staircase, had been taken over as a restaurant and the state owned and state managed facility produced a reasonable meat dish, with noodles. But what shocked us most about Vyborg was the dilapidated state of the grand 19th Century buildings. Lack of maintenance of rooves and gutters has caused water to penetrate the timbers and the walls, resulting in wet and dry rot. Since our visit, there has been some, but not very serious, debate in Finland, as to whether the Finnish Government should acquire a lease on certain properties of historic interest in Vyborg and restore them. However, the cost of bringing such degraded buildings back to life would be exorbitant. The only exception to this is the Alvar Aalto Library where Finnish donors, encouraged by President Martti Ahtisaari, have generously funded the ongoing restoration project. Karelia remains for the very practical Finnish nation a historical dream of a former fatherland that will never be recovered.

The 80-mile journey from Vyborg to Leningrad took us through an area next to the shore of the Gulf of Finland, which in the late 19th Century was a fashionable seaside resort for the wealthy of St Petersburg and also of Helsinki. Quite soon we reached Leningrad, Russia's second city, made glorious by Catherine the Great.

Before the Second World War, the city relied as much on Finland as it did on the Russian countryside to the east for its food, electricity and wood pulp. The border between Russia and Finland was a mere few miles from Leningrad. This was a big issue for the Russians, strategically and economically. Leningrad needed lebensraum. So, Karelia was in line for Soviet enlargement and was seized by the Bear when the opportunity arose.

Living next door to two large and powerful countries

When you are a small country bordering a neighbour that is much larger, you learn to live with the potential consequences. Like a smaller, younger brother, you avoid getting beaten up – if you are lucky and if you are smart. The influence of the larger neighbour is ever present and your independence is guaranteed through clever diplomacy, relationship building and alliance with other large countries. There is often a dislike of one's larger neighbour's habits and customs. And Finland has two large neighbours – Sweden, which ruled the country for centuries until 1809, and Russia, which ruled until Finnish independence in 1917. While Sweden has adopted, at least in the recent past, a neutral approach and is friendly to its neighbours, Russia has generally sought to absorb those countries on its borders. After the loss of Karelia in 1944, Finland has endeavoured to develop a modus vivendi with its eastern neighbour through a policy known as *Finlandisation*. It is the process by which a weak country is able to retain its independence from a powerful neighbour whilst being influenced by it. Today, in order to secure its future strategically, and as a safeguard against potential aggression by Russia, Finland is a strong supporter of the European Union. And, unlike the Baltic countries which have been independent from the USSR for just over 20 years, Finland has been independent of Russia for almost a century.

The country has a large Swedish speaking minority from whom many wealthy families, with their business conglomerates, are derived. For decades, Finnish business groupings, including banks, were split among linguistic lines and at one stage, there may have been some envy among Finnish Finns for the success and wealth of the Swedish Finns; this is no longer so much the case. However, Finnish people do joke about their western neighbours as being too formal, stiff and bureaucratic, a little arrogant and too soft and impractical. Stories mocking Swedes and their habits are much repeated, such as the myth that to show to prisoners how to appreciate a better life, they are incarcerated on cruise ships which ply the Caribbean during the winter months; or, that you have really arrived as a Finnish businessman in Finland when your chauffeur is Swedish. By contrast, the Swedes have a sense of superiority of culture, manners and formal etiquette which can sometimes upset their humbler neighbours. Of course, over time, encouraged by the success of Finnish industry and the growing Europeanisation of Finland through EU membership, these differences and traits are becoming less marked. But the reluctance of Sweden to come to Finland's aid in 1939 when it was attacked by Russia was an issue for the older generation.

For the first part of 19th Century, Czarist Russia's rule of Finland was benign and supportive. Much autonomy was permitted. The independent Bank of Finland was formed, with its own currency; the Finnish language became one of the official languages of administration; Finnish nationalism grew, with its own literature, music and painting. Still, even under the Russians, the Swedish language was dominant in culture, arts and business. Liberal ideas developed and then, at the turn of the 20th Century, the Bear roared. The Czars introduced a policy of Russification, designed to limit the special status of the Grand Duchy and to integrate it politically, militarily and culturally into the Russian Empire. The Finnish Army was merged into the Imperial Russian Army. As a consequence, the future great Finnish leader, Marshal Mannerheim, found himself part of the honour guard at the Coronation of Nicholas II in 1896 during his early career in the Czarist Army. While there were tensions between the two countries in 1917, at the time of the Russian Revolution and Finnish Independence, relations were good in the 1920's. However, the Soviet Union began tightening its policies towards Finland in the 1930's, for example limiting the passage of ships from Lake Ladoga to the Gulf of Finland. The Finnish defeat in the Continuation War, followed by reparations and the occupation, until 1956, of the Porkkala area near Helsinki by Russian troops, showed to the Finns that they had to respect their larger neighbour. The policy of *Finlandisation* from 1947, led by successive Finnish Presidents Paasikivi and Kekkonen, was an example of *Realpolitik*, evidencing the decision by Finland not to challenge its more powerful neighbour, yet demonstrating its national sovereignty. Thus, it was not until the mid-1980's and the Gorbachev era that Finnish media had the courage to begin to criticise Communism in Soviet Russia. Even now, while a member of the European Union, Finland has held back from seeking NATO membership partly because of concern over the Bear's reaction. But, in private, Finns have little time for their eastern Slav neighbours, in terms of culture, work ethic and approach to life. Despite its cultural history, Russia is not seen as an exemplar.

<u>Leningrad (now renamed St Petersburg, Catherine the Great's city)</u>

Our journey though Karelia and the outskirts of Leningrad demonstrated the depressed and depressing state of the Soviet economy. Grey soulless buildings of an architectural design that we learnt was referred to as *constructivist* gave a regimented air, which was not enhanced by rubbish in the streets and unshaven men standing on street corners with bottles in their hands or wandering aimlessly about. A glimpse of grand 18th Century palaces gave hope but these were in the most appalling state of repair. And, then there was our hotel for the night, the monolithic Hotel Pribaltiyskaya designed by the Soviet architect Baranov. Constructed in the 1970's by the Swedish construction company, Skanska, the hotel was functional and clean and better than other hotels we were to encounter. But there was little else to commend it. At that stage the city had not renovated its grand palaces and traditional hotels such as the Astoria, the Grand and the Lion Palace. That was to come a decade or so later, in the wake of the change in image when the inhabitants decided in the 1991 referendum to change the city's name back to St Petersburg. But, in 1990, Leningrad was still very Soviet.

The food at the Pribaltiyskaya was basic and the bar was frequented by many not so nice looking ladies of the night. I am sure they would have looked even worse during the day but, thankfully, we never found out. Our other hotel companions were sailors from Russia's Baltic fleet who hadn't yet learned to control their alcohol intake and who kept rushing out of the restaurant looking rather green. One could not have described the Pribaltiyskaya or its clientele as five star.

Since Rauma-Repola had business activities in Russia, Heikki was combining business and pleasure during our week long journey. And so we were taken to a joint venture on the outskirts of the city where the company's forest products division had a furniture making factory. The Finnish manager in charge of the activity was at his wits' end. There had been no power supplied to the factory for weeks and he could not get the state owned electricity company to fix the problem. He complained about the lack of incentive in Russia to get anything done and the lack of understanding, amongst his employees, of the profit motive. The joint venture was loss-making and was, indeed, closed down not long after our visit.

By contrast we were impressed by the Peterhof Grand Palace with its cascade of fountains leading to the shore of the Gulf of Finland. Almost entirely destroyed by the occupying German Army in WWII, the Grand Palace and its gardens have now been meticulously restored. As the Army approached in 1941, thousands of Soviet workers took precious paintings, porcelain and tapestries away for hiding. After the war they were returned to the Grand Palace as part of the restoration. At the nearby Catherine Palace at Tsarskoye Selo, the Amber Room, which had been described as the Eighth Wonder of the World, fared less well. It was looted by the Nazis, never to be seen again. But even that has now been rebuilt using amber from the original mines in Kaliningrad, formerly in East Prussia.

In the time available, we paid a short visit to the Hermitage and were astonished at the volume and quality of the collection. As is well known, it takes days even to sample the treasures amassed in the Hermitage over the two centuries since it was founded in 1764 by Catherine the Great. We confined ourselves to French impressionists Cezanne, Degas, Gaugin, Monet, Pissarro, Renoir, Sisley and Van Gogh and were not disappointed.

Despite its lack of maintenance and despite its grubbiness, in 1990, Leningrad exuded grace and charm. There were some stunning buildings dating from the 18th and 19th centuries. It had been a place of great wealth and fine culture. In one of the squares, just off Nevsky Prospekt, there was an open air market, at which we acquired two charming icons which had been looted, no doubt, from an Orthodox church. At another stall, our son Jamie acquired the first of many military watches which he sold to friends back at school – demonstrating the business acumen that he possessed even then.

The road to Moscow via Novgorod, one of Russia's treasures
After a second night at Leningrad's unlovely hotel we were pleased to set off for the ancient city of Novgorod, some 100 miles to the south east. The main road was in poor condition, with large potholes. Lorries littered the side of the road with punctures and engine problems. The occasional "rest stop" served little more than a cup of tea.

Novgorod is a very ancient city and was the capital of Western Rus, as the country was known, until 882 when Kiev took that title. Throughout its history Novgorod has prospered from trade, being on the River Volkhov and at the north eastern end of the Silk Route. It was one of the Hanseatic League towns, particularly well known for its fur trade. It is also famous as the centre of iconography in the 12th to 14th centuries and infamous for the massacre of the boyars and merchants by Ivan the Terrible's Army in 1570. Following the onslaught by Ivan the city never fully recovered its grand position as Russia's second city.

Today, Novgorod is a typical Russian provincial city, with a glorious past and long history. The city's walls and Kremlin are still intact (or have been well restored) and the Icon Gallery has some stunning exhibits. In old Russia the icon was the commonest form of figurative art. It was a visual demonstration of several concepts: faith in love and charity; the triumph of justice; and the victory of Good over Evil. The icon was an ever present companion, at home, in church, on journeys and in times of war.

Our hotel for the night in Novgorod was the Intourist Hotel, well located, but with little else to commend it. Dinner was very basic and the plates and the cutlery had not been properly washed. Worse still, there was no alcoholic beverage. However, we learnt that outside the hotel on the front steps it was possible to buy Georgian champagne and Russian vodka from a street seller – and each bottle cost US$1. So, armed with a fistful of dollars, our 13 year old Jamie was despatched to the hotel lobby to find the street traders and then to bring back what he could find. We hadn't appreciated that Mars bars were also on sale as well as liquor, for the same price. Jamie returned with five Mars bars, a bottle of vodka and just one bottle of champagne.

Even that was not enough to hide the taste of the simply appalling dinner. Lesley remembers waking up the following morning hungry and yet not being able to eat breakfast which comprised cucumber marinated in vinegar, stale black bread and some dried sausage that had seen better days. When she returned to the UK, she found that she had lost seven pounds in weight.

By now, Natasha's shell suit had changed in colour from lurid lavender to a lurid green. Jääskö was disappearing for hours at a time – seeing *friends* no doubt. The Finns were drinking the remains of the contents of the bus's fridge. And Veho, who had seen it all before, just drove the 330 miles from Novgorod to Moscow – carefully, to avoid even more potholes.

As we approached Moscow, still in the countryside, we passed Tchaikovsky's summer dacha, an attractive, grey painted building in a well tendered garden. The gate was locked and, in an attempt to get closer to the house, I climbed the fence, only to be escorted away by an official whose job it was to prevent tourists seeing this important residence rather than facilitating access. Tourism was not, at that stage, a priority for any Eastern block country.

Moscow, the capital city of a very large country

If you think that I have a fixation about awful hotels in Russia in 1990, it is because they were simply dreadful. In Moscow, we had been booked into the Belgrad 2, which seemed to live up to its name of modern Slav architecture and service. It had no charm and everything in it was ready to be replaced. The bedroom curtains were in shards, the bath towel was the size of a tea towel and there was a surly floor lady, the *dezhurnaya*, whose job was to guard the bedroom keys and, allegedly, the morality of its occupants. At least that's what we all thought, until I heard a different story from a journalist friend. Arriving back at his hotel late one night after an enjoyable dinner, he politely asked the *dezhurnaya* for the door key and thought there was a strong smell of alcohol as he passed the desk. Seconds later, as he unlocked the door, he was pushed into his room and then onto his bed by a lady twice his weight. She wouldn't get up, while exclaiming in very broken English how she *"lurved Breetish gentelmens"*. Somehow he managed to wriggle free and escape. He never recounted what happened next but I don't think he returned to that hotel again.

After one night in the Belgrade 2, with light pouring through the curtain-less windows at three in the morning – there is little darkness at night in a Russian midsummer – I decided to try and find better lodgings for our second night in Moscow. We had heard about a grand old hotel, The Savoy, which had been built in 1913 right in the centre of Moscow. In 1987, Finnair had acquired a 49% interest, with Intourist owning the remaining 51%, and a major programme of renovation had been undertaken. Jamie and I went to inspect The Savoy, which had indeed been renovated and looked quite acceptable. We ran the gauntlet of children begging at the hotel entrance. On enquiring at reception as to availability, I received the perhaps not unexpected *"Niet, we heave no roums free"*. We learnt by now, after a few days in Russia, that *"niet"* was a fairly standard answer when one asked for anything. The hotels and restaurants possessed what might only be described as a non-service approach to customers. Based on our limited experience, and the receptionist's tone of voice, I had an inkling that the answer I received was not strictly accurate. So I beckoned Jamie to come and sit with me on the sofa in reception and I spoke quite loudly to him about what a wonderful hotel the Savoy was and how everyone had extolled its virtues. After 15 minutes of praiseworthy comments, I saw the receptionist walking towards me and then heard *"When looking more, I heave found one veery nice roum"*. Lesley, Jamie and I shared a rather better room for our second night in Moscow. But, in the morning, I noticed in the corridor outside the room that water was dripping through the ceiling onto the brand new carpet below. I pointed this out to the receptionist. Three hours later when we returned to check out, water was still dripping through the ceiling onto the brand new carpet. Not even a bucket had been put in place to catch the drips. It was clear the Communist culture was alive and well at Finnair's joint venture.

Meanwhile, Rauma-Repola's representative in Moscow showed us the sights.

The city has some splendid early Soviet era buildings, known as the *Wedding Cakes* because of the ornate nature of the top part of each building. They are also referred to as the *Seven Sisters*, each of which was built in the 1940's and 1950's and are described as Stalinist architecture.

Moscow's main attraction is the Kremlin and the adjacent Red Square. There are several cathedrals within the Kremlin itself. The Cathedral of the Assumption is the oldest with wonderful icons and the church where Russian czars were traditionally crowned. For Lesley and me, the Armoury was very special with its substantial collection of non-ecclesiastical 16th and 17th Century English silver. In England, silver was melted down in the Civil War and again in the 18th Century to be reused in the designs of the time. Church silver had a better fate. There is therefore very little Elizabethan and Jacobean domestic silver remaining in the UK. But, today, perhaps the finest examples are to be found in the Kremlin, having been acquired by Czars or been given to them as presents from British merchant adventurers or British monarchs or ambassadors. One of the most exciting exhibits is a three foot high silver sculpture, made in about 1600, of a panther holding a huge shield.

On our second evening in Moscow, we were thrilled to be taken to the Bolshoi for a performance of the *Stone Guest* by Dargomyzhsky. This is a piece which is not performed often and, perhaps because of its lack of popular acclaim, Lars Blomquist found himself drifting off to sleep. The Bolshoi reeked of unpleasant bodily odours and this together with the choice of opera meant that it was not, for us, one of life's highlights.

<u>A night in Pskov</u>
We had decided to return to Finland via Estonia. The city of Pskov en route from Moscow to Tallinn was the obvious next stopping point.

It was a long journey – 465 miles – on roads which were as bad as we encountered thus far. By now we had become accustomed to the fact that travelling through Russia was hard, mirroring the life of so many of its people. En route, we stopped at some of the roadside stalls to buy strawberries and some delicious mushrooms which were, unbelievably, cooked for us by an attendant at a nearby service station. This was undoubtedly the best meal we enjoyed during our whole time in Russia.

Like Novgorod, Pskov is a very ancient Russian city which traditionally performed a role as bridge to the west. Also a member of the Hanseatic League, it was western thinking in an otherwise eastern Russian orthodox world. After Peter the Great's conquest of Estonia and Latvia during the Great Northern War of the early 18th Century, Pskov's role as a fortress town declined. But it still remained important as a staging post to the west.

Today, Pskov still retains its medieval walls and has many attractive buildings, such as Trinity Cathedral and the Cathedral of St John, both dating from the 12th Century. There are many other smaller 16th Century churches and merchants' houses, examples of the wealth of the city at that time.

In Pskov, we encountered our least lovely hotel of the whole journey, the Rizhskaya, built in the Soviet era, as a square mass of concrete exterior and concrete interior. By now the concrete was beginning to deteriorate. It became apparent that our accommodation had been designed for visiting commissars from Moscow. We each had, on different floors, an en suite bedroom, a living room and a dining room, with small kitchen area. Each living room possessed a very large sofa and a grand piano which was hopelessly out of tune. And the plumbing was not in the best condition. The Blomquists' bathroom was vertically above ours. Lars had a refreshing shower on arrival, after the long day's travel from Moscow. But the pipes must have been poorly connected and most of the water finished up in our bathroom directly beneath his. The dinner and breakfast menus were as awful as those experienced at previous hotels.

But, as ever, there was plenty to see – the city's walls, the river views, cathedrals and churches, and the sad intrusion of Soviet buildings.

Leaving Russia for Estonia

It was time to leave Russia and reach the safe haven of Tallinn in the Baltics, just 200 miles away. As we approached the Estonian border we could see that the fields and the gardens looked to be better tendered and better looked after. The gardens were full of vegetables and flowers. The houses looked to be in better condition and better maintained. The streets were cleaner. The public buildings were in good shape. It was clear that we were entering Europe and leaving Russia. Roman Catholicism and Puritanism replaced Eastern Orthodoxy. Democracy replaced authoritarianism and autocracy. Free trade replaced centralised command control. Private enterprise replaced state ownership.

Although Estonia was yet to escape the blanket of the Iron Curtain, the difference in culture and attitude was already apparent. It was refreshing to cross the border.

But, in 1990, Tallinn still looked a little depressed, with Soviet style apartments in the new town. The old town (both the lower medieval part and the upper 18th Century part) had survived the onslaught of Communism and, today, after much restoration is one of the most attractive Hanseatic cities in Western Europe and much visited.

After a quick (two hour) view of Tallinn, the Finns decided that they had enough of the USSR and that we would take the evening ferry to Helsinki. Meanwhile Veho drove the bus back to Finland via Karelia.

We have been back to Estonia many times subsequently. The Baltic resort of Pärnu is worth a visit and the charm of Tallinn will never wear off.

It had been a fascinating six days in the Soviet Union. It had not been at all luxurious. The hotels, meals and service had been most unappetising. But we had learnt a huge amount and seen some extraordinary sights – ancient and modern.

Life was to change, at least for the major Russian cities of Moscow and St Petersburg, and, of course, for Estonia, over the next 20 years. Certainly, the opportunity for tourism and sightseeing has improved and they are stunning places to visit. In 1990, we had the feeling of being pioneers.

Five Years in the Middle Kingdom – 1994 to 1999

The *Opening-Up*

At the end of the Civil War in 1949 when the People's Republic of China (PRC) was founded, the country adopted a Chinese version of Marxist-Leninism. The East became *Red*. Private enterprise ceased and property was confiscated following what was deemed to be a Workers' Revolution. The State thereafter owned the assets and determined how people should live and work.

Then, the *Great Leap Forward* in the 1950's was a disaster of unimaginable proportions when an estimated 45 million people died through starvation. Fearful of being dismissed, provincial officials reported to Beijing that harvests were greater than had actually been achieved. Centralised planning, based on these incorrect reports, led to erroneous decisions about the availability of food and about investment in agriculture. It was a disaster.

The *Cultural Revolution*, launched in 1966, caused a further massive social upheaval. Intellectuals, or merely those who had been educated, and those who were privileged, were sent to the countryside to undertake menial tasks. Productivity fell, the economy suffered and China stagnated.

It should be emphasised that, in the first three decades of Communist rule, there was some progress. During this time, the country was unified after more than a decade of war. Education and healthcare were extended to very many people and the role of the woman in China was enhanced. Foot binding, for example, came to an end. But these early years of Communist rule were painful. The country and its people suffered too many hardships.

The death of Mao Zedong in September 1976 and the subsequent ousting of the "Gang of Four", who were prominent in the country's *Cultural Revolution*, created the right environment for significant change.

To begin with, Mao's successor, Hua Guofeng, as Chairman of both the State and the Party, made modest reforms but he was a traditional

Maoist. Then, in December 1978, he was outmanoeuvred by Deng Xiaoping, who introduced far reaching changes – the *Opening-Up* of the economy; rapprochement with other countries in Asia and the West; and the encouragement of foreign expertise and investment. This was the beginning of a massive improvement in China's economic fortunes such that the lives of its people have, today, been fundamentally transformed for the better, and China has become a key player on the global stage.

In 1700, China's share of Global GDP was around 22%, while the whole of Western Europe accounted for not much more than 15%. America did not even feature. By 1980, following the decline of the Qing Dynasty, the Civil Wars, World War II and 30 years of disastrous Communist economic policies, China's share had been reduced to just 5%. The turnaround since then has been nothing short of miraculous, such that China's share is now back at nearly 17% and the country's economy has already overtaken that of the US by size in purchasing power adjusted GDP.

Economic growth in the early years of *Opening-Up* was actually quite slow as the Government's initial priority was to reform the agricultural sector. Foreign Direct Investment (FDI) rose very gradually in the 1980's from around US$0.5 billion each year to US$3.0 billion per year over the decade. Multinational corporations were initially reluctant to take the plunge.

Notable exceptions to this were General Motors, Johnson & Johnson and Pilkington Glass who followed overseas Chinese and Japanese companies in forming joint ventures with PRC partners, almost all of whom were State owned. The June 1989 *Tiananmen Incident*, as it is referred to in China, resulted in foreign investment stalling and even some, particularly US, companies closing their operations in the country.

But Deng Xiaoping made a famous, highly publicised tour of Southern China in the Spring of 1992, stressing the importance of continuing economic reform. The overseas Chinese immediately picked up the significance of this tour, which concluded in Shanghai, and they began to invest. FDI shot up, from US$4.4 billion in 1991 to

US$11.2 billion in 1992 and then to US$27.5 billion in 1993. As the pace of urbanisation and industrialisation quickened, China's exports to the rest of the world grew, fuelling yet further economic growth. The development of the private sector resulted in the State's share of economic activity and employment reducing – somehow strange for a country ruled by a Communist Party. Yet the Party had begun to appreciate that Socialism and a Capitalist (albeit a controlled) Market Economy can exist together and can bring great benefits to the People.

<u>The People's Republic of China in 1994</u>
By 1994, when I was asked to become the Executive Chairman of Coopers & Lybrand in China, the *Opening-Up* policy and the export led growth were transforming the lives of ordinary Chinese, particularly in the South Eastern Province of Guangdong, around the former 19th Century East Coast Treaty Ports, as well as the more Northern cities of Beijing, Tianjin and Shanghai.

The pace of change was, however, patchy, with certain regions (particularly the East) benefitting enormously, mainly from the establishment of *Special Economic Zones* which encouraged private enterprise and foreign investment through tax incentives and a reduction in red tape. By comparison, the ageing industrial North was suffering from factory closures, which adversely affected whole communities, and the backward West and South West were undeveloped. Average earnings and average wealth showed disparities of 10 to 1 across the country. China was becoming less of an egalitarian Marxist-Leninist country. It was being described as a Socialist Market Economy yet, in reality, it was becoming a State controlled Capitalist Economy.

The opportunities in the country were mindboggling. Foreign, as well as Chinese, manufacturing companies took advantage of the well trained but low cost labour. Multinational consumer companies were mesmerised by the thought of a market of 1.3 billion mouths or, in the case of the cosmetic industry, 2.6 million arm pits.

The world and his wife wanted to invest in and do business with China. Global companies such as Bayer, Ford, General Motors,

Glaxo, HSBC, Johnson & Johnson, Marsh, Nokia, Novartis, Peugeot, Prudential, Standard Life, Unilever, United Technologies and all the accounting and law firms were rushing to establish a presence in China. They wanted to get there quickly and take advantage of the cheap manufacturing environment, the growing service industry and the enormous developing domestic market.

As a professional firm dedicated to helping global and domestic businesses achieve their strategic objectives, Coopers & Lybrand wished to be part of this gold rush and assist its clients to enter into joint ventures, achieve legal status and establish operations in the country. Foreign companies needed help in negotiating with the tax authorities in an ever changing fiscal environment; they needed help to establish accounting and reporting systems; they required their financial statements to be audited; and then, if they were fortunate to make a profit, they sought advice on how to repatriate dividends to the parent company.

A Far Eastern Base – Hong Kong, Shanghai or Beijing?
In the 1980's and early 90's, all of the global accountancy firms provided advice to companies operating in China using Hong Kong as their base. Small representative offices had been established in Beijing, Shanghai, Shenzhen and Guangzhou with direction, management and expertise from their Hong Kong offices. Coopers & Lybrand followed this pattern, starting in 1981.

In 1992, the PRC Government introduced legislation requiring foreign accountancy firms, who wished to provide audit services, to establish a joint venture with a local firm of approved Certified Public Accountants (CPAs). Coopers & Lybrand (International) commissioned an international working party comprising four partners to examine how to respond to this. The four were Mike Stillwell (UK), Dean Yoost (US), Fujimori Nakamoto (Japan) and Marina Wong (Hong Kong). Initially, it was suggested that they might seek to try to reduce the funding of C&L's operations in China. However, having appreciated the enormous growth potential and having considered available Chinese organisations with whom to partner, the working party recommended that C&L should increase its investment in China and should joint venture in Beijing with CIEC

CPAs, part of the massive State owned and prestigious CITIC group. It was believed that partnering with a strong, well respected entity would bring status and would ensure contacts at the highest level in the Chinese Government. This did, indeed, bring advantages. But, as we discovered later, a strong partner can sometimes be a disadvantage when business objectives begin to diverge.

The recommendations of the working party were accepted. A joint venture agreement was signed in 1993 as part of a broader plan, approved by the Executive Committee of Coopers & Lybrand (International), to create a large presence in China. From 1994, international funding (from all C&L Member firms around the world) was put in place, together with a board to approve the strategy and monitor the investment and performance of C&L China.

The main question was who from C&L was to lead the China operations, oversee the investment and grow the business? Various names were suggested but none of these was acceptable to both the US and UK firms of Coopers & Lybrand. Having worked with the Chairmen of both the US and UK firms of C&L, and having spent time working on Public Listings, Corporate Finance deals and with the Management Consultancy company as well as having a background in Financial Reporting and Auditing, I was asked if I would consider the role.

At that stage in my career, I had been a partner in C&L UK for 24 years, with responsibilities for marketing in UK and Europe (for 8 years) and head of the UK's Scandinavian Desk (for 10 years). It was time for a change and the challenge of growing a business in China was an attractive proposition. From a family perspective, our two boys were on the verge of leaving school and going to university and could cope with, even benefit from, their parents being away in China for many months of the year. A life changing move was about to take place.

When I was asked to lead and develop the firm in China, a key question for me was where to live and where to base my office. C&L Beijing had the largest presence, with 35 people employed by the joint venture, while C&L Shanghai had just 12 people and C&L Guangzhou and C&L Shenzhen had together less than 10.

I was advised by Marina Wong, a senior tax partner in C&L Hong Kong, who had overseen the development thus far of C&L in China, that I should seriously consider Shanghai. Her reasons were several: Beijing was bureaucratic and I might find the joint venture challenging; she could look after Guangzhou and Shenzhen from neighbouring Hong Kong, while Shanghai offered the most opportunity; Shanghai had become the attractive location of choice for foreign multinationals following the decisions of Zhu Rongji, its reformist Mayor from 1987 to 1991, to create the right environment for FDI. Major global companies such as AIG, Ford, Pilkington and Unilever had established their China headquarters in Shanghai and there were plans to develop Pudong, the area to the east of the river Huangpu, as a major international financial centre with a brand new international airport. With its large foreign community in the pre-Communist era and being by the sea, Shanghai looked outwards to the rest of the world, while Beijing was much more national in its outlook. Beijingers wanted to legislate and to control; Shanghainese wanted to find a way around the controls in order to make money; they also had a keen sense of humour and were less serious than the Beijingers. Shanghai seemed my sort of place.

And so I decided that I would ask my Deputy, an American, Dean Yoost, to base himself in Beijing and continue to build relations with CIEC as well as the US business community, many of whose China Presidents had offices there. My office would be in Shanghai and Marina Wong would look after the Guangzhou and Shenzhen offices from Hong Kong.

Learning about China
A further key consideration was how I could get up to speed with understanding China and the issues facing C&L and its clients. In this, I was helped by two "China experts", Ken Dewoskin and Gordon Barrass.

Ken was a professor of Sinology at the University of Michigan and had advised US companies working in Taiwan and China for over 30 years. A Mandarin speaker, he understood the Chinese well and was hired by C&L in the US to advise the US firm in its dealings with China. He was able to educate me about Chinese values and behaviour patterns. During one master class, he explained the importance of *control* in Chinese society and how it was almost a sixth sense. And he evidenced this with an example – on a hillside where farmers are growing paddy rice, they need water at the right time and in the right quantity to ensure that their crops thrive. They accept that the responsibility for water management is assumed by the village leader, who therefore has control over the situation. This relinquishment of control on the part of the paddy farmers is predicated on the village leader ensuring that water is appropriately provided. If it is not, the leader is changed. *Control* is an important element in Chinese political and business life. Ken continued to provide helpful advice as well assisting in developing our consultancy business in China. But he was wary of Chinese joint ventures and skeptical of their motives and ambitions. He believed in being resolute with Chinese in negotiations and not showing signs of weakness as these might be used to advantage by the Chinese partner.

Gordon was a former senior civil servant in the UK Foreign & Commonwealth Office and his career included a spell in the Cabinet Office as Chief of the Assessments Staff. He had married a talented American lady who had a career as a museum director and wanted to live in the UK. Gordon decided to leave the FCO to avoid further postings abroad and he became the senior international adviser to C&L in the UK. Also an excellent Mandarin speaker with time spent in China, he knew the Chinese well and complemented Ken's guidance to me. Being a former diplomat his approach to joint ventures was more conciliatory, seeking to understand their objectives and to find compromises and areas of mutual interest. He developed a good relationship with CIEC's Chinese board members and managed to persuade them to arrange a high level meeting in Beijing with the PRC Premier, Li Peng, when the C&L International Board met there in 1995. He later helped the firm in China in its regional expansion programme (see below) and also in penetrating the banking and insurance sectors. And, apart from being a mentor, he became a good friend – not least being one of the team of five who travelled from Peking to Paris in 1997 in my 1934 pink Rolls-Royce.

<u>**Shanghai in 1994**</u>

Despite early enthusiasm by the Communist Party leaders, the *Opening-Up* of the economy in Shanghai was delayed until the mid-1980's, when Zhu Rongji came to power locally and gave it a shot in the arm. The story goes that the leadership in Beijing was uncertain as to the impact of giving the Shanghainese a freer rein than they had been accustomed to under the tight control during the 30 years post the Revolution. After all, Shanghai had been a truly international city in the 1920's and 30's and the Shanghainese were very entrepreneurial, as the Hong Kong Cantonese found out in the 1950's, when many of the great Hong Kong companies were established by those fleeing the Communist regime. Beijing was fearful of the consequences of letting Shanghai loose and fearful of losing control.

In 1994, the once prosperous Bund, which resembles the waterfront in Liverpool, looked shabby and tired and the houses in the former French and International Concessions had not seen a lick of paint in 45 years; their once spacious gardens had been infilled with functional brick built accommodation for the growing population. The streets were poorly lit and there was rubbish everywhere. Yet the enterprising spirit of the local people had led to the establishment of small businesses, street stalls and a desire to earn money, despite the legacy of four decades of State ownership and control.

Shanghai was full of bicycles, millions of them, but few cars, as the automotive industry in China had not at that time been given the green light for expansion. That was to come later after the country's roads were improved and after China was satisfied that automotive components could be sourced locally rather than being imported at great cost from abroad. Yet the streets were clogged with carts and bicycles and a journey across town could take a good two hours. In my chauffeur driven Lincoln Continental, purchased at huge cost because of the high tax on imported vehicles, I would take my laptop computer and compose reports and e-mail messages in the rear seat of the car; these could only be transmitted when I returned to the office or visited a hotel linked internationally via the telephone system. Transmission was intermittent and took an age. In 1994, the World Wide Web had been invented by Tim (now Sir Tim) Berners-Lee, but there was only a small number of active websites and China had to wait until the Millennium before it could be fully linked in. International communication had moved on from the telex and the fax but was still slow and unreliable.

There were a few centres of Western comfort in Shanghai. The pre-War buildings were in a state of decay and there had been little new construction in the 1990's. The Hilton Hotel, located in the former French Concession, and The Garden Hotel, originally the French Club built in 1926 and now Japanese managed, stood out as pleasant places to stay. If you wanted to be slightly more adventurous, the State managed Jin Jiang Hotel, formerly the 1930's Grosvenor House apartments, offered excellent Chinese food; and the Peace Hotel, formerly the Cathay Hotel on the Bund, had a stunning art deco interior. Built by Sir Victor Sassoon, and where Noel Coward once stayed and wrote *Private Lives*, the Peace Hotel had a jazz band made up of grandpas who had, allegedly, performed there in the 1940's. The hotel also had a great view of the Bund waterfront facing the Huangpu River and a small private dining room, once part of Sassoon's private quarters, on the top floor. At that time the hotel had not been refurbished and it was still possible to see Sassoon's bathroom with its original sea green sanitary fittings, a feature of 1930's interior design.

It became quite clear, in the first half of 1994, that there was no accommodation in Shanghai (either a renovated 1930's house or apartment) that was suitable as a permanent Far Eastern residence for Lesley and me. The construction of houses and apartments of an international standard, a feature of Shanghai just two years later, had, by that time, barely started.

Some Western businessmen found suitable new houses in gated developments and, in most cases, they had families and travelled little in China as their business activities were confined to Shanghai. I had to spend time in Beijing and in other Chinese cities such as Dalian where we opened an office later that year. And the links with C&L Hong Kong had to be maintained, not least because many PRC companies were listing their shares on the Hong Kong or New York Stock Exchange and the work had to be carried out by the more experienced Hong Kong partners and staff. While my base was to be Shanghai, I had identified a young C&L partner from the UK, Chris Merry, to take charge of developing the Shanghai office and he soon recruited many bright staff fresh out of university and found larger, modern premises in the Shartex Plaza Building in the Hongqiao area, to which I moved my office.

At the outset of my appointment, Lesley and I had agreed that she would spend a good chunk of the year back in the UK at our home in Totteridge, to provide a base for our university age sons during the vacation. She would spend term-time in the Far East and the holidays back in the UK. All we needed in China was a small apartment, comfortable by Western standards. But in Shanghai there was none to be had.

At the suggestion of Ruby Chin, the comprador supreme of the C&L Shanghai office, we looked, with some horror, at the Xijiao State Guest House. It sat in spacious grounds not far from the main Shanghai airport, which was then based in the West of the city, at Hongqiao. The Xijiao was very institutional, with faded carpets and a lingering smell of yesterday's dinner. Her Majesty Queen Elizabeth had stayed there on her momentous State Visit in 1986, but that was eight years ago and the quality of the hotel and its rented apartments had suffered. There is a well-known expatriate myth that, in those days, when cleaners in China washed a carpet with a mop, they would first pour clean water into a bucket; very soon, after a couple of washes, the dirty water from the mop would be squeezed back into the bucket and then taken up again by the mop and used to wash the next area of carpet. In this way, dirty water ensured that the carpet was not actually cleaned but that dirt was transferred from one part of the carpet to another. Certainly that is what appeared to have happened when you looked at any Shanghai hotel carpet, on which dirty stain marks were quite visible.

A skyscraper flat in Hong Kong
And so, we gave up the search for accommodation in Shanghai and, instead, sought an apartment in Hong Kong.

We quickly found an attractive split level flat with two bedrooms on the 32nd floor of an apartment building, De Ricou, in Repulse Bay. The view looking out to sea was sensational and changed daily with the weather and as different ships passed by the island on their way to Hong Kong Harbour. With a swimming pool and tennis courts, and with an excellent Asian restaurant (Spices) in the newly refurbished Repulse Bay Hotel, De Ricou was a pleasant location and suited us well from Summer 1994 until December 1996 when we moved our Far Eastern residential base to Beijing.

But this meant a fair amount of air travel. C&L China Board meetings were variously held in Hong Kong, Beijing and Shanghai. C&L CIEC Board meetings took place quarterly in Beijing. The search for new office locations in China necessitated visits to, inter alia, Chengdu, Chongqing, Dalian, Hangzhou, Nanjing, Tianjin, Wuhan and Xian. And, then there were regional meetings in Kuala Lumpur and Singapore, as well visits to the UK. I became accustomed to early starts on a Monday morning to catch the Dragonair flight to Shanghai (where I stayed in the Westin Hotel in Hongqiao) or Beijing, returning to Hong Kong on Friday evening from wherever I had been in China. The Air Miles ramped up.

I knew the Hong Kong partners well – Marina Wong and Eddy Fong were old friends from my time as a locum in Hong Kong for three months in 1980/81 – and I played squash regularly with the senior partner, Roderick Chalmers, who occasionally invited me to play golf at Shek O in the South Eastern part of the island. In those days the Union flag fluttered outside the colonial looking club house and there was a full English breakfast to be savoured after an early nine holes, which was the norm on Sunday mornings.

And, of course, Hong Kong is noted for its food. The Cantonese like their ingredients to be fresh and a visit to local markets will find the animal produce alive and wriggling and the vegetables and fruit freshly harvested. On our previous visit to Hong Kong in December 1980, we rented a flat close to the LRC (Ladies Recreation Club) where the amah had quarters behind the kitchen. There, she and her young son kept a goldfish in a bowl and we assumed that this was the family pet. Its disappearance, one day, led us to a different conclusion when she announced that they had enjoyed a delicious small fish as a starter for lunch.

To make life outside work even more agreeable, I became a life member of the China Club in Hong Kong. Created by David (now Sir David) Tang (knighted at the same ceremony as me in 2007), the Club is situated on the top storeys of the former Bank of China Building and takes its décor from China in the 1950's with priceless Revolutionary paintings and other images. The food, both Cantonese and Sichuan cuisines, was delicious. Through my then membership of the Naval & Military Club in London we had reciprocal rights to the very English Hong Kong Club. But this lacked atmosphere in its rather bland new quarters, a sad replacement to the wonderful Victorian building that preceded it. This heritage building was sacrificed to Mammon when its members decided that it should be redeveloped and they lined their pockets accordingly.

Saturdays in Hong Kong were spent playing tennis or walking on Hong Kong Island – either a coastal walk around the headland or on the hills above, part of the Hong Kong Trail. And there was a ritual every Sunday afternoon when we would descend on the Mandarin Hotel in Central for a copy of the *Weekend Financial Times* to be read while savouring a scone and cream tea, with delicious rose flavoured jam, in the mezzanine floor of the Clipper Lounge. Not far away on the same floor is the renowned tailor, A-Man Hing Cheong, who supplied all my light weight suits and still makes my excellently tailored shirts, and the shoe shop, Mayer, which similarly makes bespoke shoes to order.

Meeting (the now disgraced) Bo Xilai in Dalian

The area around modern day Dalian, at the southern tip of Liaoning Province, was Chinese for many centuries. But, from 1895 to 1950 it was occupied and controlled, intermittently, by Russia and Japan. The latter invested heavily in the region in the 1930's and, thus, Japanese companies developed quite close ties with, and a historical knowledge of, this area.

These ties were resuscitated after the *Opening-Up* began and FDI from Japan flowed into the Dalian Peninsular during the 1980's and, more so, in the 90's. By 1994, Coopers & Lybrand's Member Firm in Japan, Chuo Audit Corporation, wished to open a representative office in Dalian to service its Japanese clients and began discussions with the local Municipal Finance Bureau. Progress had been such that it was deemed appropriate that I, as Chairman, should pay a courtesy visit on the Mayor of Dalian, then Bo Xilai, in October.

Bo Xilai is the eldest child of Bo Yibo, who was a General on the celebrated *Long March* and one of the *Eight Elders* of the Chinese Communist Party. As a *Princeling*, Bo Xilai's elevation within the Party came easily and was enhanced by his intellect and by his charismatic image which he cultivated with the media. After a period of success as Mayor of Dalian, he was promoted to Governor of Liaoning Province and then Minister of Commerce in the Central Government, prior to being made Party Secretary of Chongqing, one of China's four direct-controlled municipalities. His extraordinary downfall in 2012 resulted from the subsequently proven claim that he sought to use his power to prevent an enquiry into his wife's murder of an Englishman, Neil Heywood. He was stripped of all Government positions, expelled from the Party and later convicted of bribery, embezzlement and abuse of power. He was sentenced to life imprisonment and all his property was confiscated.

But, in 1994, Bo was riding high and would go higher. The meeting was friendly and he spoke openly about what he was trying to achieve in Dalian of which he had become Mayor some nine months earlier.

He was aware of the historical interest by Japan in Dalian, just two hours' flying time away, and he explained that he had set up special incentives for Japanese investors, with a development zone and high-tech park. He had made himself available to the Presidents of top tier Japanese companies. He was in the process of ensuring that Japanese businessmen would have creature comforts in Dalian with karaoke bars and plans for a *Pebble Beach* style golf course along the coast. This strategy was beginning to work. Many leading Japanese high-tech and software firms, as well as manufacturing companies, had established operations in the Dalian area.

But his eyes really lit up when he boasted that Dalian's soccer team had beaten Shanghai the previous evening and when he spoke of the quality of the city's parks with grass seed imported from Australia. And they lit up even further when he spoke about his policewomen on horseback patrolling the streets and his plans for an international fashion show in Dalian. As for an accountancy firm establishing a representative office in Dalian, the answer was, *"well of course"* – Coopers & Lybrand would help facilitate FDI and help create the right environment for Dalian's economic success.

The meeting achieved its objectives and was celebrated, with officials from the Municipal Finance Bureau, over a dinner of several courses and, with evil effect, several toasts of Maotai. This, for the unenlightened, is the most awful concoction, a spirit distilled from fermented sorghum with an alcohol content of 53%. Apart from the disastrous consequences for the head, and no doubt the liver, the smell permeates through the blood stream and remains on your skin for at least two days afterwards. I had the most appalling return trip to Shanghai with a most uncomfortable two hour wait at Beijing airport, recovering from this ordeal. But another goal had been achieved and Coopers & Lybrand's office in Dalian duly opened.

As a sequel to this interesting meeting with Bo Xilai, I had the occasion to meet him again a few times in the years ahead – when I was a board member of the China Britain Business Council in the UK and also during an official visit I paid to Beijing as Lord Mayor when he was Minister of Commerce. On this latter occasion, as we approached the end of a very productive meeting, during which he spoke in Mandarin, which was translated for me into English, he turned to me and announced in perfect English that I was very *"handsome"* and *"what good skin I had"*. At this, my accompanying UK delegation, including the British Ambassador Sir William Ehrman, burst out laughing. He had meant to say that I was looking good. I replied to him that most people had not said this before about me but had instead commented on the attractiveness of my Mayoral badge replete with diamonds. The meeting ended on a high.

Indeed, Bo Xilai liked riding high and was extremely ambitious. In floating and fighting his way to the top he inevitably trod on a few toes and he made enemies. Perhaps these were contributory reasons for his sudden and dramatic downfall from power, his life imprisonment and the confiscation of his wealth.

Jing Shuping and Emily Ou

Born in Shanghai into a hardworking and successful family, Shuping and Emily were brother and sister. Yet their lives took them in very different directions, before coming together to help develop Coopers & Lybrand's presence in China.

Jing Shuping studied at the Anglican St John's University in Shanghai. Graduating in 1939, he worked in various managerial roles in the tobacco industry, so following his father whose Shanghai tobacco factory was bombed by the Japanese. After 1949, Jing rose steadily in the Communist Party serving as Chairman of Shanghai Tobacco Industry Association, China Democratic National Construction, Secretary General of Shanghai Municipal Committee, Deputy Secretary General of the Shanghai Federation of Industry and Deputy Secretary General of the Shanghai Political Consultative Conference. He was a shrewd businessman and had a good political nose. He was a listener, quiet, reflective and unassuming. But he was wise, astute, and he had great authority. A protégé of China's Vice President, Rong Yiren, who had also studied at St John's, Jing Shuping's star rose in the 1990's as the *Opening-Up* accelerated. In 1993, he became the Chairman of the All-China Federation of Industry & Commerce and he later established China's first private sector bank, China Minsheng Banking Corporation. He was a senior figure in the Party and was a member of the Preparatory Committees for the handover of both Macao and Hong Kong.

Several years younger, Sister Emily was sent to Taiwan at the time of the Revolution in 1949, where she attended school before emigrating to the United States. In 1979, Emily was working for Coopers & Lybrand in New York and was able to introduce the members of a Coopers & Lybrand delegation visiting Beijing to her brother. Jing Shuping was most helpful and, in 1981, Coopers & Lybrand established a representative office in Shanghai. Then, some 12 years later, Jing, who was working in a senior capacity at CITIC, founded by Rong Yiren, arranged for CITIC's accounting firm (CIEC CPAs) to form a joint venture with Coopers & Lybrand in Beijing. Emily occasionally visited China from New York and worked periodically in C&L's Shanghai representative office in a liaison capacity. And she recruited a number of local Shanghainese, one of which was the invaluable Ruby Chin.

Travels with Ruby Chin

Ruby Chin had grown up in Shanghai in the 1930's and 40's. She had witnessed the transition from a thriving international city to one downtrodden by three decades of Communist rule. And, now, she was delighted with the changes taking place in China. With a good command of English and a good understanding of both pre- and post-War Shanghai, she proved invaluable as a comprador. Dealing with the complex regulations and stifling bureaucracy was frustrating. Ruby could fix any problem with the local authorities and she could obtain any licence that was required for C&L to operate in Shanghai. To use the words of Gordon Barrass who reviewed a draft of this chapter: *"I was pleased to see what you said about Ruby, whose name matched her gem-like qualities and whose quiet charm concealed her Sunzi-like deviousness. I remember you telling me about when our (Chinese) partners in Shanghai were being difficult she went to check which firm's name the members of staff were registered and that swung things to your advantage. And I think it was after that you gave her an office of her own and suddenly she transformed herself into a self-confident and fashionably dressed lady who for the first time ever invited me to lunch"*.

From the outset, I had the idea that C&L might grow in China through associations with local PRC accounting firms. This was to prove mistaken as the Chinese firms in question derived from the local Finance Bureaus. They knew nothing of double entry booking or of auditing standards and their culture and values were bureaucratic, insular and difficult to change. Ruby accompanied Gordon on many visits to provincial cities for discussions with local accounting firms. And, on occasions, I had to visit the leaders of these firms and took the opportunity to indulge in a day or two's sightseeing, when Lesley also joined me.

<u>**Sichuan Province and the Three Gorges**</u>
Meeting with local CPA firms in Chengdu, Chongqing and Wuhan afforded us opportunity of travelling down the Yangtze River, before the construction of the Three Gorges Dam, rather than flying between the cities. The river journey was another experience of a lifetime.

But first, we flew China Southern Airlines to Chengdu, the capital of Sichuan Province, with its own language, culture and distinctive food. China Southern had a reputation for hard landings at airports as most of its pilots had trained with the PRC Air Force and were used to taking jets down suddenly and at high speed. This led to a fairly abrupt and uncomfortable landing but also caused frequent problems with the undercarriages of the airline's planes.

The Paramount Leader, Deng Xiaoping, came from Sichuan and could not be parted from its cuisine. His favourite venue for family gatherings in Beijing was the Sichuan Provincial Guest House, now the China Club, of which I am a life member. At this former Royal Palace, built in the 17th Century, you can enjoy excellent Sichuan cuisine in one of the many courtyard dining rooms. My favourite dish was *si ji dou*, which is green beans cooked in garlic, ginger, chillies, and green onions, added to which are small pieces of pork. This is stir-fried with soy sauce and chicken powder. There is absolutely nothing to beat it.

Our arrival in Chengdu in 1995 was greeted with some pomp. Here was a potential investor and a foreign organisation that would transfer technology – in this case, international accounting and auditing standards. A Mayoral reception ensued, with television cameras capturing every moment. Then, there was the usual celebratory banquet (on a floating restaurant by the river), and the signing of a cooperation agreement between C&L and Chengdu CPAs. The dishes were spicy, flavoured with red chillies, and were washed down with the local beer. And for those that wanted something non-alcoholic, there was a very special local drink by the name of *Eight Treasures Tea (Ba Bao Cha),* which was made up of green tea, dates, berries, licorice root, ginseng, dried fruit, rock sugar and chrysanthemum flowers, poured from long spouted kettles. It was delicious and complemented the spicy dishes from Sichuan.

A visit to the offices of Chengdu CPAs was less inspiring. They were shabby and poorly lit. In the corner of one room, there was an empty box in which a new telephone had recently been delivered – presumably aimed at impressing the foreign visitor. But Chengdu CPAs was the only show in town and so plans were laid for a training course in Shanghai and for a staff member of Chengdu CPAs to be seconded to Shanghai for work experience.

Although Chengdu is the capital of Sichuan, Chongqing is the more important city. Given special status by Beijing, as one of the four directly controlled municipalities (the others being Beijing, Shanghai and Tianjin), the Chongqing area has a population of over 30 million. In 1995, it looked distinctly 19th Century. Banks by the side of the Yangtze River were covered in mud over which labourers carried goods on their heads and on yokes around their necks from the barges moored alongside primitive wharves. There were a number of high rise office blocks but most had been built in the 1950's or 60's and their age had resulted in an air of decay which seemed to characterise Chongqing. Our visit to Chongqing CPAs replicated that of its equivalent in Chengdu – small, shabby offices, but with a warm welcome, since C&L would, after all, be bringing much needed knowhow if Chongqing was to be developed into a modern city.

It might be recalled that when the Japanese invaded China and, successively, took Shanghai and Nanjing, the Chinese Republican Army moved south and were based for many years in Chongqing. Some distance away from Japanese airfields, the Chinese Army built defensive positions into the hills separating the two great rivers, the Yangtze and the Jialing. They were also assisted by the weather, as Chongqing is often clouded in thick fog which impeded the Japanese bombers. The city has one of the lowest annual total of hours of sunshine of any city in China and, like Wuhan and Nanjing, it is referred to as one of the Three Furnaces of the Yangtze River, as temperatures can reach well over 40 degrees in the Summer. Of historical interest is the house occupied by General Joseph Stillwell (known as *Vinegar Joe*) as his headquarters, from 1942 to 1944, when he was Allied Chief of Staff in the China Theatre of Operations and Commander-in-Chief of the American Army in the China Burma

India Theatre. He famously fell out with the Nationalist leader Chiang Kai-shek, whom he accused of hoarding supplies under the Lend Lease scheme from America, in order to be prepared for the forthcoming civil war with the Communist Army after the Japanese had been defeated. Vinegar Joe's house is now a museum, furnished in 1940's style, and contains photographs and accounts of his posting, which US Army Chief of Staff, George Marshall, described as *"one of the most difficult"* assignments of any theatre commander.

Chongqing is a major port on the Yangtze River and access to large cargo vessels has been made easier following the construction of the Three Gorges Dam. In 1995, when we sailed down the Yangtze River from Chongqing to Wuhan, roughly 450 miles, construction of the dam had only just commenced. As a result, the height of the Three Gorges above the river level was much greater and therefore much more impressive than it is today. Our river cruiser left Chongqing in the early evening, after we had been assisted by barefoot porters to cross the mud that separated the shore from the ship's boarding planks. Our cabin was spacious, with a telephone socket that enabled me to receive and send e-mails. The food was not gourmet but local Chinese and very acceptable. We had learnt that this ship was the most luxurious on the river and, by the standards of the day, was quite comfortable. Ruby Chin had a separate cabin and we met up for meals and occasionally on deck as the ship cruised downstream through the Gorges which were mind blowing.

The first Gorge, Qutang, is the most spectacular as it is the narrowest (just 500 feet wide) with the sides of the Gorge towering above. It is at its most dramatic as one enters the Gorge through the Kuimen Gate, with the mountains reaching 4,000 feet above. The Qutang Gorge is just 5 miles long which adds to its impact. There were some extraordinary sights.

- The Chalk Wall which is a white cliff face on the southern bank with nearly 1,000 Chinese characters carved into the rock, many by famous Chinese calligraphers and some dating from the Song Dynasty (960-1279). This wall has now been submerged under the river following the construction of the Three Gorges Dam.

- The Meng Liang Staircase comprising holes carved into the rock face for wooden poles to hold a zig-zag staircase from the river to the town above.

- The Ancient Pathways which are a series of narrow footpaths built in the Han Dynasty (206 BC to 220 AD) and which were maintained and improved until the middle of the 20th Century. The original purpose was to provide a foot path for bargees to pull boats upstream. Thus the paths were always alongside cliffs next to the river. Travelling upstream, rowers were no match for the rapid current. Thus gangs of bargees, harnessed to a tow rope, hauled the boats upstream. These haulers needed a path along the steep cliffs to walk on. Thus the Ancient Pathways were built. Over the years, these paths were expanded and improved. In addition to paths for haulers, paths were built for hauling goods up mountains. Sadly, the construction of the Three Gorges Dam has resulted in many of these ancient pathways being submerged and lost forever.

- In one part of the Qutang Gorge, there are coffins which hang from the rock face. These hanging coffins are a method of ceremonially placing the corpses of the deceased upon cliff sides, an ancient funeral custom of some minority groups, especially the Bo people of southern China. Coffins of various shapes were often carved out of a whole piece of wood. Either they are hung on beams projecting outward from the cliff's vertical faces or they are placed in caves in the face of cliffs or on natural rock projections on the mountain faces.

Travelling downstream, the ship then reached the Wu Gorge, much longer at over 30 miles. The sides of the Gorge are less steep, but equally dramatic. In the Gorge are the city of Wushan and the tributary, the Daning River, which we viewed via a smaller boat which could be hired at Wushan. The town which we visited in 1995 has now been abandoned as it was submerged under the rising waters and a new town has been constructed on the hills above.

The final Gorge, Xiling, is the longest – some 40 miles – and the shallowest, but equally impressive. One has the sense that the ship has passed through the most extreme of terrains before it approaches the plains of Hubei Province, where rice grows in abundance. But before reaching our destination of Wuhan, we saw the construction site of the Three Gorges Dam in the Xiling Gorge. Xiling was known for being the most dangerous of the three gorges to travel through, with frightening whirlpools and strong rapids. The reservoir dam was completed in the summer of 2006, and the water quickly reached the maximum level of 350 feet above the original height of the river. The whole project was completed by the end of 2008.

The Three Gorges Dam has had a massive impact upon the region's ecology and people, involving a mass relocation of towns and villages. The higher water level has changed the scenery of the Three Gorges, so that the river is wider and the mountains appear lower. However, the mountains still tower above the river, and the Gorges continue to offer spectacular views.

At the end of our journey lay Wuhan, a huge industrial city where, in the Summer, the temperature and humidity soar. A visit to Wuhan CPAs followed a similar pattern to the firms visited in Chengdu and Chongqing. The local television station was on hand to record this special meeting and I was presented with two most attractive book ends, with lions on the top, ornately carved from soapstone. The same invitation was extended to Wuhan CPAs to become involved in a training programme with C&L and this was later taken up.

Wuhan has been described as the Chicago or the Birmingham of China, with its large steel and automotive manufacturing capability. The Metropolitan area comprises the three cities of Wuchang, Hanyang and Hankou, the last of which became well known to the 19th Century English as the port from which the tea clippers sailed. And, it was Wuchang where, in 1911, revolutionaries began their Uprising that led to the overthrow of the Qing Dynasty. In 1926, Wuhan became the capital of the Kuomintang Government and in 1938 was the scene of a fierce battle with the Japanese invading forces who suffered over 100,000 casualties, thus slowing their progress through China. Then in 1944, the city was virtually destroyed by US bombing. The city has, of course, recovered and has been rebuilt. It is now one of China's most important manufacturing hubs, as well as being a centre of literature and the arts.

Apart from Wuhan's fascinating history, there were some memorable sights, not least the Yellow Crane Tower, first built in 223AD and then rebuilt in 1981. The PRC authorities think nothing of pulling down a centuries' old structure if it is unsafe and then building a replica. Legend has it that the tower was constructed to commemorate two incidents: an immortal by the name of Wang Zi'an rode on a yellow crane from Snake Mountain; and then, after becoming an immortal, Fei Wenyi, would ride a yellow crane and often stop on Snake Mountain for a rest. A famous poem was written, in the 8th Century by Cui Hao, entitled *The Yellow Crane Tower*. This subject matter was later used by other poets, as is often the case in Chinese literature after successive Emperors asked for a modern version of a poem or calligraphy about a well-known scene, place or theme.

Another famous such subject that comes to mind is *The Orchid Pavilion Gathering* of 353AD when poets, writers and calligraphers celebrated the arrival of Spring on the third day of the third month by meeting in an act of purification by the side of a river. The gentlemen engaged in a drinking contest, involving rice-wine cups being floated down a small winding creek as they sat along its banks. Whenever a cup stopped, the man closest to the cup was required to drink the contents and then write a poem. By the end of the day, 26 of the participants had composed 37 poems. Later Emperors asked their calligraphers to draw their own interpretations of this event and many of these works can be seen in the National Museum in Taiwan, having been taken there by Chiang Kai-shek's army when they fled China in 1949.

Hangzhou

Hangzhou is the capital city of Zhejiang Province and is one of China's ancient and beautiful towns. The province lies to the south of Shanghai and Hangzhou is situated at the end of the Grand Canal which enables waterborne traffic from Beijing to access the East China Sea via the Qiantang River.

For many centuries, Hangzhou has been an important city. Indeed it was the capital of China in the 10th Century. Today, Hangzhou is attractive as a result of its many temples and the famous Xi Hu or West Lake, which is partly man made as a result of dykes and which is surrounded by a range of hills on which pagodas are perched. It is a stunning place to visit, particularly in the Spring when the ornamental trees come into blossom and the willows produce fresh green shoots. The West Lake provides the traveller with an opportunity for a tranquil promenade around the lake and along raised walkways over the water. And, a must stop on an island in the lake is the renowned restaurant, Lou Wai Lou, where one can savour Zhejiang cooking, regarded as one of China's eight great regional cuisines. Two particular dishes which Ruby recommended were Fried Shrimps with Longjing Tea Leaves and Dongpo Braised Pork. Longjing Tea is grown on the hillside to the east of the lake and has a particularly delicious taste when new tea shoots are picked. It received acclaim when, legend has it, Emperor Qianlong passed through on an inspection, and after tasting the tea, stamped it as *The Imperial Tea.*

But the main purpose of our visit was to meet Hangzhou CPAs and Zhejiang CPAs, the local accountancy firms carved out of the municipal and provincial finance bureaus. Unlike those in Chengdu, Chongqing and Wuhan, the firms in Hangzhou were more sophisticated and collaboration developed with some notable trainees joining the C&L network.

Nanjing

Three Chinese cities, Chongqing, Wuhan and Nanjing, are referred to as the three furnaces because of the unbearable heat in the Summer months. The best time to visit Nanjing is the Spring. In the month of March, tens of thousands of ornamental plum trees burst into life and the blossom fills the streets, the parks and the 250 acre Purple Mountain. Before the Revolution, wealthy families (such as the Rongs) kept their own plum tree orchard purely for the plum blossom. Later in March the peach, pear and cherry trees also come into flower and the air in this crowded, bustling city is perfumed, while the colours herald the arrival of Spring.

Nanjing is a very ancient city whose origins date back to the 5th Century BC. Over the centuries, it has been China's capital many times and its name means, literally, southern capital. Most recently Nanjing was selected by Dr Sun Yat-sen as the capital of the new Republic of China in 1912, although the capital was moved to Beijing shortly afterwards. But Nanjing was chosen again by Chiang Kai-shek in 1927. During the war with Japan, the city was the site of systematic and brutal massacres by the invading forces, events which are remembered as *The Rape of Nanjing*. It is estimated that, in total, between 300,000 and 350,000 Chinese were killed.

Today, Nanjing is a thriving commercial centre, benefitting from its location by the Yangtze River and as the capital of Jiangsu Province, one of the largest economic zones in China. The centre of the city has been rebuilt with high rise skyscrapers but suffers badly from smog in the winter months. Its economy is based around electronics, automotive manufacturing and assembly, steel and petrochemicals and has attracted foreign investors such as Volkswagen. Meetings with the local Jiangsu CPAs and Nanjing CPAs yielded yet more long term relationships for the C&L network.

Our prime tourist objective was to visit Sun Yat-sen's Mausoleum situated on Purple Mountain. Born in 1866, Sun spent much of his life away from China, in exile, plotting the overthrow of the Qing Dynasty. As a result of his efforts he is known as the Father of the Nation in Taiwan and the forerunner of democratic revolution in the PRC. He was the first provisional President of the Republic of China when it was founded in 1912 and cofounded the Kuomintang. His legacy is also the development of the political philosophy *"The Principles of the People"*, which are nationalism, democracy and the people's livelihood.

No mention of Sun Yat-sen is complete without mention of the three Soong sisters. Their father was an American educated Methodist minister, Charlie Soong, who made a fortune in banking and in printing bibles. All three sisters attended Wesleyan College in Macon, Georgia in the United States. Throughout their lifetimes, each of the sisters followed her own beliefs supporting the Kuomintang (KMT) or the Communist Party of China. In the 1930's, the eldest, Soong Ai-ling, was married to the richest man in China and its finance minister, HH Kung. Her sister Mei-ling married Chiang Kai-shek, who was the leader of the Nationalist cause. Ching-ling married Sun Yat-sen, Father of Modern China. She became joint President of the People's

Republic of China and Honorary President in 1981, just before her death.

After Sun Yat-sen's death in 1925, plans were drawn up for his final resting place. A grand mausoleum on the side of a hill was completed in 1929, with 392 steps leading from the square below to the tomb. Under the tomb in the hall of sanctuary stands a marble effigy of the great man who is wearing a long gown, with an open book on his lap, demonstrating his wisdom and vision. From the terrace in front of the great hall, there is a commanding view of the surrounding countryside which, at the time of our visit, was full of colour from the blossom on the trees. It is a grand setting, befitting someone around whom a personality cult had developed. During my time in China I was to observe this characteristic that some Chinese leaders sought to emulate – Mao, of course, and then more recently Bo Xilai.

Building C&L's capabilities in China
Travelling around China was pleasurable, although sometimes arduous if one was not travelling first class on domestic airlines. These journeys gave Lesley and me a better understanding of this huge country with so many diverse ethnic groups, languages and cuisine. It helped me build a base of knowledge which greatly assisted in developing my thoughts on the strategy for our business.

My objective as Chairman of C&L in China was to build a firm of auditors, business and tax advisers and management consultants to serve both international and domestic clients at the same level of competence as in other C&L firms around the world. The task was almost overwhelming, as there were no accountants or consultants in China trained to international standards. One literally had to start from scratch, recruiting bright university graduates and training them.

Partners and managers were needed from other C&L firms around the world, preferably those who spoke Mandarin, to train the recruits from Chinese universities. Localisation was the key objective for many reasons. First, it was expensive to employ partners and managers from other countries, sometimes with wives and families. In the mid 1990's, the PRC was considered to be a hardship posting and additional allowances had to be paid, including incentive bonuses, cars, chauffeurs, housing allowances etc. At its peak, C&L China was losing US$15 million each year (a lot for a professional services firm), mainly because of high expatriate employments costs, which had to be funded from the international network. But the real aim was to develop PRC nationals who could, one day, become partners in the firm and own and manage it, in the same way as, say, C&L France is owned and managed by French nationals.

There were many expatriates who contributed to the development of the firm in China and it is not possible to mention everyone. The following stand out as having a significant impact, in addition to those already mentioned above:

- Chris Merry, a young partner from the UK whose first role as a partner was to head up and grow the small Shanghai office and to act as Finance Director for C&L China
- Joe Ragg, a more experienced partner from Philadelphia, who helped steady the relationship with CIEC in Beijing and develop the office in the capital city
- Eric Goujon, a French partner who was married to a well-known Chinese singer
- Kent Watson, a good Mandarin speaker who was the second in command of Price Waterhouse in China, becoming Managing Partner after our merger in 1998 when I became Chairman. Kent took over from me in 1999 when I returned to the UK

In order to attract the best graduates into the firm, relationships were formed with the major universities. In Shanghai these were Fudan, Jiao Tong and Shanghai University of Finance & Economics (SUFE). And in furtherance of this objective C&L China sponsored the first ever university chair in China since the Revolution – for the princely sum of US$5,000 per year. Professor Lou Er-Ying became the first Coopers & Lybrand Professor of Accounting & Auditing at SUFE. This was widely reported in the media and led to the firm recruiting many talented youngsters from that university.

Another key platform of our strategy was developing the training capabilities of the firm. As part of this, a Training Centre was established in the firm's new Shanghai offices. In addition, each year, as many as 15 bright recruits were identified, after spending 12 months with the firm in China, for secondment abroad, to receive further training and to gain an understanding of how international businesses operate and what their needs are. After being closed for 30 years, China had suffered through lack of contact with the outside world. This programme of overseas experience for one year was to prove invaluable. Secondments took place to Australia, Canada, Hong Kong, Netherlands, Singapore and the UK. Many of these early secondees stayed with the firm and are now partners in PwC China.

Recruiting partners and managers from other C&L firms to act as mentors was less easy. The firms in the C&L network were quite happy to offer their less able people and, in some cases, they provided most unsuitable candidates. One in particular stands out – a US citizen of Chinese race, who was offered as someone who was a qualified American accountant (a CPA), but who spoke no Mandarin. He began language lessons and, after a while, was tested by Emily Ou in our New York office, who deemed this to be an impossible task. But the final nail in the coffin was after I suggested he might think about a spell in Singapore to improve his language skills and he responded *"you mean Singapore, Alabama?"*

The move to Beijing
By the end of 1996, the Shanghai office was beginning to grow well under Chris Merry's leadership. Meanwhile, in Beijing, there were issues to be resolved with our joint venture partner, CIEC CPAs (see further below).

The city of Shanghai was developing and becoming more acceptable as a place for foreigners to live. The ring road around Shanghai speeded up traffic considerably. The new city of Pudong was taking shape, with plans for a high speed train to a new airport. The Shanghai Museum, with its impressive collection of bronzes, was always a pleasure to visit. New international restaurants were being opened up, such as *M on the Bund* on the top floor of a former bank building on the Bund, with a magnificent view of Pudong across the Huangpu River. It was a wrench for me to move my office from the relative modern environment of a C&L 100% owned representative office to the less modern offices of our joint venture, C&L CIEC CPAs, in Beijing.

Our apartment in Hong Kong had also worked well, enabling Lesley to have the comforts of an international city while facilitating contact, for me, with the Hong Kong partners. But the firm in China was growing and there was less need for me to have a residence in Hong Kong.

So, I moved my office to Beijing, where we took a top floor apartment in the Palace Hotel, a joint venture with the Peninsular Group from Hong Kong. Living in a service flat in a hotel is very convenient, as one can devote one's entire energies to managing the business. A spare bedroom, which I used as an office, also afforded a base for occasional visits by our two sons and friends.

Most of the Presidents and Chairmen of our client companies were based in Beijing and most clients visiting from other countries tended to come to Beijing first. Thus it was a natural base from a client perspective. Lesley gave accompanying wives tours of the Imperial Palace or the Temple of Heaven or the Silk Market, while I talked business and entertained at the China Club. We played golf at the Beijing International Golf Club near the Ming Tombs. And Lesley went off on expeditions with some of the Finnish wives to unusual sites rarely visited by tourists.

While we were in Beijing, we had the pleasure of a company car with a driver, Mr Zhang. He spoke little English, but just enough to understand our destination and length of stay. He was delighted when Lesley started Mandarin lessons and asked her, after each lesson, what she had learnt. On one occasion, he was most amused when she responded, in acceptable Mandarin, *"It is very convenient to ride a bicycle"*. He was utterly reliable and loyal. On one occasion, we travelled from Beijing to Shanghai to attend the wedding celebration of my former secretary, Shirley. The return flight was delayed due to fog affecting the incoming aeroplane, whose passengers refused to disembark until they had received compensation in cash for the delay. We waited in a cold first class lounge in Shanghai airport until 03.30 in the morning when the plane finally took off. When we arrived in

Beijing at 05.00, Mr Zhang was there, waiting for us, having spent six hours in the car.

And my car? Well, it was a Hongqi Red Flag, developed originally in 1959 for the high ranking Party elite. This version was built in 1996 and had a huge rear passenger compartment where one could really stretch out. As with American cars of the 1950's, on which the design was based, it had long fins at the front and rear. In the middle of the front of the bonnet was an illuminated red light and on the right fin was a flagpole, from which we used to hang a red flag with the initials "*C&L*" embroidered on it in white letters. At junctions in Beijing where traffic police were on duty, Mr Zhang was duly waved through in the belief (mistaken or otherwise) that the occupant was a high ranking official.

As an indication of commercial opportunism in China at that time, the car possessed a foreign engine which had not been licensed by the First Auto Works, the manufacturer of the Hongqi Red Flag. We learnt this as we entertained a senior official from Volkswagen over a delightful dinner at Beijing's China Club. I had congratulated him on the success of the Red Flag with its robust Audi engine, which he denied had ever been used in the car. After dinner, we went to open the bonnet and he was horrified to discover that the engine was indeed an Audi and should never have been incorporated into the car. I never heard the outcome of this piratical anecdote.

The car had a rather primitive tape player and our selection of music included *Zadok The Priest* which Mr Zhang frequently played. It was incongruous listening to Handel while being wafted through Beijing's dusty streets. But, it should be noted, the Chinese are very fond of Western classical music.

Balancing the competing politics
Growing a business from scratch in a foreign country is tough. It is tougher when the culture, as in China is so different. It is even tougher when the stakeholders have different objectives. They often say that a joint venture with a Chinese partner is like sharing the same bed but having different dreams. The situation I found myself in was even more complex.

There were many parties to our China initiative and each had different objectives and perceptions. Managing these was more difficult than recruiting and training bright people and in servicing clients. And each stakeholder had their own ideas about the China operations and how it should be run and developed.

The Chinese

As represented by CIEC CPAs, an arm of CITIC, the Chinese had three objectives: (1) Transfer of technology, so that Chinese accountants could be trained and could fulfill the role played by international accounting firms; (2) Profits from the venture, to provide for further investment in the economy; and (3) The C&L Chinese entity would be owned, controlled and managed by PRC nationals (and therefore the Chinese State/China Communist Party).

In the short term, it was clear that you cannot grow an accountancy firm in a country with few accounting professionals who can operate to international standards, without the significant involvement of foreign nationals. This requires huge investment, thus postponing the day when a surplus might arise and also when PRC nationals can take a leadership role and control the Chinese firm. However, CIEC wanted a quick financial return. They did not fully appreciate or wish to acknowledge the time taken to train accountants to an international standard. They imagined this could be done overnight whereas in every country in which C&L operated it was generally recognised that it takes 10 years at least to develop someone to operate at partner level. They also wanted to control appointments in the firm and run the HR function following practice adopted by the China Communist Party, who knew that you can control an organisation if you control the people. They would not accept the joint venture being charged with a fair share of overhead expenditure incurred in managing the business. Through the joint venture vehicle, they had enabled C&L to access the China market and they wanted to be paid for this.

So a showdown was inevitable and this came at a board meeting of C&L CIEC CPAs in Beijing when C&L was accused by Yao Jinrong of being disingenuous, fraudulent and untrustworthy. It was the shock tactics similar to those used in the *Cultural Revolution*, aimed at denigrating and disgracing. Yao Jinrong had been educated at Fudan University in English and English Literature, in which he excelled. He was recruited into the PRC Ministry of Foreign Affairs and, I understand from him, sent to North Africa to spread Communism. Yao recounted that during the *Cultural Revolution* he was brought back to China and worked in the countryside as a farm labourer. In 1971 when Kissinger made a secret visit to China to prepare for President Nixon's momentous visit in 1972, he told me that he was brought to Beijing to act as an interpreter and then returned to the countryside. After the *Opening-Up*, he was recruited by Jing Shuping to join CITIC and had, by 1994, become the equivalent of an investment banker. Yao was clever, smart and a great negotiator. He once told me that he liked staying with Billy Graham, the evangelical preacher, in the US so that he could better understand the Western mind. He told me that Westerners suffer from a guilt complex, based on the Christian religion, whereas Chinese do not. At the board meeting he let rip, seeking to make us feel guilty and that there had been a breakdown in the relationship. I stood my ground, apologizing and, at the same time, refuting all allegations.

Marina Wong, being of a pacifist disposition, was shocked. Nakamoto quaked, never having seen such an open haranguing as, in Japan, problems are hidden and issues resolved in private – or perhaps not resolved at all. I briefed my colleagues on the board of C&L China. There were calls from the Americans for me to step down as Chairman of C&L China, but Gordon Barrass intervened and urged calm. To change the C&L Chairman at this stage would be taken by the Chinese as a sign of weakness. It was necessary for C&L (International) to show support for me and then allow me to get on and negotiate the right way forward. Yao and his colleague, Chao Xueren, began to appreciate that their tactics had had limited effect and accepted that they had to deal with me as C&L's representative. Strangely, after this incident, they became quite supportive, probably appreciating the inevitable – that I had the backing of our international firm who held me in high regard. They therefore had to deal with me and to get on with me. Relationships improved. Later, in 1998, after the merger between C&L and Price Waterhouse, the combined firm had an alternative joint venture partner in Shanghai and was therefore able to effect a separation from CIEC. Of course this was achieved at some cost. And another lesson was learnt. When operating through a joint venture in China, there is a price to pay to form it, a cost each year of being a partner in a joint venture and, finally, a price to exit. Through PRC legislation requiring certain international organisations to operate through a joint venture, the cards can be stacked against the foreigner.

The American firm of Coopers & Lybrand

As the largest contributor to the investment in C&L China, the Americans wanted the largest say. They had demanded an American to become Chairman of the China operation, but had not put forward anyone who was acceptable to the other C&L firms, least of all the Brits. I was a candidate acceptable to both the UK and US firms, but when my promoter, the Chairman of the US firm, Gene Freedman, retired, the Americans began to question the competence of anyone who was British. They sought to influence managerial decisions in China and took every opportunity to make demands. I managed to keep the senior US representatives on side by listening, by being polite and by offering objective and non-emotional responses. In the end I was acceptable, even highly regarded. And from this experience, I learnt that many Americans in business are prone to personalising issues rather than seeking to deal with the facts. I began to realise how Montgomery must have felt in WWII when faced with similar behaviour by some US generals.

The Hong Kong firm of Coopers & Lybrand

Traditionally, the partners in Hong Kong had regarded China as "their" territory. Cantonese can be rather short term in their business dealings and, with a street trading mentality, want a quick buck immediately. The Shanghainese, by contrast, are prepared to be entrepreneurial and to invest for the longer term. The concept of a strong independent C&L firm in China was difficult for some Hong Kong partners to accept, although that changed subsequently when the Hong Kong and China firms merged. But, at the time of my tenure as Chairman of C&L China, the Hong Kong partners resented not being able to seize work opportunities in China without reference to the management of the new, internationally funded, China firm. Managing these expectations was not easy but my personal relationships with Hong Kong partners, Eddy Fong and Marina

Wong, with whom I had worked in the 1980's, and with the Chairman, Roderick Chalmers, helped defuse tensions.

The Japanese firm of Coopers & Lybrand (Chuo Audit Corporation)

Chuo saw the main role of C&L China as serving Japanese clients with high quality service, at high cost and inevitably at a loss. This latter was at variance with the financial objectives of both C&L (International) and CIEC CPAs. My occasional visits to Tokyo to have Kobe beef and a bottle of Lynch-Bages with Ueno, the Chuo Managing Partner, helped build relationships and manage expectations. Our common interest in cars and in golf also assisted.

The problem of stakeholders with conflicting objectives was compounded by the fact that my immediate report (boss) changed so often: Gene Freedman (US), then Bill O'Brien (US), then Pat Sherry (UK), then Bruce Townsend (US), then Jim Clarke (US). I had five bosses in five years. Each time there was a change, I had to explain the situation and issues in China and then to seek acceptance of the previously agreed strategy. It was, at times, extremely stressful. But I really began to understand diplomacy, how to build relationships, and how to handle stakeholders with very different objectives.

The "Regulator"

China is a highly regulated country and the regulations for foreign enterprises seemed tougher than for domestic firms. I counted no fewer than 33 licences that we had to obtain and comply with in order to undertake our business in the PRC.

For the international accounting firms in China, as well as the domestic CPA firms, the regulator of our business was the Chinese Institute of Certified Public Accountants (CICPA). An arm of the Chinese Ministry of Finance, the CICPA's role in life was to ensure transfer of technology from the international firms to create large, competent, domestic firms of accountants. Pressure was put on the international firms in a variety of ways:

- Licences for new offices were dependent on training courses being held for local provincial or municipal firms of accountants (ex civil servants)

- The number of foreign accountants was restricted, in order to advance the position of domestic CPA accountants
- The number of PRC partners in a firm had to be increased so that the international firms operating in China became PRC owned and controlled

While all the international firms had, as their goal, the localisation of their practices in China, the CICPA either did not believe this or, alternatively, wished to speed up the process. At the heart of the matter is the Chinese desire to control the operations of the major auditing firms in the country, coupled with an innate mistrust of the foreigner. The self-belief of the Chinese leadership was evidenced two centuries ago in the unsuccessful mission by Lord Macartney in 1793 when his efforts to open up trade between England and China were dismissed by Emperor Qianlong. The mistrust is born of contact with the foreigner in unpleasant circumstances – the Opium Wars, the Boxer Rebellion, the development of Shanghai in the 1920's and 30's with separate foreign quarters and discrimination against Han Chinese and, of course, the West's political and military support for Chiang Kai-shek and the Kuomintang.

The response on the part of the international accounting firms to the views of the CICPA was to band together, to the extent that competition law in China permitted, to agree a common approach to the PRC authorities. It should be said that all foreign companies in every industry in China experienced these regulatory constraints. Fortunately, the efforts of the PRC to join the World Trade Organisation (WTO) afforded an opportunity for the common voice of the international accounting firms to be heard. I was appointed the chairman or spokesman by the other firms (Arthur Andersen, KPMG, Deloitte, Ernst & Young and Price Waterhouse as well as C&L) to brief the European Commission and the US Trade Representative on the matters affecting the international accounting firms. I attended meetings in Brussels and New York, as well as working with the EU Embassy in Beijing. Progress was made. However, even after China's Admission to the WTO, I understand that the CICPA has backtracked on some of the issues agreed, in favour of their nationalist objectives.

The CICPA (of which I was made an Honorary Member) sought to hasten a natural course of events, namely the localisation of the accountancy firms in China, and this created antagonism with the international accountancy firms, which did not aid the measured achievement of this long term objective.

The attitude of the CPA began to change when one Secretary-General, Ding Pingzhun, a hard line Party apparatchik, retired. He was succeeded by Li Yong, who was carefully handpicked for the job after spending time and gaining experience with the World Bank in Washington. The situation stabilized further when a new Vice-Minister of Finance, Wang Jun, a protégé of Premier Zhu Rongji, was appointed to oversee development of the profession. Wang Jun was made an Honorary Member of the Institute of Chartered Accountants in England & Wales in recognition of his efforts to develop and modernize the accounting profession in China.

In my dealings with the CICPA and the Ministry of Finance, I received thoughtful and knowledgeable advice from Qian Ning, the son of the Foreign Minister, Qian Qichen. Qian Ning had studied for an MBA in the States and was recruited by C&L Shanghai on his return to China. He was an excellent interpreter as well as a skillful go-between in my discussions and negotiations with PRC officials. He paved the way for fruitful dialogue and was able to present our views so that there was no misunderstanding, even if there was disagreement.

The Legacy

Notwithstanding these difficulties, Coopers & Lybrand and its successor firm, PricewaterhouseCoopers (PwC), grew from just 60 in four offices when I began in 1994 to over 1,200 in five when I left in 1999. We had recruited and trained hundreds of bright Chinese graduates and had thereby helped build the accountancy profession in the PRC.

Today, in February 2015, PwC has 12 offices in China with over 10,000 employees who operate to international standards serving both domestic and international clients.

As a personal legacy I wrote a book, *The New Silk Road – Secrets of Business Success in China Today*, based on interviews with 11 Presidents and Chairmen of multinational corporations who had invested heavily in China. This was published by John Wiley & Sons in 2000 and is still available for sale.

And for Lesley and me? Well, we developed an understanding of a very ancient civilization and learnt to respect the culture of the Chinese people, their strategic thinking and their tactical behaviour, and to appreciate the diversity and the pleasures of the countryside, the many historical sites and buildings, the ethnic groupings and, of course, the food. The business environment was challenging and our five years in the Middle Kingdom were an enriching experience.

And the future? I remain extremely optimistic about China's prospects. The values which the people hold dear are conducive to favourable social and economic development. The Chinese people believe in the importance of the family, education, hard work and saving. They are proud of China and increasingly less suspicious of foreigners. Their self-confidence is growing as their standard of living improves. Much has been written about the lack of democracy and that this omission will prevent further progress. I am not so sure. The Chinese people accept a large element of control on the part of their leaders, providing they deliver benefits to the people. The CCP is changing, with many successful businessmen now part of the ranks and the leadership of the Party. The Government has demonstrated, over the last 35 years, a competence that has not been replicated in other countries to quite the same extent. Their strategy and its implementation are greatly to be admired.

Lesley made notes contemporaneously, in journal form, while in China. They complement and add a different perspective to the chapter *Five Years in the Middle Kingdom – 1994-1999*.

<u>Impressions of China after our first two visits in May and October 1994</u>

Shanghai is big and bustling and buildings are sprouting upwards. We were told that there were 9,000 construction sites in Shanghai and that a large percentage of the world's tallest cranes were in China to cope with the building boom. On subsequent visits to Shanghai it seemed that a new stretch of motorway had been opened every month.

The traffic in 1994 was appalling, especially on Nanjing Lu, the main shopping street that leads down to the Bund. Traffic there is usually locked solid, even on a Sunday when it is quieter elsewhere. No one seems to be aware of anyone else on the road and pedestrians collide with cyclists who cut across cars. Junctions are mayhem.

There are millions of cyclists pedalled by young and old - ladies with white gloves, girls in very short skirts, children perched precariously in front or behind, and bicycles loaded to the gunwales or pulling other wheeled contraptions laden with everything imaginable from livestock to furniture. There are very many motorbikes too, some with sidecars.

The pedestrians charge across the road oblivious to the dangers. We saw one crocodile of kindergarten-age children led across a busy street, with each tiny tot clinging to the overall of the tiny tot ahead, all threading their way between the cars.

Given the traffic conditions, we have seen surprisingly few accidents. When there is a collision, crowds quickly gather and eagerly take sides to apportion blame and arrange the outcome of damage compensation. Hence, few foreigners drive themselves, most preferring to employ a driver. We have heard it said foreigners are sometimes driven into on purpose for financial gain.

<u>**Staring**</u>
Most of the time, we don't seem to excite much notice especially in the big cities where most foreign tourists and businessmen are found. But occasionally we are subjected to stares, usually I suspect by country folk fresh into town. We were dining in a restaurant one evening with C&L Shanghai partner Betty Ko when a man noticed us and came and literally pressed his nose against the window in order to get a better view, and he stayed there for about ten minutes. Last weekend in Shanghai we were in a souvenir shop and again were subjected to close scrutiny by another man. He went round to check our back view too and then went to fetch his friend to come and watch. They are completely unselfconscious about staring. Many expat children get really upset about this. And the Chinese have an unfortunate habit of pinching the cheeks of very little children. Chris Merry's son, Hugh, aged three, started to hit out if he ever saw a Chinese bending towards him. Blonde hair also attracts stares and our son, Jamie, and his girlfriend, Natasha, were frequently asked if they could be photographed.

Around the sights in Beijing there are often groups still dressed in Mao suits (and smelling of BO) who have come up from rural areas to visit the capital. They also stare a bit, but seem as overawed by their surroundings (the Forbidden City etc) as by foreign tourists. Then there are the usual group photos, and panic breaks out when someone loses his or her group. I was literally pushed out of the way at the Summer Palace by a chap anxious not to become separated from his group. Pushing and shoving is a way of life - it happens in Hong Kong too. I got really good at it and had to remember to keep my elbows in whenever I came back to London. Five years later you hardly ever saw Mao suits in the cities, except worn by the elderly.

I was expecting vestiges of regimentation and loudspeakers exhorting the masses but that all seems to have gone, although a few quirks remain like the "talking" litterbins in the Summer Palace. I assume the taped message is asking people to dispose of their rubbish carefully. The loudspeakers beneath the street lamps leading up to Tiananmen Square are still in place. Haranguing seems to be a national characteristic - John was on the receiving end several times from his Chinese joint venture partners (especially the one whose job in the 1970's had been to foment unrest in North Africa). At the school next to the Palace Hotel, where we lived in Beijing, the children were drawn up in lines in the playground for regular haranguing.

Children

The one child per couple policy is breeding a nation of spoilt (male) brats. I was particularly aware of it on a Sunday morning strolling round the Summer Palace. Each tiny tyrant had two doting parents in tow, and sometimes grandparents as well, pandering to their every whim and plying them with food. They say that nowadays no Chinese girls ever have elder brothers - if you have a son first, there is no need to face the economic penalties of trying for a second child. But there are also stories of young girls being closely guarded in villages as there are no girls of marriageable age. Adverts are placed in newspapers in other Asian countries, particularly the Philippines, for brides in China. Kidnappings are also reported.

The toddlers don't wear nappies. Their trousers are slit open at the bottom for quick relief and one never sees accidents, but quite often a parent holding the child over the edge of the pavement, to do their business in the gutter.

Expat Housing

When we were in Shanghai in October 1994, Ruby Chin took us house hunting. Ruby had been with C&L for very many years and acted as a comprador or fixer. Although some of the Western hotels have long-stay guests in suites, prices are high. We looked at two Chinese hotels which were much more reasonable. Both were called *State Guesthouses* and had a main hotel building with restaurant and a number of individual houses dotted around a landscaped garden area. They were both on Hongqiao Lu, the main road out to the airport and therefore close to the Shartex building where the C&L Shanghai office is situated. The Hongqiao State Guesthouse was smaller and more down market. It reminded me of some of the Eastern European hotels: rather bleak, a hatchet-faced unresponsive receptionist, and a garishly lit bar and utilitarian fittings. It was being renovated and so was empty.

There were ten or so houses in the grounds. The only vacancy was in newly built *villas* near the road. They were extraordinarily ugly, faced in white tiles, a building style currently much favoured in Shanghai. John was really taken by house no. 9, large, three storeys, standing in lovely gardens and built in a sort of fanciful colonial style with verandahs and arches. We managed to persuade the staff to let us look round. It was dark and depressing inside - curtains and blinds drawn as if it was unoccupied, but rooms furnished Communist party style with chairs ranged along the walls and heavy dark wood furniture and antimacassars.

Xijiao (meaning *Western Suburbs*) State Guesthouse was much grander, with bigger and better gardens, tennis courts and a much lighter atmosphere. We saw one two-room suite, which was nice and spacious. At that time they had full occupancy but we put ourselves on a waiting list for a suite. This is the State Guesthouse where Queen Elizabeth stayed in 1986 and there are photographs of other visiting VIPs. The security was excellent and we were warned that we would have to move out during state visits. The few houses were large, well screened by trees and all occupied. We were subsequently offered a suite, but when John saw it, he said it was very dark and dingy so we continue to use the Westin Hotel opposite the office whenever we come to Shanghai. I think we would have found Xijiao very difficult as we did not speak Mandarin and they served only Chinese food, including congee (rice porridge) for breakfast.

We then saw two of the developments purpose built for expats. Elegant Gardens was next to the Xijiao. It was in the first phase of construction, about 40 of the planned 400 villas completed and not all yet occupied. There were three basic types in pastel pinks or yellows with pillars and gables. It reminded me of Noddy and Big Ears in Toy Town, where each new occupant goes off to get his set of toy bricks and build himself a house just like his neighbours'. Subsequent developments were built in much the same style but grander, with names like Fortnum & Mason's Christmas hampers *The Windsor* or *The Gloucester*. Inside they had wood block floors but untreated wooden glazing bars, cheap looking kitchen units and very low sinks (not designed for tall Westerners) and green fluorescent doorstops. It will be fascinating to visit when they are all furnished – and it was.

There were wonderful artists' impressions of the clubhouse (still not built by 2000). The early inhabitants, including a large contingent from Ford, had major problems with the management. One very annoying difference with the Chinese was the understanding of the word *contract*. In China contracts can be terminated and changed at will, so Ford executives frequently found themselves renegotiating rent. Another early tenant, the Danish consul, having refused to pay more than he had negotiated, found his electricity cut off. So he ran a wire down the road to the American consul and sat it out.

In the afternoon we went to Green Valley where Chris and Julie Merry have taken a house. It is owned by the PLA (People's Liberation Army) who have extensive business interests. They were also the joint venture partner, with Peninsula Hotels of Hong Kong, of the Palace Hotel in Beijing where we ended up living. Green Valley is a much longer established expatriate development and consequently there are mature trees in the grounds. Again there is strict security at the entrance gate. The layout of the development is such that houses are separated from each other but there are no individually fenced gardens, just open areas with trees. The houses are a pastiche of the 1930's houses in the former French Concession, which themselves were a pastiche of Metroland. They looked insubstantial, like a cardboard film set. The area is very green - it was built on a former swamp and is prone to mosquitoes and there is a pig farm to one side. There is a central clubhouse with pool, gym and supermarket. Julie gave me a quick, guided tour - it looked very limited.

The new C&L Shanghai office is almost ready. There is tight security and the doors to the central lift area are kept locked after hours, as petty pilfering is rife. Even the loo rolls have to be removed or they would disappear and the computers are chained down. There are two security men who speak a little English and are said to be university professors needing a second job. All the professors seem very young by our standards - it was one of the professions targeted in the *Cultural Revolution* and many were killed. There is also fire-fighting equipment as the office is on the seventh floor and the fire brigade apparently would not be able to reach it.

I went to the cashier's desk in the Westin Hotel to change money - one hundred pounds sterling into Chinese currency. The girl regarded the British notes with the utmost suspicion, counted them, recounted them, recounted them again, held each up for scrutiny and finally rejected a ten pound note with a figure written on it. I explained it would have been written by a bank clerk to aid counting. But no, it was not acceptable. So I agreed to take it back and change just ninety pounds, for which I was handed the filthiest bunch of bank notes imaginable, all dog-eared with creases and bent corners. We soon discovered that Chinese loyalty is to the employer and not the customer, so the concept of service is difficult.

In early November we paid a visit to the Shanghai Golf Club. It was very busy as it was a Saturday and competition day, but it looked well cared for. All the caddies wore tin hats like upturned enamel basins and, as it was hot, most had a cloth over the hat for shade. We were shown round by one of the receptionists who found numbers difficult. She informed us that the cost of membership was in the million US dollar range, but that she had a boyfriend who could do a deal for hundreds of thousands of dollars and he could slip us onto the course unchallenged. She then rather charmingly added that the next nearest golf course was 25 kilograms (*sic*) away.

There is a dual carriageway out to the club, a good fast road, with much building going on and vast pyramids of bamboo waiting to be used as scaffolding. It seemed to be a good growing area too with small cultivated plots. We turned off down a narrow country road to the club and people were piling heaps of rice straw on the road - whether to dry out or act as a way of winnowing by car we were not sure.

January 1995 - Chinese New Year
It was decided that we should hold Chinese New Year office parties in both Shanghai and Beijing as a way of establishing a feeling of community as both offices have expanded so rapidly. Unfortunately this year the festival was on 31st January, which coincides with the business year end and a busy time for auditors. Hong Kong has been trumpeting *"Kung Hei Fat Choy"* ever since Christmas with thousands of pink furry toy pigs to usher in the Year of the Boar and

red paper packets for lucky money - new bank notes preferably, also red, for children and for the people who work for you.

The party in Shanghai was held in a private room in a restaurant on Nanjing Lu and consisted of a banquet, soft drinks, and speeches by John and Chris Merry and raffle prizes, which were very popular. There was a table prize of a cardboard throwaway camera with just one film. One or two took their prize home unused, but most wanted to snap away and all wanted to be photographed standing next to John.

The party in Beijing was for many more people and was much more sophisticated. Again, there was a banquet and speeches, but this time alcohol was served and consumed in vast quantities. A particular trick is for a group to keep toasting and plying new expatriate recruits with drink, to get them legless. Chey Chor Wai (the Managing Partner on secondment from C&L Singapore) and a new manager were targeted. There was a floorshow of Chinese dancing and the final dance required the presence of an Emperor and Empress on stage - John and me. We had to wear long robes and ornate headdresses - mine was very heavy, very precariously perched and made my ears stick out. I was most uncomfortable but John loved being back on stage. Then various party games were organised - the more raucous and childish, the better they went down. We had an even more embarrassing experience at a subsequent Beijing Chinese New Year party. We were just finishing the meal, when the lights went low, the music started and one of China's prizewinning ballroom dancing couples came on to give a display. Ballroom dancing is very popular here and you often see people hang a tape recorder on a tree in a park and start dancing. We all duly applauded and then the couple headed for our table. It was too late to escape. John and I had to take the floor partnered by the champions. I did better as he steered me around and could count in English. John found it much more difficult and said his partner had heavily calloused hands.

The next day we drove out to the Great Wall on a cold clear day with bright blue skies. Hardly anyone else was there - China closes down for New Year, which is the big holiday period when everyone travels back home - and even the Kentucky Fried Chicken Restaurant was closed. The postcard sellers on the Wall pursued us with desperation - they were obviously not going to get much custom. There was tremendous admiration for John's Finnish fur hat, a very superior model to the rather tatty Chinese or Mongolian fur hats for sale - and the sellers were keen to know where it came from and how much it had cost. We were amused by the signs saying *Police Admonishing: Beware of Pickpockets*, the translator had got the wrong sense of warning.

Back in Shanghai I was allowed to borrow Ruby Chin and one of the office cars (a very comfortable imported American Ford Lincoln) and a driver for a few hours' sightseeing. I asked if we could go to the Marble Hall, which was built for the Kadoorie family between 1918 and 1924. With the Sassoons and Hardoons, the Kadoories were one of the Jewish families who arrived in Shanghai via India from Iraq and became incredibly wealthy. They gave the house to the municipality to be used as a Children's Palace when they left Shanghai for Hong Kong, presumably in 1949. It is on Yan'an Xilu, one of Shanghai's three main roads through the centre to the Bund, and opposite the Equatorial Hotel. Many grandiose residences were being built at that time but I still found the concept of a classical European-style mansion faced in white marble mind-boggling - rather like the Getty Museum today. It is on an extremely grand scale, a long building with a raised terrace running the entire length. Two statues of an idealised boy and a girl, both Young Pioneers with their trademark neck scarves, have been placed on the steps leading to the terrace. Inside a marble staircase, deep ornate classical friezes, ornamental plaster ceilings in some rooms, wood block parquet flooring, and an elliptical hall with niches for statues opening onto a covered entrance where cars could pull up. I later met a Kadoorie relative who told me that, when his aunt went back to see the Palace, she remarked that the bedrooms still had the same colour and coat of paint on the walls. It is certainly looking rather tatty now. The garden has been turned into an adventure playground with a central stage where loud music was being broadcast. As it was holiday time over the New Year, the garden was full of school-age children on a day out. Ruby managed to persuade the man on the gate to let us in and she explained that the building was normally used for out of school activities for children who were especially talented. Inside rooms were devoted to arts, crafts, music and drama. Although this was a holiday time, various activities had been set up for children as a whole. There was one room with dark wooden panelling, which was being used by a class of specially selected girls. They were rehearsing a dance sequence and we were allowed to go in and watch (we were clapped in and waved out by 40 or so smiling girls aged from about 8 to 14). They were being trained to become professional dancers, with one of their teachers walking the part as they rehearsed. They wore bright orange practice trousers and were very well drilled.

Ruby always links arms with me when we go out. I think this is partly not to lose me and partly because she has realised how hopeless I am at crossing roads. She kept a firm grip on me when we got to the Yu Yuan Bazaar Gardens, as it is very popular and usually very crowded. It is on the edge of the old Chinese quarter and an area of old (restored) shops, temples and teahouses. The most famous teahouse, Huxingting, is five-sided and lies at the edge of a pond with the famous Nine-Twists zigzag bridge leading to the Mandarin Gardens. Apparently the bridge used to have beggars lurking in the angles. It was the inspiration for the Willow Pattern design. The gardens have small enclosed areas leading one off another, with pavilions in some, and plenty of rockeries, false mountains and pools. There are some trees and shrubs but Ruby told me that the Chinese consider that a garden should have rocks, effectively a mini landscape. I later learnt that the pictograph for garden is a rectangle (enclosure) containing the symbols for a building or pavilion, a pool or lake and a plant or rock. Some of the gardens are enclosed by dragon walls: a wall with an undulating tiled top to represent the dragon's back and a carved head at one end. A revolutionary group called the Society of Small Swords used to meet here in the mid-19th Century, which explains why the Red Guards left the gardens intact during the *Cultural Revolution*. We went to the Green Wave Gallery for lunch. Shanghai is famous for its snacks, a bit like Cantonese dim sum, and Yu Yuan Bazaar is the best place to find them. We had a set lunch consisting of about a dozen different snacks, some in a bun or doughy casing, some in crispy pancake or pastry like one crescent-shaped snack called *eyebrow cake*. Most were savoury, but the sweet fillings were very sweet. Ruby comes equipped with plastic bags and after she has pressed the leftovers on me and I have thought up some good reasons for not needing them, she sweeps everything into her doggy bag and carries it away. We soon learnt that in China it is impolite to refuse something when offered for the third time and this can often lead to misunderstanding.

When we flew into Beijing airport just before the New Year party, we found it much busier than usual. We had a long wait for luggage to emerge and not a trolley to be seen. It is traditional for people to return home for the New Year and it was estimated in one newspaper that 200 million people would be travelling that weekend. Most of course would go by train, not air.

There was a huge ice sculpture being carved in front of our hotel, which turned out to be a large ice piggy. As it was mild for the time of year, above freezing during the day, it would get a bit runny and then firm up overnight. The traffic was extra heavy as people shopped for the coming holiday. There were huge red lanterns everywhere. We managed to buy two from the Friendship Store where they formed part of the decorations. The sales assistants explained that they weren't for sale but the manager was only too happy to sell us a couple.

John had dinner in Beijing recently with some of the Nokia men and their wives. One of the wives is a painter and has been attending an art school. She told John that the female models must pose in the nude but the males are allowed to pose in underpants - chauvinistic and not so easy to draw.

<u>May 1995 – A week in Beijing</u>
The first Sunday in May was the start of the kite-flying season. People were out in droves, flying kites from the bridges over the ring roads and along the main roads and packing into Tiananmen Square, ice creams in one hand and kite strings in the other with obviously no thought of any political significance of the Square. Now there is a giant clock in the square counting down the number of days to 1st July 1997 and the return of Hong Kong. The clock was taken up to the Great Wall after the handover and replaced with one counting down to the return of Macau. The Square is regarded as the centre of Beijing and used for political events - the Great Hall of the People is

there - and for spontaneous gatherings of people, particularly after the deaths of popular politicians, as with Zhou En Lai, and the start of the student demonstrations in 1989. But also, during the handover of Hong Kong, ceremonies were held in the Square and, in the evenings leading up to the event, it was crowded.

We toured some of the antique markets: Liulichang is an area of restored shops, rather touristy, but some interesting objects and a wonderful old paint shop where I used to buy excellent dirt cheap brushes for Daddy, and Chaowai which is a huge building with individual stalls selling antique porcelain and a lot of copies. There is also a furniture hall. It lies beyond an area of clothes markets where we spotted quite a few Russians buying box loads to transport back. Chaowai has since closed down but more markets kept popping up.

I also went with Marja Helenius, on holiday in China with Antti (a colleague of John's) from Finland, and another Finn, Raija Teerikangas, to a hutong development. The Beijing hutongs are tiny alleys around which are built the courtyard houses for extended families. Many of these single storey houses have become separate flats, instead of one big extended family house. We walked around an area where traditional housing had been demolished, and new housing built in the old style and we were taken into one of the flats. The couple there had a small living room (with TV), kitchen with calor gas for cooking, bathroom and one bedroom. It was fairly cramped and the furniture was utility style but they said they liked the layout of the flats. Each had a balcony with plants and looked over a small parched garden area. Later when we were deciding where to live in Beijing, we went with Tony Walker, *The Financial Times* correspondent, to an area behind Beihei Park, close to where all the Government officials live, to look at a courtyard house that had been renovated and was being offered for rent. It was very picturesque, but isolated and expensive and I didn't think I would be able to cope with liaising with the Chinese owners.

There has been an attempt to replant trees around Beijing. When the trees were cut down in the *Cultural Revolution*, Beijing became vulnerable to dust storms coming off the desert, but you still wouldn't call it a particularly green city. Even so, one keeps coming across things we grow at home: wisteria, azalea, Banksia roses, peonies and so on, and then realising that of course they were introduced to our gardens from China.

Dean Yoost's wife, Mei Chang, took me to a shop to buy silk. There were overhead wires and when you paid, the notes were clipped to the wire and sent off to the cashier's desk for change. I remember that sort of system in the 1950's in a few shops, particularly department stores, in the UK.

May 1995 - Chengdu and Lhasa

We spent a few days in Chengdu, the capital of Sichuan Province. Sichuan is the most fertile province in China, roughly the size of France but with twice as many people, around 100 million.

We flew in over rice paddies and farmland. The airport was fairly simple: a man with two discs to direct planes to parking places, with his bicycle leaning against him. The cleaners for the planes also rode bicycles carrying their mops. And on the way back, we flew in from Lhasa (domestic) and had two hours before the Hong Kong flight (international) left and had to stand outside the international part of the airport, which was locked until 90 minutes before take-off. (Later during one Chinese New Year holiday in Hua Hin in Thailand we found ourselves sitting next to an employee of British Airways who had worked in Chengdu. He regaled us with some hair-raising tales about Chengdu airport and China Southern, mainly involving aircraft over-shooting the runway and not reporting the incident in order not to foul up the statistics. Next morning he asked us to forget the conversation.)

Chengdu has broad tree-lined streets with bicycle lanes - we took a cycle rickshaw in the rush hour and it was fun being swept along with the crowds. There is far less new construction than in Shanghai, although a second ring road had just been opened. Chengdu was only *opened* to foreigners in the mid-1980's, some time after Guangdong and the East Coast, and this is evidenced in the relative lack of sophistication. But the amount of spending power is obviously increasing and there was a large range of different types of food available in the department store which we visited.

John was visiting a couple of CPA firms and also a Vice Mayor. I was involved in one of the meetings visits because it took place in our hotel room. The boss was rather overwhelmed and made it plain he did not think he was ready for any kind of international contact just yet - and that his office was not up to a visit from us. The head of the second firm had been on a C&L training course and was much more outward looking and gave a banquet for us - plenty of courses of spicy Sichuan food, including turtle which tasted better than it looked.

The visit to the Vice Mayor was very interesting. The Government offices were on a grand scale and surrounded by very well-tended gardens with pools and bonsai trees and little hedges. We were shown into a large audience room, leather sofas ranged round the sides of the room with two grand chairs at one end, for the Vice Mayor and his most important guest, forming a U-shaped configuration, with little tables on which we were all served tea. The Vice Mayor was smartly dressed. He and John conducted formal discussions through interpreters on the extent of foreign investment and the role which C&L could play. Occasionally the formality was broken by the Vice Mayor's relaxed manner and sense of humour. At the end we were all filmed shaking hands and this apparently went out on local TV news. Since the figure of public access to TV in China is estimated at about 86%, that's the best coverage I shall ever get.

John's interpreter was Teddy Tang who works for C&L in Shanghai and speaks excellent English as he spent a year with the firm in London. He was one of the brightest students of his year who each took a series of exams to determine who should be selected for an overseas bursary. One of his friends from that time, Mr Wu, came with us and interpreted for the Vice Mayor. Mr Wu told us that he had studied optical physics at university, came through the same selection procedure as Teddy but didn't get funding to go overseas. So he returned to Chengdu. He had had to change career as there were too many graduates in his speciality and he had been directed to join the body advising overseas firms wanting to establish a place of business in Chengdu. We asked him to lunch but he felt unable to accept since his boss could not also accept, as he had to go home to look after his young child. Teddy said that this was quite common as the extended family is not always able to help. Teddy's son is cared for by his parents in his hometown of Wuhan.

Teddy arranged for me to go to the Panda Research Centre with an appropriately named Miss Xiong (translated as Miss Bear) since a panda is *xiong mao*, a bear cat). Her English name, given in English classes at school, was Kate. Sometimes these names are chosen because they sound like Chinese names, sometimes they are chosen on the basis of alliteration with the family name.

During the drive to the Panda Research Centre, Kate told me that she had changed her name to Joy. This was because she had become a Christian. There seemed to be a small but very fervent group, thanks to an American exchange lecturer, and every now and then Kate/Joy broke into evangelical hymns.

The Research Centre had a well laid out museum recording details of the breeding programme. The Chinese have had some success in breeding pandas in zoos, but the numbers of pandas in the wild have diminished rapidly. We then walked through the grounds to an area where there were a number of cages. Some held one panda and some two – there were about half a dozen altogether. They were all awake - one or two pacing about and looking rather distressed while others lay back, tucking into bamboo shoots. The cages had glass fronts and we were able to walk right up to them. When there are pandas at London zoo, the public is kept well back and the pandas are usually asleep in the daytime. One panda was let out into a big grass enclosure, where he was much photographed. There were other enclosures with smaller red-coated panda-related animals and a hospital where injured pandas were brought in from the wild. This was not open to the public but we walked round it and could just make out darkened individual rooms and hear laboured panda breathing.

We flew from Chengdu to Lhasa. The flights from Beijing to Lhasa stop in Chengdu and at present Chengdu is the only place in China with direct flights to Tibet. It is a stunning flight - at times we were above the cloud but could see snow covered peaks sticking through the cloud layer. There were tiny little settlements, mainly along river banks and, occasionally, along a winding road. But there is a great sense of isolation and of flying over the roof of the world.

Lhasa airport is some way outside the town where there is a plateau between mountains safe enough for landing. Most of the taxis from the airport into Lhasa are four-wheel drive and the road into town is terrible - frequent potholes and landslips and gangs of road builders, male and female, hard at work.

Lhasa itself is 14,000 ft high and we were both affected by the altitude, feeling headachy and breathless and having difficulty sleeping. You are advised to drink plenty of extra water and to take things slowly at first to give the body (or rather, the blood) time to acclimatise. As we only had three days, we wanted to sightsee straight away. We stayed at the Holiday Inn - well run and well stocked and decorated in Tibetan style. After the *Opening-Up* began, the Holiday Inn Company built a number of hotels in China of a high standard. In Lhasa the hotel used to have piped oxygen in the rooms to counter the adverse effects of altitude, but now they had oxygen pillows - refillable rubber pillows with a tube that you held over your face while the weight of your head released a slow trickle of oxygen - but we still felt dreadful.

On the first afternoon, we commissioned a jeep and a guide and we made our way to the Barkhor market and the Jokhang. The market was busy. All over Lhasa there are scores of upcountry pilgrims with their prayer wheels, some prostrating themselves. The girls usually have long black plaits, but so did some of the men. John used the term *noble savage* to describe them and it was very apt - they had great dignity. The Barkhor had religious items for sale - white scarves which are a traditional gift, packs of smelly rancid yak butter to keep candles burning, and prayer flags in bright colours - blue representing sky, white - cloud, red - fire, green - water and yellow - earth. There were also household items for sale and cheap clothes. It was exceptionally hot and John bought a sun hat for 10 pence. There were also felt trilbys and we subsequently came across a group of Chinese tourists all wearing Tibetan trilbys. With their thin faces and cheap sunglasses and suits, they looked as shifty as the weasels in the National Theatre production of *Wind in the Willows*.

You have to progress clockwise, out of respect, and as close to the edge of a room as possible, with the result that some pilgrims will crawl under and over furniture placed against a wall.

The Jokhang temple was dark and airless and the candles smelt of yak butter. Apparently, because of the smell, I went rather green, but managed to walk out into a little courtyard and get some fresh air. Then we went out onto the roof from which there were superb views of the surrounding mountains and little monks learning to blow the long, rude-sounding horns (a bit like Alpen horns).

The following day we visited the Potala Palace. The street to the Potala was being re-built. Previously there had been three giant stupas, which had been destroyed during the *Cultural Revolution*. These were now being replaced with replicas in time for the forthcoming celebrations of 30 years of Chinese rule, in August 1995. This was also the reason for repairs to and re-routing of the road from the airport. The Potala had always been a mixture of sacred and secular: the home of the living God, the palace of the Dalai Lama, and the seat of Government. Only a small number of rooms among the labyrinth is open to the public and only at certain times. These include some of the Dalai Lama's living quarters and the large audience chambers, as well as shrines. The Potala Palace is still a Mecca for pilgrims, a number of whom asked if we had photographs of the Dalai Lama to give them. A few years after this, such photographs were outlawed by the Chinese.

We were informed that the entrance money at all the monasteries still goes to the monastic coffers, but at the Potala it now goes to the Government. We were very impressed at the state of repair of the Potala - there were humidity controls and video security cameras. Everything seemed in good order with restoration work going on. Besides the many Buddha and Dalai Lama statues, there were thousands of scrolls of illuminated scriptures. We asked how they had survived the destruction wrought by the *Cultural Revolution* and were told that they had been removed to Beijing but subsequently returned.

As well as the Tibetan pilgrims, there were also quite a few Chinese tourists, which I hadn't expected, and many of them seemed devout.

There were also Western tourists, mainly in groups and also a few independent like us and a few backpackers. A couple of years later the Chinese government clamped down on visas for independent travellers. Needless to say there is always an enterprising Chinese trying to get round the regulations and we heard that the backpackers would go to Chengdu, contact a particular hotel, be banded together with other independent travellers as a *tour group* and thus qualify for a group visa. We observed one American tourist walking with great difficulty, supported on crutches. We wondered at the wisdom of her travel agent, as there was not only a great deal of walking necessary to visit Lhasa, but also some very steep ladders from one floor to the next and onto the roofs of the Potala.

In front of the Potala a huge square was being built in readiness for the August 1995 celebrations. We heard that this had caused great resentment as an area of housing had had to be cleared to create the square. That said, the houses were apparently small and overcrowded but the standard of living had risen under the Chinese. There are now more schools and hospitals and these are no longer under the control of monasteries, which were once all-powerful. There were Chinese soldiers everywhere and the Chinese PLA is still an army of occupation. Our Tibetan guide was very discreet but very anti-Chinese. However, friends who visited Tibet with a Chinese guide reported no resentment on the part of the Tibetans.

That afternoon we went to the Norbu Lingka Summer Palace. It was wonderfully shady - Tibet was exceptionally hot while we were there with temperatures of 27 degrees and the sun is extra fierce at that altitude. Since the whole of China is on the same time zone (set for Beijing's convenience), the sun does not set in Tibet on the western edge until 20.30 or 21.00 in the evening. In the grounds of the Summer Palace we came across the first of many solar heaters. A kettle was suspended above a shining metallic disc and you could feel the heat of the sun coming from it.

Our final day in Tibet was spent at two of the important monasteries close to Lhasa, Drepung and Sera. Both had been destroyed in part and the numbers of monks was only a small proportion of what it had been pre 1959. Drepung had a very beautiful audience hall and was in a lovely position high up on the hillside. Besides the many statues and scrolls, there were some amazing suits of chain mail armour, absolutely filthy, thick with dust and straight out of Tamburlaine. We also went into the kitchens, positively medieval, with enormous vats around a wood burning fire and huge wooden churns for the ubiquitous yak butter.

Sera is famous for its debating. The young monks take it in turn to question and answer and the questioner has to be very fierce and clap his hands in front of the answerer's face. It was all done with lots of posturing for the benefit of the supervising older monks and us, the visitors, who were watching. But there were also quite a few giggles, especially from the younger ones. We noticed a very charming child-like side to many Tibetans, not just among the up-country people who wanted to stare at us and touch our cameras and try and see through them, but also there was a lot of horseplay among the people in Lhasa. The most popular form of this were the water fights in the Barkhor, where someone was always tip-toeing up behind someone else with a bowlful of water causing great mirth among the on-lookers.

We had to get up early to catch the 'plane back to Chengdu. But our driver did not turn up. So we were invited to join a Chinese passenger, who spoke good English, in a car with his Tibetan driver. He drove incredibly badly, seeing the potholes either at the last minute or not at all. In the end the Chinese made him stop the car, and took over the driving himself with all the superiority of the master race.

Perhaps even more than the roof of the world, Tibet feels like the edge of the world. We also visited the offices of the only CPA firm in Lhasa and met a Chinese who had attended a training course in 1994 managed by Simon Anderson. He very much wanted us to visit his office.

November 1995 - Xian
We went to Xian with Jill and Pat Sherry (John's new boss) at the start of their business trip to China. The main reason, of course, was for us to see the terracotta army, but John and Pat were also planning

to visit a client, Xian Janssen (Janssen is the Belgian arm of Johnson & Johnson), which is one of the largest and most successful joint ventures in China. It is now Chinese run and has a large site in the pharmaceutical quarter of Xian - opposite the old Chinese medicine market.

Xian was a former capital of China (Cha'An) and still has its old walls and bell tower and drum tower standing (bell at dawn, drum at dusk) as well as a fascinating Moslem area of narrow cobbled streets, bazaars and an attractive mosque, all in Chinese style.

Chris Merry told us subsequently that Xian is the execution and murder capital of China and that when he was there, he was advised by Xian Janssen staff to be careful when he was out at night. We were blissfully unaware of this at the time and Jill and I had no problems touring the city on our own during the day.

All the guidebooks advised that the official tours to the terracotta army also took in the Banpo Neolithic village and the Huaqing Pool. We had our own guide and car and we asked to see the warriors and a city tour only, and lo and behold, we were taken to the Banpo village, the terracotta warriors and the Huaqing Pool. The same thing happened on Jill's and my city tour on the next day when we listed a few places we would like to see and the driver stuck to his predetermined route.

John is always very cautious about which airline to fly. Air China was broken up some time ago into different airlines, to fly internally, and some of these are a great deal better than others. The golden rule is to avoid those airlines which fly second hand Russian made aircraft, such as Tupolevs. Xian Air is one to avoid. Its call sign is XO and there are jokes about the pilots' constant need for brandy when seeking to fly high. So we had been careful when flying from Hong Kong and used Dragon Air, operated by Cathay Pacific. We flew out of Xian on China Northern to Beijing, first class, with excellent service, but I noticed, as we were landing, three air hostesses on seats for two, so one was not wearing a seat belt.

We took Jill and Pat on a quick tour of Beijing and Shanghai. We took the usual plan of going to the Great Wall and as we wanted to go on to the Summer Palace without returning to the centre of Beijing, we needed to find somewhere for lunch. There was a nice tearoom - but no food and the only dish available was some rather unsavoury looking noodles from a mobile kitchen. So we decided to go to the Kentucky Fried Kitchen Restaurant just down the road. These restaurants are now all over China. We arrived to find some American girls in front of us getting very angry - they wanted drumsticks and there were none - KFC had run out of chickens. We settled for chicken burgers and chips and they were jolly tasty. I was interested to see what the loos would be like - clean and Western style I imagined. I was wrong. They were Chinese style and as filthy as everywhere else in the country.

It was cold and windy on the Great Wall and most tourists were well muffled up. But we saw one Chinese lady who made us feel rather under-dressed - she wore a black Lurex sweater, tight black trousers and stilettos. We later discovered that honeymoon couples, brides in particular, go sightseeing in their finery to the Great Wall and, of course, to be photographed.

In a Chinese restaurant, the plates are frequently cleared and a clean bowl or plate is placed in front of you while you are mid-meal. And, sometimes, not just empty plates are cleared away. This idea has now been extended to the restaurants serving Western-type food and I find it very disconcerting, especially at breakfast in a hotel, either to find my plate disappearing to be replaced by an empty one or trying to eat with one hand on my plate when all around me is being cleared away.

<u>February 1996 - Visits to Shanghai and Beijing</u>
The new museum in Shanghai is open. Apparently the old one was dark and badly displayed, which was a shame for one of the best collections in China. During the fighting in the 1940's many national treasures were crated up for safety and taken to Nanjing and then Chongqing. When the Kuomintang fled to Taiwan, they took all the crates with them. So, today, they have the best collection in the world. When John was looking for office space, the old museum building was available but he ruled it out as being too gloomy.

C&L were also approached for money towards the cost of construction of the new museum but declined. C&L was loss-making at that time and could not afford charitable donations. No expense was spared in the construction of the museum. 14% of the US$70 million cost of the building came from private foreign donors. The building is magnificent. It is in People's Square, the new square behind Renmin Park, which was the old racecourse in Shanghai. It has municipal buildings as well as the museum and, subsequently, the Grand Theatre was built on this site. The museum building itself looks like one of the bronzes it houses but is meant to represent the Chinese saying *"the sky is round, the earth is square"*.

Outside is a polished stone surround (which became very slippery in the rain) and bronze burners modelled on those in the Forbidden City. When we visited the museum on a cold day in February, incongruously, the ubiquitous loudspeakers were playing the Theme from a Summer Place. The museum is situated in a park which is attractively laid out with flowerbeds containing strange flowering plants that look like cauliflowers and purple brassicas.

Inside the building is light and airy with marble floors, huge pillars and a central atrium under the dome. There are 14 galleries, all well lit and with clear explanations in Mandarin and English and room for the displays to be changed from time to time. So far, bronzes, porcelain and statues are on display. The bronzes are magnificent. We were astounded by the diversity and sophistication of such ancient pieces. And there were some humorous pieces too, with feline figures clambering up the side of water containers and peering over the edge.

The museum expects to have an annual budget of US$1.8 million compared to the Sackler in Beijing University with just US$25,000. The entry price in Shanghai was 40 yuan for foreigners and was 20 at the Sackler. The Shanghai Museum introduced an excellent audio tour, held visiting exhibitions in some galleries, and the remaining galleries gradually opened over the next few months. I returned again and again, sometimes spending the whole day there. A good bookshop also opened. The museum was well attended by local people, schools and many elderly couples who spent hours admiring and scrutinising the porcelain.

Another, more popular, landmark has also recently opened. The new television tower in Pudong, called Pearl of the Orient, is always busy with local sightseers. It is 263 metres tall and elevators whisk crowds up to the enclosed viewing area for a 360 degree bird's eye view over Shanghai. It affords a wonderful view of the Huangpu River and of the Bund and Pu Xi.

The ring road is also up and running which seems to have helped the traffic flow and a new flyover will take passengers to the airport - rather close to the vast expat housing development at Gubai. All the expat housing is being concentrated on the airport side it seems. Gubai was particularly popular with overseas Chinese and there were reports of a young child being kidnapped and held to ransom.

In Beijing too, a massive expat development is going up near the airport. In fact it is three separate developments, funded respectively by Singaporean, Hong Kong and Taiwanese money, all with better workmanship than the developments in Shanghai but still some bad planning - low kitchen units based on oriental height, steep steps down into guest cloakrooms, high ceilings with impossible to reach windows and front doors opening straight into living areas - and in a very cold climate - and boxes for the maid's room. I wondered where all the maids would come from (in Hong Kong and Singapore they are now mostly Philippinos). In China most of the maids came in on a daily basis. There are already water and electricity supply problems and only the first phase of each development is so far completed. They were little boxes crammed as close together as possible - a bit like a seaside tourist development. And there are some double garages in a country where most expats fear to drive.

We visited the Sackler Museum at Beijing University. After the Tiananmen Square Incident in 1989, the university was off-limits to foreigners, when special permission to visit was required. This now seems to be relaxing but Raija had telephoned ahead just in case, and indeed we all needed to show our IDs. At first our taxi took us to the wrong gate where a very young pimply sentry became very agitated at the sight of four large Western culture vultures. However we eventually found the right gate and our driver was allowed in. The

University was a real surprise - a most attractive campus, with some of the artifacts apparently taken from the grounds of the Summer Palace. So there were attractive gardens, grass, rocks, pools and trees. Many buildings were in traditional style with pitched roofs with curved ends with animal figures and painted beams and "chinoiserie" windows. There were also less attractive buildings like the huge blocks put up for the foreign, mainly African, students.

The Sackler Collection spans the Neolithic to the Qing period with most space devoted to the Neolithic. There are very many bones and some lovely early pottery and bronze and some later jade. Like all Chinese public buildings, it was not heated and we were soon shivering. Even the Finns felt cold.

We explored the big Foreign Language Bookstore in Wangfujing, the upmarket shopping street. It has an impressive number of dictionaries, technical translation aids, teaching books and classics in English. We also discovered a number of books in the interpreting section called *Olympic 2000* with questions and answers that an interpreter during the Olympics might need. We could not tell when they had been printed, but they had been produced on the optimistic and perhaps premature assumption that Beijing would win the competition to host the 2000 Olympics.

One day John and I walked in Jingshan Park, which has the famous Coal Hill. You can climb up the steep man-made hill (the spoil from the moat dug around the Forbidden City) for a wonderful view over the Palace. On the east side of the Park was a locust tree from which the last of the Ming Emperors hanged himself rather than see the Forbidden City raised by the Manchus who founded the Qing dynasty in mid-17th Century. A new tree has been planted on the spot because the old one was hacked down during the *ten year struggle period* as a little sign tells you. It took us some time to realise this was a reference to the *Cultural Revolution.*

April 1996 - Hangzhou
Hangzhou is a famous beauty spot near Shanghai and the time to visit is April. We were overwhelmed by the sight of so much fresh brilliant green foliage. Beijing has few trees, Shanghai does have

streets lined with plane trees but the impression is of dusty greyish leaves and most Chinese gardens have rocks and buildings rather than flowers. Hangzhou has trees and flowers in abundance.

The West Lake (Xi Hu) has ten scenic spots around it, each with wonderfully descriptive names made up of four Chinese characters. Everyone takes boat trips - there are packed large boats, smaller boats with one or two boatmen paddling, rowing boats on the inner lake and a strange electrically powered boat that looks like a train or a tram mounted on a wooden hull.

The lakeside gardens are spectacular - there are six public gardens on one side of the lake, a line of alternate willow and peach blossom and gardens with banks of azalea, wisteria, peonies, roses, camellias and ornamental red maple.

Hangzhou is also a tea-growing area centred around the village of Lung Ching. The tea is cultivated on small round bushes, some terraced on the hillside above rice paddies. April is the picking season, usually starting around the Ching Ming (*Sweeping Graves*) Festival, but this year it was late due to cold weather. The leaves have to be dry when picked and this is all done by hand with the pickers wearing large straw hats. The land is owned by the State and leased out to the villagers. As we drove through the village we could see the tea leaves in large wicker trays and most households were beginning the drying process. This is done in large wooden tubs with a metal lining that is electrically heated. The leaves are put in these tubs three times for about fifteen minutes each time and have to be constantly turned by hand. There is a hissing and crackling sound as the moisture evaporates - and hands get blistered. We stopped at one house to watch the process and were offered a taste and an opportunity to make purchases. Because of the late Spring, there will be less superior quality tea this year but we were shown, and selected, some of the best. Purchases are made by the *catty* or by the ounce. The ounces were weighed on a hand-held scale of bowl and moveable weights, tied up in a paper parcel and then put in a plastic bag that was sealed over a lighted candle flame. Then we (Ruby Chin and I) drove back to Hangzhou along the hikers' route to the suburbs called Nine Creeks which was a rough cobbled track crossing the stream nine times leading through tea bushes and trees. I don't know how the car managed it. I saw an old man carrying a bamboo pole across his shoulder with two baskets each containing a kid goat packed in a cardboard box.

There is an excellent museum in Hangzhou, with a history of tea culture. China was the original tea producer, exporting to Japan and all places West. As part of the exhibition was a mock-up of interiors showing how the ethnic minorities, including Tibetans, took their tea.

Hangzhou is a popular honeymoon destination and despite the rain and mud, there were a few girls in cocktail attire.

Gordon Barrass was also in town and we bumped into him lunching with Chinese friends, one of whom had studied Art History at Oxford. His Chinese friend spoke excellent English as indeed did his daughter. She was six when they went to Oxford and is very musical. She had caught the accent at her Oxford pre-prep to a tee and spoke a perfect unaccented English with a plum in her mouth.

May 1996 - Yangtze River Trip

As John had business interests in Chongqing and Wuhan, we decided to travel between the two by boat, to see the Three Gorges before the new dam is finished. The area has subsequently been very badly flooded in Summer 1996.

Ruby had again arranged my programme in Chongqing. A day trip was suggested to see some wonderful Buddhist cave paintings at a place called Daza - 100 miles away on bad roads. I would have loved to have gone, but John was concerned about the drive as we were due on the Yangtze boat that night. We tried to voice our concern by saying that we thought the journey might take too long both ways, only to be assured by our hosts that it could be done in 2 hours. I was terrified at the thought of driving at 60 mph on bad roads but, without loss of face all round, it was impossible to refuse. So I got up early next morning only to find it had rained heavily and luckily there had been an enforced change of plan.

That night we were met by a representative of the boat company and escorted to go on board - fortuitously as it turned out. It was a very steep road down to the water's edge and we arrived in a pitch black parking place to find a couple of crew from the boat waiting to help with our luggage and a motley crowd, also more than keen to take our luggage. I think that this latter group would probably have offered to carry luggage on board for a fee but possibly would have made off with anything valuable such as cameras or John's computer. One man was so keen to help that he had a fistfight with one of the crew over John's suitcase. It was rather like arriving on a film set - an impression I felt throughout the trip. The scenery was magnificent, unreal, just like all those Chinese paintings, and some of the scenes of boatmen hauling their craft up the Lesser Three Gorges looked just like a film.

We had a really good time on board - John thought it was one of the best trips we had ever experienced. We had expeditions off the boat every day and masses to see from on board besides the scenery - this included John spotting a corpse floating downstream and we saw a boat full of pigs - not so much a cruise, more a way to the dinner table. The trip up the Lesser Three Gorges was spectacular. We stopped for lunch and, when we got back on board, a very young policeman came and sat down next to me but disembarked just as our boat was leaving.

In Yue Yang we were taken to the Dongting Lake by coach. On the way back we were travelling along a two-way road of four lanes, two lanes in each direction. Suddenly there was a hold-up and we found four lanes of traffic coming towards us. Total gridlock ensued. Our enterprising driver turned onto the pavement only to find traffic coming down the pavement towards us. We then got thoroughly stuck trying to get back onto the road between the telegraph poles. No wonder the bus had a cracked windscreen.

I learnt that animals, particularly the ones associated with the zodiac, all have their birthdays on the same day each year. For example, all Chinese pigs have their birthdays on the same day and to my delight all water buffaloes gain an extra year on 8th April, my sister, Judy's, birthday.

<u>**Interesting Conversational Snippets**</u>

Living in China can be fascinating and amusing, with the following interesting examples:

- Mrs Redfarn's ayi, late 20's, married, but childless: *If I don't start a baby soon, one morning I will find someone has left a new-born baby girl on my doorstep.*

- Long-stay resident: *When we first arrived, the Ming tombs were one of the few places we were allowed to go to* which explains why this is still a favoured place for picnics. Foreigners' movements were very closely monitored just after the *Open Door Policy* in the late 1970's. When John was working in Hong Kong in 1981, he came with a tour group. Independent travellers were discouraged. Michael and Francine Clarke, the first C&L Western staff in Shanghai, lived in the Jin Jiang Hotel and say they were constantly harangued by staff in their own apartment as to what they were and were not allowed to do.

- Ambassador's wife: *When we left the UK, we rented out our house. We had to find a flat for my mother who has cancer and had been living with us.* What about the children I asked. *Oh we put their possessions in a warehouse where they can go and get things if they need to. Our stuff is in locked storage.*

- Ann Hu (parents from Shanghai, born in Taiwan, raised in USA) whom we met holidaying in Bangkok: *I refuse to visit the Chinese pavilion at the Thai Summer Palace because it is Qing.* The Qings ousted the Ming dynasty in 17th Century after invading from Manchuria and were regarded as foreigners. They were also hated for their lavish spending (Dowager Empress Cixi used money raised to pay for a navy to embellish the grounds of the Summer Palace) and for the fact that during the 19th Century China was forced to submit to a number of unequal treaties ceding land, including Hong Kong, and opening up trading concessions

- Louisa Paul is the Cantonese wife of the Senior Partner of Price Waterhouse's Hong Kong firm. She told me her grandfather had six wives and 25 children. Her grandmother was the second wife (so effectively regarded as a concubine). She was unusual in that she was wealthy in her own right and had three maids but she had refused to have her feet bound and so was not considered beautiful – she was a sort of damaged goods as her feet were not deformed!

- Betty Ko told us that she was on a visit to Taiwan in June 1989 where she first heard about the Tiananmen Square Incident and her reaction was that it was Taiwanese propaganda against the mainland. Then she travelled to Hong Kong and discovered the facts. When returned to Shanghai, people were aware of what had happened and were talking about it openly. After that she went to Beijing where no one was saying anything.

Adoption

In the mid 1990's, the UK's Channel 4 television broadcast a documentary, shot in a Shanghainese orphanage, showing the appalling conditions the baby girls endured. Connie Watson (wife of Kent, John's colleague in Beijing) told me, a propos a conversation about the official line banning meetings of more than 15 people, that a big fund raising event was to be held for the orphanages, to be addressed by the Chinese American author, Amy Tan. But, at the last moment, it was forced to cancel.

Adoptions had been going ahead before then. I met an English girl in Shanghai with her recently adopted baby who seemed to be thriving. They did not know how old the little girl was exactly, probably around 15 months. There is now a steady stream of prospective Western parents coming to China. We saw three well-built middle-aged Caucasian women with tiny Chinese babies in baby slings taking a trip out to the Great Wall, presumably doing a spot of sightseeing before taking the babies back home. I heard that the Canadian Government is being particularly helpful in providing back up - they have recently had a very open immigration policy and many Chinese, especially from Hong Kong, have settled in Vancouver.

In October 1998 we met John's partner, Vaughan Thomas, and his wife Christine, from the UK, who were hoping to adopt a Chinese baby. They were very pragmatic about the problems, particularly health problems, which can occur. A lot of the babies have been found to be HIV positive. We had heard that lead poisoning was also a problem as there is still a lead content in paint, but this can easily be reversed with the correct diet. With help from Qian Ning, son of the Foreign Minister and one-time employee of C&L in China, the adoption formalities were completed and they came out again to collect their baby in May 1999, just after the bombing of the Chinese Embassy in Belgrade by NATO. Luckily this did not interrupt the adoption process and we met little Francesca just before she was taken back to the UK. She was about nine months old then, very docile, eating and sleeping as though there had been no major disruption to her routine, but curled around her new parents like a baby monkey as at last she had something to hug. We saw her six months later back in London. She had put on lots of weight and was interacting with her surroundings and was much livelier.

When John and I returned to China in 2007, as part of a Mayoral visit, I met representatives of the charity *Care for Children* and found that the Chinese Government was cutting down on foreign adoptions and arranging more fostering programmes within China. With the *One Child* policy, there were many families willing to give a home to orphans without incurring financial penalties for having a larger family.

<u>October 1999 - 50th Anniversary Celebrations</u>
In October 1999 the 50th anniversary of the proclamation of the foundation of the People's Republic of China will take place. A number of large building projects in Beijing are expected to be completed by then, in particular the new terminal at the airport and a huge new shopping and office development to be called Oriental Plaza on the corner of Wanfujing Dajie and Chang'an. When we first came to Beijing this prime site had the first McDonalds in Beijing at one corner. Then the whole area was sold to Li Ka-shing of Hong Kong to develop. McDonalds protested that they had a contract for their tenure and for a while refused to move as the surrounding buildings were levelled and huge cranes and pile drivers brought in. In the end, McDonalds had no option but to leave when the whole area became fenced off. A new subway station is also being put in and the western end of Wangfujing soon became a morass of mud and boarded over holes yet cars, cyclists and pedestrians still picked their way along it.

Oriental Plaza and countless other new developments have caused a huge influx of farmers turned labourers, estimated to be about 3 million in Beijing alone according to China Daily. Some of them look ridiculously young. They are bussed in from dormitories every day. They worked on a huge block of serviced apartments, which sprouted next to the Palace Hotel. I could have set my watch by them - each evening at exactly 18.00 a huge roar went up as they downed tools and rushed for the bus!

Tiananmen Square is among the landmarks getting a facelift. It was fenced off in November 1998. We hear that it is to be repaved in pink granite and some areas will be grassed over. This very conveniently meant that the Square was boarded up during the 10th anniversary of the Tiananmen Square Incident. Mao's Mausoleum in the Square was temporarily closed recently, and then opened again to the usual long queues. Recently, advertisement hoardings around the Square and in streets leading to it have had to start coming down.

On our return trip in April 2000 we used the new airport - a great improvement. There is also a new motorway built for the 50th anniversary to whisk VIPs from the airport directly into Jianguomenwai and straight to Tiananmen Square. Wanfujing is now repaved and has buses but no other traffic along it. But Oriental Plaza is a mass of empty skyscrapers surrounding a building site.

Cabbages
Connie Watson, who arrived in Beijing in 1992, said her first impression was one of cabbages. They were one of the few winter vegetables available and people were exhorted to buy them in huge numbers in the Autumn to store through the dry Winter. Connie says that what is now Silk Alley, the clothes market, was then wall-to-wall cabbage. In a way it still is, as *cabbage* is the rag trade name for the extra garments made on the side of an estimated production run and sold off on the cheap.

On our first Winter-time visits, it was easy to spot great mounds of cabbages outside residential buildings, but with growing purchasing power and better distribution, the range of vegetables available in Winter had increased dramatically by 1999 and the cabbage mounds had disappeared.

In 1997 we read in China Daily that there was a glut of cabbages in the Beijing area as subsidies had encouraged the farmers to plant too many. As a result, the rules banning the farmers bringing their produce individually to the capital were relaxed and, for a few weeks, traffic was snarled up by tractors pulling loads of cabbage to the markets. Chinese never do things by halves - why pull one ton of cabbage when you could pull two? – and, on the road to the Great Wall at Mutianyu, we passed some precariously overloaded cabbage trailers, including one farmer on his tractor with an enormous mound of cabbages on the trailer with his wife lying spread eagled on the top to keep them from falling.

Walking in Beijing

One Sunday in February 1998 John and I went for a walk. We were trying to locate the Courtyard Restaurant, first opened during the previous year and then rumoured to have encountered licensing problems. We knew it was close to the Forbidden City so we kept diving off the main road down little hutongs. These are the narrow little streets with traditional courtyard houses packed close together. Some of the ones close to the Forbidden City are obviously very old, with carved tile-ends, and not many mod cons. They have communal public conveniences. Most still burn coal and, in the Winter, bicycle carts carry coal dust bricks for sale to the hutongs.

Many areas of hutongs are being pulled down. We used to take a short cut through a network of little streets close to the hotel. When we went that way recently the area had been flattened, devastated. There was nothing left, in preparation no doubt for some huge scheme. People are being rehoused in huge new blocks - more hygienic, less friendly and much less picturesque. And, by 1999, some of the huge shopping malls had to close and there was oversupply of office space and expat housing.

Eventually we found the restaurant by the East Gate of the Palace overlooking the moat. The ice on the moat was still very thick and two old men had hacked holes in it and were fishing. As the restaurant was only 10 minutes or so walk from the hotel, we went back in the evening. The route passes one of the evening food markets - a mass of little open air stalls producing hot noodles and other food, even in Winter. There are several large restaurants in the street. One had a large aquarium with live fish swimming about, and an equally large tank with live snakes, all ready for dinner. I couldn't look, but John was tickled pink to see a toad sitting among them. He couldn't count the snakes but on the way home, he said he was sure there was one snake less and a very replete looking toad! The Courtyard Restaurant had poached a chef from the Palace Hotel, and they lost another to the Italian restaurant at the newly opened International Beijing Club Hotel, which was used to put up the entire cast of Turandot which was played in Beijing to rapturous audiences.

That day we also discovered the very run-down former Imperial Ancestral Temple from the Ming Dynasty, now the Working People's Cultural Palace where Turandot was staged. It was once part of the Forbidden City but now, like Beihai Park, stands outside the Palace Museum area.

Reflections

All in all, it was a fascinating five years and a great learning curve. At the outset, I knew nothing of Chinese history or art and I loved learning more. I think we were there at a very interesting time, where there was much change. In the 1970's and 1980's, expatriates were very much kept apart from Chinese; but in the second five years of the 1990's there were fewer restrictions and greater access; and there were still traces of the old China before the massive international development that we witnessed taking place.

I have memories of some amusing cross-cultural instances. A wholly foreign owned enterprises is spelt *WFOE* and pronounced *"wuffy"*; when refuse carts reverse in city streets the loudspeaker plays *Happy Birthday*; in Beihai Park in Beijing, the children's carousel goes round and round to the tune of *Silent Night*. This all makes for a bit of amusement.

But I came home with a deeper understanding of Chinese civilisation and a huge respect for the Chinese people – their intellect, their resourcefulness and their enterprise.

The Centenary London to Brighton Veteran Car Run – 1996

<u>Genevieve</u>

Genevieve is the name given to a 1905 Darracq motor car and is also the title of a British comedy film, made in 1953. Starring John Gregson, Dinah Sheridan, Kenneth More and Kay Kendal, the film's plot revolves around two veteran cars and their crews participating in the annual London to Brighton Veteran Car Run. After an eventful journey to Brighton, as a result of breakdowns and arguments, the two men challenge each other to race back to London with the first over Westminster Bridge winning £100.

The two cars race neck-and-neck through the southern suburbs of London. But with only a few yards to go, *Genevieve* breaks down. As the other car is about to overtake it, its tyres become stuck in tramlines (London's tram network had closed in 1952 but many of the tracks were still in evidence when the film was made the following year) and it is forced to drive off route. The brakes on *Genevieve* fail and the car rolls a few yards onto Westminster Bridge, thus enabling the driver to collect the £100.

<u>Tommy Boothman</u>

Tommy Boothman was my father's cousin who was inspired by watching *Genevieve* to acquire a *Brighton car* of his own. He bought a 1904 Norfolk and, later, a 1902 Napier. While he owned other vintage cars, the London to Brighton Run was the annual event which he enjoyed greatly, taking his wife, Margaret, and their two sons, John and Clive, on the Run. After John and Clive had learnt to drive they in turn drove the two cars to Brighton and on other Veteran Car Club rallies. Since Tommy's death, they now own the cars jointly and still participate each year.

I was influenced by Tommy's love of cars and, to begin with, I acquired a 1934 Rolls-Royce 20/25, before later buying and restoring a 1931 Rolls-Royce Phantom II Continental. But, in 1993, I decided it was time to purchase a *Brighton car* and I found a 1904 Wolseley for sale at an auction in Hendon. Lesley threatened to divorce me if I acquired another car. Sneakily, having bid successfully for the car, I registered it in her name.

1904 Wolseley ("*Claudia*")

Lesley's car was built at Crayford, Kent and delivered new to Ireland in 1904. It is one of the oldest cars in existence that was first used in Ireland. Originally registered in the name of Justin McCarthy, Glen of the Downs, County Wicklow, the car was off the road after the Great War and then found abandoned in Sligo in the early 1950's. Restored by Willis Roycroft of County Kildare, it was given a new registration number, WR 1 (his initials), under which it was rallied extensively in Ireland in the 1950's and 1960's. The car was acquired in 1963 by the founder of the Irish Veteran and Vintage Car Club, Knollys Stokes, and given its original registration number, IK 135. This *Irish* Wolseley was repatriated to the UK in 1981 and completed 11 Brighton Runs under the ownership of Alan Curry and his son, Stephen, using a UK imported registration number, DS 6613. On acquisition by Lesley in 1993, the car was named *Claudia*; and the original number plate was restored when the UK DVLA accepted that since Ireland was part of Great Britain in 1904 they had the authority to do this.

Claudia was a single cylinder 6HP Wolseley car. It was not much larger than a dining table with two leather button backed armchairs placed on top. There was no windscreen, let alone wipers. So, it was necessary to wear goggles and to wrap up, with waterproof gear if it was raining. Sitting in an elevated position, one had a commanding view of the road and it was possible to peer over hedgerows as you sped along. With a top speed of about 25mph going downhill with the wind behind, the car could be quite terrifying, particularly since the brakes were not that good. The main brake lever was on the right hand side placed outside the body of the car, following the pattern of a horse driven carriage. There was also a foot operated transmission brake which I was advised should only be used in extreme circumstances since it might result in damage to the back axle. To start the car, the oilers (delivering oil to the engine) had to be turned on. The advance and retard lever and the accelerator (also a lever) were set to the right position and, then, the engine had to be cranked, taking care not to break your thumb or wrist in the process – the advice was to tuck your thumb away to avoid being hurt if the engine started too quickly. The two key levers were fixed to the steering column, such that you really needed three hands to operate the car. A certain amount of dexterity was required to drive it and, more important, to stop it. While its acceleration was quick, it was a challenge to stop. The car had the feel of a 1904 Mini Cooper S – speedy and a little dangerous.

Over the years, *Claudia* developed a reputation for being a very nippy car that would mount a pavement to overtake, on the inside, larger horsepower cars that were fast on the open road but quite pedestrian in heavy urban traffic. And she was reliable – completing 10 Brighton Runs out of 11 under Lesley's ownership. The only Run she failed to complete was the first one in 1993 after the big end had been replaced and, after overheating, seized. Our engineer, Roy O'Sullivan, was called to a back street in Clapham where he took the entire engine out of the car and tried to file the big end down. We limped on to Crawley where it seized again. With failing light in an early November afternoon we gave up the challenge. Lesley's father, Geoffrey, was my passenger on that occasion and, being an engineer, was quite philosophical about the whole affair. He greatly enjoyed the adventure.

<u>Locomotives on the Highway Act, 1896</u>
The *Red Flag Act* of 1865 had limited all self-propelled vehicles to a speed of 4 mph in the country and 2 mph in town. The Act also required a man with a red flag or lantern to walk 60 yards ahead of each vehicle. The 1878 Act removed the need for the flag, although local authorities still had the power to insist that a red flag should be carried. After further lobbying, the 1986 *Locomotives on the Highway Act* removed restrictions for light locomotives and raised the speed limit to 14mph, although this was immediately cut to 12mph by the powerful Local Government Board. In return for the increase in the speed limit, cars were taxed at two guineas annually and had to *"carry a bell or other instrument capable of giving audible and sufficient warning"*.

<u>The Emancipation Run of 1896</u>
To mark this *Red-Letter Day in the history of automobilism*, Britain's first motoring magazine, *The Autocar*, printed a whole issue in red ink. The notorious financial adventurer, Harry J Lawson, organised a

commemoration run from London to Brighton. Thus the first Emancipation Day Run took place, in appalling rain, on 14th November 1896. Despite the rain, huge crowds turned out to examine the 33 cars which participated and to admire the spectacle. Ever since, the London to Brighton Run has been a popular annual event in the English social calendar, attracting thousands of spectators at the start in Hyde Park, along the route, and at the finish on Brighton's Madeira Drive.

<u>The 1996 Centenary Veteran Car Run</u>

The centenary of this milestone was greeted with great enthusiasm by the veteran car motoring community. The RAC Motor Sports Association took responsibility for organising the event, in conjunction with the Veteran Car Club of Great Britain, the Police Forces en route, the Parks Office of the Department of the Environment and the Corporation of Brighton. HRH Prince Michael of Kent, as President of the RAC, wrote a Foreword to the Official Souvenir Programme. The history of the event, and subsequent Runs, and of the cars which had entered, were described in the programme. The cars were numbered in descending order of age. Thus the oldest entrant, an 1896 Panhard et Levassor, was number 1. Within each year, the smaller horsepower cars were numbered earlier in the sequence. *Claudia* was number 498 out of the 680 cars which had been entered – the cut-off date for entry being cars produced before 31st December 1904.

Lesley had yet to drive any distance in *Claudia* and agreed to be the passenger on this memorable event. The evening before the Run we dined, as had been our custom prior to previous Brighton Runs, at Green's Restaurant in Duke Street. There, potted shrimps, steak and kidney pie followed by treacle tart or syrup sponge, washed down by a white Burgundy and a red claret, set us up for the ardours of the following day. This necessitated a five o'clock start to collect *Claudia* from the underground garage, at Embankment Place, of Coopers & Lybrand (now PwC) for the short drive to Hyde Park, to line up in numerical order by the Serpentine.

Fortunately it was a fine morning and, as the dawn broke, there was coffee and bacon rolls on hand from the stalls near the lake. Then, at the appointed signal, the engines of the 680 entrants were fired up, having been cranked, since few if any had push button starter motors. Our engineer, Roy O'Sullivan was on hand to see that the engine revved and also to keep a watchful eye on the other cars he looked after (the Boothmans' and the Strangs'). The first car drove out of Hyde Park as soon as it was light and, shortly after this, we were heading for Brighton, with a band playing, policemen waving us through red traffic lights and the roads lined with enthusiastic, flag waving spectators.

Everything went fine, at least for a while. The coffee stop at Crawley gave an opportunity for a comfort break, a refreshing drink and a chance to compare notes with friends in other cars. But, then, not far south of Crawley, there was a loud bang. We had been hit from behind by a motor bike whose rider had not been able to control his machine on a patch of oil on the road. Veteran cars like plenty of oil. But, unlike modern cars whose engines are sealed, the older cars spew out oil from the bottom of the engine. The motor cyclist had been racing with his chums, skidded on the oil and, as he fell off, broke his collar bone. Being an accident in which someone was injured, the police as well as an ambulance were called. And, by law, I and the motor bike rider were breathalysed. The only occasion on which this has ever happened to me was witnessed by crowds, television cameras and veteran car friends speeding by with enormous grins on their faces. By now, it was at least 12 o'clock and, with an early breakfast and a cup of coffee, there was no trace of alcohol. The rider was similarly clear but while he was being attended to, his bike was carefully removed by his chums. One suspects that either it was not taxed or that he was uninsured or both. Names and addresses were exchanged and he was taken to hospital.

While we were OK, *Claudia* wasn't. The impact of the crash had damaged one of the rear wings but, worse, the tie rod, which separates the rear axle from the front axle and which prevents the rear axle moving forward during acceleration, had bent and was likely to snap. Roy was quickly on the scene and secured the tie rod to the chassis with a plastic tie. He assured us that we could continue but with the warning *"Take it slowly and no heroics"*. It was only afterwards that I learnt that, if the tie rod had snapped, the car would have somersaulted, were it not for the plastic tie. By that stage we were about one hour's drive from Brighton and I was determined to get there, particularly during this centenary year.

And, so, with careful driving, my peering down to check the tie rod every few minutes and a very modest speed, we made it to Madeira Drive, so completing the 1996 Centenary Brighton Run.

Peking to Paris in a Pink Rolls-Royce – 1997

It takes ten hours to fly from Beijing to Paris. The distance is approximately 6,000 miles as the crow, or perhaps a jumbo jet, flies. By land it is an altogether different story.

On 6th September 1997, 94 pre-war and classic cars lined up in Beijing. Some 43 days and 10,000 miles later, 82 vehicles drove triumphantly into the Place de la Concorde and wrote themselves into the history books.

The Peking to Paris Motor Challenge, as it was christened by the organisers, the UK based Classic Rally Association, was a competitive rally for some, but for many it was an opportunity to travel in an old vehicle through some of the world's most fascinating countries and over some of the world's worst roads. The only previous occasion on which a rally had successfully completed the journey from Peking to Paris was in 1907, when an Italian aristocrat, Prince Borghese, had finished first, out of five starters, in an Itala car.

Why was it then that our 1934 Rolls-Royce 20/25 Barker bodied sports saloon, affectionately known as *Harrison*, after the first owner Henry Harrison Stuttard, should have started every morning and not experienced a single hitch? The only problems encountered were eight punctures, a dented Chinese Beijing jeep which refused to get over to its side of the road, one dead sheep in Western China and some dents to the bodywork as the road turned into a boulder laden stream just short of the Tibetan-Nepalese border.

So, why no hitch? This is a question which Rolls-Royce 20/25 owners will not find hard to answer. After all, the car was created by the greatest motor engineer of all time. Also, the roads in Europe in the 1930's were not all that good, resulting in the need for a sturdy chassis, robust springs and shock absorbers, and a certain amount of over engineering, all of which proved invaluable on the roads of China, Tibet and Pakistan. Asian potholes, ruts, mud and streams proved too much for the Aston Martins, Bugattis, Buicks, Chevrolets, Citroens, Marmons, Mercedes, Stutzes, Vauxhalls and Volvos, but not for the 20/25. Even the thin air at high altitudes in the Himalayas did not deter the carburettor from functioning perfectly. *Harrison* just kept on going.

But, perhaps an added reason for the lack of problems was the amount of time spent in preparation. "Well begun is half done" quoted my cousin, John Boothman, who is a Derby Bentley man. *"I have to confess that when you first told me that you were taking the 20/25, I thought you were slightly mad! It seemed to me that such a refined, complex piece of machinery would never stand up to the punishment meted out by maintaining high average speeds for day after day on unmade roads. The fact that I have been proved wrong is a fine testament to the quality of the car and the skill of its crew"*. Indeed it was the preparation that was half the battle. Most of this comprised simply ensuring that the original parts were functioning correctly. Very few modifications were made to the 1934 specification.

In 1990, Ristes Motor Company of Nottingham had totally overhauled *Harrison's* engine following an inspection by the Rolls-Royce Enthusiasts Club's technical adviser, Richard Barton, soon after I had acquired the car in 1989. To use Richard's words: *"You've bought a very nice looking car, but it's totally clapped out"*. As a result, king pins and shackle pins were replaced, a new exhaust system was fitted, the radiator core was renewed, the petrol tank was removed and cleaned, the brakes were taken apart, the steering box was overhauled and an overdrive was fitted – something which came into its own on the long flat stretches of asphalt in Iran when *Harrison* would reach 75mph quite comfortably. To ensure that the car was functioning properly and totally run in, I had driven it on four rallies in Europe between 1992 and 1995 – two *Italia Classica* and two *Rallye Monte-Carlo des Voitures Anciennes*.

Of course, more needed to be done and, at the beginning of 1997, our motor engineer, Roy O'Sullivan, who was to accompany us on the Challenge, started further restoration. The one-shot chassis lubrication system was totally overhauled, a new engine vibration damper was installed, wheels and brakes came off and were scrupulously checked. Some modifications were introduced that might have put off a Concours judge, but of which Henry Royce would, I am sure, have approved:

- A bull bar was specially made and attached to the front irons. This proved essential – for nudging cattle and Beijing jeeps out of the way and for hanging rally plaques, promotional material and, at one stage, a ram's head that literally fell off the back of a lorry
- The car had, on occasions, to be capable of travelling 300 miles without refuelling. To achieve this, two five gallon tanks were fitted in the boot. Of necessity, the Autovac had to be disconnected, but left in situ for emergencies, and a separate petrol pump was installed
- A new oil filter was fitted
- A roof rack was screwed to the ash framed roof and a container fixed to it to hold our tents, sleeping bags and holdalls – one each, to conserve weight and space.

By July, the car was ready to receive its coat of salmon pink paint, at the request of the editor of the *Weekend Financial Times*, which featured *Harrison's* progress every Saturday in the *Weekend Review*. This pink colour was later to receive some flattering attention as well as some derogatory remarks, the latter typically from Australian entrants on the rally who questioned the gender of the car and its English occupants. Off then to Felixstowe and by container, care of Jeremy Barker of CARS UK, to Tianjin, a large city that acts as the port of Beijing on the east coast of China.

Harrison's crew assembled in Beijing a few days before the start. Apart from Roy, our engineer, the other three all came from international accountants, Coopers & Lybrand - Simon Anderson, a long time Coopers man, who had served in Pakistan and Iran in the 1960's and who spoke Farsi and a little Urdu; Gordon Barrass, who had worked at the British Embassy in the 1970's and spoke Mandarin; and me, then working in Beijing as Executive Chairman of Coopers & Lybrand's business in China. Four people seems a lot for a 1930's saloon car on such an arduous rally and, certainly, with three tons fully laden, we were conscious of not trying to take too much luggage. However we wanted to share the enormous cost of the undertaking and also to have different companions in the car over such a long distance. This was to prove important as the rally entered its fourth week, when some of the drivers and co-drivers were no longer on speaking terms. With four there is rarely a problem since, if one gets grumpy, the others will soon sort him out. It also helps share the responsibilities.

The organisers, the *Classic Rally Association*, had warned that four in the car was too many and that we would probably not make it to Paris, a prediction that we were later delighted to prove wrong. A fifth member of our crew, David Colvin, then the British Ambassador to Belgium, was to replace Gordon Barrass in Istanbul, as the linguistic needs of Europe replaced those of Asia.

To help pay for the cost of painting the car salmon pink, *The Financial Times* had persuaded some of its friends and advertisers to sponsor the car. They included Eagle Star, H&R Owen, Jardine Fleming and Standard Chartered. Ristes Motor Company joined them. Separately, our crew decided to raise funds for the British Red Cross in support of a disaster relief project in Nepal, in memory of Peter Walsh, a former partner and friend from Coopers & Lybrand in the UK. Peter, who sadly died of cancer in November 1996, was a great traveller and inspired others to broaden their outlook and horizons through travel. Prior to his very brief retirement, he had acted as non-executive finance director to the Red Cross. Fundraising for the Red Cross was a way of recognising Peter's guidance and charity and a way of saying *"thank you"*.

Crossing China

The People's Republic of China is a huge and populous country, as we were to find out in the 12 days it took us to cross it. With 1.2 billion people, China has about 50 million in the police and the army. We reckoned that we saw about 100,000 of them, lining the roads and cordoning off the huge crowds in the towns and villages through which we passed.

The rally began with a police escort for the 93 cars from the centre of Beijing to Badaling, where there was an official ceremony with accompanying band and lion dancing. Each competitor was given a bronze plaque to commemorate the rally. The British Ambassador,

Sir Len Appleyard, came to see us off, bowing deeply as the pink 20/25 purred past.

The first day was relatively easy, climbing into the hills to the provincial capital of Zhangjiakou. However, it was not without incident. A second pre-war Ford got into difficulties. This time a 1928 Model A Roadster broke down on the way to the Great Wall. Then, soon after the start, another tragedy occurred. The fan on Lord Montagu's 1915 Prince Henry Vauxhall came loose and tore chunks out of its radiator. With two skilled engineers to hand, Roy O'Sullivan and the Beaulieu Motor Museum's Doug Hill, the car was back on the road within three hours, but the heating system never fully recovered from this incident and the car was withdrawn two days later and shipped back to the UK. Lord Montagu hitched a lift in a 1967 Phantom V, which used to convey Queen Elizabeth on her visits to Australia, now owned by Australians John Matheson and Jeanne Eve. This was later to break its main spring in a pothole in Western China but, after emergency repairs in Kathmandu, it was driven successfully to Paris.

The next few days took the rally into the arid plains of Inner Mongolia, near the Gobi Desert, where the scenery varied between heavy industry and stunning landscapes dotted with yurts, the tents in which the nomadic Mongolian people live. We followed the mighty Yellow River, which floods from time to time, causing incalculable damage and loss of life. Then, surprisingly, we found ourselves on a brand new 100 mile highway which had recently been completed and opened especially for the rally cars. There was no one else on the road.

A feature of the rally in Northern China was the huge number of people and policemen who lined the route. In one city, Linhe, we estimated crowds of over 100,000, including waving schoolchildren who had been given time off school to watch the cars go by and who threw flowers and passed messages of support in very broken English through the car windows. During the China leg alone, we reckoned that over one million people must have seen the rally, usually cheering or watching in open-mouthed disbelief.

By day five the rally had reached Langzhou, a major city on the old silk route in central China. As the cars approached the outskirts, the participants were met and escorted by police cars with lights flashing and sirens wailing. A rest day was necessary to prepare for the climb to the roof of the world.

The next five days were to prove the most challenging of the entire rally, as the roads got worse and the towns became scarcer. There were three nights camping, the highest at 16,000 feet, where it was so cold that one's breath froze on the inside of the tent. In many places the roads were being repaired, which resulted in off-road excursions through mud, over rocks and in conditions more suited to four wheel drive vehicles. During this phase of the rally more cars started to drop out – broken half shafts, damaged suspensions and engine failures were the common causes. Many of these problems could have been avoided either through better pre-rally preparation or more cautious driving. The German driver of a museum-entered 1907 La France had to be invalided out when he caught pneumonia after encountering sleet on the high Tibetan plateau. A few Brighton Runs might have prepared him better for the conditions.

We travelled on the highest road in the world – at 17,800 feet, the Tangula Pass sits on the border between China and Tibet. The scenery was quite spectacular: the attractive Kunlun mountain range, white peaks, rushing rivers, yaks and then people with beautiful costumes – as well as simply appalling roads.

It was therefore with some relief that the rally cars limped into Lhasa, the capital of Tibet, for a day's rest and much needed repair to broken cars. Much to the chagrin of other contestants, *Harrison's* crew went sightseeing but only after cleaning the inside of the car made filthy when a group of young boys hurled yak dung through the open windows as we entered Lhasa – what a welcome !

From Lhasa the road runs West, on a rough metalled surface, to Xigaze, Tibet's second city and the traditional seat of the Panchen Lama (who had recently been appointed by the PRC Government) at the 15th Century Tashilumpo Monastery. Some 175 miles from Lhasa, this small, dusty, but attractive town is the last refuelling stop on the way to Kathmandu. From here the cars on the rally had to rely on bowsers (petrol tankers) arranged by the China International Sports Travel Group, which managed the rally's efficient progress through China.

After Xigaze the villages became less prosperous. There were spacious, wide valleys and also the remains of the old military fortifications dating from a time when Tibet was stronger, both economically and politically, and sought to protect itself from foreigners – unsuccessfully as it turned out from the expansionist British Empire in the 19th Century. The road climbed to 16,000 feet until the cars reached their resting place for the night, close to Everest base camp, where the world's highest mountain can be seen – and what a sight it was, changing from white to orange as the snow on the summit reflected the sunset. It was a rare moment at the end of an exhausting day. By the following morning the cloud cover was lower and the mountain was lost from sight.

It is difficult to imagine a more barren place than the Tibetan plateau. At over 12,000 feet, there is little to support human or animal life. The occasional herd of yaks brings some movement to an otherwise desolate part of the world. Yet, it must also rank as one of the most spectacular places to visit. The awe-inspiring Himalayan mountain range with its jagged snow-capped peaks leaves one breathless with amazement and breathless as a result of the thin air. To compensate for the high altitude and to avoid mountain sickness or worse, we took daily doses of *Diamox*. It is a diuretic than needs to be accompanied by drinking lots of water, the consequences of which are obvious. There were numerous comfort stops which also afforded an opportunity to take photographs. This drug also has an effect on the senses and, listening to Mozart on *Harrison's* primitive CD player (non-standard in 1934); four grown men had tears streaming down their cheeks as they marvelled at the beauty of the mountains around them. Few people, only mountaineers and intrepid travellers, have the privilege of seeing these extraordinary sights.

It was through this semi-lunar mountainous landscape that the cars took four days to travel a mere 400 miles from Lhasa, the capital of Tibet, to Kathmandu, the capital of Nepal. This road that links the two emerging nations of the 21st Century, China and India, was then more suited to four wheel drive vehicles. Perhaps in 10 or 20 years' time there will be a four lane highway which will bring tourists in coaches to Everest base camp, but not yet. At the time of our trip, this "high road" was not for the faint-hearted.

From Everest base camp to the Nepalese border, unbelievably the road surface got worse, with rutted sections and huge potholes waiting to damage suspensions and shock absorbers. Of the 94 starters in Beijing, there were then 82 travelling under their own steam. Seven had officially retired and five were on flatbed trucks on their way to Kathmandu, either to be containered home or to visit the repair shops to try to mend broken parts.

The support crew on the rally, in their Vauxhall Fronteras, were the real heroes, pulling no fewer than 30 cars out of ditches and mud, stopping to provide emergency repairs and also giving roadside first aid. But it was on the rally's final day through China that the cars needed most help. In the last 10 miles before the Nepalese border the road dropped from 10,000 feet to 3,000 feet, down an escarpment littered with landslides. During the previous week, this road had been breached in several places and, after emergency repairs, was still only open to cars, with care.

The descent was terrifying. In places the mud was two feet deep. In other places the road was a stream, with boulders lurking to damage sumps and to hole petrol tanks. The penalty for failure was a 3,000 feet drop. Miraculously, *Harrison* survived the ordeal with little more than a dented front wing and buckled running boards. A 1929 Bentley, driven by a Dane, had a narrow escape when a slab of rock crashed down on the road shortly after he had passed under an overhang. The undercarriage of a second WO Bentley, driven by an American, became stuck on a boulder and had to be lifted off by other competitors, demonstrating the team spirit which was a feature of the entire rally.

<u>The journey through Nepal and India</u>
After the Chinese border town of Zhangmou, the frontier, in the form of Friendship Bridge, was a welcome sight. Perhaps as incredible as

the descent from the Tibetan plateau was the warmth of the welcome from hundreds of schoolchildren lining the roadside, waving Red Cross flags.

As Kathmandu approached, the roadside greetings intensified. Garlands of flowers and messages of support were showered on the cars and their occupants, who were made to feel like conquering heroes. One misspelt message seemed to capture the corporate spirit *"Peking to Perish Old Timer Car Rally"* (sic).

It was, therefore, something of a relief for the 87 cars, battered and bruised, some on trailers, to reach Kathmandu – the first car rally to cross the Tibetan-Nepalese border. It was also something of a first for *Harrison* – the first pre-war Rolls-Royce to enter Tibet from China, the first Rolls-Royce to cross Tibet and the first Rolls-Royce to enter Nepal from Tibet. There followed two further days of rest, a reception at the British Residence, and repairs to cars before the rally continued to India. We also had time to visit the headquarters of the Nepalese Red Cross and to see for ourselves the efficient organisation that would be the recipient of our fundraising efforts. There was a warehouse full of blankets, jerry cans and emergency tents for the relief of disasters, to which the country is, from time to time, subjected.

A very Western dinner at the five star Yak & Yeti was much appreciated, as was the first taste of wine for some weeks.

It was with a heavy heart that we left Nepal, but it was during this section of the rally that we had the first of our eight punctures, caused undoubtedly by the poor roads we had experienced in the previous fortnight, but also the weight of the car. The route was quite challenging as there were 13 rivers to be crossed – by going through them as there were no bridges. Fortunately there had been little rain and the water was not so deep as to cause problems. But they were wide and the fords were the longest the participants had ever experienced.

Entering India from the north is like going back to the days of the Raj. There are fine Victorian houses in hill stations with cool

climates. There are lakes and scenery that are reminiscent of Wales
and the English Lake District. On the lakes are boats shipped out
from England that are seen in the UK today only in Edwardian
photographs. At our night stop in Nainital we learnt that an early
Land Rover, driven by Nigel Challis, had been forced off the steep
road leading to the hotel by a lorry; Nigel and his co-driver had found
themselves upside down with the car against a tree which was holding
them back from the edge of a 100 foot cliff. They were slightly hurt
but able to recount what had happened. Sadly, though, the car had to
be repatriated but not before it had been stripped of all removable
parts by the local people.

As one travels south, the heat of the Punjab becomes overpowering,
as does the traffic and the number of people. Ox carts and *holy* cows
which wander in the road represent an enormous hazard for old and
new cars alike.

The magnificent sights of New Delhi, with its imposing buildings
designed by Lutyens, form a highly suitable backdrop for
photographing old cars, particularly a Rolls-Royce. After all, India
was the largest export market for the Derby manufacturer in the
1920's and 30's. The Indians know and love the Royce. Another
reception followed at the British Embassy, courtesy of the
Ambassador, Sir David Gore-Booth.

It might be remembered that Gore-Booth was a controversial
character, despite being a member of a titled Anglo-Irish family. He
caused consternation when he resigned from the Foreign Office in
1999 and his valedictory letter (from Delhi) included the following:

> *"One of the great failures of the Diplomatic Service has been
> its inability to cast off its image as bowler hatted, pin striped
> and chinless with a fondness for champagne… Indeed cocktail
> parties are death as I am sure 99% of diplomatic service
> colleagues would agree. Whoever it was who suggested an
> international treaty banning National Day receptions should
> be canonized".*

If the Tibetan roads had the worst road surfaces, then the Indian roads had the worst drivers. It is very disconcerting to be driving on a dual carriageway, on the correct side of the road, only to find that there are two heavily laden trucks coming towards you and expecting you to give way.

Three Islamic countries

Entering India from Nepal had been a nightmare, with a six hour wait, for some, at immigration and customs. By contrast, in Pakistan, the efficiency of immigration, customs and local police made motor travel into and through the country easy. Less friendly, however, were the roads, which resulted in our awarding Pakistan first prize for being the best tyre repairer of the countries visited thus far. Tyres which would fail the MoT test in the UK are kept going with the same technology I used as a teenager on my Raleigh cycle.

The reception in Lahore, the venue for another rest stop, was friendly, but our crew had to spend most of the day looking unsuccessfully for tyres for our 20/25. Rolls-Royce owners appeared with the offer of spare tyres but, unfortunately, all were of a different size, typically from Shadows and Silver Spurs. None was to be found and so the Pakistani tyre repairers did their best and one such resuscitated tyre managed to take us all the way to Paris.

It was in Quetta, in southern Pakistan, that the rally had its first and mercifully, only, fatal accident. The German driver of a Volkswagen Beetle cabriolet and his son were killed when their car went out of control coming down a hill and hit a bus. Competitive rallying was stopped for the next 24 hours as entrants recovered from the shock and realised the dangers which they were facing.

Further west, for two days before reaching the border with Iran, the rally passed through Baluchistan. We began to appreciate why this region had been ungovernable for over 200 years. Most of the area is sandy desert with very few people. Apart from the few signs of human life, the other main sight is the occasional herd of camels. There were also the remains of former British fortifications along the border with Afghanistan. And there were numerous checkpoints with rather frightening looking characters with beards and turbans carrying old and rather dangerous rifles and shotguns. Indeed, there was a flavour of being in bandit country.

These two days proved to be arduous driving and hot. We were on the road for 16 hours and 13 hours respectively. The temperatures in the Baluchistan Desert reached 40 degrees in the shade. Many cars suffered but not *Harrison*, who cruised along with the engine temperature between 70 and 80 degrees. The only problem was two more punctures and, in that heat, it is hard work changing tyres.

We entered Iran in the south-east, where the welcome matched that of Nepal, with efficient immigration and customs clearance. The rule of the religious Mullahs and Imams in Iran has created a society which has not received a good Press in the West. As a result, we saw few tourists, even at the famous historical and architectural sites. It was, therefore, an excellent time to visit Iran. The people we encountered en route were friendly and welcoming, which came as a pleasant surprise compared to the international image of a frenzied Islamic state. In almost every town and village through which we passed, there were banners welcoming the rally participants, who were flatteringly described as "athletes". Life can of course, be Spartan – no alcohol, a strict dress code (even for foreigners) and hotel staff who do not understand the concept of service. At one hotel the manager locked himself in his office rather than face some irate rally guests who were demanding their laundry before an early start the following morning.

However, this all pales into insignificance compared to the quite stunning sights. We had enough time during our four day crossing of Iran to see some memorable places. The deserted town of Arg-e Bam, which dates from the 12th Century and was a key resting point on the old silk route from China, is a Persian equivalent of Pompeii. Similar in many respects to a medieval European castle, it fell into disrepair over 100 years ago as borders closed and new trade routes by sea were opened. Bam is also world famous for its black dates, which are the most succulent and nourishing I have ever tasted. Sadly, Bam suffered badly in 2003 from a major earthquake and is now being restored. We also had time to stop at the city of Yazd, the site of a

Zoroastrian fire temple which houses a fire which is said to have been burning continuously since AD470.

But the jewel for us in Iran was Isfahan, built largely under the rule of Shah Abbas in the early 17th Century. In his day it was said that if you have seen Isfahan you will have seen *"half the world"*. With the magnificent mosque and the seven-storey palace in Imam Square, laid out in 1612, and the 17th Century double terraced bridges, it is easy to understand that it was quite stunning in its day. Isfahan is still a most attractive place to visit, particularly if one stays at the Hotel Abbasi, a former caravanserai which was converted into a hotel in the 1960's. With bedrooms and suites surrounding a main square filled with fountains and trees, it is a most delightful resting spot for the weary traveller and a convenient base from which to visit the sites.

Iran also has some excellent, albeit simple, dishes, including barley soup, fresh Iranian naan bread, kebabs and salads, the last of which are safe to eat in Iran. Surprisingly for a hot country, there is an abundance of dairy produce and some of the best yoghurt I have ever tasted. Tea taken sitting on large cushions on a mosaic floor, coupled with a mild smoke from a hubble-bubble, is also a must.

The participants on the rally voted Iran as having the best roads so far, a result of the large oil revenues from which the country has benefited.

The crossing from Iran to Turkey was memorable, not least because of the clear view of Mount Ararat, of Noah's Ark fame, some 40 kms north of the border. To have crossed Asia and made it to Turkey was quite an achievement, demonstrating the true grit of many of the participants. Some cars disappeared for days on end, only to reappear with tales of suspensions being rebuilt in the early hours in back street garages. One competitor, Gerry Acher, in his 1932 Aston Martin, the smallest pre-war car on the rally, was seriously delayed in western Pakistan, but finished up having tea and biscuits, followed by dinner with the District Commissioner in his oasis garden in the middle of the desert. Still the most amusing incident of the rally so far is that of an Italian co-driver who was lost early in the rally. At one rally control point, he needed his rally book stamped and asked a local policeman where he could get a *"stamp"*. The kindly officer took him several miles in his police car to the nearest village to find a *"postage stamp"*. This caused his compatriot and the rally organisers' great concern as they believed that he might have been kidnapped. Such are the challenges and surprises of pan-continental motor rallying.

The easy bit

After a triumphal entry into Istanbul, the journey through Greece, Italy (including San Marino), Austria, Germany and France was like a Saturday afternoon outing. My wife, Lesley, had brought a new spare tyre by plane to Istanbul and we felt safe in the knowledge that further punctures were unlikely to defeat us. After five weeks of tough road and weather conditions it was a relief to spend the last week of the rally travelling in Europe. We had time to stop for lunch and adjust to a more normal pace of life. We journeyed along Lake Garda during the truffle season. Gewurztraminer and foie gras in Alsace were especially welcome after the culinary deprivations of Tibet.

But the entry into Paris proved to be the final challenge, since the rally route book bore no resemblance to the roads in the Parisian suburbs. Many cars got lost and tempers frayed almost at the moment of triumph. However, the finish at the Place de la Concorde, with the accompanying reception in Formula One style, was a magical moment after travelling over 16,000 kms in 43 days.

The last week was not, however, without incident for many of the competitors. We had two more punctures. The car which had the closest escape was a Rover driven by a Yorkshireman, David Bull, and his accountant wife, Angela; they lost a rear wheel and a half shaft, which came loose and fell off as the car was crossing a bridge in the Austrian Alps. After numerous phone calls by another competitor, David Drew, at around midnight, a replacement half shaft was located in Vienna on an enthusiast's car; this was dismantled overnight and flown by special plane to Lake Constance, thus enabling the Rover to continue, arriving in Reims at 3.30 in the morning, before a triumphal entry into Paris.

There was also talk of sabotage to the leading car, a 1942 Willys Jeep, driven by Phil Surtees. It was reported to him that *"someone in authority"* had been bemoaning the fact that the rally might be won by a four wheel drive car rather than *"a proper rally car"*. Since sabotage was feared, the jeep was locked up for the night in a champagne cellar in Reims. On a happier note, when the jeep was experiencing clutch problems in Italy, Ted Thomas who was driving a 1950 Ford, and was in second place, stopped to help repair the clutch. This demonstrated the chivalry and camaraderie which had been features of this extraordinary event. The overall winner of the rally was the Willys Jeep.

Harrison finished well down the order, but this was due to the fact that we were in the touring category, having changed our crew in Istanbul, and also because of our decision to take it slowly. We wanted to stop and take photographs, enjoy the countryside and the scenery – and have the occasional lunch break. Out of the 94 cars which started in Beijing, 82 reached Paris, demonstrating the determination and the true grit of the participants.

Our 20/25 Rolls-Royce car, as might be expected, did not break down once, except for the punctures which delayed our progress from time to time. The fact that it came through unscathed, apart from dents acquired on the journey, is a tribute to Sir Henry Royce; but it is also thanks to Ristes Motor Company who renovated the engine in 1990, and to our motor engineer, Roy O'Sullivan, who prepared the car exceptionally well.

The other Rolls-Royce cars on the rally fared reasonably well. An Austrian entered 1950 Silver Dawn, driven by Kurt Dichtl, and a 1965 Silver Cloud III, owned by Dane Erik Christiansen, had no difficulty. Peter Noble's 1955 Bentley Continental paved its own way across Asia, ever dependable.

On the other hand, those who modified original Rolls-Royce parts experienced problems. The Australian entered 1967 Phantom V was lucky to rise again from the ashes after its main leaf spring was replaced; the addition of heavier duty modern springs caused the break on the rally. A similar problem befell an attractive 1928 boat tail Phantom I, whose German owner, Gerhard Weissenbach, had unfortunately removed the original Autovac in favour of an electric fuel pump that proved faulty; this was compounded when the electrical system failed, again as a result of modern modifications. The message is clear. Don't tamper with anything that the great master engineer spent many man years perfecting. Leave the original design and renovate the original parts, if you can, and don't try to re-engineer.

Our thanks went to the organisers of *The Peking to Paris Motor Challenge*, the Classic Rally Association. The rally was the brainchild of its Managing Director, Philip Young, who sadly died in March 2015 after a motor accident on the border between Thailand and Burma. Philip was wonderfully vague about the plans, leaving much to fate. Through Qian Ning, an employee of Coopers & Lybrand in Beijing and the son of China's Foreign Minister, we helped Philip organise the China leg and Lord Montagu facilitated contact with the Indian Government which led to permissions being granted. But without Philip's vision and chutzpah, the rally would never have happened. On an amusing note, Philip believed that of the 94 starters only a maximum of 50 cars would reach Paris and, allegedly, ordered just 50 finishers' medals; he was obliged, at the last minute, to order more so that all 82 cars that completed the distance received a medal at the gala dinner at the Intercontinental Hotel in Paris.

Ladies in the Desert
A Tour of Jordan by Rolls-Royce and Bentley cars – 1999

<u>Statues in a London park</u>

On the north bank of the River Thames, immediately in front of the Savoy Hotel, is one of London's more interesting patches of green. In a city full of history and surprises, the Victoria Embankment Gardens do not feature prominently in the tourist guides. Yet for someone with 10 minutes to spare before dinner in the Savoy's River Restaurant or wishing to walk off the after effects of spotted dick for lunch at nearby Simpsons-in-the-Strand, a saunter through the gardens will pleasantly surprise.

The statues in this small park include the Scottish poet Robert Burns, the Victorian composer Sir Arthur Sullivan, the founder of the Sunday School movement Robert Raikes and a leader of the Temperance Movement Sir Wilfred Lawson MP.

Close to the western end, near the bandstand, there is another monument which bisects the pathway that runs the length of the gardens. It is the statue of a soldier, wearing a pith helmet and uniform of the Great War, who sits atop a camel on a plinth covered with the names of those who died and of the regions in which they fought between 1916 and 1918. The memorial is a tribute to the long disbanded Imperial Camel Corps and includes the names of places we were shortly to visit: Amman, Jordan Valley, Mudawara (Hedjaz). Kiplingesque images flash by. There are memories of TE Lawrence and his role in helping the Arabs rid the Middle East of its Turkish oppressors. Their actions led to the creation of the modern Arab states, such as Jordan, with its fine Bedouin traditions, its much-loved King Hussein and its close ties with Britain.

It was to Aqaba, a city made famous in Lawrence's wartime campaigns, that 180 Rolls-Royce and Bentley enthusiasts, with their 72 cars and one support vehicle, arrived on 18 September 1999, for a truly memorable tour of Jordan.

The cars had been shipped two weeks before from Southampton on a Ro-Ro (roll-on roll-off) vessel. The vehicles had been delivered by their owners to a warehouse at the docks where Douglas Vaughan, a past Chairman of the Rolls-Royce Enthusiasts Club (RREC), and his wife Margaret had parked their caravan for three days. As participants arrived, the cars were logged in and Margaret generously dispensed ham and cheese rolls and coffee and biscuits to those who had driven down. A few wimpish owners actually trailered their cars, displaying a lack of confidence that was later to prove justified as the number of wounded cars mounted.

The Jewel that is Jordan, as the tour was named, was the brainchild of Michael Foster. An exploration-drilling engineer by profession, Michael first worked in Jordan in the early 1960's on a phosphate exploration programme. Years later he had the vision of bringing a group of Rolls-Royce cars to the country, inspired by his own interest in the marque and his fondness for Jordan and its people. He recalled the welcome afforded to visitors in Jordan and judged to be rarely equalled. The rally was Michael's idea.

An event like this, outside Europe, requires a great deal of planning and also co-ordination with local authorities. The RREC formed a tour committee to deal with shipping and insurance, the route book, hotel bookings and the like. It was all very professionally done.

Philip Hall, the Curator and Chief Executive of the Sir Henry Royce Memorial Foundation, which has a wealth of historical information about Rolls-Royce cars, prepared the rally book and was always on hand to provide invaluable data on the marque – for example to Princess Muna and Prince Faisal, whom we met on more than one occasion. BMW, the long term owner of the Rolls-Royce name, arranged for three support vehicles to be made available for the duration of the rally.

The journey to Jordan
I first met Michael Foster on the plane from Heathrow to Aqaba. Flight RJ118 of the Royal Jordanian Airlines normally flies from London to Amman via Berlin Tempelhof. On this occasion, the regulars must have been taken aback, because the flight did not stop in Berlin but flew directly to Aqaba before the short hop northwards to the capital. The pulling power of a group of 180 enthusiasts, keen

travellers to a country with an ambition to develop its tourist industry, led to a diversion from the scheduled route. I came across Michael at the rear of the plane. He had discovered a standing area near the galley – a sort of aeronautical bar – where the steward extolled the pleasures of the Middle East. "*Have you tried this red wine from the northern part of Jordan? It's called Chateau Sainte Catherine*". I did. It was a rather pleasant, made from the Cabernet Sauvignon grape. Imaginatively, a David Roberts' etching of a Biblical temple adorned the label.

The plane was full of car enthusiasts, some reading *Classic & Sports Car* or *Classic Cars*, others discussing twin carburettors or exhaust cut outs. I spotted the occasional reader of *Seven Pillars of Wisdom* or *Lawrence – The Uncrowned King of Arabia*. Most seemed accustomed to regular travel. It was a pity, I thought, that the airline had not chosen David Lean's *Lawrence of Arabia* as the in-flight movie. That would have got everyone in the right frame of mind, with the appearance of Rolls-Royce Silver Ghosts as tender vehicles. But perhaps it would have been too corny.

On the plane Michael handed out a list of helpful Arab phrases. After the obvious "*Hello*" – "*Assalamu aleikum*" – and "*Thank you*" – "*Shukran*" – the possible communications became more imaginative. "*Do not put diesel in this car*" reminded me of the Australian brain surgeon, John Matheson, who filled up his 1924 Silver Ghost with diesel at a garage on the 1998 Monte Carlo Rallye des Voitures Anciennes only to find his precious vehicle chuffing and belching like Chitty-Chitty-Bang-Bang. Actually, it looks and sounds far worse than it is; Silver Ghost engines are remarkably resilient – but it makes for an awfully red face. The next helpful hint, "*I am stuck in the sand*", is hardly necessary for the brighter Bedouin – he would probably have guessed what had happened. However, "*Please tell your camel to stop licking my Flying Lady*" was particularly appreciated, evoking the potential perils of taking favoured Rolls-Royces (and Bentleys) and favourite wives into desert country. (Note: for the uninitiated, the *Flying Lady* is another name for the mascot on the top of the radiator cap, also known as the *Spirit of Ecstasy*). The adventure in Jordan was about to begin.

On arrival at Aqaba the passengers were greeted by Jordanian dignitaries and then whisked off to the Radisson Hotel on the shores of the Gulf for welcoming glasses of fruit punch. From 15 degrees in London to 25 degrees in Aqaba the holiday mood set in immediately. That evening, sitting by the pool at one of the first of 36 buffets, there were introductions and the usual mantras of welcome. We were told that this would be the rally of a lifetime.

Aqaba – Gateway to the sea

Aqaba is situated, like it neighbour Eilat, on the apex of the Gulf of Aqaba that leads into the Red Sea. These towns, one Jordanian the other Israeli, share the same bay and are separated only by the inconvenience of an international border. For Jordan, Aqaba is of strategic importance. Over 90% of the country's trade is conducted through the sea port, linked to the other cities by road and railway, the latter with its origins in the famous Hedjaz Railway, of which more anon.

Aqaba has a long history. According to the Old Testament, King Solomon built a naval base just north of the town. The Romans had a fortification there and the town was later taken over by the Muslims who were driven out by the Crusaders in the 12th Century. They, in turn, were expelled by Saladin and the former Crusader stronghold became known as Saladin's Castle. It was during the Mamluke Egyptian rule in the 14th Century that the town acquired its present name.

But the town's rich past was not the main focus of interest as the drivers of the 72 vehicles sought to collect their cars from the Ro-Ro, inspecting each carefully to ensure that no damage had occurred on the sea crossing from the UK. The ship's captain was used to transporting Hyundai cars from Korea to Southampton. This was the first time that he had a cargo of such value.

Before the rally began, the group spent two full days in Aqaba, checking engines, water skiing and scuba diving and, also, seeing some of the town's historical remains. The Mamluke Fort is worth a visit. Badly damaged by a British warship during WWI, it was captured after TE Lawrence's surprise attack from the north (the

landward side). Above the main gate the coat of arms of the
Hashemites, from whom the present king, Abdullah, is descended, are
proudly displayed. Lunch nearby at the Mina House, a former tugboat
now embedded in concrete by the harbour, gave a pleasant
introduction to Jordanian cuisine – red snapper and emperor fish,
preceded by houmous with green chillies and olives, followed by
Turkish coffee flavoured with cardamom.

It was after this enjoyable lunch that we sampled our first hubble-
bubble. The Ali Baba Restaurant in downtown Aqaba is definitely the
place for a serious smoke. Locals outnumber foreigners by five to
one. It was here that I met Jordan's premier heart surgeon, Ibrahim
Moflab Abbadi. His advice for longevity – eat plenty of vegetables,
particularly tomatoes, take alcohol once a day, have sex twice a week
and enjoy a hubble-bubble four times a month.

<u>Wadi Rum – Valley of the moon</u>
Aqaba to Wadi Rum is just 45 miles. But the 3,000 foot climb was
enough to make some engines boil, particularly if the driver left late
and was caught in the mid-afternoon heat. We soon learnt that, in the
Middle East, it is best to journey early in the day before the sun gets
too hot.

Andy Wood of P&A Wood, the UK's premier Rolls-Royce garage,
advised: *"don't try to go too fast; change down on hills; if it's too hot,
prop open the bonnet; take extra water; if you need to top up the
radiator, make sure the engine is running to avoid a surge of boiling
water"*. These were all useful hints for anyone not accustomed to
driving in hot climates.

Wadi Rum is a village in a canyon, with 2,000 feet high vertical cliffs
either side of the valley floor. It is, without doubt, one of the most
spectacular landscapes in the world. *"The hills drive together until
two miles divided them; and then, towering gradually till their
parallel parapets must have been a thousand feet above us, ran
forward in an avenue for miles.....Our little caravan grew self-
conscious, and fell dead quiet, afraid and ashamed to flaunt its
smallness in the presence of the stupendous hills. It was vast, echoing*

and God-like". So wrote TE Lawrence in 1917 in *Seven Pillars of Wisdom*.

The ground around Wadi Rum is loose sand, over which only camels and four wheel vehicles can safely pass. The Jordanian authorities had arranged for a fleet of Toyota jeeps to be provided but even these got stuck and had to be pulled out. As we drove through the valley I couldn't get out of my head the refrain from the music hall song that Peter O'Toole sang in *Lawrence of Arabia* as he rode through Wadi Safra looking for Prince Faisal:

> *"As I walk along the Bois de Boulogne*
> *With an independent air*
> *You can hear the girls declare*
> *He must be a millionaire*
> *You can hear them sigh and wish to die*
> *You can see them wink the other eye*
> *At the man who broke the bank at Monte Carlo".*

As the end of the day approached the entourage headed for a camp sheltered under the cliffs. The camp comprised a forest of small tents, just enough for two. The tents were close together and one couldn't help overhearing sweet nothings during the night. And there were some anxious moments as well: *"Darling, I am going to have a tantrum"*, to which the response came: *"My sweet angel, there isn't enough room for a tantrum"*. In the middle of this temporary village was an assembly area covered in large carpets and surrounded by Bedouin tents opening inwards to the square. Fortified by arak, the local Bedouin desert police sang traditional songs with a repetitive theme tune, similar to the refrain of the US Marine Corps trying to build morale and a corporate fighting spirit.

When the music stopped, an extraordinary stillness settled over the camp. The sky was clear and, with no artificial light, the view of the stars was spectacular. Dawn was equally magical as the sun rose over the desert and then, just as we were enjoying breakfast, there was a small trail of dust on the horizon. Over the next few minutes, we watched as the dust became larger and then all became clear. It was the desert police arriving on their camels. Wearing the red and white checkered keffiyeh headdress, sitting astride their camels, which were also adorned with colourful harnesses, the Jordanian mounted police cut quite a dash.

The drive to our next night's stop was just 63 miles but the climb from Wadi Rum provided an opportunity for yet more cars to overheat and boil over. We reached a ridge that runs the length of Jordan from north to south alongside the Jordan Valley. Our hotel, Taybet Zaman, is a village converted into luxury accommodation.

Petra – an eternal tribute to a lost civilisation

The rose-red city of Petra was built by its Nabataean Arab inhabitants between the 4th and 1st centuries BC. The buildings are carved out of soft Nubian sandstone to a style that mixes Egyptian, Greek and Roman architecture.

The approach is dramatic, beginning with an 800 yard downhill walk from the modern town of Wadi Musa to the hills that hide and protect Petra. A gap in the mountainside leads the traveller along a 600 yard fissure, called the Siq, where there is a path no more than 20 feet at its widest, with 200 feet high cliffs on either side, forming a unique gorge. At the end, there is a crack through which you can catch a glimpse of the awe-inspiring al-Khazneh, better known as The Treasury. It is truly magnificent.

Well hidden for centuries, Petra was rediscovered in 1812 by the Swiss explorer Johann Ludwig Burckhardt. Since then, scholars have identified over 800 monuments in the Petra area. In a visit of 24 hours one can only see a few buildings. The Treasury is Petra's most famous monument, its name reflecting local legend that a Pharaoh's ransom is concealed inside. In fact it was built as a tomb for one of the Nabataean kings and was later used as a temple. Carved out of sandstone in the 1st Century it is a mixture of architectural styles and well preserved, except for the bullet holes on the façade caused by some local lads who many years ago tried to test the legend of hidden treasure by firing at the statues. They were jailed for life by an outraged people who care greatly for Jordan's past and its antiquities.

Tips for those visiting Petra include taking a stout pair of shoes, since to visit the key sites involves a walk of about six miles; also long trousers and a hat since it can be jolly hot and it is easy to get sunburnt and perhaps even sunstroke. On the day we visited Petra the thermometer reached 35 degrees. There is, however, no need to take water or food as both are provided at various points.

Below the Treasury, the Siq widens out with tombs and civic buildings on either side including an amphitheatre, fountain and church. For the energetic there is a long climb to the high place of sacrifice and an even longer climb to Al Deir, the monastery, from where the exhausted visitor is rewarded with a splendid view of the Jordan Valley. The monastery is the largest of Petra's monuments, a temple that was an important place of pilgrimage. Later, from the 4th Century, it became a Byzantine church. Nearby, a hermit, who lives in a cave on the mountain top, sells the most delicious tea, laced with sage and thyme, to the weary traveller. Sage, we were informed by our Bedouin guide, is excellent for preventing colds in Winter.

The King's Highway – Ancient and historic route

Running south to north, from Petra to Amman, is one of the oldest roads in the Middle East. There is reference to it in the Old Testament when, as early as 1,200 BC, Moses asked the Edomites if he could *"pass through their country by the King's Highway"*. The 180 mile journey from Taybet Zaman to Amman takes one through some spectacular scenery encompassing such sights as the Crusader castle of Kerak, the Mujib Valley, the ancient city of Madaba in the land of Moab and the nearby Mount Nebo, from which Moses gazed over the Promised Land.

The drive from Taybet Zaman to Kerak passed through some interesting terrain – steep hills, lunar landscape and little vegetation apart from cactus plants – until we reached Tafilah Plateau, where Lawrence fought his only pitched battle against the Turks in 1918. From here the countryside becomes kinder with hundreds of olive groves for which the region is famous.

Kerak has always been important because of its strategic position at the head of the wadi that leads west to Palestine. Dating from 1142, the castle was built to protect the Crusader kingdom's eastern flank. Surrounded by cliffs on three sides it dominated and protected the lucrative trade route. It was at Kerak Castle that terrible atrocities were committed by Crusader Reynauld de Chatillon, later avenged by Saladin, who captured the castle in 1189.

The afternoon's drive was even more spectacular. Between Kerak and Madaba, the Wadi Mujib cuts a swathe across the King's Highway. It is Jordan's answer to the Grand Canyon. The road twists and winds its way down 3,000 feet to the bottom of the wadi.

Amman and its neighbouring attractions

Our base for the next week was the Radisson SAS Hotel in Amman.

The tour became what is commonly known as a spoke rally: that is a rally based on one hotel with daily excursions. The first of these was back to Madaba, where the main attraction was the Orthodox church of Saint George. Although it dates only from the 19th Century, it incorporates the remains of the much older Byzantine church. The 6th Century Madaba map, depicting the Eastern Byzantine world at that time, must not be missed. After lunch we visited Mount Nebo, where Moses died, aged 120, after seeing his goal at the end of the Chosen People's wandering in the Wilderness.

That night a black tie reception was held at the Citadel. The guest of honour was British born HRH Princess Muna (formerly Toni Gardner), the present king's mother. She attended with her father, Colonel Gardner, and inspected four cars invited to act as a backdrop for the event. One of these was my 1931 Rolls-Royce Phantom II Continental which had won many prizes after restoration to Concours condition. In fact, it won *Best of Show* at the RREC Annual Rally at Althorp and also *Best in Class* at Pebble Beach, California, in 1994. It was later to win the Master's trophy at the RREC Annual Rally in 1996. As part of its restoration, we arranged for two whisky decanters to be placed in the headliner behind the rear seats as a tribute to the first owner who was allegedly fond of Johnny Walker Red Label. The Reception in Jordan was a *dry* event, in deference to local custom, but whisky proved something of a lifesaver for Colonel Gardner who appreciated the offer of a glass as he and the Princess inspected our car.

The Hedjaz Railway – Target of Lawrence's attacks

On the Sunday we were whisked off to the station to board the old Hedjaz Railway, the construction of which began in 1900 under the Ottoman Sultanate. Ostensibly built to transport Muslim pilgrims to Medina, political, strategic and economic factors figured prominently at a time when the Ottoman Empire was on the wane and needed propping up. Approximately 1,000 miles of track were laid through inhospitable country and some huge swings in gradients. The work was completed by the outbreak of WWI, when it proved to be a vital line of communication for the Turks. Every station was protected by a stone fort, self-sufficient with its own underground water system, and secured with barbed wire, steel shutters and firing slips.

It was the Hedjaz Railway on which Lawrence and his Arab army focused their military efforts, blowing up track, bridges and railway engines, disrupting supplies and distracting the Turkish army from the main battle front. Subsequently, the railway has been considerably reduced in length but remains an important means of transporting goods within Jordan. It is also a tourist attraction.

The Roman city of Jerash

Jerash, one of 10 Roman cities known as the Decapolis, is special because it is well preserved and one can see what it looked like and how people lived 2,000 years ago. The 30 mile drive from Amman took us north into the hills that are a continuation of the Rift Valley and one of Jordan's more fertile regions with fields of vegetables, olive trees and vines. There are also Palestinian refugee camps on the north and west approaches to the city with workshops repairing cars, fabricating iron gates and manufacturing the wonderfully coloured pots and jars.

Jerash dates from the time of Alexander the Great, around the 3rd Century BC. But what we see today dates largely from the period after Jordan was captured by the Roman General Pompey in 63 BC. Much restoration has been undertaken and some rebuilding, much to the chagrin of UNESCO, who prefer to see old monuments preserved as they are found. It is possible to see the main buildings and the basic layout of this great city which was badly damaged by a succession of earthquakes in AD749.

The entrance to the city is the triple-gated Hadrian's Arch, built in AD129 to commemorate the Emperor's visit to Gerasa, as the city was then known. Two stunning amphitheatres have been carefully restored. One is used today for the annual Jerash Festival of Culture and Arts, when Verdi operas and Shakespeare plays are performed. The acoustics in the south theatre are extraordinary. Stand exactly in the middle of the area in front of the stage and you can hear your voice as if amplified by quadraphonic speakers; move off centre and the effect is lost.

There is a magnificent view from the south theatre of the Temple of Zeus, the long colonnaded main street and the Oval Plaza, a meeting place flanked by a broad sidewalk and a fine arcade of Ionic columns. It was to the Oval Plaza that we were to return three nights later for an extraordinary black tie, gala dinner.

Safawi – an oasis on the way to Iraq

East of Amman is a desert road to the Iraqi border. In places the ground is littered with black basalt lava and then, further, with dark limestone and flint flakes. Occasionally, there is a sandy stretch. It's all pretty barren and inhospitable. Every 50 miles or so, there are the remains of oases. I say *remains* because the water table has dropped as water has been taken to provide for the ever expanding population of Amman. Before WWII, the city and its surrounding suburbs had just 200,000 inhabitants. By the time of our rally, in 1999, with increased childbirth, refugees from Palestine and the migration of people from the desert, this had swelled to two million. Water, or rather lack of it, is one of the main reasons for tension between Israel, Jordan and Syria.

En route to Safawi, we stopped at the ruins of Azraq Castle, which was TE Lawrence's home in the winter of 1917/18. In a draughty room above the gatehouse he plotted the assault on Damascus. In those days, Azraq, which means blue in Arabic, was the site of a large lake. This has now dried up due to the lower water table. An interesting feature of the castle, much damaged by an earthquake in 1927, was a huge Roman door that still turned on its original stone hinges.

Our purpose in travelling to Safawi was to see the Badia Research and Development centre aimed at improving the quality of people's lives through sustained development and through linking the economies of the desert with Jordan's national development policies. This includes combating desertification and the depletion of natural resources. Initiated by HRH Prince Hassan, the brother of the late King Hussein, the Badia Fund has an exhibition and a research centre which was formerly a pumping station of the erstwhile Iraq Petroleum Company's oil pipeline from Kirkuk to Haifa. Badia is Arabic for the semi-arid region where the annual rainfall is less than 20cms. 80% of Jordan's land is classified as Badia.

After the visit, we were treated to a buffet lunch on tables under Bedouin tents which shaded the diners from the sun. We were joined by elders from the local community. Dining Bedu style comprises eight to ten of you standing around a large circular copper dish of saffron rice and cooked lamb. The chef pours a mixture of yoghourt and the juices from cooking the lamb on top. With your left hand behind your back, you take rice in your right and then roll it into a ball before eating. Chunks of meat can similarly be taken, again with your right hand. It's very matey, but each diner has his or her own area of food on the plate and this makes it orderly. It is also rather messy. Having eaten, the diner takes a handful of sand in his or her right hand and squeezes this to soak up the remains of the food before wiping the hand on the sacking that forms the wall of the tent. As you can imagine, after a few months, the sacking desperately needs changing.

Royal Amman

The Royal interest in our rally extended to our being invited to a private view of the Royal garages, at the invitation of HRH King Abdullah bin al Hussein. We were escorted by his mother, HRH Princess Muna, who drove her own car, a 1959 Bentley S2 HJ Mulliner Continental, a wedding gift from her late husband, King Hussein.

The late king had amassed an array of cars, collected over a 40 year period, including many large engine BMW motor bikes, a demonstration of his passion for speed. There were open top Land Rovers, with bullet proof screens, used for Royal processions. Our visit concluded with a visit to the late king's grave.

Lunch was taken at the Royal Jordanian Automobile Club where our guest of honour was HRH Prince Faisal.

A gala evening in Jerash
A motor bike escort of police outriders accompanied a few chosen cars to Jerash, and back, for the gala dinner in the Oval Plaza. We drove *Harrison*, our 1934 Rolls-Royce 20/25, which had been lent to our friends David and Caroline Colvin for the rally. Being salmon pink, after *The Financial Times*, the colour makes quite a statement, particularly at night under artificial light and is most appropriate for a black tie party.

Arriving at the south gate of Jerash at any time is impressive. Arriving for a gala dinner is even more impressive, particularly when there are torch-bearing Roman soldiers as escorts and when the ancient city is lit up. We enjoyed a son et lumiere before the formal dinner, where we were joined again by Princess Muna and Prince Faisal.

On the return to Amman, I found myself at the front of the convoy, behind the leading police outrider. He kept to a slow speed for most of the journey but was amused when I overtook him and we had a game of cat and mouse all the way to the capital. At the end, he came over and gave me a big hug, reminiscent of another hug I received from a bearded Iranian policeman on *The Peking to Paris Motor Challenge* in 1997.

The drive from Amman to Aqaba by the Dead Sea
The 207 miles from the capital to Aqaba was the longest on our tour and, since we had to be there by 17.00 for the cars to be loaded onto the return Ro-Ro, there was no opportunity for leisurely stops or breakdowns. During our stay in Amman, we had spent a day at the

Dead Sea and, like most visitors, enjoyed a float in this salty water as well as a mud bath.

This was not a good day to get lost or to run out of petrol. We were amazed, and later amused, when David Colvin, driving *Harrison*, ran out of petrol not just once, but twice. The first occasion was a misfortune, as the petrol gauge became resolutely stuck at 16 gallons when dirt from the petrol tank lodged in the feed pipe. Fortunately two support vehicles were on hand to provide a much needed five gallons to start him up again. A satisfactory explanation for the second incident is still outstanding. *Harrison* again performed faultlessly.

During this stretch of the road, which was absolutely flat and straight, with few other cars on it, I was clocked by Andy Wood driving my Phantom II Continental at 100mph, the only ton I have ever done in an old car.

The development of the motor car

Karl Benz is generally regarded as the inventor of the modern motor car, a motorwagen, in 1885, although there were earlier attempts at powering vehicles with steam and electricity.

By the turn of the Century, French and German automotive manufacturers, such as Benz, Daimler, De Dion, Georges Ricard, Maybach, Mors, Panhard et Levassor and Peugeot led the field in producing cars which were acquired by the rich and famous.

The British companies lagged behind their Continental neighbours as a result of the strong railway and horse lobbies and the antipathy towards the motor car. In Britain, there was resentment towards motor vehicles and automobilists, generated by suspicion, ignorance and jealousy. Motor cars were considered to be the playthings of eccentric fat cats who, by their furious driving, scared both horses and people, slaughtered dogs, chickens and livestock, and created thick clouds of choking dust. It was also feared that they might pose a considerable threat to the vested interests of the wealthy in bloodstock and railway company shares.

The *Red Flag Act* of 1865 had limited all self-propelled vehicles to a speed of 4 mph in the country and 2 mph in town. The Act also required a man with a red flag or lantern to walk 60 yards ahead of each vehicle. The 1878 Act removed the need for the flag. After further lobbying, the speed limit was raised to 12mph in 1896. But, these restrictions held back the full development of the automobile in Great Britain, although there were exceptions - some fine cars were made by Lanchester, Napier and also Daimler, this last under licence from Germany.

The Hon Charles Rolls is recorded as saying "*People now take no notice of a bicycle going along at 20mph; they have got used to it, and it no longer shocks them. But when they see a heavy motor vehicle driven by a man in a mask, with a weird-looking shining black jacket, and overall appearance of being in armour plate, travelling at 30mph, raising a cloud of dust, and propelled by a force they do not understand, and leaving behind it a smell, which, sweeter than eau de Cologne to the motorists, is to them abominable, they naturally say that we are madmen in motors, and that such practices must end in the death of thousands of people".*

Indeed, by the turn of the Victorian Century, a large number of people in Britain had never seen a motor car. There was, perhaps, an even greater number who laughed at the idea of it ever becoming a practical or commercial success.

The Thousand Mile Trial in 1900

Since the *1896 London to Brighton Emancipation Run*, which celebrated the passing of the *Locomotives on the Highway Act* of that year, there had been no serious attempt to demonstrate the practical use of the motor car to the British public. By contrast, on the Continent, there were numerous public motor shows and automobile races and manufacturers were bringing out new models each year.

In 1899, Claude Johnson, then Secretary of the Automobile Club of Great Britain and Ireland (latter renamed the Royal Automobile Club) had the idea of organising a grand scale public demonstration of the motor car. He devised a 1,000 mile trial of motor cars around the UK, visiting the major towns and cities to show off their capabilities. The route from London to Edinburgh and back included stops in Bristol, Birmingham, Manchester, Kendal, Carlisle and, on the return, Newcastle, Leeds, Sheffield and Nottingham.

A Committee was formed to oversee the event. It included such luminaries as Sir David Salomans, the Hon Charles Stuart Rolls, Worby Beaumont, Henry Hewetson, Hubert Edgerton, the Hon Evelyn Ellis, Frederick Simms, Sir Bernhard Samuelson, the Hon John Douglas-Scott-Montagu (later Lord Montagu), SF Edge, Montague Napier, Harvey du Cross, JE Hutton, JD Siddeley (later Lord Kenilworth), EM Iliffe (later Lord Iliffe) and Henry Sturmey. Alfred Harmsworth (later Lord Northcliffe) underwrote the whole venture against any financial loss to the Club.

In total, 80 vehicles were entered for the event in which 64 actually started. Of these, 33 claimed British manufacture, although many were not of entirely British design. Most of the competitors had never driven a car as far as 100 miles in a day. Demonstrating quality, as well as endurance, after a journey lasting 20 days, 49 vehicles completed the 1,000 miles. At the various stops, local dignitaries and businessmen were given the opportunity of riding in the cars. There was enormous Press interest and a huge public turnout on the route and at the open exhibitions.

The Gold Medal for the event, presented by the Club, was awarded to the Hon Charles Rolls who had driven a 12HP Panhard fitted with a Daimler engine. This had most impressed judges with its reliability, timekeeping, hill climbing and speed capabilities.

Despite a number of accidents involving animals, the event was deemed to have been a huge success, putting motoring well and truly on the map. *The Times* pronounced that the Trial had achieved its objective of proving the car "*a serious and trustworthy means of locomotion, not a toy, dangerous and troublesome alike to the public and its owner, but a vehicle under as perfect control as a bath chair, capable of accomplishing long journeys, in all weathers and over every kind of road, with ease and safety, designed to take its place with the train and the bicycle as a common object of daily life, and as superior to them in many respects, as they are superior to the horse and cart*".

Afterwards, automotive manufacturers made improvements to the design of their cars as a result of observations made of the vehicles' performance; and pneumatic tyres were introduced. Legislation in 1903 increased the maximum speed limit to 20mph and provided that all motor vehicles in the UK should be registered and display number plates.

The Re-enactment of *The Thousand Mile Trial* in 2000

The Thousand Mile Trial in 1900 was a demonstration to the public that the motor car was a practical means of transport.

To commemorate and celebrate this milestone in the history of motoring, the Veteran Car Club of Great Britain organised a re-enactment to take place between 18th and 27th May 2000. As a result of developments in roads, such as the building of motorways and the enlargement of towns, it was not possible to follow exactly the same route as in 1900. Thus, the start was moved from Whitehall in London to the VCC's headquarters in Ashwell, Hertfordshire. Such was the interest in the re-enactment that entry was restricted to cars built prior to 31st December 1904, in order to keep the numbers within manageable bounds.

The driving force behind the re-enactment was Daniel Ward, one of the three *Ward Brothers* who had a large collection of veteran cars. As a member of the VCC, working together with the RAC, Daniel organised a memorable event.

There were 56 participants ranging from an 1894 Benz Velo to a 1905 De Dion. No 42 was my wife Lesley's 1904 Wolseley. I drove and our friend, David Colvin, former British Ambassador to Belgium, was the passenger and navigator. We were accompanied by our mechanical engineer, Roy O'Sullivan, who drove our Range Rover with a trailer and whose assistance was to prove invaluable in the days ahead.

1904 6HP Wolseley ("*Claudia*")
By the time of the re-enactment in 2000, Lesley's car, *Claudia*, had completed four Brighton Runs, including the Centenary Run in 1996. Under the Stuttard ownership, the car went on to complete six more. She was ready for the 1,000 mile challenge. Roy had ensured that she was in perfect mechanical shape. But, even he could not predict the impact of such a long journey on a car that had typically not done much more than 100 miles in a year and had never journeyed more than 60 miles in a day. *The Thousand Mile Trial* was actually 1,030 miles from our house in Totteridge to the end of the tour - the equivalent of almost 21 Brighton Runs in just 10 days.

Driving to the VCC Headquarters
The cars had to be driven to Ashwell on Wednesday 17 May, prior to the start at the VCC Headquarters early on the Thursday. My cousins, John & Clive Boothman, had entered their family's 1902 Napier and we arranged that they should stay the night with us on the Wednesday prior to the drive to Ashwell on the Thursday. While the Wolseley

had an easy run on Thursday morning, the Napier developed mechanical problems which necessitated Roy visiting a workshop in Sussex on the Friday.

The Start (Day 1)

Claudia had a good run on the first day, covering 100 miles through the attractive countryside of the Chilterns (Woburn Park, Mentmore, Kimble, Chinnor, Bledlow, Britwell Salome, Goring, and Yattendon) to our hotel, the Elcot Park, west of Newbury. En route, near Yattendon, we were treated to a champagne tea at the home of Lord Iliffe, grandson of EM Iliffe, and were shown his car collection, some of which were not exactly in Concours condition. He had seemingly kept every car he had ever owned and they were stored in a barn on the estate next to his quite modern house, erected when the Victorian pile, acquired by his grandfather, had been converted into apartments. The Boothmans, David and I dined at the Royal Oak at Yattendon where I had stayed in the late 1960's while auditing Sterling Cables at nearby Aldermaston.

Disaster strikes, but Phoenix rises (Day 2)

On the second day, the route took us through the area to the north of Salisbury Plain (near Marlborough, West Kennet, Silbury Hill, Avebury, Wootton Bassett and Tetbury) and we enjoyed some attractive scenery. We had been asked to a buffet lunch near Stroud by Charles & Ute Howard whom we had known for almost a decade on successive Monte Carlo rallies. Charles was a well-known dealer in fine vintage cars and two of my Rolls-Royces (1921 Silver Ghost 33LG and 1931 Phantom II Continental 50GX) had passed through his hands.

But our lunch stop was not to be. *Claudia's* inlet valve broke as we were approaching Nailsworth. *Claudia* was then piggy-backed to Charles' engineer who diagnosed the problem. A replacement could be made locally but certainly not at 16.00 on a Friday afternoon. Fortunately Roy was at the machine shop in Sussex where a part was being made for the Napier. Charles' engineer drew a sketch of the inlet valve and measured its dimensions. These were then faxed to Roy and a replacement inlet valve was machined that evening and brought, late at night, to the Green Dragon Hotel in Hereford, to which *Claudia* had been further piggy-backed.

The Green Dragon Hotel is one of those wonderful coaching inns with an indoor garage built over the old courtyard. It was dry, reasonably warm and well lit – an ideal location for Roy to fix the new inlet valve. After a restful night (albeit not for Roy, who worked for many hours on the car), we were back on the road the following morning.

A wet day in the West Midlands and the Welsh Borders (Day 3)
The euphoria of being mobile again quickly evaporated as the weather changed. It rains a lot in Wales and some of this drifts over to Shropshire, which is well known for its green fields and dairy herds. After the pleasant, rolling hills around Ludlow and south of Shrewsbury, the relatively flat countryside of North Shropshire is less interesting, particularly in the driving rain. With no windscreen, we were soon soaked to the skin and the journey around Whitchurch and Altrincham seemed to go on forever.

Finally, we reached Manchester and our destination, the Midland Hotel, where Henry Royce had famously met The Hon Charles Rolls in 1904. Dry clothes were produced from our escorting Range Rover with the wet ones left drying over the bedroom's radiators, while we went out for a grand dinner at the Manchester Town Hall.

Designed by Alfred Waterhouse and completed in 1877, the Town Hall is one of the finest examples of Victorian gothic architecture in the world. There is much marble and there are grand staircases and rooms. No money was spared. At a cost of around £1 million it represented several years of annual local authority revenues and was a shining example of municipal confidence and pride.

Through Lancashire to the Lakes (Day 4)
There are some delightful parts to Lancashire but the route did not take us through the most attractive, the Forest of Bowland. Instead, we skirted Swinton and Chorley and went through the centre of Preston. However, there was one point of interest. We had been invited for lunch at the home of Geoffrey Thompson, whose family

owned the Blackpool Pleasure Beach. And, Geoffrey had an extensive miniature railway around his large estate.

The scenery improved as we entered the Lake District National Park and made our way to the Old England Hotel at Bowness on Lake Windermere. In those days, when we were employed and earned large sums, we felt well-heeled enough to forego dinner at the Old England and, instead, booked a table at the Michelin starred Miller Howe. We had a delightful meal with the Boothmans.

The Longest Day (Day 5)
140 miles is a long way for a 1904 veteran car. But, the route (probably) took us through the most stunning scenery – Ambleside, Grasmere and Keswick, going up Dunmail Rise, one of the demanding hill climbs on the original route. From there we journeyed past Bassenthwaite, onto Carlisle, and then on the moorland road, the B709, to Eskdalemuir and Innerleithen. Taking this route is one of the most spectacular ways of reaching the Scottish capital.

By now, the length of the distance covered was beginning to have an effect on *Claudia*. The car's radiator is wrapped around the front of the body to ensure maximum exposure to the air and to prevent overheating. Notwithstanding this, the engine did get hot and the radiator had to be topped up with water quite frequently. The situation got worse when the radiator sprang a leak and Roy came to the rescue using plastic ties which stopped it breaking up further.

And, my passenger, David, had a close shave when I had to swerve to the left and almost into a hawthorn hedge as a large oncoming lorry took up most of the road on a narrow section 30 miles short of Edinburgh.

But we made it safely and were treated to dinner in the magnificent 18th Century Signet Law Library in Edinburgh.

Downhill all the way to England (Day 6)
The 111 mile journey from Edinburgh to the county of Northumberland takes one through some wild country in the Borders that has been fought over for centuries by English and Scots. Our

fight was ensuring that *Claudia's* radiator did not disintegrate
completely. Roy's plastic ties were the only thing holding it together,
as a major repair was out of the question. But the engine was going
well and we were able to keep up a reasonable speed.

That evening, our hotel was the castellated Slayley Hall Hotel with
spa, championship golf course and an excellent restaurant and bar.
The sight of buggies, used to ferry golfers about the course, was too
much for Lord (Edward) Montagu and we enjoyed buggy races with
him around the grounds. But these were no match for our veteran
cars.

Through Wensleydale to Harrogate (Day 7)
North Yorkshire has some very grand countryside, particularly along
the River Ure which passes through, or by, Wensley, Leyburn, East
Witton, Masham and Ripley. Apart from producing some fine cheese,
Wensleydale is also great shooting country. I have in later years often
stayed at the Blue Lion at East Witton on November shoots; the pub
is one of the least spoilt and most original country pubs I know.

And, so, on to the spa town of Harrogate and our hotel, the Old Swan,
where Agatha Christie spent 10 days in 1926 after she had
disappeared, causing consternation and a major manhunt. She had
checked in under an assumed name but was recognised by one of the
hotel's banjo players. That night, we dined with Rick (now Lord) and
Lindy Best who live in the guest wing of a stately pile near Tadcaster.

The rather miserable "South Riding" (Day 8)
It is easy to understand why there was never a South Riding of
Yorkshire as that part of Yorkshire has very little to commend itself.
Steel works, coal mines and heavy engineering dominate. And, as one
approaches Lincolnshire, the land gets flatter and the landscape seems
to go on for ever. There are some fine cities – Lincoln and Grantham
– but our route avoided these. Instead our views were of power
stations and electricity pylons. At the end of the day, the Belton
Woods Hotel was a modern, faceless golfing centre. So, we dined at
the nearby Harry's Place, without doubt the smallest Michelin starred
restaurant in the country.

<u>**The final journey to Hatfield Heath (Day 9)**</u>
On the two last days we covered over 220 miles – the equivalent of two Brighton Runs each day. How the car managed to survive is beyond us. The radiator had very nearly been destroyed and we had lost one of the front wings. Roy's sticking plaster had kept everything together. But after 10 days of constant driving with wind and rain in our faces, we were totally exhausted.

It was something of a triumph to reach the final hotel, Down Hall, at Hatfield Heath in the knowledge that, out of 56 cars that started, less than 30 completed the route. One of the smallest of these, our 1904 single cylinder 6HP Wolseley, had performed a miracle.

<u>**The gala dinner at the RAC**</u>
By contrast, the gala dinner at the RAC was something of an anti-climax. It should have been a celebration of achievement. And to a large extent it was. But there was a certain amount of backbiting, for which the VCC has become well known. There were some unnecessarily sour comments made by a former VCC President about the Ward Brothers, who had done a fantastic job in organising the event. The re-enactment was a fitting commemoration of a remarkable chapter in British motoring history and the participants and their cars in *The 2000 Thousand Mile Trial* had risen to the occasion.

Ecstasy in the Orient
A Tour of Malaysia by Rolls-Royce and Bentley cars – 2001

The British influence and Malaysia today

Rudyard Kipling wrote of Malaya, *"Into this land God first put gold and tin and after these the Englishman who floats companies, obtains concessions and goes forward"*.

It was indeed gold and tin as well as spices that lured our ancestors to the Malay Peninsula. Nutmeg and pepper could be sold in London for 100 times more than its price in the Orient. Fortunes were made and lives were lost. Those who survived the tempests, pirates and tropical diseases became hugely wealthy. In the 17th Century, the average life expectancy of a sailor was four years – the equivalent of two return journeys. The graveyard in Penang is a historical chronicle. Headstones tell of brave Englishmen lost overboard from the yardarm in the Malacca Straits or dying young of *the fever*.

The Europeans were not the first to trade and settle in the Malay Archipelago. Melanesians and Polynesians came first, followed by peoples of mixed Malay, Chinese and Indian blood, while some had Arabic and Siamese origins. The Indians and the Chinese had trading ties with the region in the first millennium and Muslim seafarers from India brought Islam at the end of the 13th Century. At the onset of the 15th Century, a Malay king established a settlement in Malacca. The Portuguese followed and a 16th Century explorer and composer from Portugal, Duarte Barbosa, wrote, *"Whoever is Lord in Melaka has his hand on the throat of Venice"*. 130 years later it was the Dutch who took possession of the Portuguese fortress and built their Empire in the Orient, until the East India Company established a settlement on the island of Penang in 1785. Then, after the Napoleonic Wars, the British became the sole colonial power. Their rule was generally benign. The local sultans held sway in their own states, with some oversight from Great Britain, who governed directly the Straits Settlements, comprising Malacca, Penang and Singapore. In 1957 the country gained its independence or freedom (*Merdeka* in Malay). Some six years later the Federation of Malaysia was formed, embracing Sarawak and Sabah, as well as continental Malaya.

At independence, the population of Malaysia was just over 10 million, comprising Malays (47%), Chinese (34%), Indians (9%) and native groups (10%). The different races and religions (Muslims, Buddhists, Confucians, Hindus and Christians) have co-existed for generations. Different groups have lived in (more or less) harmony for over 1,000 years. This multi-racial, multi-religious, multi-cultural combination has produced a fascinating and hospitable country for tourists – not least the 90 Rolls-Royce and Bentley car owners and their crews who spent an enjoyable three weeks in Malaysia in Autumn 2001.

The origins of modern Malaysia lie in the economic and social development of the country by the British in the first half of the 20th Century. At one time, Malaya produced 50% of the world's tin and 50% of the world's rubber. Rubber seeds arrived from Brazil via Kew Gardens and thrived. Revenues from tin and rubber financed roads, railways, telecommunications, as well as education, healthcare and other amenities. Pre-war Malaya must have been a hard working yet rewarding environment in which a British planter or administrator could enjoy a career. There were hardships such as malaria and the hot and humid climate, with no air conditioning. But the people were friendly and keen to learn.

For British colonials, there were the usual expatriate haunts. A senior civil servant or *tuan besar* (big boss) would spend his leisure time at the Selangor Club sometimes referred to as *The Spotted Dog* after the Club's emblem of a running leopard. Here he would sip a *stengah* (half a peck of Dewar's white label whisky with water). In front of the Club is the *Padang* (the field) where cricket is still played. Opposite is the much photographed Sultan Abdul Samad building, which houses the Supreme Court, and along the third side St Mary's Cathedral where colonial families prayed. Meanwhile, a junior district officer or *tuan kechil* (little boss) might make his way to the Coliseum Café and Hotel, founded in 1921, for many years a place where bachelors could enjoy discreet pursuits. Here he (never she) could relax with a copy of the *Malay Mail* (first published in 1896) which gave advice on such useful topics as what to do *when your servant has malaria*. A copy of one such article still hangs in the Coliseum's bar and reads: *"Immediately notify the Health Officer who will search for the breeding grounds of the anopheles in the vicinity, with the object of destroying them. Then take him to the District Hospital. Mosquito net – see he uses it. Give him quinine"*. Today, the traveller can still enjoy a *stengah* of beer at the Coliseum and also *sizzling steak* for which the restaurant is famous, cooked at your table by a waiter almost old enough to have been there in 1921. Their starched white aprons, with holes from much wear, look to be originals too.

At long weekends and holidays, to escape the heat, families would decamp to the hills. Fraser's Hill, near Kuala Lumpur, was popular, as was the Cameron Highlands with its golf course, the corporate bungalows and Ye Olde Smokehouse Inn, a fine example of 1930's Tudor-Gothic. Here you can still be pampered in colonial fashion and enjoy cream teas on the terrace, a Pimms' No. 1 in the bar before dinner of Beef Wellington or steak and kidney pie, accompanied by a passable claret, in the panelled dining room.

The British legacy was sound. Even so, the development of the country since independence has been nothing short of miraculous. Known in the 1990's as one of the Asian tigers, Malaysia has made huge advances in economic and social development. The evidence is all around – a network of motorways links state of the art industrial estates and attractive housing complexes; a modern state capital that seeks to match Lutyens' New Delhi; an impressively designed international airport with its neighbouring and equally impressive Formula One (F1) circuit; a telecoms infrastructure that is the envy of many advanced countries; and two of the tallest buildings in the world – the Twin Petronas Towers. Tin, rubber and palm oil have given way to tourism and information technology. Indeed, one Government Minister proudly told us that Penang alone now accounts for 50% of the world's computer chips.

Planning and organising the tour

The 1,000 mile Rolls-Royce and Bentley tour of Malaysia was the brainchild of Peter Cameron, formerly head of Standard Chartered Bank in Malaysia. Peter had participated on the Rolls-Royce Enthusiasts Club's (RREC) tour of Jordan in 1999 and had the idea of a Malaysian tour while camping in Wadi Rum. He and the then

RREC Chairman, Eri Heilijgers, took the key decisions with assistance from Douglas Vaughan and Philip Hall.

The tour was fortunate to have as its patron, His Highness the Regent of Selangor, Tengku Idris Shah, whom I had met on *The Peking to Paris Motor Challenge* in 1997 and whose Coronation Lesley and I had the honour of attending in 2003.

A most attractive route book was produced, beautifully illustrated with sketches, with information about the country and a selection of Malay words that might come in handy, thus:

- *Bus Sekolah* is a school bus
- *Taksi* is a taxi
- *Rumah Bomba* is a fire station
- *Kereta Api* is a train (literally flame wagon)
- While the Malay for a girl is *Chik*

It perhaps comes as a surprise that Malay has no plural form as such but involves repeating the same word twice. Thus the word for men is man-man or *tuan-tuan*, as we discovered whenever Peter Cameron delivered the usual greetings in speeches – *Tunku, Tunku, Dato Dato, Datin Datin.*

Arrival in Kuala Lumpur

As with the Jordan rally in 1999, the cars were shipped from Southampton via a Hyundai Ro-Ro vessel. Driven on and driven off, the cars were strapped down for the voyage and arrived safely in Port Klang on 23rd October 2001, after a journey across half the world.

The drive to Kuala Lumpur was short and uneventful and we checked in to the Palace of the Golden Horses, our hotel for the seven nights' stay in the city and our base for a *spoke* tour. I had brought our 1921 Silver Ghost All Weather Tourer which is, as the name implies, suitable for all manner of weather. Its windows pull up, rather than wind up, in the manner of a pre-war railway carriage window, and the hood can either be taken right back, so that the car becomes an open tourer, or fixed to the top of the windscreen, so that the car is 99% waterproof. The sun was quite fierce and so we kept the hood up for much our time in Malaysia.

There were four of us in the car: Lesley, British Ambassador to Belgium David Colvin CMG, with whom I had toured on many other rallies, and Roy O'Sullivan, our engineer, whose costs were shared with his other clients (my cousin, John Boothman & his wife Sue, and Ian & Julie Strang) who had also entered the rally.

Our Silver Ghost was ordered in 1921 by a London car dealership, Car Mart, which specified that it should have an Alpine Eagle chassis and a light body. A four seater, with plenty of legroom in the back, the car was made to look sporty, with just two doors and a most attractive V-shaped windscreen that made it immediately distinguishable and gave it a racy, Great Gatsby, appearance. The July 1921 edition of The Autocar magazine shows a photograph of the car (chassis no 33 LG), with a registration number XF 7646, and the text "*Elegant Lines. The Rolls-Royce depicted has been fitted by Car Mart, Ltd., 297-299, Euston Road, London, N.W.1, with a very smart V fronted sporting all-weather body and is being used by that firm for demonstration purposes. The coachbuilders have been particularly happy in securing a very low top line without in any degree sacrificing comfort. Access is gained by a large single door on either side of the car*". This unusual, sporty touring car was purchased by His Highness The Maharaja Sir Natwarsinhji of Porbander, KCSI, who kept the car at his London home, 82 Eaton Square, SW1. The Maharajah was then 20 years old and had just come into his title and inherited his father's estates. Five years later, in 1926, he arranged for the car to be shipped to India aboard the SS Rawalpindi, a P&O merchant ship that was later sunk by the German battleships, Scharnhorst and Gneisenau, in the North Atlantic in 1939. After use in Porbander, a city in the southern part of Gujarat, the Silver Ghost was sold in 1932 to a Bombay family, then to a family in Poona, where it was found in a dishevelled state in 1969 and brought back to the UK for renovation. I acquired the car in 2000 and the tour to Malaysia was its first big outing.

The rally began with a visit to the new Federal capital of Putrajaya which contains imposing buildings reminiscent of another grand capital, New Delhi. The Prime Minister's office is roughly 20 times the size of No 10 Downing Street and is very luxurious, as I was to find out when I visited the Prime Minister in 2007, as Lord Mayor.

Next stop was Malaysia's F1 circuit at Sepang, where our Rolls-Royces were waved onto the track for a lap of honour at a very sedate pace led by a police car. We were lying third in the convoy and I put my foot down and roared past the leading police car. The rest of the pack followed. At the end of the lap, I couldn't stop and so the whole procession completed a second lap. But, I hadn't realised just how steep the banking on the corners was and we had to slow down to 30mph per hour on several occasions. Afterwards I wondered how a Ferrari could navigate the circuit at over 100mph.

It was a happy coincidence that we were joined at the Sepang track by the then Lord Mayor of London, Sir David Howard Bt., and his wife Valerie. Also in the party were the Chief Commoner, Anthony Eskenzi and his wife Eileen, accompanied by the City Marshal, Neill O'Connor. They had been on an official tour of Hong Kong and Malaysia and were enjoying a day off before flying to Singapore. After lunch, the chairman of the company that manages the circuit, Tan Sri Basir, delayed the start of the afternoon practice session for Ferraris so that I could take the Lord Mayor and the Lady Mayoress for a spin around the track in the Ghost. It was quite a sight, as we hurtled round the circuit, to see the Lady Mayoress hanging on for dear life and, by her own admission, loving every minute of it.

That night we were entertained by Rikki Curtis, whom we had met on *The Peking to Paris Motor Challenge* in 1997. His family have been in Malaya (now Malaysia) for four generations and he is a close adviser to and friend of Idris Shah, the *Raja Muda* (or heir apparent) of Selangor. Rikki had several business ventures in Malaysia, one of which was the Asiana Restaurant in the Federal Hotel. Rikki and Idris hosted a splendid dinner for those members of the tour who had also participated in the 1997 Challenge. Idris kindly floated the idea that perhaps one day we might attend his Coronation as the Sultan of Selangor.

During our stay in Kuala Lumpur, we had the opportunity of seeing and then dining in the Petronas Towers. On the first occasion, the cars were lined up in the square in front of this iconic building, which is 1482 feet high and has 88 stories. The appalling fate of the World Trade Centre in New York, just seven weeks earlier, was never far from our mind.

I had first visited Malaysia in 1967 while I was working in Brunei as a volunteer teacher. Then, I took the train from Singapore to Bangkok, stopping in both KL and Penang. In the intervening 44 years, the country had changed immeasurably and the evidence of this change was never greater than in Kuala Lumpur. The city had, indeed, become a truly international centre. Gone were the satay stalls in the streets and the primitive air conditioning units with boxes that hung outside the walls of the buildings. Satay was still served, but in smart restaurants, and every building has purpose built integrated cooling systems. The hotels were of the quality you would find in any other modern city and the town planners had created a most attractive Asian city, with flowers and trees separating the lanes of highways and parks full of lush vegetation.

A day trip (90 miles) to Malacca (aka Melaka)

By contrast, Malacca had changed little. Travelling there took us through country roads and small villages which, similarly, had escaped the urban development we had witnessed in Kuala Lumpur. Chickens still roamed in the back yards and spilled out onto the highway. Roadside stalls still sold fruit and wickerwork. Cafes with open fronts still gave the customer the option of dining alfresco or in the fan-cooled interior. Old men and women, with their mouths stained by beetle nut, still sat lazily waiting for something to happen. The sight of dozens of Rolls-Royces and Bentleys purring past would be certainly something to relate to family, friends and neighbours for many weeks to come.

Being on the sea and almost on the Equator, Malacca is hot and humid for most of the year. As a result, sightseeing can be a sweaty business, as well as tiring. But there are some fascinating sites:

- The famous 16th Century Portuguese fortress, *A Formosa*, the only surviving part of which is the small gate house, saved by Stamford Raffles from destruction in 1810 after the Governor of Penang had ordered its demolition as part of the plan to move the East India Company's presence in Malaya to Penang

- The Dutch Square, with Christ Church and the Town Hall, Stadthuys, which dates from 1650
- The Malacca Straits Mosque, built in the early years of the 21st Century. Situated on a promontory with an isthmus connecting it to the mainland, it looks as though it is floating when the water level is high.

Malacca was listed as a World Heritage Site (together with Penang) in 2008.

Royalty at Seri Menanti, capital of Negeri Sembilan

Nine of Malaysia's states are headed by a traditional Malay ruler. Every five years, or whenever a vacancy occurs, the rulers gather together and elect the Federal monarch, known as the *Yang di-Pertuan Agong*, the King. This position was created in 1957 with Tunku Abdul Rahman, who was well known in the West, being the first person to be elected to this position. The rulers of each state are usually elected by reference to their state's position in a cycle of the nine which are eligible. Thus, each state should have an *Agong* every 40 to 45 years, or less if a ruler dies in office or is judged unfit due to illness or for any other reason.

In most states the ruler has the title of Sultan. In Negeri Sembilan, he is referred to as the *Yang di-Pertuan Besar* and is selected from among the four leading princes of the state. Seri Menanti is the site of the Royal Palace of Negeri Sembilan and lies 65 miles to the south-east of KL.

Every time we left the hotel in Kuala Lumpur, usually in convoy, we were escorted by as many as 15 policemen on motor bikes. The outriders loved every minute of it, racing between the Rolls-Royces and chatting at the various stops. Security was impressive and the Malaysian Chief of Traffic Police accompanied us for most of the tour. Our visit to Seri Menanti was no exception.

The old palace of the *Yang di-Pertuan Besar*, HRH Tuanku Jaafar, was built over a Century ago and is made out of teak, without a single nail being used. It is now a museum which displays local culture and artefacts and is a most interesting place to visit. The Tuanku was a proven Anglophile who owned a Rolls-Royce and also a golf car with a Rolls-Royce radiator. In keeping with Malay custom, we were advised to dress reasonably smartly, albeit casually, but with no yellow, as this is the Royal colour in Malaysia (and of course in China, as well). We were entertained for lunch on the *Padang* (the Malay word for a grand field) accompanied by local musicians and a colourful display of dancing. There were speeches and a generous exchange of gifts, with members of the Royal family making the presentations.

<u>The climb to a hill station</u>
Sir Henry Gurney KCMG, KStJ was appointed High Commissioner of Malaya in 1948, just as the Malayan Emergency was beginning. On 5th October 1951, on his way to Fraser's Hill, Gurney's convoy was ambushed by Malayan Communist Party guerrillas who killed Gurney, his chauffeur and five policemen. His wife was saved after Gurney had got out of the car and, although wounded, staggered forward to draw the insurgents' fire away from the car and towards him. The car, a Rolls-Royce Silver Wraith, is now in the State Museum in Penang and there are traces of the 35 bullet holes which the car suffered on that fateful day.

Fraser's Hill and the Cameron Highlands are both hill stations founded and developed by Scotsmen. Fraser's Hill is closer to KL, while the Cameron Highlands have more facilities but this requires a longer drive. Our climb to the Cameron Highlands, just over 50 years after Gurney's climb to Fraser's Hill, was to prove less eventful. The drive from KL to the beginning of the climb was straightforward. However, in 2001, before new roads were built, the only access was a windy road. It was, indeed, very windy but the Ghost took it easily, as the engine, with six cylinders, totalling almost eight litres, is very powerful.

The Cameron Highlands were unknown to Westerners until 1885, when William Cameron surveyed the area and discovered *"a fine plateau with gentle slopes shut in by mountains"*. The main town, Brinchand, has the curious atmosphere of an out of season ski resort. Its Englishness is reinforced by a penchant for mock Tudor half-timbering and what must be the densest concentration anywhere in the world of old Land Rovers. Clearly this is the place where Land Rovers come to die or, perhaps, to find everlasting life, with their rust free aluminium bodies, albeit in increasingly battered condition. It is a place to relax, play tennis or golf, and enjoy the fresh vegetables, tea and strawberries that grow for most of the year in the Tropics at this altitude.

Here, without drawing attention to ourselves so as not to upset the organisers of the tour, we did not check in at the pre-booked, soulless Equatorial Hotel. Instead we stayed at the 1930's half-timbered Ye Olde Smokehouse where, perhaps because of our means of transport, the receptionist allocated us the Honeymoon Suite. We enjoyed an English cream tea, complete with cucumber sandwiches and scones. And, we were joined for dinner by the Boothmans and the Crossley Cookes, choosing, of course, Beef Wellington, after a Pimms on the terrace. When I asked the waiter if they had mosquitoes at the Smokehouse, as quick as a flash he responded, *"Certainly sir, how would you like them?"*

North through Perak State

The journey from the Highlands to the island of Penang took us from comfortably cool to sticky hot in the space of two hours. It also took us through the State of Perak and another hugely hospitable Royal lunch at the *Istana* (Palace) at Kuala Kangsar.

Before lunch, the cars gathered under awnings on the large *Padang*, with cold drinks dispensed by volunteers. The Sultan of Perak, Azlan Muhibbuddin Shah, then arrived in a formal procession, welcomed by townsfolk waving palms. After lunch we were permitted to view the ground floor of the *Istana*. The décor was similar to what one might find in a French Palace, very much Louis XIV, with the wallpaper in a yellow flock. Since the Sultan had been *Agong* between 1989 and 1994, there were numerous photographs of him with visiting heads of state, including Queen Elizabeth II.

One of our friends on the tour, David Crossley Cooke, made a detour, with his wife Elspeth, to Taiping, to visit the grave of his father, killed in 1941 in David's presence (aged four) in Northern Malaya.

324

Since childhood, David had understood that his father had no known grave or monument. The trauma of his father's death and of the family's subsequent escape to South Africa and back to Great Britain meant that David was not inclined to go into the matter too deeply. In the course of our rally, thanks to the Defence Section of the British High Commission, David established that his father, Flying Officer KC Cooke, lay in a grave in the Commonwealth War Graves Commission Taiping Cemetery. KC was almost certainly killed when Japanese aircraft bombed and strafed 62 Squadron's airfield at Alor Star on 8th December 1941, the first day of the Japanese invasion of Malaya.

The Island of Penang

Penang was settled at the end of the 18th Century by an English trader and adventurer, Francis Light, on behalf of the East India Company. To encourage trade, it was made a free port. This led to the expansion of the settlement by Chinese and Indians who, today, predominate in the capital, George Town. In fact, Penang is no longer an island after the third longest bridge in the world linked it to the mainland in 1985.

George Town is one of Asia's gems, often described as the best preserved Chinese town in the Far East. Recently much of George Town has been restored, including the well-known E&O (Eastern & Oriental) Hotel, built in 1885 and run by the Sarkies Brothers, who also managed Raffles in Singapore and the Strand in Rangoon.

I first stayed at the E&O in 1967 when it was very down at heel, grubby and with no air conditioning. It had not received the usual 1960's makeover and there was, therefore, an authentic Somerset Maugham air to the place. When I visited the E&O again in 1993 it had been spoilt with a most unsympathetic renovation. Now, in 2001, while some of the original features had been retained, such as the entrance hall with rotunda and the terrace with its cannons and magnificent views of the Kedah Peak, it had been plasticised and was like any hotel you might find in Florida or California. The poor old dame had seen better days and the Sarkies Brothers would be turning in their graves.

By comparison, the Chinese clan houses had retained their originality and their charm. When the Chinese came to Penang, they chose to live close to each other and the extended families established temple complexes and rooms for the old folk. The most visited of the clan houses is that of the Khoo family. We enjoyed a banquet at Khoo Kongsi, the miniature clan house dating from the 19th Century, accompanied by drums, gongs, dancing, jugglers, acrobats, Chi Gong martial arts and fire-eaters. Our guest of honour was Penang's Chief Minister, The Right Honourable Tan Sri Koh Tsu Koon, who described Penang as *Heritage, High Tech and Good Food*.

The courtyard of Khoo Kongsi is dominated by the family temple. On one side, on the walls of an adjoining room, are those members of the clan who excelled at education – for example Khoo Chey Wing MA, of Trinity College Cambridge – and, on the other, memorials to those who enjoyed distinguished careers – for example Khoo Swan Jeng, High Court Judge. The temple is more than a place to worship the present. It is a place to honour ancestors and to mark their achievements.

<u>Home for a State Visit</u>
It was at this point that we had to leave the tour since I had a duty to perform. As an Alderman of the City of London I had been invited to a State Banquet at Guildhall for the visiting King and Queen of Jordan. Since I had been newly elected, it would have been inappropriate to miss the first of several State Banquets. So, regrettably, we had to fly home, from Penang to KL and thence to London.

David Colvin, my co-pilot, drove the car from then onwards, accompanied by Roy O'Sullivan, as the tour went south to the island of Pangkor Laut and then to Kuala Lumpur for the final dinner.

Footnote: A big thank you to David, not just for driving the Silver Ghost in the closing days of the tour, but also for co-authoring, with me, an account of the tour which appeared as a supplement to the RREC's magazine. This chapter is derived from the first, jointly authored, account.

<h1 style="text-align:center">Coronation in Selangor – 2003</h1>

An invitation
It's not every day that you receive an invitation to a Coronation.

I had met Sharafuddin Idris Shah, the *Raja Muda* (the heir apparent) of Malaysia's Selangor State, on *The Peking to Paris Motor Challenge* in 1997. On a subsequent car tour of Malaysia in October 2001 we had dined with him and he casually said that he hoped that one day we would be able to attend his coronation. We had not realised but at that time, Idris' father, Sultan Salahuddin Abdul Aziz Shah, had recently undergone a heart operation and died a month later, in November 2001, shortly after our tour finished.

Idris' father had been Sultan of Selangor for 40 years and *Agong* (King) of Malaysia for just two years prior to his death. Idris was 55 years of age when his father died and had plenty of time to prepare for his accession, as well as enjoying his interests of sailing, driving old cars and antique map collecting. In 1995, taking 22 months, he circumnavigated the world in his yacht, SY Jugra. He has a stunning collection of books, paintings, manuscripts and maps relating to Malaysia's history and covering much of South-East Asia.

The invitation came via Rikkee Curtis, a close adviser to and friend of Idris; Rikki's father had been the British Adviser to Idris' father and also Controller of the Royal Selangor Household. The Curtis family, which emanated from Scotland, has been in Malaysia for four generations. Rikkee had accompanied Idris on the Peking to Paris rally and helped with any contact with the UK and Idris' friends in the sailing and motoring world.

With just three weeks to go before the Coronation, I accepted immediately and booked flights for Lesley and me on British Airways to spend three nights in Kuala Lumpur.

The Carcosa
The Carcosa Seri Negara, to give it its full name, is now a luxury hotel set in grounds of 40 acres on a hill overlooking KL. It comprises two large houses, the Carcosa, which was built in 1897 as the official

Residence of the British High Commissioner, and the Seri Negara, opened in 1913, as the official guest house of the Governor of the Straits Settlement. Immediately prior to Independence, Tunku Abdul Rahman gave the Carcosa to the British Government for use by the British High Commissioner but the house was returned to the Malaysian Government in 1987 after a campaign led by Anwar Ibrahim and Dr Mathir Mohamed. Both the Carcosa and the Seri Negara now comprise this wonderful hotel. I booked, for three nights, the Grand Suite in which Queen Elizabeth II and the Duke of Edinburgh stayed during their visit to Malaysia for the Commonwealth Heads of Government Meeting in 1989. The Carcosa has the most elegant drawing room, which is a favourite for afternoon tea, a number of terraces with brown rattan furniture, balconies and acres of polished teak wooden floors.

The Grand Suite comprises an enormous sitting room, a huge bedroom and a large bathroom with a spacious balcony on which, in 2007, we were to have dinner with the British High Commissioner, Boyd McCleary and his wife Jenny, during our Mayoral visit to Malaysia. From the balcony there is a stunning view overlooking KL.

After checking in at the Carcosa, a short rest and lunch, we headed off to the centre of KL to view a collection of paintings from Idris' collection which were on view at a local gallery. The paintings comprised mainly water colours of seascapes from the 19th Century. Then, we enjoyed dinner back at the hotel and an early night before the Coronation programme began the following day.

<u>The Coronation</u>
Instructions for the Coronation were very detailed, particularly regarding dress. Men were asked to wear morning coat, with decorations. Ladies were asked to wear a long skirt and a top with arms covered. Lesley wore a stunning long turquoise blue silk dress, with her pearl choker. We both looked appropriately dressed for the occasion.

After being collected and escorted by one of Idris' cousins, we arrived at the *Istana* (Palace) for the ceremony. The Malay men wore the traditional costume, known as the *baju melayu*, which comprises a

shirt buttoned up to the collar and trousers over which is wrapped a
sarong around the hips. A ceremonial dagger known as a *keris* is
tucked in the waist band. The headdress is a cap known as a *songkok*.
The Malay women wear a knee length blouse over a long skirt. The
blouse has no collar and has long sleeves. The designs of the clothes
of both men and women are most attractive and the colours are
vibrant.

Idris was wearing traditional Malay dress but all in golden yellow
(the Royal colour), with a yellow cape and a red band across his chest
which was presumably a senior decoration. On his head, he wore a
gold crown with a sprig of diamonds at the front. He looked most
regal.

We sat in chairs around a podium on which there was a grand throne
for Idris. The ceremony was taken by the senior Imam and various
symbols of office were presented to Idris for him to touch – the
Koran, the ceremonial *keris*, the sceptre, the mace and other artefacts.
This was a very similar procedure I encountered later, in 2006, when I
was installed as Lord Mayor during the Silent Ceremony at Guildhall.
In this ceremony, various symbols of office are presented to both the
outgoing and incoming Lord Mayors to touch – *the Sword, the Mace,
the Purse and the Seal of Office*. The content of each ceremony was
remarkably the same, no doubt with its origins in some very ancient
civilisation.

Afterwards, the new Sultan posed for photographs, at the foot of a
double staircase with gold carpet, looking magnificent in his regalia.

<u>A party and then the formal Gala Banquet</u>
That evening, Rikkee held a party at his house, with his Chinese
Malaysian wife, Pin, for everyone who had journeyed from outside
Malaysia for the Coronation. Flushed with excitement from the day's
events, Idris joined us and enjoyed relaxing among friends.

The formal celebratory Banquet was held the following evening at the
Istana where Lesley and I have never seen such a display of
conspicuous wealth. It was a black tie event for the men and a similar
dress code for the ladies. And there were stunning outfits worn by the

visiting Royals. The ladies of the other Malay States were positively dripping with diamonds, pipped by the *Raja Isteri*, the wife of the Sultan of Brunei, who is a distant relation of the newly crowned Sultan of Selangor.

Despite the formality of the long tables, littered with beautiful crockery and glasses and the processions, Malay meals are in many ways very relaxed. Guests get up from their places to speak to friends. Sometimes gaps are left between diners for many minutes. The Royals were gracious and the atmosphere was friendly, with subjects greeting them and each other with respect and in genuine affection. This was an occasion to celebrate and an opportunity to indulge in the splendour of a magnificent Coronation.

By Train from Cape Town to Dar es Salaam – January 2011

Our ultimate destination - Zanzibar

I had always wanted to visit Zanzibar, after learning about the brief stay there, in 1873, by my great-great-great uncle, the Reverend James Midgley MA.

When Midgley was studying at St John's College, Cambridge, in 1857, he listened to a speech given by David Livingstone at the Senate House. Livingstone spoke about his missionary work and his travels in Southern Africa. Midgley was greatly inspired by what he heard. He took the cloth, later joining the Universities' Mission to Central Africa (UMCA) in 1872. He began his missionary life in East Africa, arriving in Zanzibar in June 1973, although his stay was short, due to the onset of malaria. But it was in Zanzibar where he was trained for missionary work, first on the African mainland and then, soon afterwards, in Brazil. For many years, the UMCA had a large mission and hostelry in Stone Town, the capital of Zanzibar.

To reach Zanzibar, we thought we might journey in the footsteps of Livingstone, who had started his life as a missionary and an explorer in South Africa – thousands of miles to the south.

Rovos Rail

Lesley and I have always enjoyed train and river journeys. We heard about a luxury train, with restored vintage carriages, that travels three times a year from Cape Town to Dar es Salaam. Run by Rovos Rail, the 3,800 mile journey takes 14 days through South Africa, Botswana, Zimbabwe, Zambia and Tanzania. We would have plenty of time to read about the history of exploration in Southern and East Africa. We could fantasise over journeys and discoveries made by Livingstone and Rhodes 120 to 150 years earlier. There would be plenty to see en route from the luxury and comfort of the train. Now in our sixties, ease of travel rather than adventure was a more important pre-requisite for exploring distant lands. On reaching Dar es Salaam, at the end, we would be able to visit the nearby island of Zanzibar. The Rovos train was an opportunity not to be missed.

Rohan Vos, a South African, has always had an obsession with old cars and old trains. With an interest in mechanical engineering and transport he began, in the late 1980's, to restore railway steam engines and then to run them, with period carriages, on the South African national rail network. Today, based from a private station in Capital Park, Pretoria, Rovos Rail (named after Rohan Vos) operates luxury train journeys throughout Southern Africa.

The journey begins

Rovos Rail has its own reception at Cape Town station for check-in and for a briefing by Rohan Vos and his team. The trains have the capacity to accommodate 72 passengers. We learnt that we would be a party of about 50, which meant plenty of space in the two dining cars, the two lounge cars and the bar. Our party comprised nationals from many countries; the common purpose seemed to be the desire for an adventurous holiday, in style.

Rohan Vos emphasised that it would be an adventure; the track in Tanzania was in poor shape, necessitating lower train speeds. Punctuality could not be guaranteed. Indeed, we might get held up for hours while the track was repaired or a derailed railway truck removed. Then, in South Africa, January was the start of the copper wire theft season, when electric cables alongside the track would be stripped, resulting in loss of power and many hours delay. He reassured his passengers by asserting that the train's staff could cope with anything.

And so they did. When a stone came hurtling through the window of the lounge car as we travelled through Worcester, not far from Cape Town, one of the train's engineers removed the entire window and replaced it from inside the moving train, in a matter of minutes.

The carriages, including the sleeping accommodation, had been restored to look like Edwardian-era trains, although we learnt that many dated from the 1930's. They were air-conditioned and the sleeping accommodation was roomy, depending on the class of cabin, and there was an air of luxury about the train, with as many staff (mainly youngsters) as passengers. The food and wine had been loaded in Cape Town into a special truck and this would last us all the way to Dar – and also for those passengers who had booked the return leg. The price for the journey included all food and all drinks, which made life a lot easier.

Matjiesfontein – a Victorian time warp

After a climb of 500 feet from Cape Town to Worcester, the train then climbed steeply for a further 2,500 feet to the Hex River Pass. At over 3,000 feet, the semi-desert region of the Karoo in the Western Cape appeared rather inhospitable. Here, in the middle of nowhere is a Victorian time warp, Matjiesfontein, created by a Scotsman, James Logan. It was a place to provide refreshments and a night stopover for those travelling by train from Cape Town to the Diamond Fields and further north. The town has been by-passed by today's transnational traffic, but has been made into a delightful, living museum. The Lord Milner Hotel looks very much as it might have done in the 1890's and, today, with electricity, takes room bookings for travellers, often honeymooners, and dinner reservations. Matjiesfontein has some splendid historic buildings which were tastefully restored in the 1970's and has been declared a national historic monument. Our train stopped long enough in Matjiesfontein for an interesting walk around town. With the potentiality for being a Las Vegas style pastiche, it has resisted this and offers a genuine retrospective of South African heritage.

The Big Hole at Kimberley

We journeyed overnight and, after lunch, the train reached Kimberley, capital of the Northern Cape Province. This was the centre of the diamond mining industry. Between 1871 and 1914, 50,000 miners dug the ground, creating the *Big Hole*, producing 2,722 kg of diamonds. The smaller mining companies were amalgamated in 1888 by Cecil Rhodes and Barney Barnato to form De Beers Consolidated Mines, which still has a major hold over the world's diamond market. We saw the *Big Hole* which was, frankly, a very big hole – but it did have exceptionally clear blue water in its base.

Pretoria

We were slightly underwhelmed by Kimberley, perhaps because we didn't see the Victorian town. Back on the train, there was time for an excellent dinner, a comfortable night's sleep and a lavish breakfast before we pulled into Pretoria the following lunchtime.

We had been introduced to Mario Pretorius, a South African telecoms magnate who had helped in the planning of Lord Mayoral business visits to South Africa. Mario and his wife, Leanette, had entertained us for lunch at the Mount Nelson in Cape Town and he offered to meet us off the train in Pretoria. Mario is descended from Martinus Pretorius who founded Pretoria and named it after his father, Andries Pretorius, who was a national Afrikaner hero after his victory over the Zulus at the Battle of Blood River.

Mario offered to show us the Voortrekker Monument and I immediately accepted. On my first visit to South Africa in 1964, I had been encouraged to believe that this monument was rather shameful. After all, the Afrikaners had fought the British in two rather nasty Boer Wars. Then, according to the English version of history, the Boers had allegedly wished to prolong slavery longer than the British people thought morally or legally acceptable. The monument was a testimony to the struggles of the Afrikaner people and these struggles were often against us, the Brits, as well as the African tribes. However, time has marched on and I was keen to learn more about the Afrikaans people, particularly since they are now in the minority in South Africa and, to some extent, the object these days of discrimination.

The monument was built between 1937 and 1949 to commemorate the life and trials of the Voortrekkers who made The Great Trek from Cape Colony in the 1830's and 1840's. The building makes a massive statement, on a hill south of Pretoria, and the design is based on Egyptian architecture and mythology. It also has links to German architecture of the 1930's and has similarities to the nationalistic Monument to the Battle of the Nations (*Völkerschlachtdenkmal)* in Leipzig, commemorating the defeat of Napoleon in 1813.

The Voortrekkers left Cape Colony because of dissatisfaction with British rule. They also wanted a better life. The land of Natal, the Orange Free State and The Transvaal was of superior quality. Inside the monument, there is a frieze of 27 bas-relief panels depicting the history of the Great Trek, including scenes of everyday life, work practices and religious beliefs of the Voortrekkers. Outside the monument, on each corner, there is a statue of the great Voortrekker leaders, including Mario's ancestor, Andries Pretorius, who famously defeated the Zulu King Dingane at the Battle of Blood River on 16th December 1838. The date was memorialised as the *Day of the Vow*, based on the oath sworn prior to the battle. It became a religious holiday in South Africa. It is still a public holiday, but has been renamed, since black independence, the *Day of Reconciliation.*

The monument certainly has the feel of a temple, glorifying the endeavours and the feats of the Voortrekkers as God's chosen people in South Africa. This was its intended purpose. Being shown the Voortrekker Monument by Mario, a descendant of the great Afrikaner hero, was rather special, given his family history and what it means to him.

I had been to Pretoria before – the last occasion was 47 years earlier, in 1964. The grid pattern of the streets and, of course, the Union Buildings, designed by Sir Herbert Baker and built before the First World War, have not changed. Because of the significance of the Voortrekker Monument and the Union Buildings, a law in Pretoria limits the height of any building between the Voortrekker Monument and the Union Buildings such that the view between them remains unobstructed.

New office blocks have been constructed in the last five decades. But today, the centre of Pretoria seemed somewhat dowdier than I remembered it. The leafy suburbs were just as well maintained, with a growing affluent African middle class being able to afford large houses in large gardens.

Mario took us for lunch at the Pretoria Country Club which demonstrated that, for some, the luxury and lifestyle had not changed since the club was built in 1911.

Rovos Rail Station
Rovos Rail has its own private station at Capital Park, Pretoria. As we arrived from Cape Town, the electric powered locomotive was

replaced by a steam engine. With smoke billowing and particles of soot falling, we chuffed our way into the gracious colonial-style railway station.

Here, engineers from Rovos Rail maintain some wonderful old locomotives and their carriages for the journeys across Southern Africa. We learnt that, due to the poor state of the track in many countries, the wheels on the rolling stock have to be replaced quite frequently. The carriages also have to be repainted on a regular basis. And the coal has to be of the right quality. Running a vintage railway company can be an expensive proposition.

To Botswana and a game park
Close to the border with Botswana lies Zeerust, in the North West Province of South Africa. We disembarked for a two-night stay at the five-star Tau Lodge in the Madikwe Game Reserve. Early mornings and evening drives are the order of the day. We had some pleasant drives in this new game park which was created from an amalgamation of a number of farms. And we saw elephants, lions, zebras, wart hogs and plenty of bird life outside the attractive rondavel shaped chalets.

Formerly the British Protectorate of Bechuanaland (since 1885), Botswana became independent in 1966. It held democratic elections and Sir Seretse Kharma became the first President. Shortly before independence, the capital was moved from Mafeking to Gaborone, where we boarded the train again.

Despite recurring droughts and increasing desertification in Botswana, the country seemed more prosperous than South Africa and, certainly, the railway track was in better shape. This was perhaps as a result of the significant find of diamonds in Botswana in recent years.

Zimbabwe and the Victoria Falls
But our comfort was short lived. Crossing the border, north of Francistown, around midnight, our ride became bumpier and the engine driver reduced speed.

It would take us almost 36 hours to cover the 300 miles to our haven (the Victoria Falls Hotel) in this poverty stricken country. Villages along the route seemed quite run down and the people looked quite impoverished. The train did not stop until it reached Victoria Falls, where we were met by a group of bare-chested dancers holding shields and spears and dressed in traditional costume.

To provide added interest on our journey, Rovos Rail had thoughtfully arranged for a guest lecturer (a historian from Pretoria University) to join the train to give lectures on travelling days in the mornings and afternoons on a variety of interesting topics: colonialisation and British rule in Southern Africa; Cecil Rhodes and De Beers; Livingstone and the search for the source of the Nile; South Africa since black independence; the Tanzam (now renamed TAZARA) Railway. They were fascinating and, by the time we reached Dar, we had learnt a great deal about the countries we had travelled through and their history.

The Victoria Falls Hotel is situated immediately adjacent to the railway station at Victoria Falls. It opened in 1904 for passengers on the newly built railway which, it was hoped, would link Cape Town and Cairo. From the terrace in front of the hotel, there is a stunning view of the Second Gorge and the Victoria Falls Railway Bridge.

In the 1930's and during post war years, Imperial Airways (and its successor companies, British Overseas Airways and BOAC) operated a flying boat service from Southampton to South Africa. One of the stopping off points, known as the *Jungle Junction,* was Victoria Falls, where the planes would land on a reach of the Zambezi River above the Falls. All this is captured in a mural in the foyer of the newly renovated hotel.

A sunset cruise on the Zambezi River, sighting hippos and crocodiles, was followed by a very pleasant dinner at the hotel. And then, the following morning, there was an opportunity to walk through the rain forest on the south side (Zimbabwean side) of the Falls from which one has the most wonderful view of one of the wonders of the world. Known as the *Smoke that Thunders* by the Kololo people, the Falls are three miles long and 360 feet high; they are only matched by the

Iguazu Falls in Brazil. We also passed the statue of David Livingstone, being much admired by parties of Zimbabwean schoolchildren.

Livingstone to Lusaka

The Victoria Falls Railway Bridge is one of the more amazing sights in Southern Africa. While the view from the Victoria Falls Hotel is spectacular, so is the train journey across the bridge, as one travels from Zimbabwe to Zambia gazing down 420 feet to the Second Gorge below. The bridge was completed in 1905, as part of Rhodes' dream to have a railway linking Cape Town and Cairo. Designed by George A Hobson of consultants Sir Douglas Fox & Partners and constructed by Cleveland Bridge & Engineering Company, the bridge was fabricated in England and then shipped to Beira in Mozambique. The huge parts were then transported on the new railway to the Victoria Falls where construction took just 14 months.

It has been said that the bridge is a man-made engineering marvel which rivals the wonder of the Falls themselves. The bridge is 650 feet long, with border posts at either end.

Although it was strictly forbidden, our engine driver stopped the train in the middle of the bridge to permit the passengers to alight and take photographs of the gorge and the river below. Since we were in no-man's land between two countries, it was unclear as to who would enforce that rule. I think the driver knew he could get away with it.

The next 24 hours were spent relaxing on the train, as we travelled through the southern part of Zambia, listening to further fascinating talks by our on board historian.

The following day we passed through Lusaka and saw the large number of people living alongside the track in slum conditions. Everyday life could be seen from the train – washing, cooking, haircutting and trading in basic goods. This was Africa at its most raw.

The TAZARA Railway

100 miles north of Lusaka is Kapiri Mposhi where Zambia Railways interconnects with the TAZARA Railway.

The Railway was financed (through an interest free 30 year loan) and built by the People's Republic of China between 1970 and 1975. The concept was to eliminate Zambia's dependence on Rhodesia, Mozambique and South Africa, all three then under white minority rule. Completion of the railway line provided Zambia with an alternative route, through Tanzania, for its copper exports. Built shortly after the independence of both Zambia and Tanzania, the railway was sometimes known as *the Great Uhuru Railway*, Uhuru being the Swahili word for Freedom.

The railway was an enormous feat of engineering. 1,150 miles in length, from Kapiri Mposhi to Dar es Salaam, the track was laid through some of Africa's most rugged terrain, rising to 4,600 feet above sea level. Its construction employed 50,000 Tanzanians and 25,000 Chinese and required the building of 300 bridges, 23 tunnels and 147 stations.

The section, in Tanzania, from Mlimba to Makambako was the most difficult part of the route, crossing mountains and steep valleys. Almost 30 percent of the bridges, tunnels, viaducts, and earthworks along the entire route were located in a 10-mile stretch of this section.

The TAZARA Railway has been a post war African wonder, providing an alternative route from the Zambian copper belt to the Indian Ocean. However, it faced operating difficulties from the outset and has never lived up to expectations. After eight years of African management, the Chinese were invited to resume control and had to assist with refinancing. However, the railway was overstaffed; estimates suggested as many as 2,500 workers would have to be laid off. Service deteriorated and there was competition from the roads, which were improved. Traffic fell from 1.2 million tonnes in 1990 to 533,000 tonnes in 2011. Declining copper prices and alternative sources of this metal's supply did not help.

In 2008, the railway's condition was described as being *on the verge of collapse due to financial crisis*, and Chinese technicians described parts of the track as dangerous. The Chinese government gave TAZARA a US$39 million interest-free loan in 2010; but TAZARA's management estimated that US$770 million would be required to make the line commercially viable. Cash flow difficulties have led to a failure to pay salaries on time, with resulting frequent strikes.

Although it remained in operation, the TAZARA Railway was, at the time of our journey, in a very poor state due to mismanagement, financial difficulties and inadequate maintenance. This was the railway line on which we were to travel for three days and, at times, the journey was quite hairy. But our South African train driver had travelled this route before and, with the help of local *pilots*, he knew when to slow down.

In several sections, where the track twisted and turned to reach the high altitudes, there were wrecked railway trucks that had fallen down ravines or lay by the side of the track. Poor maintenance of embankments and track, coupled with over confident drivers who were going too fast, perhaps to achieve time bonuses, had caused the wheels of the trucks to leave the track. Within days of an accident, the contents of each vehicle had been stripped.

A brief stop at Kasama, in north eastern Zambia, enabled us to visit the Chisimba Falls, which were picturesque and provided a break in the three days of travelling on TAZARA. Each station looked as though it might have been in China. Architects from the PRC who worked on TAZARA's construction clearly had standard designs, which they considered entirely appropriate for rural Africa. In many ways, this mirrored the colonial architecture left by the British.

We journeyed to Makambako in Tanzania, where we were able to spend an hour wandering through the streets of this dusty town in the Southern Highlands. Paul Theroux in his book *Dark Star Safari: Overland from Cairo to Cape Town* described Makambako as "*a collection of hovels on a stretch of paved road where idle people sat or stood*". It seemed to us that it was quite busy. There were more shops selling mobile phones than anything else, showing the reach of cellular telephony in some of the poorest parts of the world.

As we descended from the high pass to Mlimba, there were yet more wrecked trucks on either side of the track, their wheels and bogies rusting away. Soon, we were crossing the huge plain through the Selous Reserve and the Mikumi National Park with wild animals peering at our train as it roared through.

The final night before we reached Dar was the most nail biting. We picked up speed on the flat, but the track was in no better condition, so that the carriages rocked from side to side in a most alarming manner. At one stage during the night I seriously thought that we might topple over. However our experienced driver knew his stuff and we arrived safely at the TAZARA station in Dar, elated by our train journey through the heart of Africa.

It had been quite an adventure, as predicted by Rohan Vos. It had been fascinating to learn about the Victorian explorers and to follow in their footsteps. We had enjoyed good company on the train and excellent food and wine.

To cap it all, on the station platform, we were welcomed by the Dar es Salaam Police Band, in fine, white colonial uniforms. They played, with enormous enthusiasm but hopelessly out of tune, a memorable rendition of *The Hallelujah Chorus*. For a moment the colonial clock was turned back.

Postcript on TAZARA

I was pleased to read that, in November 2011, TAZARA and the Chinese authorities had reached a US$42 million agreement to enable Chinese companies to help with the rehabilitation of the ailing railway. TAZARA said that *"funds provided by China to the Tanzanian and Zambian governments under 15 different protocols will keep the railway in operation over the next three years while the two African governments complete a desperately-needed programme of recapitalisation, reconstruction and restructuring"*. Let's see what transpires. My hunch is that TAZARA will keep stumbling along.

The Reverend James Midgley, Missionary (1832 – 1922)

James Midgley was born on 4 March 1832 at East View in the Chapelry of Cross Stone, Todmorden in the West Riding of Yorkshire. His father, William (1797–1850) and mother, Ann (1799–1836) lived at Keb Cote, a lonely farm on the moors above Burnley and Todmorden. Keb Cote became a pub and is now known as the Sportsman's Inn.

James was four when his mother died and so his sister Mary (1823–1891) looked after the young boy and his father. She continued to do so even after to her marriage to Joseph Crossley (1821–1901), who came to live at Keb Cote and who was a stone carrier as well as a farmer. Later Joseph and Mary were to move to Stones Grange Farm above Walsden.

As a boy, James was educated at the grammar school at Heptonstall. This involved a five mile walk each way along the moorland road high above Todmorden. From there he went on to Bingley School. James was baptised at the age of 16 on 26th October 1848 at Cross Stone Church situated above Todmorden almost on the moors and close to Todmorden Golf Club. Cross Stone Church was deconsecrated in the late 1970's, as its foundations were unstable and the building was thought to be in danger of collapsing. It did not, however, collapse and was later converted into flats.

In 1854 James went up to St John's College, Cambridge to read moral science. He graduated in 1858 with first class honours, obtaining an MA from the university in 1866. It was during his time at Cambridge that Midgley was inspired with missionary zeal, after hearing David Livingstone's Address at the Senate House on 4th December 1857. Livingstone had undertaken his first pan-African journey, from west to east, between 1853 and 1856. He wrote an account of this journey *Missionary Travels and Researches in South Africa,* which was published by John Murray in 1857.

After graduating, James Midgley entered the church and was ordained as a Deacon at Ripon in 1859. He was a Curate at St James' Church,

Bradford, from 1859 to 1861, and Curate in charge of Ickham, Kent, for twelve years from 1861 to 1873.

It was in 1873, the year of Livingstone's death, that Midgley began his overseas missionary work. In January of that year he joined the Universities' Mission to Central Africa (UMCA), perhaps after reading Stanley's account, published in July 1872, of his celebrated meeting with Livingstone in November 1871. After a brief stay in London, probably about two months, undergoing familiarisation with the Mission, Midgley sailed for Zanzibar in April. Arriving in June, he took up a post as a missionary teacher, based at the headquarters of the UMCA at Changani House in Zanzibar Town. Apart from acting as administrative headquarters for the missions to Africa, Changani House ran a school for freed slave boys and girls, at Mbweni. It was these young slaves that were probably the Reverend Midgley's first pupils in Africa.

Changani House had been built between 1847 and 1850 and was occupied by the UMCA from 1854. It was sold to the British Government in 1874. It became a European hospital in 1926. The UMCA moved initially to Mbweni and later to Mkunazini which is the location of the Anglican Cathedral. Changani House then became the Office of Administration for Public Records. At the time of our visit to Zanzibar in February 2011 the building was empty, pending planning permission for development as a hotel. It is a protected building, whose preservation is supported by UNESCO, as Stone Town is a world heritage site.

In July 1873, the UMCA received a request to strengthen the missionary presence at Magila, a substantial village in the Usambara Mountains, south west of the port of Tanga in Tanzania. Reverend Midgley was selected to go to Magila and so he left Zanzibar at the age of 41 after only one month's teaching.

The first mission at Magila had been established in 1867 by the UMCA to administer to a relatively populous region. However a series of tribal wars in 1869 and 1870 depopulated the area and the mission was abandoned in 1870. Two years later, in October 1872, the Zanzibar Headquarters sent four sub-deacons back to Magila –

Samuel Steere, Francis Mabruki, John Swedi and Benjamin Hartley. They found the work quite difficult and requested that a senior man be sent to the mission. This man was James Midgley who arrived in 1873 and took charge of the mission.

The Reverend Midgley had quite a material effect at Magila. He was responsible for building a small hospital surgery and a series of rooms for villagers and travellers. He did not build a church, but probably erected a small portable altar in the rooms for church services. Most of his time was spent travelling through nearby villages preaching. Unfortunately a disastrous fire in 1885 destroyed most of Magila and with it all of the Reverend Midgley's buildings. However, two photographs have survived of the hospital and two rooms that he had built.

While at Magila, the Reverend Midgley suffered repeated attacks of malaria and it was with regret and after heartfelt searching that he decided to leave the mission field. He resigned from his post at Magila in April 1874, returning to Zanzibar and immediately to England. During the voyage home, two members of the mission died from the fever that had also attacked James Midgley.

Midgley's time in Africa (June 1873 to April 1874) coincided almost exactly with the extraordinary journey made by Livingstone's servants who carried his body from the interior to the coast. David Livingstone had died on 1st May 1873 and was found by his servants, Susi and Chuma, kneeling across his bed in prayer. After cutting out the heart and viscera, they dried the body in the sun for a fortnight, wrapped it in calico and bark, and carried it over 1,000 miles to the Indian Ocean. The journey took 10 months and was a miracle of a kind bearing in mind the nature of the countryside and the number of tribes that lay in wait for every wayfarer that came by.

Such devotion among primitive and uneducated men can hardly have been inspired by any ordinary emotion. Susi and Chuma and 60 odd men who had remained faithful to the end reached the coast at Bagamoyo on 15th February 1874. The body was taken across to Zanzibar and then transhipped to England where Livingstone was buried in Westminster Abbey on 18th April 1874. Thus Midgley did not meet his inspirer, Livingstone, in Africa, although James, lying ill in bed with fever in Magila, was less than 60 miles away from Livingstone's body at Bagamoyo, shortly before it left Africa. The name of the village was changed from Magila to Msalabani in 1900.

After convalescence in England, the Reverend Midgley was appointed consular chaplain in Recife, Pernambuco, Brazil, taking up his post in 1875. Here he led a healthier life, playing tennis, often with the German consul, in addition to teaching and preaching.

During his 17 years in Brazil, he probably lived in Rua Padre Ingles in Recife. The church in which he worshipped was pulled down many years ago, but the British Cemetery, at which he undoubtedly officiated, is situated on the main road to Olinda. During my Mayoral year, I paid an official visit to Brazil and visited Rua Padre Ingles and the British Cemetery in Recife.

In 1892, aged 60, James Midgley retired to Todmorden. On his return to England, he lived first at Stones Grange Farm, above Walsden, where his sister and brother-in-law, Mary and Joseph Crossley had resided. During this time James and Joseph (Mary had died in 1891) were looked after by Joseph's daughter, Hannah (1851–1929). Hannah's husband, Frank Whitehead, had also died in 1893.

About the turn of the Century, the family moved to Wood Cottage, which was the dower house of Scaitcliffe Hall, in Ewood Lane, opposite Mons Mill, Todmorden. As Hannah in turn grew old, the management of the house devolved on Emily Whitehead (1882–1973), Hannah's third child and the only unmarried daughter. Emily nursed her mother and her great uncle James for the next 20 years.

During his retirement, the Reverend Midgley's interest in the Church and religious education continued. He took up a post as a licensed preacher in the diocese of Wakefield in 1894, which role he continued until his death in 1922.

He assisted local clergy at Todmorden Parish Church, Christchurch, and was a frequent attendee at Harley Wood Parish Church (now demolished). He was one of the earliest members of Todmorden Golf

Club and, apart from golf, his other favourite pastimes were tennis and whist. He had a kind and generous nature and on his death he left most of his money to endow honorary canonries of Wakefield Cathedral and to increase the stipends of the poor clergy of the Deanery of Halifax. He left his military style mahogany desk to his great-niece, Emily. This desk together with his top hat and leather hatbox are now in the author's possession.

James Midgley died of bronchitis aged 90 on 31st May 1922. He was buried alongside his father in the graveyard of Cross Stone Church, Todmorden, where a memorial tablet was erected at one end of the church in his honour.

After the decision to deconsecrate Cross Stone Church, this memorial tablet was removed and, with the help of the Venerable Alan Chesters, then Archdeacon of Halifax and later Bishop of Blackburn, we managed to arrange for it to be transferred to Halifax Parish Church (now Halifax Minister) where the tablet was rededicated on 25th October 1987. I attended this service together with Lesley and our two sons, Tom and Jamie, who were then aged 12 and 11 respectively.

We had always wanted to discover more about James Midgley's time in East Africa. Our train journey to Dar es Salaam gave us this opportunity.

<u>Travel to Zanzibar</u>
After our 3,800 mile train journey from Cape Town, we stayed the night in one of Dar's better (but hardly luxurious) hotels. The following morning we took the twin engine plane to Zanzibar, a magical island in the tropics.

Zanzibar conjures up an image of exoticism and adventure – tropical fruits and spices; the centre of the Omani Empire and of slave trading for many years; the gateway to Africa for Burton, Speke, Grant, Livingstone, Stanley and other explorers and missionaries; and, in the 1970's and 1980's, a place not visited by tourists following a bloody revolution and the formation of a Marxist nationalist government. A country being out of bounds for a while always excites the interest of the intrepid or discerning traveller. These days it is also well known as the birthplace of Freddy Mercury.

Zanzibar is a fascinating place in which to spend a few days. The capital, Stone Town, has narrow streets and ancient houses with ornately carved wooden doors. It retains its medieval character, full of atmosphere, and was, interestingly, the first place in Africa to enjoy electric lighting (in a former Sultan's Palace). It is full of old buildings. One of these is now a hotel, Africa House; built around 150 years ago, its original owner was a wealthy slaver trader from Oman. Shortly before his death he gave it to the Sultan. In 1888, it became the first English Club of East Africa. Then, after the Revolution in 1964, the Club was abolished by Presidential Decree and the building became a State run hotel. Over the years, it fell into disrepair and was taken over by an Omani investor who arranged its renovation into a charming hotel, which retains the original character and is set in a stunning location for a sundowner. Despite being Muslim, the island is not dry.

Today, Zanzibar is easy to visit as a tourist destination. It has attractive sandy beaches and a soft, warm climate beside the Indian Ocean. Our hotel, the Zanzibar Serena Inn, in Stone Town is probably the best on the island as well as being in a very convenient location from which to visit the old Omani capital. Situated at Shangani Point, a promontory to the west of the town, the hotel overlooks the sea and the old fort. Our balcony had a stunning view over the gardens and the trading boats sailing by.

The hotel is also adjacent to Changani House, the site of the UMCA's first headquarters in East Africa. The building was sold to the British Government in 1874, when the UMCA moved to Mbweni, where a mission was built for freed slaves. The UMCA was the result of collaboration between the faculty and alumni of Oxford and Cambridge universities, who were soon joined by enthusiasts from the universities of Durham and Dublin. Christian missionary fervour was encouraged by the speech which David Livingston gave at the Senate House in Cambridge in 1857, appealing for missionaries to go to Africa. He believed that slavery could only be ended through

Commerce and Christianity. My Uncle James, the Reverend James Midgley MA, had responded to this call.

Intrigued to ascertain if there was any record of Uncle James being in Zanzibar, we set off for the Zanzibar National Archives Building. Here we found the dates of James Midgley's arrival in 1873 and departure in 1874. We also learnt more about the UMCA and its activities in Zanzibar and on the mainland of Africa.

Of interest in this connection is the Anglican Cathedral in Mkunazini, Stone Town. Construction began in 1873, the year that James Midgley arrived in Zanzibar. The third Bishop of Zanzibar, Edward Steere, was the instigator of this building, which occupies an area where the town's biggest slave market used to be. It was placed there to celebrate the end of slavery. Inside the church is a cross made from the wood of the tree that grew on the place where Livingstone's heart was buried, in Zambia. During our visit to the Cathedral we met the present Bishop of East Africa and heard him speak about the UMCA.

We felt that, in Zanzibar, we had come to the end of a particular journey, in search of Uncle James. Perhaps this was also a fitting moment to begin to reflect on, and to write about, travels in my lifetime, inspired by the accounts of my intrepid ancestor.

India in the second half of the 19th Century

by Louisa Edith Harcourt-Ranking, Great-Great Grandmother of Lesley Stuttard

<u>Introduction</u>

I have included as an Annex this account of her experiences in India written by Louisa Harcourt-Ranking, Great-Great Grandmother of my wife Lesley. It makes fascinating reading and reveals some of the pleasures, difficulties, hardships and emotions of a member of our family in a bygone era and in a world which has disappeared – that of the British Raj.

Some of the countries I visited in the second half of the 20th Century are no longer as safe or accessible. Hitch-hiking in Southern Africa and travelling through Eastern Ethiopia, Sudan and Western Pakistan today would be hazardous, to say the least. Despite this, during this period, other countries, such as Vietnam, Indonesia, the Baltic countries and the Balkans have now become popular destinations for global travellers.

Travel in India is now quite popular and relatively safe. However, in the period in which Louisa lived in and journeyed through India (1865 to 1869 and 1877 to 1891) life was very different, as her account reveals.

<u>Louisa Edith Harcourt-Ranking</u>

Louisa Edith Harcourt-Ranking was born in Bury St Edmunds on 4th October 1845, daughter of Dr William Ranking a Cambridge-educated physician and editor of a medical magazine. He worked at the Suffolk General Hospital and then at the Norfolk & Norwich Hospital. Her Mother, Louisa Leathes (nee Mortlock) was the daughter of Sir John Cheetham Mortlock. Also Cambridge educated, Sir John had trained as a barrister and became Commissioner of Excise as well as serving as Mayor of Cambridge. His father had founded Mortlock's Bank, the first bank in Cambridge, in 1780.

Tragedy struck the family in 1864, when Louisa was just 18 years old. Her mother died and her father suffered a stroke, after which he was an invalid and confined to a home. As a result, she was sent to India to stay with her uncle, (James) Lancaster Ranking, who was Surgeon General in Madras. Within a year she was married to an Army officer, Major Robert John Baker of the 32nd Madras Native Infantry. Robert was the son of Richard Baker, British Chaplain in Hamburg, and grandson of Sir Robert Baker, a bencher of the Inner Temple and Chief Magistrate and Treasurer of the County of Middlesex.

Robert and Louisa had three sons and five daughters between 1867 and 1884. Their eldest child, Edith Louisa Violet (known as Violet), was born on 29th September 1867 at Hoshungabad, Central Provinces, India. Violet married Joseph William Howard in 1919 and their only daughter, Joan (born in 1892), is Lesley's grandmother.

Louisa's account of her journey to India and of her time there was written when she was an elderly lady living back in England. It is not known when she wrote this, nor where or when she died. A photograph taken of her by Nicholas Brothers of Madras still exists as does a photograph of her daughter and Joseph Howard taken by ATW Penn and of the Lancaster Rankin family, showing Lancaster Rankin, his wife, Sophy, Louisa and Marion in Madras.

An account of the travels of Mrs RJ Baker (nee Louisa Edith Harcourt-Ranking)

I think you might like to read of my travels to India and the reason why I went.

Well, to begin with, I may as well say that I was born in Bury St Edmunds on 4th October 1845, my father, William Harcourt-Ranking, being a physician there. My mother was Louise Mortlock, daughter of Sir John Cheetham Mortlock.

When I was two years old, we went to Norwich and I lived there till 1864. That year my father's health gave way (he had a stroke) and we, or at least some of us, Elinor, Marion, Lertia and I went to

Guernsey. The other children, Florence, Emily and Mabel, went to school or to our grandparents, Mr & Mrs Ranking.

In 1864, my Mother died and we (Elinor had meantime married) returned to England and I went to live with our uncle and aunt, Mr & Mrs Philip Rose. (Uncle Philip was afterwards made a Baronet through the influence of his friend, Disraeli). Meantime, our Father, whose mind had become very feeble, was taken care of in a private asylum, where he remained till he died in 1867.

We had an uncle, Lancaster Ranking, Surgeon General in the Madras Medical Establishment who, hearing that it was proposed to make me and Marion into governesses, said that while he lived none of his brothers' girls should work like that and asked for the two of us to be sent out to him. At that time it was proposed that I should be sent to Brussels and there to be educated to be a governess, but my Aunt Margaret decided that I was too good looking. Then as I had a fairly good voice, my Uncle Philip asked if I would like to go abroad and have it trained and renewed his offer starting from Gravesend to sail for India. I believe my Father was averse to this (former) – anyway I declined and Marion and I were put on board the *Lord Warden*, one of those Green Line Company sailing ships and away we went.

In those days people furnished their cabins and, money not being plentiful, we had our bunks, as they were called, roughly made more like coffins than anything. They had one side to let down and the mattresses and pillows were, I am sure, stuffed with dry seaweed; chests of drawers and so on were fitted into the cabin and, as far as I can remember, we had no baths, only a foot bath; And all this for a three month voyage. There were about 60 passengers and some were very kind to us.

Oh, how seasick we were; I did not get over it for a month; and what cured it was an unlimited quantity of sweets. The food was fairly good; fowls were kept in coops on deck running along both sides and they were gradually moved away as the fowls were consumed. Great was the excitement when one day an egg was found in one of the coops. A cow was brought on board but died, poor thing, very soon.

The *Lord Warden* was a fine three-masted vessel and, being a sailing ship, there was no disagreeable smell like steam vessels.

The Captain rejoiced in the name of John Smith and was a kindly man. The table for meals was a T-shaped one and he thought it his duty to keep Marion and me under his eye; so he placed us opposite him. Opposite me was a missionary, the greediest man I think I have ever met. He would take meat, pudding etc on his plate all at once and pass it up to be refilled before he had finished what was on it. Sharing his cabin was a young Artillery Officer, being sent out in a hurry because he gave his people so much trouble. He came on board for a three months' voyage with clothes enough to last one week. He was a dirty creature and when he got to Madras found his battery under orders for home and returned in the same vessel.

At the end of the first month a ceremony took place called *"Throwing away the dead horse"*. The sailors, having had advances of pay, worked for nothing the first month and only began to work for pay at the commencement of the second. A stuffed representative of the horse (I think the skin of the dead cow was used) was fastened to the end of one of the yardarms and, at a signal, amidst cheers and singing, was cut adrift and fell into the sea. We had no piano on board but one lady, who had a good voice, had a guitar and a concert was got up – the only entertainment I remember the whole three months. I was asked to sing and sang *Auld Robin Gray*. I was told I looked miserable and Mr Kelso, who subsequently married Marion, nicknamed me *"Robin"*.

When we crossed the *line*, the ceremony of *Neptune and his wife* coming on board took place. Two men dressed up and carried tridents etc and brought letters for passengers. A sail was rigged up and filled with water and the men passengers, or some of them, were *ducked* and made to pay their footing. As far as I can remember the ladies had to pay also.

The next excitement was waking up one morning to find another ship, homebound with troops, becalmed near us. We were in the doldrums as it is called - an odd experience in mid ocean and miles and miles from land. The Captain of our ship sent an invitation for passengers to lunch with us; and asked for the bagpipes to be sent (It was a Scottish Regiment). The invitation was joyfully accepted. There were only four ladies on board and two of them would not speak to the other two; so they were glad enough to speak to the ladies on our ship. A big luncheon was arranged on deck and the pipers marched round playing during it. It was the only time I have heard bagpipes near at hand and I don't think I want to repeat the experience. Towards evening our guests returned to their own ship (I have forgotten the name) and a breeze sprung up in the night. We parted company. By the morning the other ship was out of sight.

On the whole the weather was good and it was delightful when we got into the trade winds and sailed along going at such a slope that it was difficult to keep our feet. One night though we were asked to go on deck, where we had to hold on, to see the wonderful sight of the waves running up as high (apparently) as the mast top and curling over, as if they must come down to sink the ship. It was a moonlit night and a sight not to be forgotten. First, we went up on the crest of the waves and then down in a trough, into the waves looking as though they must crash down on us.

As we neared India, we just escaped a cyclone; another ship which got in just before us, coming from Burma, had her masts broken off.

I forgot to mention that we sailed on 10th September 1865 and did not land till 18th December. All that time we never sighted land or, if we did, it must have been at night. So, you can imagine our joy when Madras was in sight. It was a Sunday evening and a young clergyman, Mr (now Canon) Sell, was reading the evening service and giving a sermon (he was not, and is not, much of a preacher) when a man put his head through the skylight and announced that the Madras light was in sight. I'm afraid that not more attention was paid to Mr Sell's sermon. It was too late to land then but next day a Captain Edgecombe came on board with a letter from Uncle Lanc (sic), who asked him to meet us. Our Captain was very particular and questioned him before he allowed us out of his care; but at least he was satisfied.

The next thing was how were we to land? We did not go through the surf, as was usually done, but a cask had one side taken out and a seat put across; this was slung from the yardarm and we were lowered into a boat and taken to the pier.

I was quite proud of myself, for I was able to walk the length of it on one plank. Generally people coming off a long voyage find it very difficult to walk straight.

It was odd to part with people with whom one has been living in close companionship for three months, and all to go in different directions. The only ones I have met of our fellow passengers since were Mr Sell and Mr Browne. The latter was a Major when I met him again and I had been married for many years.

We found we were to go to Captain and Mrs Edgecombe for a short time till arrangements could be made for us to go to the Hills, where Aunt Sophy was living. Our baggage had to be landed, an Ayah engaged, and so on. We stayed with the Edgecombes at Chepank House for a fortnight and, to the best of my recollection, went to one ball. Mrs Edgecombe drove us about Madras; but I'm afraid she must have found me a very stupid guest; in those days I was very shy and had nothing to say for myself. After being in Madras for a fortnight, Marion and I were started off with the Ayah.

At the end of the fortnight, Marion and I set off by train, the Ayah in another compartment, and next day got to Pudami, where we had to get into a bullock coach. The Ayah, accustomed to such a conveyance, and not having been told how to get in, we lay down with our heads towards the bullocks. Consequently, when in the middle of the night we stopped for the bullocks to rest, the pole subsided onto the ground and then we were head downwards. However we righted ourselves and next morning started at the foot of the Ghaut. It was quite an adventure for us two girls, strangers in a strange land, and not able to speak one word of the language. The Ayah, of course, was miles behind and no help to us in travelling.

At Kour, at the foot of the Ghaut, we found two wretched ponies waiting for us. Coolies took our belongings, and we mounted the poor little beasts, but got off and walked a good part of the way. The road was so steep we pitied the ponies, though neither Marion nor I weighed much in those days. On our way up we met an elephant, fortunately a tame one.

It must have taken us some time to get up to Connor where we had a carriage ready for us. Away we drove, in more or less comfort, to Ootacamund, to *Ottley Hall*, where Aunt Sophy was living with two children, Walter and Minnie, both of whom ought to have been home at school. Aunt Sophy was a very queer tempered woman, what is called "*four annas in a rupee*", and very difficult to please. I found she was fond of gardening and, by doing a little work in the garden when she was in a temper, I managed sometimes to keep in with her. Uncle Lancaster was a dear kindness itself. She was very jealous of him; he was a favourite everywhere.

I suppose we went to dinners and so on, but I do not remember any. I became engaged on 9th June 1866. Robert was then a Major. We were married on 14th July, the same year, and spent a fortnight honeymoon at a shabby hotel in Connor, situated in or near a tea estate, but so dirty that unmentionable insects used to perambulate my dressing table. There was nothing to do and nowhere to go and I was glad to return to Ooty. I remember I ate apples and sang all the way in. Robert's sister was waiting for us in a house called *Glyn Creek* above what is now the Gymkhana ground. Later on, we all moved over to a bungalow in *Silks Hotel* compound. My chief recollection of that was they gave us black cherry jam at nearly every meal and I got so tired of it. I hardly ever ate it again.

I find that I have omitted to say that from *Glyn Creek* we moved first into a house called *Glenburn*, on the Connor road. Whilst we were there the house was broken into, by whom we never found out. Robert was gone out shooting for two or three days, leaving Carrie, his sister, to look after me. Subsequently being interested in the Backbay Reclamation Scheme, Bombay, we went there *sub rosa* travelling, I think, as Mr Butcher. It was a waste of money, as the scheme went *phut*.

In April 1867, we started for Hoshangabad in the Central Provinces. I begged Robert to arrange for Carrie to stay behind. I found that servants were saying that I was not mistress in my own house, and so on. She was at least 14 years my senior and, though she afterwards married, was very *old maidish* and I longed for a house, alone. We drove to Connor and there I got into a *toujon*, a sort of sedan chair, carried on a pole by two men in the front and two behind. Robert walked alongside. I found it a very uncomfortable way of travelling as I was seated at a steep angle and kept slipping forward.

At the foot of the Ghaut we got into a one horse vehicle, something like a hansom cab. In this we went to Corimbatore, I think, and thence by rail to Beypore. It was very hot. At Beypore we had to cross a river to Calicut, and then embarked. I indulged in some pineapples and we had to go in a small boat two miles; I was deadly sick before I got on board.

We had five days journey to Bombay and I was alone in my cabin most of the time, very sick. By the time I got to Bombay I was looking pretty bad, so much so that a gentleman, a friend of Carrie's, wrote and told her that he thought I was dying. We went to a hotel and arranged for the continuation of our journey. I knew nothing about travelling and Robert never thought of telling me to take a pillow; nor did he think of taking any ice. Fortunately for us, a gentleman I had known slightly in Ooty, Captain Boo Stewart, was on the train and he gave me a pillow and a syphon with sherry and water and ice in it.

Our first stoppage, next day, was at Klundwal which was as far as the line was finished. There we mounted a trolley, having two chairs fastened on it and were run along the line at night by coolies. In this way we got to Bhosawal and were told that further along the line we should find a railway engineer encamped and that, no doubt, he would let us rest or share his tent; but though Robert went and explained that I was on the trolley he would do nothing. I don't think he even gave us a cup of tea. So, in the blazing sun we had to start off again and further along came by a wayside station and there we took refuge. I was so worn out and I slept on the veranda with no punkah, and of course no ice all day. Robert said it was a wonder I did not die of heat apoplexy.

When it got cool we started off on a coolie train; I had to crawl up on a truck as best I could and it was a marvel I survived the journey. Soon after starting there was a great whistling and the engine and trucks were backed. It was then I discovered the driver was drunk and another train was coming towards us on the same line. Finally we got on safely and our next halt was at Husdat where we found some railway people had taken up their abode in the *dak* bungalow. However Robert insisted on their turning out of one room and we had a rest and a wash. Arrangements had been made for a bullock coach to come from Doolungabad for me but it did not turn up; and as Robert had to get to Doolungabad by next day a country cart was procured, lots of straw and mates put in, and into this I got. What a jolting I had. The cart wheels were solid and the road very bad. Fortunately for me the bullock coach met me and I got into it, Robert telling me that if I wanted water I must ask for *pani* and that was the only word of Hindostani I knew. He came on in a cart. I was at the mercy of the bullock men and the coolies but managed to sleep a little.

Early next morning I was challenged by a Sepoy but managed to make him understand that the *Major Sahib* was coming along and I was allowed to pass; I got to the mess bungalow which we were to share with Jock & Emily Macdougall, the latter my cousin, Uncle Lancaster's eldest daughter.

My first requirement was a bath and, as there was only one bathroom, for Robert and myself, I had to hurry and as quickly as I could came out to breakfast. Robert arrived directly after; and while we were seated at breakfast we heard a commotion in the bathroom and on Robert going to investigate we found that a large cobra and ever so many young ones had been curled up under the bath (a large wooden cask) and there it, no doubt, had been all the time I had been bathing. On the bath being lifted, it reared itself up, but Robert dropped the edge of the bath on it, so it could only wave itself about and we soon despatched it, the young ones too, anyone of which would have killed a man had it bitten him.

We remained with the Macdougalls some months and, on 29th September, my first child, Violet, made her appearance. Why she had not been born in the middle of our journeyings, I don't know. I had our Quartermaster Sergeant's wife as nurse; she was not certified but in those days people were stronger than they are now; and in a fortnight I was up and about. Our Colonel's wife, Mrs Williams, came to look after me and presently we were ordered off; but much to my joy got counter orders. I thought I must learn to wash my baby, but I was so nervous I wonder I did not drop her in the bath; and as next day we received our counter orders, I never in my life repeated the experiment.

Aunt Florence came and stayed with us for a time. There is nothing much to record of these months. Doonlungabad was such a small station very little went on. There was a croquet ground opposite the house we moved into, one the Colonel had had. It was on the bank of the River Nerbudda, one of the sacred rivers, which in the rainy season was about half a mile across but in the dry weather only a small stream with rocks in it onto which crocodiles came to bask in the sun. In the rains all sorts of things were washed down, including corpses.

In February 1869, Harry was born and as a small child was very ill. Violet too got out of health and was liverish. At last the doctor said we must take her home, that she could not live if she remained out another hot weather season. This doctor used to say these things and that we must be careful of her diet; yet he came to tea and lunch and stuffed with cake and sweets. She was very fond of sweets and helped herself plentifully to them.

We had a horse for riding and driving – a brute which bolted with Florence one day. I was never a good rider. I used to ride Robert's charger, a flea-bitten grey, I nicknamed *Granpus* as he used to puff and blow so much. I also rode a white Arab belonging to the Colonel, not a safe mount for a lady, and once I was chased by a wild pony (a *tat*) but Mr Hicks who was with me headed it off. Had it come up with me I should probably have been torn out of the saddle. Later on, Robert bought me a pretty little Gulf Arab from our doctor. I have a photo of me on him wearing a riding habit nearly touching the ground.

At last it was decided that we should go home and Florence went to Uncle Lancaster and Aunt Sophy at Ooty. Robert got medical certificates (he had varicose veins and made the most of them) but anyhow as he had not been home for 13 years would not have been refused. By this time the railway was finished as far as Hurdah, 10 miles off. Robert went on ahead to Bombay to see about passages leaving word at Hurdah that I, the children and the Ayah were to have a carriage to ourselves; but when we got there we found there was no accommodation except with some people who resented our coming with the carriage and were so unkind and disagreeable. I was obliged later on to appeal to the station master and he put another carriage on.

Never shall I forget that journey of 24 hours. Both children were ill and the heat torture. It was April and in one place we stopped near some white rocks off which the sun radiated enough to kill one. I thought of course to find Robert at the station; but he was not there and I did not know what to do. I don't think I had money with me, anyway not much, but I imagine I knew the name of the hotel (*Adelphi*), as I started walking carrying Violet with the Ayah following with Harry. Fortunately just after we had started, Robert came gaily to the station driving with some man. I was so cross with him, I fancy I let him see it.

We sailed in *Candia* and at Suez transhipped into a train and so went to Alexandria. There we went on board an old paddle boat, one of the last to ply, I should think.

We landed at Southampton; I was too sick to do any packing till we got into Southampton Water; but made a good tea of bread and butter at the station and then we took our departure for London. I think it was May, but very chilly, and there was snow on the ground the next day.

We went to one of Robert's uncles, Mr Charles Baker, in Bloomsbury Square and, after refuelling ourselves, went to the lodgings they had taken for us – *such* lodgings with other occupants! Poor Violet was dreadfully bitten and we moved to others also very insanitary. Meanwhile Robert was enquiring for a house and took one about a mile out of Bath, in a village called Charlcombe. The house had been a farmhouse but the farmer's people only lived in part of it. We had nice rooms, one of which was a square hall with a fireplace in it where we sat in the Winter. Before going there we stayed a short time with the Roses in Buckinghamshire. Robert had a sister and other relatives in Bath. I never liked the place as it is too enervating.

In September, Eddie was born and christened in Charlcombe, said to be the smallest church in England.

We remained in Charlcombe Manor till October 1871, when we moved to 2 Sidley Place in Bath itself and there remained till it was time for Robert to go out to India again. After hunting in vain in Bath for a suitable house, for me and the children, I took one in Norwich, 5 Carlton Terrace, Heigham. My old friend, Mrs Robinson, arranged everything for me, engaging servants etc and I had nothing to do, but to take possession. The house furnished came to £82 a year. There I remained till the end of '76. Robert then came home, I thought for two years' leave; but the morning after his arrival he announced that he had bought *Tudor Hall* (or as it was called *Tiger Hall*) tea estate in Ooty and was returning in March. I did not at all like the idea of settling out there, but it had to be done. I could not leave till the end of the year, as Millie was on the way and arrived in September. I was to have gone out as soon as I was strong enough, and book passages in the *Merkain*, but, just before the final arrangements were made, the children got measles and then whooping cough. I had arranged with kind Mr & Mrs Fritten to make a home for Violet and Harry, and all in the bitter cold. Violet had to go on the box seat of the carriage, as she turned so sick and green if she went inside.

The parting was a sad one. Harry was then about seven and I did not see him again till he was about 21. He had then before passed into the West Indian Regiment and having nearly died at Sierra Leone from fever was shipped off home and went to Marion. Eventually he went into the 23rd Carnatics (Note: which became the 31st Madras Native Infantry).

But, to resume to my adventures. I got my passage arranged to a small vessel called the *Scotland* with only 16 passengers. Millie was desperately ill with bronchitis, so bad that the doctor (as I heard afterwards) said she would give a champagne lunch if she lived to Suez.

We touched at Colombo and I asked the Captain, who went on shore, to send a telegram to Robert, but either he forgot or it was not sent, as it never arrived. When we got to Madras, early in March, I of course thought that I should find Robert there; but he did not come down, only arranged for money to be given me; and the evening we landed I set off again, Millie still anything but strong. Robert met us at Mettapollund and we travelled up the Ghaut in bullock coaches. From Connor on, Evie, Millie, the Ayah and I went in a carriage and a pair of horses and Robert and Eddy in another. Poor Evie was in a great state of alarm as it began to get dark and she thought a tiger would spring on us. It was quite dark when we got to Charing Cross, Ooty, where the carting company had their stables; then Robert had to get a lantern and walk ahead of the carriage, up an awful road to *Tudor Hall*. We did not get there until ten at night and, what with the cold and the indifferent milk, Millie got ill again and I had to rout Robert up and get a doctor. For some weeks after, Millie was very delicate.

At that time, Robert's nephew, Raymond Brasley, was with us as an assistant.

The morning after our arrival, I caught sight of a pair of ponies, a white and a dun, which were a great delight to me. I was also initiated into the art of making tea which in those days was done in a very primitive way. The top of the sprays of leaves was nipped off by women, each woman carrying a big basket. She had to bring in a certain weight, but was paid extra for overweight. After being weighed the leaves were spread out on mats under a glass roof, like a greenhouse. There they remained to wither. Had they been rolled unwithered they would have been broken into dust. When sufficiently withered, they were taken into the tea house, where there was a long table about 2½ feet wide. Coolies stood on either side and a large bunch of leaves was taken by the first and rolled in his hands, then passed to the next, and so on to the end coolies. The tea juice was running out all over their hands, not a very clean way of doing things. The leaf was then put in a warm building to ferment and get a brown colour. It was then put on sieves and roasted over fires of glowing heat. When done it was sieved through sieves of varying fineness, the various grades of tea being a matter of sieving. The tea was called *Orange Pekoe, Pekoe, Pekoe and Gunpowder*, the latter being the dust sieved out. It was stored in large tin-lined boxes and afterwards packed and sent to England. But a good deal was kept for consumption in India and many is the pound I have packed in paper packets, which had our label of a tiger's head put on. We also had some *Cinchone Bark* and planted out more. The Government said they would not interfere with private enterprise, but they did not keep their word and threw so much on the market that the price went down from ten shillings a pound to two. They also cut down and sold timber and tea was overdone; consequently we found ourselves in difficulties and had to mortgage the place. I was obliged to give up my ponies and, one day, Robert went down to see his lawyer, Mr Cowdell, and sent me up a note to say that if he could not furnish a certain amount of money in a few hours he would be put in jail. Imagine my feelings. All I could do was to tie up the small amount of jewellery I had and send it down to him (it was subsequently returned) and tell him to let the mortgage. A Mr Rogers had the carriage and the ponies. This was agreed to and Robert came back in the evening. We never again referred to this incident. The only thing to be done was to try and sell the place. General Clementine had a second mortgage on it and (so I learned afterwards) had intended foreclosing and told people his son Mark would take on the estate. But just in the nick of time we heard of a purchaser, a man called *Sabability Ayhah* and were able to pay off old Clementine and have a small sum left over.

For about a year Robert continued to manage the estate, which by that time had proper tea making machines erected but Mr Sabathy got word of two unscrupulous Englishmen who contrived to oust Robert. (Both these men committed suicide eventually).

We lived on the estate for 11 years and, in the meantime, Eddie and Evie had gone home to school. Violet had come out and Lily, Wilfred and my youngest baby had been born. As you all know *Tudor Hall*, I will say no more about it. Towards the end of our stay there, at the

instigation of Mrs Cornish, I had started selling milk and butter; and I
kept on at it till Wilfred had left Sandhurst. People were very glad to
have clean and good dairy produce. I began with my own cows, but
as the business grew, I hired others and housed them at Prospect
Lodge, where we moved to. I managed to make enough out of it to
furnish the house, based on dairy produce, and to sell enough to pay
for clothes.

I ought to say something about the difference in Ooty itself from the
time Marion and I first went there, till I returned in March 1877. The
church, St Stephen's, had no chancel, only an apse, and the vestry
was on the right hand side, where the ayam now stands. Mr John
Pope, son of Dr GM Pope, who kept a boys' school at Snowdon, was
the organist. A propos of the Snowdown School, one Sunday
afternoon, when Aunt Sophy, Marion and I were there for afternoon
service, we saw a lady there whom we learnt afterwards was the
widow of Sir John Franklin, the great Arctic explorer; she was staying
with the Bishop of Madras and his sister, to whom she was related. St
Thomas's church had not then been built. The Library was where
Bayly's shop now is, one end of it was for the coolies, the other for
papers and tables, where then as now people met and talked. The Post
Office, a very small building, was where the present one is. There
was a flagstaff on which a ball was hoisted when the English mail
came in; and many people came up and fetched their own letters. I
remember on one occasion being at a dance given by Mrs (can't
remember) at Rosemount, till 6am; finding it was then light, I made
up my mind not to go to bed, but dressed and walked to the Post
Office, from Ottley Hall, with Mrs Matthews. I tried to keep awake
all day but don't think I did.

For many years, the only way of coming up the Ghaut was by
tonegan, a two-wheeled vehicle, with seats back to back, and drawn
by wretched horses who were flogged with going two miles at full
gallop; in the season they were frequently made to take on the next
tonegan with hardly any rest – and some dropped down dead.

I have rather wandered away from my original purpose in writing
these memoirs, so I will hark back to the time I arrived in Ooty for the
second time, in 1877. Lily was born that year, on 10th December, and

was a delicate child; I had many an anxious day with her and Millie, who did not grow strong till she was about three years' old. We lived a quiet life and the roads were very bad. One very wet evening, Captain Digbie gave a dance in Gorse House and I had to ride down to it.

Robert got fruit trees out from England and planted them in a walled garden, alongside the house, but gooseberries, currants, cherries, greengages, peaches and plums were a complete disaster. Captain de Montgomery gave us some strawberry plants, but they were not a success. The whole question of fruit growing was, at that time, anyhow for us, of an experimental nature.

Evie and Eddie went home to the Wilsons at Fritton, Norfolk, in 1881, weeping floods of tears, which however dried up when a friend, Mrs Campbell, appeared on the road near the toll bar with plantains etc.

In 1882, Wilfred was born and from the first was a strong child and gave no trouble. Violet came out (to India) soon after, I forget the year, travelling as fellow passenger with a Miss Judy Plummer, daughter of the Chief Justice of Mysore. Robert went down to Madras to meet her, having asked the Cornish's to put her up. When he met, he kissed as was natural, but she had not recognised him and was very irate. She was very tired when she arrived and fainted. I am afraid she must have had a dull time, but made friends with the Sheens, who gave lots of Badminton parties, followed by dancing for which I played a good deal. Robert was a very good Badminton player, but I never shone much at the game. There were courts at the Club (Archery, Badminton and Cricket) and the Duke of Buckingham, who was Governor, being very fond of the game played there once or twice a week. There were *At Homes* at Government House every week, and people were invited on alternate Tuesdays.

About the Author

John Stuttard was born in Burnley in 1945. From the age of eight, he was sent away to boarding school, initially on the Wirral in Cheshire and then to Shrewsbury School, prior to graduating from Churchill College, Cambridge University. As a result, he was used to travelling and living away from home at an early age.

He was greatly influenced by his great aunt's stories of her great uncle's travels as a missionary. While at Cambridge, John Stuttard travelled widely and then spent a year in Borneo in the mid '60's, teaching English with Voluntary Service Overseas at a secondary school in Brunei.

After qualifying as a chartered accountant in London, he spent many weeks on assignments in Europe (particularly Finland), the United States, Iran and South Africa. Business travel was complemented by holiday travel to some remote places and to geographical areas which are not easily accessible to the cautious traveller.

As Lord Mayor of London in 2006-07 he visited 23 countries, spending more than 100 days abroad, promoting the City of London and the financial services industry. The details of this business travel are recorded in a separate book *Whittington to World Financial Centre – The City of London and its Lord Mayor*. After serving as Lord Mayor, he was knighted in January 2008 for *Public Service*.

His experience of travel in the 50 years (1964 to 2014) was typical of many of his generation. Few countries and geographical areas were too dangerous or out of bounds. Travel was, relatively, much safer than it seems to be 50 years later when this book was written.

The accounts of his travel experiences provide a picture of the environment in which adventurous travel in the second half of the 20th Century could take place.